The Oxford Picture Dictionary for the CONTENT AREAS

Teacher's Book

Dorothy Kauffman
John Rosenthal
Marilyn Rosenthal
Gary Apple

OXFORD

UNIVERSITY PRESS

Oxford University Press
198 Madison Avenue
New York, NY 10016 USA

Great Clarendon Street
Oxford OX2 6DP England

Oxford New York
Auckland Bangkok Buenos Aires Cape Town Chennai
Dar es Salaam Delhi Hong Kong Istanbul Karachi Kolkata
Kuala Lumpur Madrid Melbourne Mexico City Mumbai Nairobi
São Paulo Shanghai Taipei Tokyo Toronto

OXFORD is a trade marks of Oxford University Press.

ISBN 0-19-434340-5

Editorial Manager: Shelagh Speers
Editors: June Schwartz, Paul Phillips, Charles Flynn Hirsch
Production Editor: Joseph McGasko
Associate Production Editor: Peter Graham
Elementary Design Manager: Doris Chen Pinzon
Designer: Nona Reuter
Art Buyer: Stacy Godlesky
Production Coordinator: Shanta Persaud
Production Manager: Abram Hall

Printing (last digit): 10 9 8 7 6 5 4

Printed in China.

Acknowledgement:
The authors wish to thank Linda Butler, Grammar Consultant, for her contribution to this book.

Oxford University Press is a department of the university of Oxford. It furthers the University's objective of excellence in research, scholarship, and education by publishing worldwide

TABLE OF CONTENTS

UNIT 1 PEOPLE AND PLACES

UNIT 2 THE U.S. AND ITS NEIGHBORS

UNIT 3 U.S. HISTORY AND GOVERNMENT

UNIT 4 THE HUMAN BODY

UNIT 5 LIVING THINGS

UNIT 6 THE PHYSICAL WORLD

UNIT 7 THE EARTH AND THE SOLAR SYSTEM

UNIT 8 MATH AND TECHNOLOGY

SYLLABUS

UNIT 1 PEOPLE AND PLACES

TOPIC	CONTENT	LANGUAGE
1 THE CLASSROOM *Page 2*	Classroom objects	• There + BE (*there is/there's/there are*): *There is one teacher.* • Cardinal numbers: *There are ten students.*
2 THE SCHOOL *Page 6*	Places and people at school	• Prepositions of place (*in, on, in front of, near*): *The coach is in the gym.* • Habitual present: *The students eat lunch in the cafeteria.* • Ordinal numbers: *The gym is on the first floor.*
3 THE HOUSE *Page 10*	Rooms of the house	• Prepositions of place (*at, above, below, between, in, on, over, next to*): *There is a roof over the house and a roof over the porch.* • Present continuous: *She is sleeping.*
4 THE FAMILY *Page 14*	Family members and family relationships	• Possessive adjectives: *This is my family tree.* • Possessive nouns: *My sister's name is Rosie.* • Comparative and superlative adjectives: *Danny is younger than Eva./She is the oldest.*
5 THE CITY *Page 18*	Places in the city	• Prepositions of place (*across, at, behind, between, in front of, on, over, near, under*): *The subway is near the police station.* • There + BE (*there is/there's/there are*): *There's a newsstand on the corner.*
6 THE SUBURBS *Page 22*	Places and items in the suburbs	• Adjective + noun: *There are clean streets and friendly people.* • Present continuous: *Sam Jordan is washing his car.*
7 THE COUNTRY *Page 26*	Places in the country	• Adjectives for colors (*blue, green, red, white, yellow*): *The barn is red.* • There + BE (*there is/there's/there are*): *There are no cars on the road.* • Prepositions of place (*across, behind, inside, next to, outside, from, into, over*): *There is hay inside the silo.* • Present continuous: *Arthur Sampson is driving his tractor.*
8 THE HOSPITAL *Page 30*	Health workers and medical items	• Present continuous: *The nurse is helping him.* • Future with *going to*: *She's going to see her parents today.*
9 PEOPLE AT WORK *Page 34*	Occupations	• Habitual present: *Mechanics fix cars.* • Present continuous: *The messenger is riding a bicycle.*

UNIT 2 THE U.S. AND ITS NEIGHBORS

TOPIC	CONTENT	LANGUAGE
10 THE UNITED STATES *Page 38*	Political maps and compass directions	• Comparative and superlative adjectives: *Canada and China are larger than the U.S., but Russia is the largest country in the world.* • Compound sentences with *but*: *Montana is a very large state, but Texas is larger than Montana.*
11 THE NORTHEAST *Page 42*	States, features, and landmarks in the Northeast	• Verb + infinitive: *Traders try to buy stocks at low prices.* • Habitual present: *They work in studios.* • Adverb *too*: *A trader is a businessperson, too.*
12 THE SOUTH *Page 46*	States, features, and landmarks in the South The food processing and manufacturing industries	• Logical connector *such as* + noun phrase: *Goods are products such as furniture and clothing.* • Habitual present: *Workers make sugar from sugarcane.*

TOPIC	CONTENT	LANGUAGE
13 THE MIDWEST *Page 50*	States, features, and landmarks in the Midwest The agriculture and dairy farming industries	• Future with *will*: *Bakeries will make bread with the flour.* • Present continuous: *These farmers are getting milk from the cows.* • Quantity expressions *some of, many*: *Some of the grain will become flour.*
14 THE WEST *Page 54*	States, features, and landmarks in the West The mining and ranching industries	• Present perfect: *Ranchers have lived in the West since the 1800s.*
15 THE NORTHWEST *Page 58*	States, features, and landmarks in the Northwest The logging, fishing, and canning industries	• Habitual present: *Lumberjacks cut down the trees with chain saws.* • Compound words: *There is a lot of sawdust at sawmills.*
16 THE SOUTHWEST *Page 62*	States, features, and landmarks in the Southwest Natural resources	• *So...that* (*so* + adjective/adverb + *that* + result clause): *It is so beautiful that millions of people visit it every year.*
17 THE WEST COAST AND PACIFIC *Page 66*	States, features, and landmarks on the West Coast The technology, tourism, and entertainment industries	• Correlative conjunctions *both...and*: *Both California and Hawaii border the Pacific Ocean.*
18 CANADA AND MEXICO *Page 70*	Features and landmarks of Canada and Mexico Maps	• Expression *stand for*: *On these maps, a thick red line stands for a national border.* • Prepositional phrases in initial sentence position: *On the map of Mexico, dotted lines stand for borders between states.* • Modal *can*: *You can find totem poles in Canada.*

UNIT 3 U.S. HISTORY AND GOVERNMENT

TOPIC	CONTENT	LANGUAGE
19 THE NATIVE AMERICANS *Page 74*	The Native American groups inhabiting North America before European exploration	• Simple past: *They made boats, houses, and masks from wood.*
20 EXPLORATION AND DISCOVERY *Page 78*	The explorations of Leif Eriksson, Christopher Columbus, and Ponce de León	• Common and proper nouns: *Many European explorers came after Columbus.* • Past continuous: *They were looking for wood.* • Compound sentences with *but*: *Each one followed a different route, but they all came on ships.*
21 THE SPANISH MISSIONS *Page 82*	Daily life in and around the Spanish missions	• Passive voice, simple past: *Many of the buildings were made of adobe.* • Spanish words in English: *adobe, patio, San Francisco, pueblo*
22 COLONIAL LIFE *Page 86*	The life of the pilgrims in colonial America	• Simple past: *Apprentices learned their jobs from the workers./The cobbler made shoes.* • Compound words: *The courthouse was for the government.*
23 THE REVOLUTIONARY WAR *Page 90*	The events leading up to and including the Revolutionary War Weapons used in battle	• Adverbial clauses and phrases of time with *when, before,* and *after*: *When England charged a tax on tea, the American colonists were angry./After the war, America was a free country.*
24 A NATION IS BORN *Page 94*	People and events connected with the Declaration of Independence	• Adverbial clauses of purpose with *so* (*that*): *They declared independence from England so that the thirteen colonies could form their own government.* • Simple past: *He wrote the Declaration of Independence.* • Roman numerals I-X

TOPIC	CONTENT	LANGUAGE
25 WESTWARD EXPANSION *Page 98*	Pioneer life during the period of westward expansion	• Adverbial clauses of reason with *because*: *Many wagons traveled together in wagon trains because it was safer that way.* • Prepositions of place (*across, along, through, onto, into, on, in, under, over, by*): *The pioneers drove the wagons along trails and over mountain passes.* • Compound words: *They rode on flatboats, steamboats, rafts, and canoes on rivers and canals.*
26 THE GOLD RUSH *Page 102*	The lives of the people who migrated west during the California gold rush of 1848	• Direct object gerunds (verb + gerund): *The headlines started appearing in the New York papers in 1848: "Gold!"*
27 THE CIVIL WAR *Page 106*	People and events of the Civil War	• Simple past: *They wore blue uniforms.* • Emphatic *own* (possessive adjective + *own*): *They created their own government, elected their own president, and made their own flag.* • Appositives: *The U.S. President, Abraham Lincoln, wanted to keep the southern states in the Union.*
28 U.S. GOVERNMENT *Page 110*	How the government of the United States works	• Passive voice, simple present: *One branch is called the executive branch. It is governed by the President.*
29 PEOPLE IN U.S. HISTORY *Page 114*	Famous men and women who shaped the history of our country	• Verb + infinitive of purpose: *Frederick Douglass fought to end slavery.*

UNIT 4 **THE HUMAN BODY**

30 PARTS OF THE BODY *Page 118*	Learning the parts of the body	• Modal *have to*: *Sam has to use many parts of his body.* • Conjunction *or* (*else*): *Sam has to bend his knees, or (else) he will fall.*
31 INSIDE THE HUMAN BODY *Page 122*	The functions of the human body	• *Wh-* questions with *what*: *What does the heart do?* • Possessive adjective *your*: *The skull protects your brain.*
32 THE SENSES *Page 126*	The five senses	• Imperatives: *Look at the stars.* • Linking verb + adjective: *They look bright.* • Adverb *also*: *The sun is also bright.*
33 FEELINGS *Page 130*	Feelings and emotions	• BE + predicate adjective: *He is lonely.* • Intensifier (*really, very*) + adjective: *He's really hungry.*

UNIT 5 **LIVING THINGS**

34 EXPLORING SCIENCE *Page 134*	Basic principles of the scientific method	• Modal *might*: *You might use a hand lens.* • Noun forms of specific verbs: *planning, observation, classification, measurement, experimentation, reporting* • Imperatives: *Plan your work.*
35 LIVING ORGANISMS *Page 138*	Living organisms: monerans, protists, fungi, plants, and animals	• *Have* as a main verb: *Monerans and protists have only one cell.*
36 PLANTS *Page 142*	The different parts of various kinds of plants	• Stative verbs (*smell, have, be*): *Pecan trees have short, flat leaves.* • Action verbs (*make, carry*): *The plant's leaves make food with sunlight, air, and water.*
37 VEGETABLES *Page 146*	Various kinds of vegetables	• Count and noncount nouns: *Mrs. Ruiz buys some celery and a pound of string beans.* • Quantity expressions: *some..., a head of..., a pound of..., a bag of...*

TOPIC	CONTENT	LANGUAGE
50 ENERGY AND MOTION *Page 198*	Energy and motion in daily life Simple machines and how things move	• Verb + noun phrase + infinitive for expressing purpose: *It uses magnetic force to move things.* • Adverbial clauses of time with *when*: *When you put a wedge under a wheel, it doesn't roll.*

UNIT 7 THE EARTH AND THE SOLAR SYSTEM

TOPIC	CONTENT	LANGUAGE
51 THE UNIVERSE *Page 202*	The planets of the solar system The stars and other astronomical phenomena	• Simple present: *The Earth is just one planet. All the planets go around the Sun.* • Ordinal numbers: *The Earth is the third planet from the Sun.* • Superlative adjectives: *Pluto is the farthest planet from the Sun.*
52 THE EARTH AND ITS LANDFORMS *Page 206*	Geographic features of the Earth	• *Have* as a main verb: *The Earth has many different landforms.* • Prepositional phrases: *An ocean is a very large body of salt water.*
53 CLIMATES AND LAND BIOMES *Page 210*	Climates and environments	• Adverbs of frequency *always, usually,* and *never*: *The weather is always hot and dry. It never snows.*
54 WEATHER *Page 214*	Weather descriptions and forecast A weather map	• Future with *going to*: *The snow is going to stop this evening.* • Expressions: *How's the weather?*

UNIT 8 MATH AND TECHNOLOGY

TOPIC	CONTENT	LANGUAGE
55 EXPLORING MATH *Page 218*	Whole numbers, fractions and simple mathematical functions	• Modal *can*: *You can add numbers.* • Direct and indirect objects: *You give each friend 2 sweet rolls.* • Math expressions: *Seven minus three equals four.*
56 GEOMETRY I *Page 222*	Plane figures, solid figures, lines, and dimensions	• *Have* as a main verb: *Plane figures have two dimensions.*
57 GEOMETRY II *Page 226*	Angles, areas, and other advanced geometric functions	• Simple present: *The circumference is the distance around the outside of the circle./The diameter passes through the exact center of the circle.* • Modal *must*: *She must multiply the width by the length.*
58 MEASUREMENT *Page 230*	U.S. customary system and the metric system	• There + BE (there is/there's/there are): *There are 100 centimeters in a meter.* • Simple present: *A thick pencil is about a centimeter wide./The metric system measures length in meters.*
59 NUMBER PATTERNS, FUNCTIONS, AND RELATIONS *Page 234*	Number patterns, tables, and graphs	• Adjective clauses with *that*: *Graphs are pictures that compare numbers.*
60 COMPUTERS AND CALCULATORS *Page 238*	Components of computers and calculators	• Imperatives: *Sit in front of the computer./Let's try it.* • Modal *can*: *You can also use the arrow keys on the keyboard.* • Expressions: *upside down*

INTRODUCTION

About *The Oxford Picture Dictionary for the Content Areas* Program

The Oxford Picture Dictionary for the Content Areas, with its accompanying components, is a conceptual vocabulary development program designed to present and reinforce language and concepts from the content areas of social studies, history, science, and math. It is intended specifically for ESL students in elementary and middle schools.

The *Dictionary* contains more than 1,500 high-frequency content words presented in the context of detailed, full-page color illustrations. The content words and concepts presented in the Dictionary are based on research and analysis of the major content area textbooks used throughout the United States. The selection and presentation of these content words and concepts is also based on interviews and focus groups with ESL teachers, content area teachers, and mainstream teachers.

The purpose of the *Oxford Picture Dictionary for the Content Areas* program is to help ESL students acquire fluency in academic content as they develop fluency in English. Internalization of the words and concepts presented in the Dictionary can lead to improved comprehension of the academic subject areas and serve as a bridge to the mainstream curriculum.

Organization of the Picture Dictionary

There are eight units in the Picture Dictionary, each covering a specific content area. Within each unit are a series of topics of two pages each. On one page is a full-color illustration depicting the content of the topic. Facing this page is a numbered list of the topic's content words, each accompanied by a small illustration that duplicates the individual object or action in the large illustration. These "callouts" help students to define the words, enabling them to understand the meaning individually and then in the context of the large illustration. There are generally 12 to 22 numbered words and callout illustrations for each topic.

The topics and themes of the Dictionary progress from the small-scale world of the family, neighborhood, and school to large-scale areas of geography, U.S. history, and scientific exploration. Although there is a logical progression of content within each unit, the topics are self-contained and can be presented to students in any order. Topics can be selected to coincide with mainstream content instruction, to present particular language structures, or to suit students' interests and needs.

An *Appendix* at the back of the Dictionary serves as a ready reference for newcomers. It is also an excellent review of basic topics. The Appendix includes *Numbers, Time, Money, The Calendar, Colors, Opposites, Food, Clothing,* and a *World Map*.

Following the Appendix is an alphabetical *Word List* which lists all of the content words found in the Dictionary, as well as words that appear in a topic's title or as a label on an illustration. Words that appear in the illustrations but are not included in the text are listed in pink.

Use of the Picture Dictionary Program

The Picture Dictionary, with any or all of its components, can be used in a variety of ways. Teachers can determine the most effective way to use the materials based on the needs of their students. For example, if the goal is vocabulary development in a particular content area, the dictionary can be used by itself or with the workbook for additional practice with the content words. If the goal is to create a whole course for language development, the Dictionary can be used with its full range of components. It can also be used with any or all of its components to supplement an already existing ESL course. Teachers can decide how much time to spend on each topic and activity. There is enough material in the Teacher's Book to expand any topic into many hours of study.

The Dictionary program is appropriate for use with any level of language proficiency. The detailed illustrations in the Dictionary make academic content accessible to students of varying language levels. Each page presents opportunities for students to engage in language and conceptual development, whether they are responding non-verbally, identifying basic vocabulary, learning the use of sentence structure, or developing more elaborate expressions for their thoughts and feelings. At each of these language levels, the skills of listening, speaking, reading, and writing can be fully developed through the use of the Dictionary and the accompanying components.

The Teacher's Book provides suggestions for both language and content activities. Using these suggestions, teachers can build a course tailored to the language abilities and academic needs of their students. The following pages describe the components and how to use the Teacher's Book.

COMPONENTS

▶ Picture Dictionary

The *Picture Dictionary* presents more than 1,500 high-frequency vocabulary words for 60 content area topics. Each topic features a page of content vocabulary words alongside a detailed, full-page illustration that depicts the words in context. The content words are accompanied by small illustrations derived from the larger illustration. These "callout" illustrations help students to identify the content words in the main illustration.

▶ Teacher's Book

The *Teacher's Book* presents techniques and strategies for using each component of the program, as well as specific ideas for teaching each topic. These ideas include suggested activities for the Word and Picture Cards, Content Readings, Content Chants, Worksheets, and Workbook pages. The Teacher's Book also contains extension activities and annotated listings of selected literature to support each topic.

▶ Workbook

The *Workbook* is a book of reading and writing activities, word games, and puzzles designed to reinforce the content words. There is one page of activities for each topic in the Dictionary. Activities can be used for homework or for in-class pair and group work.

▶ Wall Charts

The *Wall Charts* provide enlarged versions of the Dictionary illustrations. They can be used for whole class and group work, as well as for student dramatizations and role plays.

▶ Transparencies

The *Transparencies* provide versions of the Dictionary illustrations on transparent pages for use on an overhead projector. Like the Wall Charts, they can be used for whole class and group work, as well as for student dramatizations and role plays.

▶ Reproducibles Collection

The *Reproducibles Collection* is a boxed set of four books of reproducible pages:

- The *Word and Picture Cards* book contains pages of word and picture cards that match each topic's content words. Each page can be copied and cut to assemble individual card sets. The word and picture cards can be used to introduce, practice, and reinforce the content words and concepts.

- The *Content Readings* book contains a one-page reading for each topic. The readings bring the Dictionary illustrations to life in clear, simple explanations of the academic content. The readings are good models for language use and can be used to explore the featured grammatical structures used in each topic.

- The *Content Chants* book contains one chant for each topic. The content chants, written by Carolyn Graham, help students acquire the natural rhythm and stress of many content area words and expressions.

- The *Worksheets* book contains one worksheet for each topic in the Dictionary. The *Worksheets* reinforce the language structures and content presented in the content readings through reading and writing activities, puzzles, and games.

▶ Cassettes

The *Cassettes* provide listening practice for all of the components of the Dictionary program. They present clear, natural speech models for the content words, content readings, and content chants. They can be used for the initial presentation of the material, as well as for individual listening discrimination practice and reinforcement in a listening corner or language lab.

HOW TO USE THIS TEACHER'S BOOK

The Oxford Picture Dictionary for the Content Areas Teacher's Book is a resource from which teachers can select lessons and activities that match their students' needs and interests.

Topic Plans

The main body of this Teacher's Book (pages 2-241) consists of specific suggestions for each topic presented in a four-page *Topic Plan* (see "Organization of Each Topic Plan" below). The general overview page is followed by suggestions for different kinds of lessons (Words, Content, and Chants) plus Extension activities and Literature ideas.

Techniques and Strategies

The Techniques and Strategies section of this book (pages xiv-xxii) is a resource for suggested listening, speaking, reading, and writing activities that can be used with any topic. The section is organized to match the kinds of lessons (Words, Content, Chants, Extension, and Literature) shown in the specific Topic Plans. It is recommended that teachers read, re-read, and refer back to the general strategies and techniques while making lesson plans for each of the topics.

Teaching Language through Content

Throughout the Teacher's Book, language activities are interwoven with the academic content presented in the Dictionary. For each topic, one to three grammatical structures have been selected. The content reading for each topic combines natural use of the content words in context, along with repeated use of the featured grammatical structures.

Each grammatical structure in a topic is listed on the overview page, followed by an example sentence from the content reading (see example below). An overview of the content and language in all of the topics can be seen in the Syllabus in the front of this teacher's book (pages v-ix). An alphabetical listing of the grammatical structures is also included in the Index of Featured Grammatical Structures at the back of this book (pages 260-261) so that the teacher may select a particular topic based on the grammar as well as the academic content.

Organization of Each Topic Plan

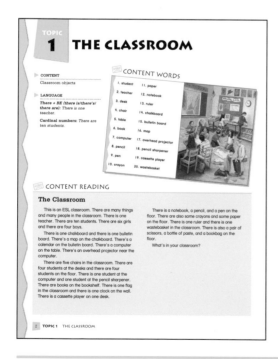

Overview Page

The content covered in the topic is listed, followed by the grammar structures that are featured in the content reading.

The list of content words from the topic is shown beside a reduced version of the Dictionary illustration.

The content reading from the Reproducibles Collection is also shown on this page for easy teacher reference.

The cassette icon indicates that the content words and the content reading are recorded on the cassette.

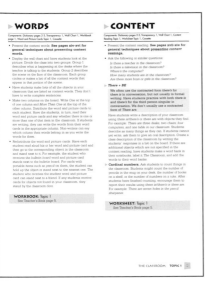

Words

The first column offers specific activities for presenting and practicing the content words for that topic. Language notes which address issues of spelling, pronunciation, or meaning of specific words are included where appropriate.

Content

The second column presents activities for addressing the academic content and the language featured in the content reading. Activities which help to practice specific language structures are marked with a ▶. Where appropriate, a highlighted box includes a simple grammatical explanation of the featured language structure. A list of basic comprehension questions for the content reading is also included. These are general as well as detailed comprehension questions. They include *Yes/No* questions and *Wh-* questions based on the content reading. Many of the questions are intended to elicit answers that use the featured grammatical structures. These questions can be used for listening, speaking, reading and/or writing activities.

Chants

The content chant from the Reproducibles Collection appears on this page for easy teacher reference. Specific suggestions are given for teaching the chant, including ways to practice the rhythm, how to break the sentences into smaller chunks, and how to divide groups for chanting.

The cassette icon ▭ indicates that the content chant is recorded on the cassette.

Extension

Extension activities are included which expand the topic beyond the Dictionary presentation with suggestions for additional classroom and community activities or research projects using books, magazines, encyclopedias, and the Internet.

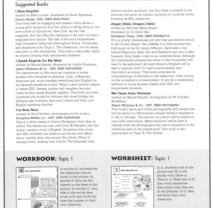

Literature

Each topic has an annotated list of suggested literature for students that includes both fiction and nonfiction books related to the topic. With this list, teachers can begin a classroom content library to encourage further reading about the topics.

Workbook and Worksheet

The Workbook page for the topic and the Worksheet page from the Reproducibles Collection are shown on this page, along with brief explanations and instructions.

Answer keys for the Workbook and Worksheet pages are provided at the back of this book.

TECHNIQUES AND STRATEGIES

▶WORDS

Components: Picture Dictionary, Transparency, Wall Chart, Cassette, Word and Picture Cards, Workbook

The following are techniques for presenting the content words of any topic. As you plan your lessons for each topic from the ideas presented in the specific Topic Plan, refer back to this section for basic techniques on how to present the words. Pick and choose from the following sections on *Listening*, *Speaking*, *Reading*, and *Writing* according to the abilities or current needs of your students.

WORD AND PICTURE CARDS

The *Word and Picture Cards* book is one of the four books in the Reproducibles Collection. For each topic, there are pages of words and pictures that match the topic's content words. To make cards, photocopy the pages for the topic, color the pictures, and cut apart the squares. Students can help with cutting and coloring. To make sturdier cards, glue them to poster board before cutting, or mount them on index cards after cutting. If desired, laminate the cards. Many card games and activities work best with separate word cards and/or picture cards, but you can also make two-sided cards with the words on one side and the corresponding pictures on the other side. To do this, make a double-sided copy of the page; be careful to turn the book so that the words and pictures match up.

There are numerous activities for the word and picture cards on page xvi, as well as specific suggestions within each Topic Plan. You may want to enlarge the cards for some activities and make several sets for each topic.

Preview

- Display the wall chart or the transparency. If possible, bring in actual objects of the pictures in the wall chart or transparency and have students observe them and handle them. Point to the topic title and read it aloud. Encourage students' comments and ask students questions to assess their prior knowledge and experiences. For example: *Have you ever been to a farm? Which animals do you see in the picture?* If students' language level permits, ask questions which require them to interact with the topic, to make predictions, and to engage in higher-level thinking. For example: *What are the people doing? What three things are made of metal?* Frame questions so that students with varying proficiency levels can participate and experience success.

- Encourage students to name the words they know in their native language(s) and share that information with others in the class. Point out any cognates.

Listening

- Play the cassette or read each word so that students have a chance to listen to the pronunciation. You may want to do this several times or with a group of only a few words at a time. Introducing five to seven words may be enough for students to handle at once. Use your judgment, depending on the needs of your students.

- During the reading, point to the illustration of the word as it is named. There is enough space on the cassette after each word so that students can repeat the word.

- Invite individual students to take turns pointing to the words on the wall chart or the transparency as they hear each word on the cassette.

- Divide the class into two groups or teams. Have group/team members take turns pointing to each illustration as it is named. If appropriate, make this into a game with scores of one point for each correct response.

- Have students open their Dictionaries and point to each illustration as you call out the vocabulary words.

Speaking

- Replay the cassette and ask the class to repeat each word as it is spoken. Do this again with pairs of students and finally with individual student volunteers.

- Have the class name each object as you point to it on the Wall Chart or Transparency. Then have individual volunteers point to the objects as other students name them.

- Divide the class into two groups or teams. Assign each group/team a section of the wall chart and have its members identify and name all the content words in that particular section. The other group or team listens for accuracy and corrects any errors.

- Students in groups or teams look at the wall chart for one full minute, close their eyes, and then, in turn, try to name as many words as they can remember.

- Circulate through the room and point to specific illustrations in each student's Dictionary. Have students name the objects. More advanced students can ask and answer questions about the words or use the words in a sentence.

- Have students look at the Words page in their Dictionaries. With students, categorize the content words using a chart or web with as many categories as are appropriate. (The Words section of many of the Topic Plans gives specific suggestions for categorization activities. For example, in Topic 5, the notes suggest an activity using the categories *Buildings* and *Vehicles* as column headings on the board.) Students can dictate which words go in each category while you write them on the web or chart, or they can place their word and picture cards in the appropriate category on the graphic organizer. For some topics, students may be able to propose their own categories.

- Use the word and picture cards to provide hands-on practice and reinforcement of the words and concepts (see the Word and Picture Card activities on page xvi).

Reading

- Many of the activities with the word cards (see page xvi) can be used to improve students' word recognition and reading skills with the content words.

- Practice word recognition skills such as spelling, consonant clusters, blends, syllabication, and pronunciation. Many specific ideas are given in *Language Notes* in the Words column of each topic.

- Have students practice syllabication and word stress by tapping out the rhythm with a pencil or ruler after your model. Then have students do it without your model while other students try to guess which word is being tapped out.

- Conduct a spelling bee of the content words. You may want to combine the content words from two or three related topics.

- Have students find and copy sentences in printed material using as many of the content words per topic as they can. Encourage students to look in newspapers, magazines, textbooks, encyclopedias, and on the Internet. On chart paper, they can list the word, the example sentence, and where they found it. Group students of varying language ability together for cooperative learning.

Writing

- Have students alphabetize the content words on each page.

- Form groups and have students make their own semantic webs or charts categorizing the content words.

- Dictate the words to the students as they write them in a notebook or journal. Encourage students to select their favorite words in each topic and mark them with a symbol or a decorative border. More advanced students can write sentences with their favorite words. Have students share this information with the entire class.

- Have students make personalized dictionaries with two pages for every letter. Encourage them to look up the words in a standard dictionary to find additional forms of the words to include in their personal dictionaries. Encourage more advanced students to try to define a content word in their own words, and have them share their word and definition with the entire class.

- Students can make their own personal *word banks* with index cards in an index file box or a shoe box. Have students make a card with a tab for every letter in the alphabet. Encourage students to add new words (perhaps not found in the Dictionary) to their word banks as they explore the topic. Students can personalize their word banks or journals by decorating the cards or pages.

- Divide the class into small groups. Distribute writing paper and pencils and have students sit in group circles. Have each student choose a vocabulary word and use it in a sentence. Have students pass their papers to the student on their right, who writes a different sentence using the word. Students continue passing the papers until they are returned to the owners. The owners read the sentences aloud.

USING THE WORKBOOK

The Workbook provides additional practice with the content words through interesting illustrations, word puzzles, and games. First preview the workbook page with the students and make sure they understand the directions and the tasks. Give an example if necessary, or have students give examples in their native language(s). Vary the use of the workbook pages. Assign them for homework sometimes, and at other times, have students work in pairs with each member of the pair checking the other's work for accuracy. At times, have two teams challenge each other to see which one can complete the workbook page more quickly and accurately. Be sure to consult the teaching tips for each specific workbook page on the last page of each Topic Plan in this Teacher's Book.

See page xvi for suggested activities using the Word and Picture Cards.

WORD AND PICTURE CARD ACTIVITIES

These activities utilize listening, speaking, reading, and/or writing skills.

Color and Match: Have students color and cut out the picture cards. Practice language while students work. For example: *Who has a blue tractor? What color is your tractor?* When the cards are finished, have students take turns placing the picture cards in their appropriate place on the wall chart. Students can also do this with word cards. (The cards can be temporarily fastened with tape.)

Share and Pair: Distribute the word cards to one group of students and the picture cards to the other group. Students walk around the room and ask each other questions about which cards they have until they find the student with the matching card.

Ready, Set, Match!: Divide students into pairs or small groups. Shuffle two sets of word cards and picture cards and put them facedown on a table. Students take turns placing two cards faceup and saying the word(s). If the picture card matches the word card, the student removes them from the set. When all the matches have been made, the student with the most cards is the winner. To increase the language difficulty level, have students also use the words in sentences.

The Secret Card: One student picks a card and stands in front of the class without showing the card. Students take turns asking *Yes/No* questions to figure out what the card is. Questions can vary according to students' language levels. For example: *Is it a barn? (Yes, it is./No, it isn't.)* or *Does it have wheels? (Yes, it does./No, it doesn't.)*

Word and Picture Card Bingo: Have students select at least nine picture or word cards and place them in equal rows faceup on a table. Mix another set of cards and place them facedown. Draw a card and pronounce it or have a student "caller" say the word. Students place a marker, button, or paper square on the matching word or picture card. The winner is the first student to cover all of the pictures. To increase the language difficulty level, ask the winner to use a designated number of the words in sentences. To make bingo game boards that can be used again, glue the cards to paper or paper board. For sturdier boards, laminate or cover with clear adhesive plastic.

What's Missing?: Place four or five word or picture cards on the chalk tray facing the class. One student is "it." That student comes up to the chalk tray and looks at the cards. Then, the student turns his or her back to the cards while another student removes one of the cards. The student who is "it" then asks *Yes/No* questions to determine which card was taken. For example: *Did you take the tractor?*

Go Fish!: This game can be played with two players or a small group. Shuffle several sets of picture or word cards. Give each student seven cards. Shuffle the remaining cards and put them facedown in a "fishing pond." The object of the game is for students to collect as many pairs as they can. First students put aside any pairs they already have. Then they take turns asking for cards to match the single cards they still hold. On each turn, a student picks another student and asks, for example, *Do you have a silo?* If the answer is *yes*, the second student gives up the card and the first student gets the matching pair. If the answer is *no*, the second student says, *No I don't. Go Fish!* and the first student fishes for a card from the fishing pond. If there is a match, the student goes again. When everyone is out of cards, the player with the most pairs wins.

Riddle Rebus Reading and Writing: Write rebus sentences on the board or on sentence strips using picture cards as the rebus. Read the sentences aloud or have the students read them aloud. Students then select the appropriate word card and place it under the rebus in the sentence. If students' language level permits, divide them into small groups and have them write additional rebus sentences using the picture cards for the rebus. Then groups trade and each group selects the appropriate word card for the rebus and reads the sentences aloud.

▶ CONTENT

Components: Pictures Dictionary, Transparency, Wall Chart, Content Reading, Worksheet, Cassette

The following are techniques for presenting the content in any topic. As you plan your lessons for each topic from the ideas presented in the *Content* section of the specific Topic Plan, refer back to this section for basic techniques on how to present the content. Pick and choose from the following sections on *Listening*, *Speaking*, *Reading*, and *Writing* according to the abilities or current needs of your students.

CONTENT READINGS

The *Content Readings* book is one of the four books in the Reproducibles Collection. There is one reproducible content reading for each Dictionary topic. Each content reading explains the meaning of the academic content in the topic's Dictionary illustration (and on the wall chart and transparency).

The content readings are written at a high-beginning/low-intermediate language level in order to make the academic content more accessible to students. The content reading for each topic combines natural use of the content words in context along with repeated use of the featured grammatical structures. (See the *Syllabus* for an overview of the content and grammatical structures featured in each topic. See the *Index of Grammatical Structures* in order to select a content reading based on the language structures it contains.)

Preview

- Using the transparency (which has the individual words and the illustration side-by-side), point to and say the topic title. Briefly recap the background information and experiences shared by students during the Words activities. Have students say each word chorally as individual students point to or circle the words (with a washable marker) on the transparency.

- Have students take turns placing either picture cards or word cards in the appropriate places on the wall chart. (The content words are listed on the back.) Students pronounce the word as they place the card on the chart.

- Before they listen to the content reading, ask students questions about what they think the picture is about. Encourage them to make predictions based on their prior knowledge.

- Make a *K-W-L* (Know, Want to Know, Learned) chart on chart paper like the example below. Ask students to share and record on the chart what they already *Know* about the topic. Encourage students to brainstorm questions regarding what they *Wonder* about or *Want to Know*, and record those questions in the second column. At the end of the lesson for each topic, elicit from students what they feel they have *Learned*, and record their information in the last column on the chart. Keep the chart on the bulletin board and use it for discussion and review.

KWL Chart		
Know	Wonder (or Want to Know)	Learned

Listening

It is important to play the content reading from the cassette (or read it aloud to students) several times so students have an opportunity to focus on the content concepts as well as the content words and language structures. The listening activities below provide a variety of different things students can do as they listen repeatedly to the cassette.

- Play the cassette. Select one or two students to point to the illustration of each content word as it appears on the wall chart and/or the transparency as they hear each word being said on the recording. At the same time, the rest of the class points to the objects on their Dictionary illustration pages.

- Play the cassette. Have students listen and raise their hands as they hear each content word in the reading used on the cassette. A variation of this is for students to clap or hold up the appropriate word or picture card as they hear each content word in the reading used on the cassette.

- Play the cassette. Have students listen and then try to recall one or more pieces of information mentioned in the content reading. Make a list on the board afterwards of as many items as students can recall.

- Distribute copies of the content reading to the students. (You may want to make multiple copies of the text for different activities.) Play the cassette again and have students underline the content words where they appear in the text as they are listening. You can also do this with some of the featured grammatical structures in the content reading after you have presented them to the students.

Speaking

- Play the cassette. Have students listen and then retell the reading in their own words.

- Have students respond to the comprehension questions about the content reading listed on the second page of the Topic Plan. Ask additional questions. If it is appropriate to the language level of your students, challenge them to ask and answer additional *Yes/No* or *Wh-* questions about the content reading.

- Pair students and have them interview each other to find out what each partner understands about the topic.

- Encourage class discussion about the topic. Many of the topics reflect a distinctively American cultural viewpoint. For example, our culture determines our attitudes about the types of food we eat, the animals we consider pets, the government documents which we consider most important, and how we treat our environment. Ask students to talk about how American culture is different from their native cultures. There are a number of questionnaires for the students, their friends and families, and the community throughout the teaching suggestions in this Teacher's Book that deal with cultural differences. Encourage students to raise questions and discuss these differences in order to appreciate them.

- Point out the featured grammatical structures in the content reading. After students have identified them (see reading and writing activities below using the featured grammatical structures), have the students use the structures to talk about the content or about their own lives experiences related to the topic.

- Have individual students or groups, in turn, describe the illustration in their own words as they point to various sections of the wall chart or transparency. This is different from describing the content reading in their own words. Encourage students to add information not apparent in the illustration and make judgments and inferences about the illustration.

- When applicable, have students dramatize the page using the wall chart or transparency as a backdrop. Encourage students to go beyond the obvious information and use their imaginations to construct lively dramatizations or role plays based on the illustration.

Reading

- Using their copies of the content reading text, have students read along silently as they listen to the text being played on the cassette.

- Play short sections of the cassette, stopping the tape to have students read each section aloud.

- Have groups take turns reading the content reading (or sections of it) chorally. Encourage each group to use appropriate sound effects to dramatize their reading.

- Pair students and have them take turns reading the text aloud, alternating sentences or paragraphs.

- Provide one or two examples of the use of the featured structure(s) in the content reading. Have students identify all instances of the grammatical structure(s) in their own copies of the content reading by circling, underlining, or otherwise highlighting the sentences containing these structures. Students then read these sentences aloud to the class.

- Cut each sentence of the content reading into two or more pieces. Distribute the pieces among the students, and have them ask questions and read to find the piece(s) they need in order to reconstruct the sentences. Then have students display the complete sentences and read them aloud in the order of the content reading.

- Have students work in groups and cut a copy of the content reading into sentence strips. The groups then paste the sentence strips onto poster board in the correct order. If appropriate, make this a timed activity. The first group to rearrange their sentence strips in the correct order in the time allotted is the winner.

- Copy one or more paragraphs of the content reading onto sentence strips. Display the strips and read the text aloud (or have a student read it). Tell students to close their eyes. Remove one or more of the strips from the text and move the remaining strips to fill in the empty spaces. Have students refer to their copies of the text to identify what's missing.

Writing

- Dictate some lines or a section of the content reading as students write what you say. This can also be done with the cassette. Dictation gives students practice in associating the oral and written language while practicing the word order and general sentence structures used in the reading. A variation of this is a CLOZE dictation practice in which you leave a blank for every seventh word or leave certain classes of words blank, such as nouns or verbs, and have the students fill them in as they are writing the dictation.

- Have students in groups or pairs write ten questions about the content reading for the other groups or the other member of the pair to answer. Students check each other's answers for accuracy.

- Have students write ten sentences about the content using the specific grammatical structure(s) presented in the content reading. For variation, have students write ten sentences about their friends, family, or another aspect of their lives using the grammatical structure.

- Reproduce the content reading on an overhead transparency or on chart paper. Cover the text and gradually reveal it section by section as you read it aloud. Ask students to identify the first main idea with a colored mark and circle the details with a second color. Continue with the remaining main ideas and details in the other sections of the text. Next, write a skeleton outline on the board or on chart paper. Display the marked text and ask individual students to use it to complete the outline.

- Have individual students or students working in pairs write their own descriptions of the Dictionary illustration. Encourage students to make inferences and state their opinions about certain characters, if applicable, as well as write complete descriptions of the scene.

USING THE WORKSHEETS

The *Worksheets* book is one of the four books in the Reproducibles Collection. There is one worksheet for each topic.

The worksheet provides additional practice and reinforcement of the language structures and content presented in the content reading. The worksheet can be used at any time during the lesson once the content reading and the featured structures have been presented.

Preview the worksheet with the students and make sure they understand the directions and the tasks. (Consult the description for the worksheet on the last page of each Topic Plan.) Give an example, if necessary. Vary the use of the worksheet. Assign it for homework, group work, pair work, or independent work. In addition to giving students writing practice with the language structures and content, the worksheets can be used for informal assessments. Students can present their answers orally in class and have other students check for accuracy.

►CHANTS

Components: Picture Dictionary, Content Chant, Cassette

The following are techniques for presenting the content chants in any topic. As you plan your lessons for each topic from the ideas presented in the *Chants* column of each Topic Plan, refer back to this section for basic techniques on how to present chants. Pick and choose from the following sections on *Listening*, *Speaking*, *Reading*, and *Writing* according to the abilities or current needs of your students.

CONTENT CHANTS

The *Content Chants* book, by Carolyn Graham, is one of the four books in the Reproducibles Collection. There is one chant page for each topic. The content chants teach the natural rhythm, stress, and intonation patterns of English. Practicing the content area language in the context of a chant makes the language more accessible and more enjoyable to learn.

Note that an asterisk (*) used in the chant indicates a clap. Rhythmically, the asterisk indicates another beat.

The content chants present conversational content language. While there are strategies listed here for listening, speaking, reading, and writing activities, the primary focus of the content chants is spoken language.

Preview

- Point out the title of the chant and ask students for their reactions or predictions. Students might predict which content words are in the chant by listening to the title.
- Ask students if they know chants, songs, or poems about the topic in their native language(s).
- Encourage students to bring in rhythmic instruments, especially those indigenous to their various cultures, to enhance the natural rhythm of the chants as they perform them. For example, students might bring in maracas, tambourines, wood blocks, or bells.

Listening

- Play the cassette several times as students listen to the entire chant. After the first or second listening, have students clap or tap the rhythm with a pencil or a ruler, or use their instruments to join in with the beat. If there are some more difficult sections of the chant, play just those sections so students can listen closely to them.

- Encourage students to pantomime the action words in the chant as they listen, or guide them in creating interesting movements to go with the rhythm of the chant.

Speaking

- *Chunking*

  Practice *chunking* the more difficult words or phrases in the chant. A language *chunk* is any meaningful utterance in the language. It can be a word, an idiom, an expression, or a phrase that can be isolated from the larger sentence and still retain its meaning. It is often useful for students to practice the language of the chant with various small chunks before trying to chant whole sentences. Suggestions are provided in the Chants column of each topic for specific chunks of the language which might be useful for practice. However, teachers may want to select other language chunks, depending on the needs of the class.

  Have students practice these chunks of language first chorally or in groups and then individually. Choral chanting gives the students confidence until they feel comfortable with the language. In the specific Topic Plans, it is often suggested that different groups chant different lines simultaneously while becoming familiar with the rhythm. This helps build students' confidence and concentration, as they have to maintain their own lines while others are chanting different ones.

- *Backward Buildup*

  When students are practicing long sentences, it is often helpful to break the sentence up into smaller chunks and practice *backward buildup* from the end of the sentence. With this technique, students repeat each phrase and then tack it onto the previous phrase. This technique helps students maintain the sentence rhythm and intonation. For example, in the sentence *And lots of constellations will be out tonight,* backward buildup would work as follows:

  (Repeat each chunk before adding the next)

  out tonight

  will be

  will be out tonight

  constellations

  constellations will be out tonight

  and lots of

  And lots of constellations will be out tonight.

  Some sentences for which backward buildup is useful are presented in the chant sections of each topic, but the teacher is encouraged to use this technique as necessary, depending on the needs of the students.

- Make a transparency of the chant for those students who may want to refer to it, but practice speaking the chant first and not reading it. Otherwise, students could get lost in the written word and not concentrate on the rhythm and intonation of the spoken language.
- Before students read the chant, divide the class into groups and have each group chant along with various stanzas on the tape. Or, stop the tape periodically and have students repeat the line(s) or stanza they just heard.
- Assign various verses to small groups first, and then later have students in pairs or individually take different roles or verses or lines in the chant.
- Change the roles periodically so that each group can take turns chanting the different types of language in the chant.
- Have each group practice chanting their lines alone, starting slowly and softly and then increasing the volume and speed as they feel more comfortable with the language of the chant. Often groups take turns chanting their parts, particularly in question and answer chants. Other times, you might have groups chant their parts simultaneously.

Reading and Writing

- Distribute the content chant at any time you feel that it is appropriate.
- Explain the meaning of any words that may be new.
- Have students cut the chant reproducible into strips and hand the different strips out to pairs or individuals who chant their lines or stanzas in turn.
- Encourage students to write their own chants, substitute their own words for words in the chant, or add verses that maintain the same rhythm of the chant and use the same language patterns, if possible. For example, in the content chant *Sixteen Ounces, One Pound*, one of the stanzas is :

Two pints of milk
   One quart
Four quarts of milk
   One gallon.

Students could rewrite the chant using other units of measure taught in the lesson. If possible, have students write, perform, and record their chants for the class, the school, or other visitors.

▶ EXTENSION

Components: Picture Dictionary, Transparency, Wall Chart, Word and Picture Cards

Extension Activities provide expansion and reinforcement of the language and concepts introduced in the lesson. They help students internalize the language and content, and apply what they have learned to life outside of the classroom.

The Extension activities are geared to students of mixed levels. Many of these activities, such as group discussions, debates, and research projects, involve group work in which students at different language levels can work to achieve the same goals. As you have groups work together in these activities, select group leaders and group recorders. The leaders try to ensure that all students are participating. The recorders report the progress of the group.

Activities for Language Practice

There are numerous Extension activities for language practice. Some involve using the featured grammatical structure creatively in oral or written work. (For example, students might use comparative and superlative adjectives to talk about each other, their friends, or their family members.) Other activities involve language games. Still other activities involve discussion and debate about the content or a particular point in the lesson, with students expressing their opinions, talking about their various cultural points of view, or interviewing each other and then analyzing and reporting the data.

Activities for Content Practice

The Extension activities help students to explore the content more extensively. Supportive group and pair work is encouraged in research projects that motivate students to find specific types of information in books, journals, magazines, almanacs, and on the Internet, as well as in school, at home, and in the community. These extension activities encourage students to find information and report it through posters, graphs, charts, and oral and written reports.

► LITERATURE

Each topic in the Teacher's Book includes an annotated list of suggested *Literature* for students. The list provides a detailed summary of each book, including its plot or theme, its reading level, and its relationship to the topic. Suggestions for activities based on the selection are also provided. The literature list includes both fiction and nonfiction books. The books frequently address issues relevant to newcomers, such as bilingualism and cultural differences.

Preview

- Establish a reading corner or class library where students can read quietly by themselves, in pairs, or in small groups. You can also read to them, depending on the needs of the class.

- Engage students in an activity that elicits interest, taps prior knowledge, or addresses the background necessary for understanding the particular literature selection.

- Display the cover of the book and point out the title, the name(s) of the author and illustrator, the table of contents, and the index, if there is one. Share and discuss any other features of the book which will directly contribute to students' understanding and enjoyment of the text (for example, the illustrations, the captions, graphic organizers such as tables, graphs, etc.). Have students make predictions about what they think the book will be about.

- Encourage students to hold the book and look through it, especially if they are choosing their own selection.

Listening

- If the book is short enough, read the story straight through as students listen or point to the pictures. If the book is too long, have students listen to various chapters or to certain selections from the book.

- If a recording is available, have students listen to it several times. You can also make your own recording. At the outset, the primary goal is to have students listen and/or read along to enjoy the selection.

- Pair students with mainstream students who will read aloud or record the selection.

Speaking

- After the initial reading, read the selection again, stopping at various points for students' reactions, opinions, and questions and answers. Ask *Wh-* information questions about the book.

- Have students retell the story in their own words.

- Encourage students to share events from their own lives that have been suggested by the reading.

Reading

- Have students do shared reading in groups or pairs.
- Provide independent silent reading time.
- Encourage students to select books to take home so they can share their reading with parents or friends.

Writing

- Have students write short book reports describing the book as well as their reactions to it. Student can read their reports to the class and/or put them in a file box for other students to check if they are doing independent reading.

- Have students write some of their favorite ideas from the book in their journals. They can also add new words to their word banks.

- Encourage students to write and illustrate a related story about their own lives, individually or as a group, and share their stories with the entire class.

- Have more advanced students try to use some of the sentence patterns from the book. Suggest a sentence pattern to the students and have them compete to see who can create the funniest or most interesting sentence. This technique often improves both spoken and written fluency.

ASSESSMENT

A variety of assessment techniques can be used in conjunction with any program built around *The Oxford Picture Dictionary for the Content Areas* and its components. Assessment measures such as focused observations, portfolios, learning logs, and checklists work well with the variety of activities presented in the Teacher's Book. Described below are some ideas for assessment techniques that can be used for continuing evaluation of students' oral and written performance as they work with the Dictionary and the accompanying components. Following the ideas are descriptions of four reproducible assessment pages included in this book.

Assessment Ideas

- Distribute the content reading reproducible, the content chant reproducible, or uncut copies of the word and picture cards. Pronounce the words in random order as students identify the content word by cutting it out or underlining it wherever it appears in the various texts or pictures.

- Draw a graphic organizer such as a word web or Venn diagram on the board. Label the sections and have students place the picture and/or word cards in the appropriate sections.

- Using the content reading, cover selected content elements or selected sentences illustrating the featured grammatical structures and have students say or write the missing words.

- Ask students to describe the content topic orally or in writing using one of the featured grammatical structures in a sentence(s).

- Have students refer to the wall chart or transparency and use their own words to describe, dramatize, or role-play the Dictionary illustration (or sections of it).

- Have students keep journals in which they draw and/or write about the topic they are studying. Periodically, read the journals and write responses to students' entries, including suggestions for improvement. Make notes of difficulties students have with either language skills or content concepts and make a plan for subsequent instruction.

- At the beginning of a topic, pair students with a "study buddy" and have them use learning logs to complete a *K-W-L* chart (see page xvii). Students list words and/or facts they already know. Then they write one or more questions they have about the topic. At the end of the activities, students write the answers to their questions and record one or more pieces of information they learned. Students discuss their entries. You can use K-W-L charts for the entire class as well.

- Have students make a T chart like the example below and list what they *understand* and *don't understand* about the topic.

Understand	Don't Understand

Students compare and discuss their charts and then revise their lists. Hold conferences with students periodically and examine these entries together to identify problems. Address these needs as you plan further instruction.

- Portfolios are tangible records of students' progress over time. Portfolios usually contain a variety of items ranging from simple pictures and lists of words to journal entries, maps, stories, and written reports, including first drafts, revisions, and final forms. Both teachers and students should agree on what is kept in the portfolio. By reviewing the portfolio contents, teachers, parents, and the student can assess the progress made and identify further instructional needs.

Reproducible Assessment Pages

Topic Tracking Chart (page xxiv)
This grid helps teachers keep track of which topics and which elements within a topic each student has worked on or completed. The teacher lists student names on the left, writes the topic number or name in the spaces, and puts checkmarks under each element or component.

Student Self-Assessment Checklist (page xxv)
This checklist is intended for students to use with each topic. It enables them to become involved in the assessment process. Students check off how well they think they can do each of the skills listed.

Checklists of Oral Language Skills and Written Language Skills (pages xxvi-xxvii)
These checklists are informal measures for recording observations made throughout the school year. They can be used during or immediately following instruction to note students' progress. Teachers can adapt the checklists to the needs of their own classes. The first checklist is for recording the observations of various listening and speaking skills. The second checklist is used for recording observations of reading and writing skills. The teacher marks whether students "rarely" or "usually" are able to do these skills at the time the observation is made. Teachers can note students' progress by comparing observations made at different times in the school year.

TOPIC TRACKING CHART

Student Names

												TOPIC
											Word Cards	
											Picture Cards	
											Content Reading	
											Content Chant	TOPIC
											Worksheet	
											Workbook	
											Other	
											Other	
											Word Cards	
											Picture Cards	
											Content Reading	
											Content Chant	TOPIC
											Worksheet	
											Workbook	
											Other	
											Other	
											Word Cards	
											Picture Cards	
											Content Reading	
											Content Chant	TOPIC
											Worksheet	
											Workbook	
											Other	
											Other	
											Word Cards	
											Picture Cards	
											Content Reading	
											Content Chant	TOPIC
											Worksheet	
											Workbook	
											Other	
											Other	
											Word Cards	
											Picture Cards	
											Content Reading	
											Content Chant	TOPIC
											Worksheet	
											Workbook	
											Other	
											Other	

The Oxford Picture Dictionary for the Content Areas

Name _____   Date _____

Topic _____

Things I Can Do:	☆☆☆☆☆ Wow!	☆☆☆ Great	☆☆ Okay	☆ Try Again
1. I can read all the content words.				
2. I can match the content words and pictures.				
3. I can understand and describe the wall chart.				
4. I can read the content reading aloud.				
5. I can understand the content reading.				
6. I can use the content words in sentences.				
7. I can chant the content chant.				
8. I can write about the topic.				
9. I can understand the topic.				
10. One more thing I can do is _____.				

CHECKLIST OF ORAL LANGUAGE SKILLS

Student _____

Oral Comprehension/Listening	Rarely	Usually	Date
1. Observes but does not participate			
2. Responds verbally to simple greetings			
3. Responds to questions with nonverbal responses			
4. Responds to questions with appropriate verbal responses			
5. Understands content information and participates in discussions			

Oral Expression/Speaking	Rarely	Usually	Date
1. Observes, but does not participate			
2. Attempts to speak in group or choral activities			
3. Speaks in single words or short phrases			
4. Pronunciation has many errors which interfere with communication			
5. Pronunciation has some errors which don't interfere with communication			
6. Pronounces words and sentences accurately and uses correct rhythm, stress, and intonation			
7. Speaks about or reports information using two or three sentences			
8. Speaks about or reports information using five or more sentences			
9. Asks questions to gather information			
10. Asks questions to clarify information			
11. Speaks independently without prompting or questions			
12. Uses common idioms			
13. Is able to explain and rephrase difficult content concepts			
14. Communicates with other students with difficulty			
15. Communicates creatively, effectively, and fluently			

CHECKLIST OF WRITTEN LANGUAGE SKILLS

Student _____

Reading Skills	Rarely	Usually	Date
1. Identifies letters of the alphabet			
2. Recognizes letters of the alphabet in words			
3. Recognizes common consonant sounds			
4. Recognizes common vowel sounds			
5. Reads words for common objects and actions (sight vocabulary)			
6. Identifies and reads content words			
7. Reads simple sentences			
8. Reads and follows simple directions			
9. Reads new sentences created by recombining or rearranging known words			
10. Reads titles, heading, and/or captions and makes predictions about content			
11. Identifies main ideas and details			
12. Categorizes words and concepts			
13. Understands and interprets charts, diagrams, and other graphic organizers			
14. Identifies events in a sequence			
15. Identifies cause and effect relationships			
16. Draws conclusions and makes predictions			
17. Responds to text with original ideas			
18. Uses reference materials successfully			
19. Reads fluently			
20. Selects books and reads independently			

Writing Skills	Rarely	Usually	Date
1. Writes name			
2. Copies words correctly			
3. Writes dictated words, phrases and sentences			
4. Writes simple words			
5. Writes content words			
6. Writes phrases and sentences			
7. Writes answers to questions in single words or phrases			
8. Writes answers to questions in simple sentences			
9. Writes sentences with correct spelling, capitalization, and punctuation			
10. Independently writes recalled content information in three or more sentences.			
11. Writes original thoughts in a paragraph using five or more sentences			
12. Uses paragraph conventions of main and subordinate ideas in writing			
13. Writes an outline of content information			
14. Writes research reports			

▶ **CONTENT**
....
Classroom objects

▶ **LANGUAGE**
....
There + BE (there is/there's/there are): *There is one teacher.*

Cardinal numbers: *There are ten students.*

 CONTENT WORDS

1. student
2. teacher
3. desk
4. chair
5. table
6. book
7. computer
8. pencil
9. pen
10. crayon
11. paper
12. notebook
13. ruler
14. chalkboard
15. bulletin board
16. map
17. overhead projector
18. pencil sharpener
19. cassette player
20. wastebasket

CONTENT READING

The Classroom

This is an ESL classroom. There are many things and many people in the classroom. There is one teacher. There are ten students. There are six girls and there are four boys.

There is one chalkboard and there is one bulletin board. There's a map on the chalkboard. There's a calendar on the bulletin board. There's a computer on the table. There's an overhead projector near the computer.

There are five chairs in the classroom. There are four students at the desks and there are four students on the floor. There is one student at the computer and one student at the pencil sharpener. There are books on the bookshelf. There is one flag in the classroom and there is one clock on the wall. There is a cassette player on one desk.

There is a notebook, a pencil, and a pen on the floor. There are also some crayons and some paper on the floor. There is one ruler and there is one wastebasket in the classroom. There is also a pair of scissors, a bottle of paste, and a bookbag on the floor.

What's in your classroom?

▶ WORDS

Components: Dictionary pages 2-3, Transparency 1, Wall Chart 1, Workbook page 1, Word and Picture Cards Topic 1, Cassette

- Present the content words. **See pages xiv-xvi for general techniques about presenting content words.**

- Display the wall chart and have students look at the picture. Divide the class into two groups. Group 1 describes what is happening at the desks where the teacher is talking to the students. Group 2 describes the scene on the floor of the classroom. Each group circles or makes a list of all the content words that appear in that portion of the scene.

- Have students make lists of all the objects in your classroom that are listed as content words. They don't have to write complete sentences.

- Make two columns on the board. Write *One* at the top of one column and *More Than One* at the top of the other column. Distribute the word and picture cards to each student. Have the students, in turn, read their word and picture cards and say whether there is one or more than one of that item in the classroom. If students are writing, they can write the words from their word cards in the appropriate column. Non-writers can say which column their words belong in as you write the words for them.

- Redistribute the word and picture cards. Have each student read aloud his or her word and picture card and then go to the corresponding object in the classroom and stand next to it. For example, the student who receives the *bulletin board* word and picture card stands next to the bulletin board. For cards with portable items such as *pencil* on them, the student can hold up the object or stand next to the nearest one. The student who receives the *student* word and picture card can stand next to a friend. If any students receive cards for objects not found in your classroom, they stand by the classroom door.

WORKBOOK: Topic 1
See Teacher's Book page 5.

▶ CONTENT

Components: Dictionary pages 2-3, Transparency 1, Wall Chart 1, Content Reading Topic 1, Worksheet Topic 1, Cassette

- Present the content reading. **See pages xvii-xix for general techniques about presenting content readings.**

- Ask the following or similar questions:

  Is there a teacher in the classroom?
  Is there a television in the classroom?
  Where's the computer?
  How many students are in the classroom?
  Are there more boys or girls in the classroom?

▶ *There + BE*

> We often use the contracted form *there's* for *there is* in conversation, but not usually in formal writing. Have students practice with both *there is* and *there's* for the third person singular in conversation. We don't usually use a contracted form of *There are.*

Have students write a description of your classroom using *there is/there's* or *there are* with objects they find. For example: *There are three desks, two chairs, four computers, and one table in our classroom.* Students describe as many things as they can. If students cannot yet write, ask them to give an oral description. Create a class description of the classroom by writing the students' responses in a list on the board. If there are additional objects which are not specified in the content reading, have students make a word bank in their notebooks, label it *The Classroom*, and add the words to their word banks.

▶ **Cardinal numbers.** Ask students to count things in the classroom. Students might count the number of pencils in the mug on your desk, the number of books on a shelf, or the number of numbers on a ruler. After students have finished counting, encourage them to report their results using *there is/there's* or *there are*. For example: *There are seven holes in the pencil sharpener.*

WORKSHEET: Topic 1
See Teacher's Book page 5.

►CHANTS

Components: Dictionary pages 2-3, Content Chant Topic 1, Cassette

 ## CONTENT CHANT

Classroom Chant

Computer, * overhead projector,
pens, pencils, books, and crayons.
Computer, * overhead projector,
pencil sharpener, bulletin board.

> Is this your classroom?
> > Yes, it is.
>
> Are these your books?
> > Yes, they are.
>
> Is this your pen?
> > Yes, it is.
>
> Are these your crayons?
> > Yes, they are.

Pens, pencils, books, and crayons.
Pencil sharpener, bulletin board.

> Is there a computer in the classroom?
> > Yes, there is.
>
> Is there a cassette player?
> > Yes, there is.
>
> Is there an overhead projector?
> > Yes, there is.

Wow! You have everything!

Computer, * overhead projector,
pens, pencils, books, and crayons.
Computer, * overhead projector,
pencil sharpener, bulletin board.

- Present the content chant. **See pages xx-xxi for general techniques about presenting chants.**

- Before distributing Content Chant 1, establish the rhythm of the chant. Begin by having the entire class chant *Computer, (clap) overhead projector* repeatedly. Then divide the class into two groups. Group 1 repeatedly chants *pens, pencils, books and crayons.* At the same time, Group 2 repeatedly chants *pencil sharpener, bulletin board.* Increase the volume and the speed as students become more familiar with their parts, but maintain the rhythm. Then, have each group chant their parts in turn.

- Now distribute Content Chant 1 and model the chant as all students repeat after you. Then, Group 1 chants all the questions and Group 2 chants all the answers. Groups exchange parts and repeat the chant.

- Select one student to shout out the line that begins with *Wow!* Then Groups 1 and 2 take their parts as above for the last stanza.

►EXTENSION

Components: Dictionary pages 2-3, Transparency 1, Wall Chart 1, Word and Picture Cards Topic 1

- Write *There is 1 _____.* on the board. Underneath it, write *There are 2 _____.* Continue for all numbers up to ten. Students copy these lines in their notebooks or on pieces of paper. Then they fill in the blanks with the names of the appropriate objects found in the classroom. For example: *There is 1 <u>teacher</u>,* or *There are 4 <u>chairs</u>.* After students have found appropriate objects for all ten numbers, they exchange papers with their neighbors, who check them for accuracy.

- Pair students. Have them take turns asking and answering questions about classroom objects with *how many* and *there is/there are.* For example, if Student A asks *How many wastebaskets are in the classroom?,* Student B says, *There are two wastebaskets.*

- Distribute one word and picture card to each student (excluding *student* and *teacher* cards). Each student reads the word and picture card and tries to explain what one does with the object shown on the card. For example, for the *pencil* card, the student writes or says, *This is a pencil. I write with a pencil.*

- Ask students to close their books. One student comes to the front of the class and holds up or points to one of the objects shown in the dictionary illustration. The other students try to name the object without looking in their books. The first student to name the object correctly comes to the front of the class and points to or holds up another object shown in the picture.

- **Game: It's in This Room.** Select one student to be "it." Have the student who is "it" leave the room while the rest of the class decides on one content word object to hide. The student who is "it" has to guess which object is hidden and where it is. He or she gets a total of 15 guesses. Encourage the student to ask *Yes/No* questions about the object and its location, such as *Is it a _____?* and *Is it near the wall?*

► LITERATURE

Suggested Books

I Hate English

written by Ellen Levine; illustrated by Steve Bjorkman.
Demco Media, 1995. ISBN 0606076840
This book tells an engaging and realistic story about a young girl's transition from her school in Hong Kong to her new school in Chinatown, New York. As the title suggests, she has difficulty adjusting to her new country's language and culture. The text of the story emphasizes high-frequency verbs and interrogative forms. Vocabulary and situations from Topic 1, The Classroom, can be easily identified in the illustrations. This book is especially useful for shared reading with mainstream students.

I Speak English for My Mom

written by Muriel Stanek; illustrated by Judith Friedman.
Albert Whitman & Co., 1989. ISBN 0807536598
The experiences in this story are common to many families who emigrate to America. Lupe, a Mexican-American girl, must translate everything into English for her Spanish-speaking mother. When Lupe's mother begins to attend ESL classes, mother and daughter become closer as they speak English together. This book provides a positive role model for children who must bridge the bilingual gap between their new culture and their non-English speaking families.

I'm New Here

written by Bud Howlett; photographs by the author.
Houghton Mifflin Co., 1993. ISBN 0395640490
This is a photo-essay of Jazmin Escalante's first days at school. Her family has just come from El Salvador and she doesn't speak a word of English. Situations that many new ESL students can relate to are shown and talked about: finding their way around the school, filling in strange forms, making new friends. The language may

require teacher guidance, but the ideas conveyed in the pictures will serve as realistic prompts for students newly entering an ESL classroom.

Angel Child, Dragon Child

written by Michele Maria Surat;
illustrated by Vo-Dinh Mai.
Scholastic Trade, 1989. ISBN 0590422715
Ut is a young Vietnamese girl who has just started school in the United States. She dislikes it at first because the kids laugh at her for being different, especially a boy named Raymond. After she and Raymond get into a fight, however, they finally come to an understanding. Although the Vietnamese phrases and some of the vocabulary will need to be explained, all newcomers to English will be able to identify with Ut's self-consciousness and discomfort at school. This book promotes an understanding of diversity in the classroom, with a focus on the acceptance of newcomers. It can be a meaningful addition to social studies classes with ESL and mainstream students.

We Came from Vietnam

written by Muriel Stanek; photographs by W. Franklin McMahon.
Albert Whitman & Co., 1987. ISBN 0807586994
This book's black-and-white photographs and simple text tell the story of a Vietnamese refugee family's adaptation to life in Chicago. The section on school will be helpful to read with newcomers. Many students will be able to identify with the photographs that show situations in the classroom and on the playground. This book is also appropriate for Topic 4, The Family.

WORKBOOK: Topic 1

In activity A, students list the classroom objects found in the picture. In activity B, they list the objects on the desk in the picture. In activity C, they refer to the words they wrote in B, and circle the ones that appear in their own classroom.

WORKSHEET: Topic 1

In A, students look at the picture and fill in the blanks with *There is, There's,* or *There are.* In B, they write sentences describing what they see in the pictures. In C, they tell about their own classroom.

2 THE SCHOOL

▶ **CONTENT**
....
Places and people at school

▶ **LANGUAGE**
....
Prepositions of place (*in, on, in front of, near*): *The coach is in the gym.*

Habitual present: *The students eat lunch in the cafeteria.*

Ordinal numbers: *The gym is on the first floor.*

CONTENT WORDS

1. playground
2. office
3. principal
4. secretary
5. cafeteria
6. gym
7. coach
8. hall
9. water fountain
10. locker
11. boys room
12. girls room
13. custodian
14. auditorium
15. stairs
16. library
17. librarian
18. media center

CONTENT READING

The School

This is a school. There are three floors in the school. There are many different rooms and many people.

The cafeteria is on the first floor of the school. Many students are in the cafeteria. The students eat lunch in the cafeteria. The gym is on the first floor. The coach is in the gym. Students play basketball in the gym. The office is also on the first floor. The principal is in her office. The principal is the head of the school. The secretary works near the principal's office.

The hall is on the second floor. The girls room and the boys room are in the hall, too. There is a water fountain in the hall. There are lockers in the hall. The custodian is in the hall. The custodian cleans the school. The auditorium is also on the second floor. There is a concert in the auditorium.

The library is on the third floor. The stairs are near the library. The librarian helps the students. Students read in the library. The media center is in the library. Students watch videos in the media center.

The playground is in front of the school. The students play in the playground. They swing on the swings and they slide on the slide.

There is a new student at the front door. He is with his parents. Today is his first day at this school.

▶ WORDS

Components: Dictionary pages 4-5, Transparency 2, Wall Chart 2, Word and Picture Cards Topic 2, Workbook page 2, Cassette

- Present the content words. **See pages xiv-xvi for general techniques about presenting content words.**

   Language Note: Note that *gym* is short for *gymnasium. Custodian* is another word for *janitor. Assistant* is sometimes used as another word for *secretary. Water cooler* is another word for *water fountain. Corridor* is another word for *hall. Lunchroom* is another word for *cafeteria.* People often use the word *bathroom* to mean either the boys room or girls room.

- Display the wall chart and have students look at the picture. Divide the class into two groups. Group 1 describes what is happening on the second and third floors of the school. Group 2 describes what is happening on the first floor and outside the school. Each group circles or makes a list of all the content words that appear in their section.

- Have students make lists of all the people, places, and things in your school that are listed as content words. They don't have to write complete sentences.

- Make three columns on the board. Write *People* at the top of one column, *Places* at the top of the second column, and *Things* at the top of the third column. Distribute one word and picture card to each student. Have each student, in turn, read the word and picture card, and say whether it is a person, place, or thing. If students are writing, they can write the word in the appropriate column on the board. Non-writers can say the word and tell you where to write the word for them.

WORKBOOK: Topic 2
   See Teacher's Book page 9.

▶ CONTENT

Components: Dictionary pages 4-5, Transparency 2, Wall Chart 2, Content Reading Topic 2, Word and Picture Cards Topic 2, Worksheet Topic 2, Cassette

- Present the content reading. **See pages xvii-xix for general techniques about presenting content readings.**

- Ask the following or similar questions:

   Is there a cafeteria in the school?
   Is the librarian in the cafeteria?
   How many students are in the hall?
   Where is the auditorium?
   Where's the custodian?

▶ **Ordinal numbers, Prepositions of place.** Distribute one word and picture card to each student, and divide the class into two teams. A student from Team 1 asks *Where's the _____?*, using the word from the card. For example: *Where's the principal?* A student from Team 2 says where that word can be found in the picture, using ordinal numbers and/or prepositions of place. For example: *Her office is on the first floor.* Then a student from Team 2 asks a question, and a student from Team 1 answers. Continue the game until all students have read and answered at least once.

▶ **Ordinal numbers.** Divide the class into two teams. Each team stands in a line facing the other team. Introduce ordinal numbers from *third* to *tenth*, and beyond *tenth* as appropriate for the number of students in the lines. Ask a student from Team 1 to name the fourth student from the left on Team 2. The student calls out the name. If the student names the correct person, Team 1 gets a point. If not, Team 2 gets a point. Now ask the fourth student from Team 2 to name the seventh student from Team 1. If she says the name correctly, Team 2 gets a point. If not, Team 1 gets a point. Continue the game (choosing the ordinal numbers at random) until all students have named another student.

▶ **Prepositions of place *in* and *on*.** Put a pencil in a cup and a book on a desk. Ask students to describe the position of these objects using the prepositions of place *in* and *on*. For example: *The pencil is in the cup. The book is on the desk.* Have students describe other things in your classroom using *in* and *on*. Each student should try to describe a different group of items.

WORKSHEET: Topic 2
   See Teacher's Book page 9.

►CHANTS

 ## CONTENT CHANT

Where's the Coach?

Where's the coach?
He's not in the gym.

> There he is!

That's not him!
That's the custodian. That's not him.

Where's the coach?
He's not in the gym.

> Here he comes!

That's not him!
That's the librarian. That's not him.

> Look on the playground.
> There! With Tim.

That's not the coach. That's not him.
He's not on the playground. That's not him.

Where's the coach? He's not in the gym.

- Present the content chant. **See pages xx-xxi for general techniques about presenting chants.**

- Before distributing Content Chant 2, establish the rhythm of the chant. Divide the class into two groups. Group 1 chants *Where's the coach?* Group 2 chants *There he is!* A male student from Group 2 role-plays the coach and waves. Then, the groups switch parts. Group 2 chants *Where's the coach?* and a female student from Group 1 waves as Group 1 says *There she is!* Continue this type of word play with other content words such as *principal, custodian, secretary* and *librarian*.

- Now, distribute Content Chant 2 and divide the class into two groups. Group 1 chants the first two lines. Group 2 or an individual student chants *There he is!* and Group 1 continues *That's not him! That's the custodian. That's not him.* Continue the pattern for the entire chant. Then have the groups switch parts so that Group 2 has a chance to do the longer parts.

- Adapt the chant by using the names of students in the class. Start students off by mentioning a name. Student A chants, *Where's Yukio? He's not in the gym.* Encourage Yukio to respond *Here I am! I'm not in the gym.* Then Yukio chants the name of another student. *Where's Alicia? She's not in the gym.* Alicia continues the chain. Continue until all students have had a chance to question and answer. Make further adaptations with the names of personnel in your school.

►EXTENSION

- Write the name of each student on the board in alphabetical order. Ask students to describe this list using ordinal numbers. For example: *Alfredo is first, Yang Foo is second*, etc. Now arrange students in some other kind of order (by height, by birth dates, by shoe size, etc.) and have students describe this new list, again using ordinal numbers.

- Have students describe the locations of various rooms in your school using the content words. They can also use other words they know. For example: *The office is on the second floor. The principal works in the office. The auditorium is on the third floor.* Encourage students to use as many of the content words as are appropriate to your school.

- Pair students. Have them take turns asking and answering questions about school rooms, using the prepositions of place *in* and *on* and actual information about your school. For example: *Where's the gym? It's on the third floor.*

- Pair students again. Have each student build a tower of classroom items, using books, papers, notebooks, pens, pencils, rulers, and other items. Students may use no more than one of each item. After each student builds a tower, the partner describes the tower using *on*. For example: *The pencil is on the card. The card is on the paper. The paper is on the book. The book is on the desk. The desk is on the floor.* After each student has built a tower and described a partner's tower, compare the heights of the towers. The student who builds the tallest tower that does not fall over is the winner.

- Have students talk or write about their favorite room in the entire school. They should say where this room is and why they like it the best. For example, they may like to see their friends in the cafeteria or hear music in the auditorium.

► LITERATURE

Suggested Books

School Bus: For the Buses, the Riders, and the Watchers
written and illustrated by Donald Crews.
Mulberry Books, 1993. ISBN 0688122671
This simple, direct book offers students an introduction to school buses, traffic, and safety. The text's repeated word patterns and short declarative sentences ensure that the entire book can be read aloud quickly. Most of the vocabulary can be found in Topic 1, The Classroom, and Topic 2, The School. However, some high-frequency verbs need to be introduced in order for students to understand the text. The colorful art is suitable for all students, although the book, as a whole, is best-suited to beginners.

Lilly's Purple Plastic Purse
written and illustrated by Kevin Henkes.
Greenwillow, 1996. ISBN 0688128971
The young mouse, Lilly, has just started school and she loves her new teacher, Mr. Slinger. When Lilly plays with her new purse during class, however, Mr. Slinger takes it away. Lilly gets angry, although her feelings of anger quickly change to remorse when Mr. Slinger returns the purse with a gentle note and a treat. This best-seller has become a favorite in schools everywhere. Students are sure to identify with Lilly or with the "Lilly" in their classroom. The humorous illustrations reinforce the topic's vocabulary and also help beginning students learn additional language related to their new school.

Oxford American Children's Encyclopedia
Oxford University Press, 1999. ISBN 0195110811
This nine-volume set is an excellent resource for ESL students in search of information or clarification of content-area vocabulary. It presents accurate and clearly-written articles for all subject areas, including social studies, history, geography, language arts, science, and math. It also includes many one-word entries that define and illustrate the content words in the Dictionary.

Check It Out!: The Book About Libraries
written and illustrated by Gail Gibbons.
Harcourt Brace, 1988. ISBN 0152164014
In this informative book, Gail Gibbons introduces ESL students to one of the most important and useful places in their school and community: the library. The clear pictures and text teach the basic vocabulary that students will need to know in order to use the library. When read aloud, particularly in a school library or media center where students can make visual connections, this book invites discussion about what a library is, what it does, and how it works. After students have enjoyed this book, teachers may want to follow up with a class visit to a local library.

Miss Nelson Is Missing
written by Harry Allard; illustrated by James Marshall.
Demco Media, 1985. ISBN 0606044000
Miss Nelson Is Missing is a clever mystery about the disappearance of the nicest teacher in the school. When the mystery is solved, Miss Nelson's students learn an important lesson about how to treat others. Useful language structures featured in the story include *Wh*-questions and exclamations. Students will appreciate the humor in the drawings, and the simple text can be used for read-aloud or read-along sessions.

WORKBOOK: Topic 2

In A, students write the words for the numbered people and places in the picture. In B, they refer to their answers in A. They circle words for places, and underline words for people.

WORKSHEET: Topic 2

In the first activity, students identify the floor on which the people or rooms are, and fill in the blanks. In the second activity, they look at the picture and fill in prepositions using the choices in the word box.

▶ **CONTENT**
....
Rooms of the house

▶ **LANGUAGE**
....
Prepositions of place *(at, above, below, between, in, on, over, next to): There is a roof over the house and a roof over the porch.*

Present continuous: *She is sleeping.*

CONTENT WORDS

1. porch
2. window
3. door
4. basement
5. kitchen
6. cupboard
7. living room
8. floor
9. bathroom
10. toilet
11. sink
12. bathtub
13. shower
14. bedroom
15. closet
16. wall
17. ceiling
18. attic
19. roof
20. chimney

CONTENT READING

The House

The Johnson family lives in this house. The house has many windows and a red front door. There is a roof over the house and a roof over the porch. There's a chimney on one side of the house.

The attic is on the top floor of the house. It's above the bathroom and the bedroom. The bathroom is next to the bedroom.

Jimmy Johnson is in the bathroom. He is washing his face at the sink. The sink is between the toilet and the bathtub. The bathtub has a shower.

Janet Johnson is in the bedroom. She is sleeping. There are pictures on the wall above her bed. The closet door is open. There's a light on the ceiling.

Mrs. Johnson and Tanya are in the kitchen. Mrs. Johnson is eating breakfast. Tanya is getting a plate from the cupboard. The kitchen is next to the living room. It is below the bathroom.

Kevin and Troy Johnson are in the living room. They are watching TV. There's a rug on the floor. The living room is below the bedroom.

Mr. Johnson is in the basement. He's doing laundry. The basement is below the living room and the kitchen. The dog is watching him.

Pete Johnson is on the front porch. He's going to school.

▶ WORDS

Components: Dictionary pages 6-7, Transparency 3, Wall Chart 3, Workbook page 3, Word and Picture Cards Topic 3, Cassette

- Present the content words. **See pages xiv-xvi for general techniques about presenting content words.**

- Display the wall chart and have students look at the picture. Divide the class into three groups. Group 1 describes what is happening on the first floor of the house. Group 2 describes what is happening on the second floor of the house. Group 3 describes what is happening in the basement and outside the house. Then each group circles or makes a list of all the content words that appear in their portion of the scene.

- Make four columns on the board. Label the columns *Kitchen, Living Room, Bedroom,* and *Bathroom.* Remove the cards with those words from the set of word and picture cards. Also remove the cards for *attic, chimney, porch,* and *roof.* Distribute the remaining cards, one to each student. Have each student, in turn, read a word and say in what room(s) the item can be found. For example, if the word on the card is *floor,* the student says, *There's a floor in the bedroom, the kitchen, the living room, and the bathroom.* You (or the student) then write the word under all four columns. But if, for example, the word on the card is *toilet,* the student says, *There's a toilet in the bathroom.* You (or the student) then write the word *toilet* only in the *Bathroom* column.

- Distribute all the word and picture cards, one per student. Have each student read the card and say whether that word can be found in the school. For example, windows, doors, basements, floors, and bathrooms can all be found in schools, but most schools don't have living rooms, bathtubs, showers, or bedrooms.

> **Language Note:** *Cellar* is another word for *basement. Cabinet* (or *kitchen cabinet*) is another word for *cupboard.* There may be variations with other words in this topics according to region. Discuss these differences with the class.

WORKBOOK: Topic 3
See Teacher's Book page 13.

▶ CONTENT

Components: Dictionary pages 6-7, Transparency 3, Wall Chart 3, Content Reading Topic 3, Word and Picture Cards Topic 3, Worksheet Topic 3, Cassette

- Present the content reading. **See pages xvii-xix for general techniques about presenting content readings.**

- Ask the following or similar questions:

    Is Jimmy Johnson in the attic?
    Are Kevin and Troy watching TV?
    Is Mr. Johnson doing the laundry or eating breakfast?
    Where is Tanya?
    What is Tanya doing?

▶ **Prepositions of place.** Distribute one word and picture card to each student. Divide the class into two teams. A student from Team 1 reads the word from the card. A student from Team 2 says where that object can be found in the Dictionary illustration by using prepositions of place. For example, if the word is *sink,* the answer is *The sink is between the toilet and the bathtub.* Then a student from Team 2 reads a word. Continue the game until all students have read and answered at least once.

▶ **Prepositions of place.** Divide students into two teams. Each team tries to describe a room in the house on the wall chart, using as many prepositions as possible. Students describe the room's location in the house: *The bedroom is above the living room and next to the bathroom.* They also describe the items in the room. *There are pictures on the bedroom wall. There's a lamp on the table.* Appoint one person from each team to count the actual numbers of prepositions used in student descriptions by the opposite team members. Score one point for each preposition. The team with the most points in 10 minutes wins.

▶ **Present continuous.** Divide students into two teams. A student from Team 1 pantomimes an action from the picture, such as getting a plate from the cupboard, or watching TV. A student from Team 2 says what the action is, using the present continuous tense. For example: *She's washing her face.* If the student guesses correctly, the next student from that team pantomimes an action and a student from the other team guesses the action. Continue until all students have pantomimed or guessed an action.

WORKSHEET: Topic 3
See Teacher's Book page 13.

►CHANT

Components: Dictionary pages 6-7, Content Chant Topic 3, Cassette

 ## CONTENT CHANT

There's a House

There's a house. * There's a big, white house.
There's a bathroom in the house,
    In the big white house.
There's a sink in the bathroom,
    In the big white house.

There's a boy at the sink in the bathroom in the house.
He's washing his hands,
    In the big white house,
At the sink, in the bathroom,
    In the big white house.

There's a bedroom in the house,
    In the big white house.
There's a bed in the bedroom,
    In the big white house.

There's a girl in the bed in the bedroom in the house.
She's taking a nap,
    In the big white house,
In the bed, in the bedroom,
    In the big white house.

- Present the content chant. **See pages xx-xxi for general techniques about presenting chants.**

- Before distributing Content Chant 3, establish the rhythm of the chant. Have the entire class chant *In the big white house* repeatedly until they are comfortable with the language. Now select one student to chant *There's a bathroom in the house.* The rest of the class responds with *In the big white house.* Continue with other rooms of the house, with the entire class responding each time.

- Invite individual students to invent introductory lines to the chant such as *There's a person in the house,* or *There's a TV in the house.* The class responds *In the big white house.*

- Distribute Content Chant 3 and have students, in groups, practice individual phrases from the longer sentences of the chant before they chant the entire sentences. For example, for the sentence *There's a sink in the bathroom in the big white house,* Group 1 chants *in the big white house,* Group 2 chants *in the bathroom,* and Group 3 chants *There's a sink.* Each group chants their language chunks individually, and then they put their parts together to chant the entire sentence. Continue this procedure with other long sentences in the chant.

►EXTENSION

Components: Dictionary pages 6-7, Transparency 3, Wall Chart 3

- Have students draw their own houses or apartments and label the things in each room. They may use the content words, as well as any other words they know. Encourage them to make their drawings large enough to fit all the furniture in each room.

- Have students talk about the different things they do in each room of their house or apartment. Students say or write lists of three or four things they do in the kitchen, in the living room, in the bedroom, and in the bathroom. Compare students' lists and encourage them to talk about the differences.

- Pair students. Student A tells Student B about the location of rooms in his or her house or apartment as Student B tries to make a drawing of these rooms. They use words only and no gestures or pointing. Student B can ask questions such as *Where's your bedroom?* Student A answers *It's between my parents' room and the living room.* When Student B finishes the drawing, Student A checks it for accuracy and they make adjustments, if necessary. Then they reverse roles.

- Ask students to describe a house they would like to live in. How many rooms would it have? What would be in each room? What would each room look like? Where would the house be? Who would live in the house with them? Encourage students to write the answers to these questions in a short essay entitled "The Perfect Home." Non-writers may draw pictures of their perfect home.

- Bring in a big bag with hundreds of tongue depressors, ice cream sticks, or other wooden building materials. Invite students to build model houses with ice cream sticks and glue. They should leave room for windows and doors, but not attach a roof. After students have finished building their houses, they can show them to the class. Ask them to point out the different rooms in their houses. After students have shown their houses to the class, they may wish to add roofs to their houses.

► LITERATURE

Suggested Books

This Is the House That Jack Built
written and illustrated by Pam Adams.
Child's Play Intl. Ltd., 1995. ISBN 0859530752
A popular nursery rhyme outlines the events that occur
one day at the house that Jack built. The colorful
illustrations are humorous enough to engage younger and
older students alike. Clever cut-out sections of each page
reinforce vocabulary and identify the various characters in
the text. The story can be read aloud with many pauses to
identify vocabulary illustrated on each page. Repetitive
language patterns in the story can be used as a fun
classroom chant.

Amelia Bedelia
written by Peggy Parish; illustrated by Fritz Siebel.
HarperCollins Juvenile Books, 1992. ISBN 0064441555
Like many ESL students, the popular character Amelia
Bedelia has limited English proficiency when it comes to
idiomatic expressions. Through Amelia's adventures as a
maid in Mr. and Mrs. Rogers' house, students will be
introduced to many instances of conversational English.
Amelia's literal interpretations of idiomatic expressions are
amusing and educational. New students will certainly
identify with her misunderstandings. The repetitive text
constructions and cartoon-like drawings make this difficult
aspect of learning English easy and fun.

Houses and Homes
written by Ann Morris; photographs by Ken Heyman.
Mulberry Books, 1995. ISBN 0688135781
The creators of this book take readers on a photographic
journey around the world to see the various houses that
people call home. These glimpses of how people live will
certainly prompt students from other countries to speak
about places in their home countries. The poetic text is
short, so teachers may want to read this book aloud many
times, in whole or in part. Students may be grouped so
that they can share a book, engaging them in both seeing
and hearing it.

The Little House
written and illustrated by Virginia Lee Burton.
Houghton Mifflin Co., 1978. ISBN 039525938X
This story of a little country house that is gradually
enveloped by a growing city has been a classic since it
won the Caldecott Medal in 1943. In simple yet vivid
language, the author describes the coming of the road,
the shift from a rural to a suburban to an urban landscape,
and the ever-passing seasons. The illustrations can be
used to foster student discussion about their environment.
This book may also be used in conjunction with Topic 5,
The City; Topic 6, The Suburbs; and Topic 7, The Country.

WORKBOOK: Topic 3

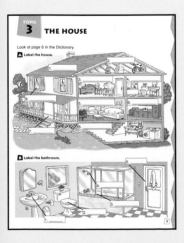

In A, students label the
rooms of the house. In B,
they label the objects in
the bathroom.

WORKSHEET: Topic 3

In A, students search the
picture for various letters.
They fill in each letter and
the prepositions listed in
the word box to tell where
the letters are in the
house. In B, they write the
letters in the appropriate
blanks to spell the word
cupboard, where the
mouse can find its
cheese.

▶ **CONTENT**
....
Family members and family
relationships

▶ **LANGUAGE**
....
Possessive adjectives: *This is
my family tree.*

Possessive nouns: *My sister's
name is Rosie.*

**Comparative and superlative
adjectives:** *Danny is younger
than Eva./She is the oldest.*

CONTENT WORDS

1. grandparents
2. grandmother
3. grandfather
4. parents
5. mother
6. father
7. baby
8. sister
9. brother
10. aunt
11. uncle
12. cousins

CONTENT READING

The Family

My name is Mario. My family and I are at a
barbecue with all my relatives. This is my family tree.
All my relatives are in my family tree.

My grandparents are at the bottom. Carlos is my
grandfather. Laura is my grandmother. Carlos and
Laura have two children. They are Joe and Maria.
Joe is my uncle. Maria is my mother. Joe is older
than Maria.

Joe married Christina. She's my aunt. Their two
children are Eva and Danny. Eva and Danny are my
cousins. Danny is younger than Eva.

Maria married Mike. Mike is my father. My parents
have three children. I have a sister and a brother. My
sister's name is Rosie. She is the oldest. My
brother's name is Peter. He's a baby. He's the
youngest. I'm older than Peter, but I'm younger than
Rosie. Can you find me?

▶ WORDS

Components: Dictionary pages 8-9, Transparency 4, Wall Chart 4, Word and Picture Cards Topic 4, Workbook page 4, Cassette

- Present the content words. **See pages xiv-xvi for general techniques about presenting content words.**

  Language Note: We use certain alternate words to identify family members. For example, *grandma* and *nana* are other words for *grandmother*. *Grandpa*, *granddad*, and *grandpa* are alternate words for *grandfather*. *Mom*, *ma*, and *mama* are alternate words for *mother*. *Dad*, *daddy*, *pop*, and *papa* are alternate words for *father*. Most of these words are used as terms of affection when addressing the individual directly. Generally, we use the more formal terms such as *grandmother*, *grandfather*, *mother*, and *father* to refer to the individual in the third person. *Aunt* may be pronounced *ant* or *ahnt*.

- Display the wall chart and have students look at the picture. Divide the class into two groups. Distribute a set of word and picture cards to each group. Using chart paper, students draw an outline of the family tree like the one on the wall chart. Students paste the appropriate word and picture card on these drawings in the same position as they are in the wall chart. For example, they place the word and picture card for *baby* in the top right position on their trees. Plural words such as *grandparents* should go underneath the cards for *grandmother* and *grandfather*. *Parents* should go underneath the cards for *mother* and *father*. Then each group compares their trees for accuracy. Save these family trees for later activities after students complete the content reading.

- Form two groups. Have students from Group 1 and 2 work together as they look at the bottom of the wall chart picture. Students in Group 1, in turn, point to each person in the picture and name the relationship of that person to Mario. For example, the student in Group 1 says, *This is the father*. The student from Group 2 tells what that person is doing in the picture. For example: *The father is cooking* or *He is cooking*. Students who are writing can label the bottom of the chart with written word and action labels.

WORKBOOK: Topic 4
See Teacher's Book page 17.

▶ CONTENT

Components: Dictionary pages 8-9, Transparency 4, Wall Chart 4, Content Reading Topic 4, Worksheet Topic 4, Cassette

- Present the content reading. **See pages xvii-xix for general techniques about presenting content readings.**

- Ask the following or similar questions:

  Is Maria older than Joe?
  Is Rosie Joe's mother?
  Who is Mario? Who is Carlos? Who is Laura? Who are Maria and Mike?
  Who married Christina?
  Who is the youngest person in the picture? Who are the oldest people in the picture?

- **Possessive nouns.** Distribute the family tree drawings students made earlier. Students in each group say and then write the name of each person in the family tree on their drawing in the appropriate places. For example, *The baby's name is Peter* or *This is Peter*. Each group compares their labeled drawings for accuracy.

- **Possessive adjectives.** Write the names of all the people from the reading on the board or on pieces of paper (except Mario): Carlos, Laura, Maria, Joe, Christina, Danny, Eva, Mike, Rosie, and Peter. Have one student stand under each name or hold one piece of paper. Now ask each student, in turn, to pretend to be Mario and to describe his relationship to the person on the board or paper. For example, the student standing under *Carlos* should write or say *Carlos is my grandfather*.

- **Possessive adjectives.** Extend the above activity to practice possessive adjectives in the third person. Assign one student the role of Mario. Have the other students describe the relationship of each person to Mario. For example: *Carlos is his grandfather*.

- **Comparative and superlative adjectives**

  Comparatives use the comparative adjective form plus *than* (*older than*). Superlatives use *the* plus the superlative adjective form (*the oldest*).

  As in the two activities above, assign one name of a character to each student, pair, or group. Ask each student to tell about the age of that character using comparative or superlative adjectives. For example: *Danny is younger than Eva*. Students may want to refer to the content reading for some of the characters.

WORKSHEET: Topic 4
See Teacher's Book page 17.

►CHANT

Components: Dictionary pages 8-9, Content Chant Topic 4, Cassette

 ## CONTENT CHANT

Father, Mother, Sister, Brother

Father, mother
Sister, brother
Grandma, grandpa
Uncles, aunts

Nephews, nieces
Cousins, babies
Cats and dogs
and books and plants

Uncle Larry's very hairy.
Cousin Joe is big.
Aunt Eileen looks like a queen
in her purple wig.

Uncle Willie's very silly.
Aunt Marie is very smart.
Every Sunday she recites
the alphabet by heart.

Father, mother
Sister, brother
Cats and dogs and books and plants
We're so happy in our family,
Grandma, grandpa, uncles, aunts.

- Present the content chant. **See pages xx-xxi for general techniques about presenting chants.**

- Before distributing Content Chant 4, establish the rhythm of the chant. Divide students into four groups. Group 1 chants *father*, Group 2 chants *mother*, Group 3 chants *sister*, and Group 4 chants *brother*. Have each group chant in turn, increasing the volume and pace until a steady rhythm is achieved. Now proceed to the next two lines of the chant, splitting the four words again by groups. Again, have each group chant in turn. Now put both halves of the first stanza together and chant the entire stanza in groups.

- Now distribute Content Chant 4. Chant the first stanza in the same groups, as well as the first two lines of the second stanza. For the remaining stanzas, have the entire class chant together, or select individual students to chant one line at a time. Return to the four groups for the first two lines of the last stanza. Have the entire class chant the last three lines.

- Explain the concept of knowing something "by heart," or from memory. Talk about things people know by heart, such as songs, names and numbers, or birthdays. Ask students what they know by heart, such as their address, their phone number, or the alphabet.

►EXTENSION

Components: Dictionary pages 8-9, Transparency 4, Wall Chart 4

- Introduce additional relationship words and explain their meanings: *son, daughter, child, children, niece, nephew, grandchild(ren), grandson, granddaughter, husband, wife, son-in law, daughter-in law, mother-in law, father-in law, stepfather,* and *stepmother.* Explain that each person can have different relationships with different people. For example, Maria is Carlos and Laura's daughter. She is also Joe's sister, Mike's wife, Mario, Rosie and Peter's mother, and Eva and Danny's aunt. Make a chart on the board listing the name of each person in the wall chart family tree. Students list as many relationships as possible under each name.

- Have students draw their own family trees and label the members of their family, both by name and by relationship to themselves. They may do this with words, simple drawings, or pictures from home. Pair students so that they can ask each other questions about their family trees. For example, one student might ask *Who's Teddy?* The other answers *He's my uncle.* When students know the basic information, they ask and answer additional questions, such as *How old is Teddy?* or *Where does he live?* Then sets of partners make groups of four. Within the groups, each student tells a new partner about the family of his or her previous partner.

- Ask students to bring in pictures of their family members. Pair students. Each student gives the pictures to his or her partner, along with the family tree from the activity above. The partner must try to figure out who's who in the picture, and what that person's relationship is to the student.

- Ask students to talk about their pet names for special family members. Some students will have nicknames or pet names for the actual names of some of their family members. For example, *Ken* for *Kenji,* or *Bob* for *Roberto.* Others will have pet names for the relationship of certain family members. For example, *Mamasita, Pop-pops* or *Popito.* Ask students to explain what these pet names or nicknames mean.

- Ask students to line themselves up according to their birthdays from youngest to oldest. Then, as each student calls out his or her birthday, you or another student writes a list of the names and birthdays. Then, have students describe themselves relative to the ages of some of their classmates. For example: *I am older than Jin Foo, but I am younger than Klaus* or *I am the oldest student in the class.*

- Display the list from the above exercise. Choose any three students to come to the front of the class. Select a fourth student to describe their age relationship. For example: *Klaus is older than Jin Foo. Lucia is younger than Jin Foo. Klaus is the oldest. Lucia is the youngest.*

LITERATURE

Suggested Books

Family Pictures/Cuadros de Familia
written and illustrated by Carmen Lomas Garza.
Children's Book Press, 1998. ISBN 0892391529

In My Family/En Mi Familia
written and illustrated by Carmen Lomas Garza.
Children's Book Press, 1996. ISBN 0892391383
The stories in these companion books are drawn from the life of the author/illustrator, who grew up in a Mexican-American family in Texas. Each vignette is accompanied by a vivid folk-art illustration. The artfully-placed text appears in both English and Spanish. For an extension activity, the stories and illustrations can be used as prompts for students to create their own family albums. These books are particularly recommended for classrooms with Latino students.

Families: A Celebration of Diversity, Commitment, and Love
written by Aylette Jenness; photographs by the author.
Houghton Mifflin Co., 1993. ISBN 0395669529
This collection of personal stories from parents, children, and guardians captures the diversity that is reflected in the families of students today. Most students will find a story or photograph that matches their own family situation. This book's sensitivity to diversity will encourage all students to speak and write about their own families.

Fathers, Mothers, Sisters, Brothers: A Collection of Family Poems
written by Mary Ann Hoberman; illustrated by Marylin Hafner.
Puffin Books, 1993. ISBN 0140548491
These twenty-six, lively, happy, and sometimes serious poems are about a wide variety of families and family life. The vocabulary in Topic 4, The Family, appears throughout the poems. In addition, the repetitive and cumulative structure of some poems provides many opportunities for language learning. The poems can be used to introduce or reinforce vocabulary for a variety of other topics including, clothing, food, the seasons, and parts of the body.

How My Family Lives in America
written by Susan Kuklin; photographs by the author.
Simon & Schuster Children's Books, 1992. ISBN 0027512398
Food and family life are the common themes in this photo essay. The author profiles three families and shows how each family's distinct heritage influences their adaptation to American life. The documentary photographs are filled with examples of words that can be matched to many of the word/picture cards. Family recipes are also provided as a bonus. This book can also be used with Topic 37, Vegetables.

One Hundred Is a Family
written by Pam Munoz Ryan; illustrated by Benrei Huang.
Disney Press, 1998. ISBN 078680405X
This illustrated poem provides an opportunity for students to practice using numbers (see Topic 59, Number Patterns, Functions, and Relations, and the Appendix) while learning about family life. The text counts—by ones and by tens—the love, friendships, traditions, and communities that make up a family. The illustrations help students understand unfamiliar words.

WORKBOOK: Topic 4

On this page, students use the family tree to fill in sentences with the words for family members.

WORKSHEET: Topic 4

In A, students look at the picture to determine who is older or younger. They fill in the blanks with choices from the word box. In B, they fill in possessive adjectives, choosing from the word boxes provided. Then, in C, they tell about their own families.

► CONTENT
....
Places in the city

► LANGUAGE
....
Prepositions of place (across, at, behind, between, in front of, on, over, near, under): *The subway is near the police station.*

There + BE (there is/ there's/there are): *There's a newsstand on the corner.*

 CONTENT WORDS

1. restaurant
2. newsstand
3. hotel
4. post office
5. department store
6. office building
7. apartment building
8. church
9. mosque
10. temple
11. parking garage
12. bank
13. movie theater
14. police station
15. subway
16. bus
17. taxi
18. garbage truck
19. helicopter
20. traffic light

 CONTENT READING

The City

This is a very busy city. There are many buildings and many people in this city.

There are two policemen in front of the police station. The subway is near the police station. The subway goes under the street.

There is an office building across the street from the subway. There's a very good restaurant on the first floor of the office building. There's a newsstand on the corner. People buy newspapers at the newsstand.

The hotel is between the office building and the post office. There is a mailbox in front of the post office. People mail letters and buy stamps at the post office.

The department store is near the post office. People buy clothes and shoes at the department store. There's a helicopter flying over the department store.

There's a church behind the department store, and there's an apartment building behind the church. People live in the apartment building. A mosque and a temple are near the department store, too.

The parking garage is across the street from the post office. The bank is across the street from the hotel. The movie theater is across the street from the restaurant.

There are cars and taxis on the street. There's a garbage truck, too. A bus is waiting at the traffic light.

▶ WORDS

Components: Dictionary pages 10-11, Transparency 5, Wall Chart 5, Word and Picture Cards Topic 5, Workbook page 5, Cassette

- Present the content words. **See pages xiv-xvi for general techniques about presenting content words.**

- Display the wall chart and have students look at the picture. Divide students into three groups. Group 1 looks at the people and buildings on one side of the street. Group 2 looks at the people and buildings on the other side of the street. Group 3 looks at the people and cars in the middle of the street. Each group describes what is happening in its area. Then, the students write down or circle all the content words that appear in their areas.

- Draw two columns on the board. Label one column *Buildings*. Label the other *Vehicles*. Explain that a vehicle is something that moves and carries people or cargo, such as a car, bus, or truck. Distribute one word and picture card to each student. Have each student read his or her card aloud; then, write each word on the board in the appropriate column. Note that the *helicopter* and *subway* cards might cause some confusion, especially if students live in areas without subways. Explain that a subway is a train that runs underground. Then ask the class whether a subway is a building or a vehicle. Note also that the traffic light is not a building or a vehicle and should not be included.

- Collect all the word and picture cards and redistribute them again, one per student. Ask each student, in turn, to say what happens at the building shown on his or her card, or to explain what the vehicle on his or her card does in the city. For example: *People eat dinner at a restaurant*, or *The garbage truck picks up the people's garbage*. If students are writing, they may write their answers instead of saying them.

- Draw two lines on the board to indicate a street. Pair students. Distribute sets of picture cards to half of the pairs, and sets of matching word cards to the other pairs. Have one pair of students with picture cards come to the board and arrange six cards in any order on the street. A pair of students with word cards then comes to the board, finds the matching word cards for those pictures, and arranges the words in the same order. The class then names the buildings or vehicles the students have chosen.

WORKBOOK: Topic 5
See Teacher's Book page 21.

▶ CONTENT

Components: Dictionary pages 10-11, Transparency 5, Wall Chart 5, Content Reading Topic 5, Worksheet Topic 5, Cassette

- Present the content reading. **See pages xvii-xix for general techniques about presenting content readings**.

- Ask the following or similar questions:

  Is the subway near the temple?
  Where's the mailbox?
  What's between the office building and the post office?
  What's across the street from the parking garage?
  What do people buy at the department store?

- ▶ **Prepositions of place.** Distribute one word and picture card to each student. Ask each student to make up sentences about the buildings and vehicles that are *near* the object on the picture card in the dictionary illustration. For example, the student who has the *police station* card says or writes *movie theater*, *subway*, and *restaurant*. Then ask students to make a list of the buildings or vehicles that are *in front of* or *behind* the object on the word and picture card. For example, the student with the *bus* card says or writes *The garbage truck and the traffic light are in front of the bus. A car and the subway are behind the bus*.

- Pair students. One student describes what happens in a particular building without naming it. The second student must name the building based on the clue. For example, the first student may say *People live here*. The second student responds by saying *It's an apartment building*.

- ▶ **Prepositions of place.** Pair students again. One student describes a building by what it is near, next to, across the street from, in front of, or behind. For example, the first student says *This building is across the street from the bank and is near the post office*, and the second student responds *It's the hotel*.

WORKSHEET: Topic 5
See Teacher's Book page 21.

Components: Dictionary pages 10-11, Content Chant Topic 5, Cassette

Components: Dictionary pages 10-11, Transparency 5, Wall Chart 5

 CONTENT CHANT

I Like the City

I like the city.
　　I do, too.
　　There's so much to see,
　　so much to do.

Look at the buildings
touching the sky.
I love the city.
　　So do I.

　　　I like department stores.
So do I.
There's so much to look at,
so much to buy.

If you love the city,
follow me.
Summer or winter,
that's the place to be.

Yellow taxis,
Neon light.
My favorite city
is up all night.

- Present the content chant. **See pages xx-xxi for general techniques about presenting chants**.

- Before distributing Content Chant 5, establish the rhythm of the chant. Divide the class into two groups. Group 1 chants *I like the city*; Group 2 chants *I do, too*. Then Group 1 chants *I love the city*, and Group 2 chants *So do I*. Each group chants in turn, increasing the volume and pace until they achieve a steady rhythm.

- Now distribute Content Chant 5, and begin the chant. Group 1 chants the lines that start at the left-hand margin; Group 2 chants the indented lines.

- Explain that neon light is a type of very colorful, bright light used to attract attention to a sign at night. Big cities have many neon lights. Bring in pictures of New York or Las Vegas that show neon lights.

- Explain that the phrase *up all night* means that people stay up very late at night or don't go to sleep at all. If a city is *up all night*, it means that stores and restaurants stay open late, and people can be seen on the streets at late hours. Ask students if they know a city that is up all night. Is their city or town up all night?

- Ask students to tell about the things they would do if they could stay up all night. Where would they go? Would they be with friends or family?

- Divide students into two teams. Each team stands in a line facing the other team with an aisle of about three or four feet between the lines. Explain that the aisle represents a street. Choose one student from the first line to answer a question about the position of a student in the second line, using *between* and *across the street from*. For example: *Lisa is across the street from Doug. She's between Michael and Mercedes.*

- Divide the class into two teams. Try to make sure that each team has approximately the same number of students at various language levels and that each team includes students who can read and write. Give students a time limit of 10 minutes. Each team looks at the wall chart and makes a list of all the signs on buildings or anywhere else they can find. For example, *Police, Madison, Boyd Bank, Bus Stop*, etc. The team with the most signs wins. Note that *U.S. Post Office, Star Theater,* and *News* each count as one sign, regardless of the number of words in each.

- Pair students. Tell each student to make a list of things his or her parents do on Saturdays, such as mail letters, buy clothes, eat lunch, see a movie, buy a newspaper, etc. Students exchange lists with their partners and write the name of the appropriate building next to the action on their partners' lists. Example: *mail letters— post office*. Then, once the lists are completed, students can make sentences: *They mail letters at the post office.*

- Ask students about traffic lights. Questions might include: *What do traffic lights do? How many traffic lights are in your city? What would happen without traffic lights? What does each color light mean?*

- As a class, invite students to recreate a busy block in your city or town. Students can draw a map on the board or chart paper, or make a three-dimensional model with construction paper, building blocks, or cardboard. Students can color their maps or models with chalk, crayons, or paints. Once the city block is completed, help students to fill in the names of local businesses, restaurants, and offices. Then have them describe the block using *there is, there's,* or *there are* and as many of the content words as possible.

► LITERATURE

Suggested Books

Sky Scrape/City Scape: Poems of City Life
edited by Jane Yolen; illustrated by Ken Condon.
Boyds Mills Press, 1996. ISBN 1563971798
Poets such as Langston Hughes, Carl Sandberg, and Lilian Moore evoke the hustle and bustle of life in the city. Teachers may select particular poems, such as "The Streetcleaner's Lament" or one of the four skyscraper poems, to give the content words from this topic a visual context different from that of the Dictionary. The poems and their illustrations can also serve as models for students' own illustrated poems about city life.

Town & Country
written by Alice Provensen; illustrated by Martin Provensen.
Browndeer Press, 1994. ISBN 0152001824
In this journey of discovery, life in a busy city is compared to life in the countryside (see Topic 7, The Country). Much of the detailed text is presented in the second person. This language structure provides opportunities for expanding vocabulary, as well as modeling and building grammar. The illustrations can be related to numerous other Dictionary topics. The visuals can be useful especially for connecting this topic to Topic 9, People at Work.

Tar Beach
written and illustrated by Faith Ringgold.
Dragonfly, 1996. ISBN 0517885441
Cassie Louise Lightfoot is an eight year old who enjoys family outings on "Tar Beach"—the rooftop of her family's Harlem apartment building. Cassie imagines that she can fly over the city and lay claim to all she sees. This popular book is well-suited for learning through acting-out activities. Students can pretend that they are flying over their own neighborhoods and point out the things and places they see.

Abuela
written by Arthur Dorros; illustrated by Elisa Kleven.
Puffin, 1997. ISBN 0140562257
This imaginative adventure of a young girl and her grandmother, Abuela, is written in simple language. The text models the language pattern, "If I could fly...I would...." The collage illustrations, packed with details of an urban environment, can be used to extend vocabulary and spark conversation. Spanish words and phrases are scattered throughout the book. Students may talk about what it means to speak more than one language. A glossary of Spanish terms is included at the end of the book.

A Year in the City
written by Kathy Henderson; illustrated by Paul Howard.
Candlewick Press, 1996. ISBN 1564028720
A Year in the City takes children on a month-by-month trip through the seasons in a city. The beautiful illustrations show how city dwellers adapt to the seasons, such as turning up their collars in the winter cold and going to a park to take in the summer air. The illustrations may inspire students to talk about changes in the weather and the natural world. Students can point out and describe the distinct faces in the crowd scenes and identify many of the vocabulary words throughout the unit.

WORKBOOK: Topic 5

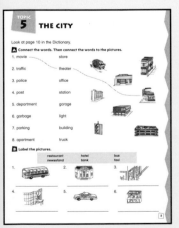

In A, students connect each word to a related word in the middle column, and then to a picture. In B, they label the pictures with words from the word box.

WORKSHEET: Topic 5

For each number in A, students circle the sentence that correctly describes the picture. In B, they follow the path of the girl in the picture and choose prepositions from the word box to fill in the blanks in the paragraph.

6 THE SUBURBS

▶ **CONTENT**

Places and items in the suburbs

▶ **LANGUAGE**

Adjective + noun: *There are clean streets and friendly people.*

Present continuous: *Sam Jordan is washing his car.*

CONTENT WORDS

1. street
2. sidewalk
3. crosswalk
4. corner
5. block
6. stop sign
7. mailbox
8. fire hydrant
9. yard
10. garden
11. garage
12. driveway
13. park
14. swimming pool
15. gas station
16. van
17. car
18. motorcycle
19. bicycle
20. basketball

CONTENT READING

The Suburbs

Welcome to the suburbs. This neighborhood is in the suburbs. There are many beautiful blocks. There are big houses with nice yards and tall trees. Some houses have beautiful gardens with pretty flowers and vegetables.

This is a quiet neighborhood. There are clean streets and friendly people. People walk on the sidewalk. They cross the street at the crosswalk. There is a fire hydrant on the corner near the stop sign.

It's Saturday morning in the suburbs. Mr. Morse is riding his motorcycle. Paul and Brian are playing basketball in the driveway in front of the garage. Brian's bicycle is on the sidewalk.

Mr. Clarke is mailing a letter at the mailbox. Sam Jordan is washing his car. Mr. and Mrs. Turner are walking on the sidewalk. Mrs. Lopez is buying gas for her van at the gas station.

Some people are playing baseball in the park. Some people are swimming in the swimming pool. It's a beautiful day in the suburbs. Everybody's having fun.

▶ WORDS

Components: Dictionary pages 12-13, Transparency 6, Wall Chart 6, Workbook page 6, Word and Picture Cards Topic 6, Cassette

- Present the content words. **See pages xiv-xvi for general techniques about presenting content words**.

- Display the wall chart and have students look at the picture. Divide the class into two groups. Group 1 looks at the people and the houses on the left side of the long vertical street in the middle of the picture. Group 2 looks at the people and houses on the right side of the street. Each group describes what is happening in their area of the picture. Then they write down or circle all the content words that appear in that area.

- Draw three columns on the board. Label Column 1 *Driving/Riding*, Column 2 *Walking*, and Column 3 *Driving/Riding or Walking*. Explain that some of the content words involve driving or riding, some involve walking, and some involve driving, riding or walking. For example, a person walks in a garden, but almost always drives or rides to a gas station. Distribute one card to each student. Have each student read his/ her card, then place it on the board in the appropriate column. Note that there may be more than one correct answer for words like *corner*, *block*, and *street*.

- Direct students' attention to the stop sign on the corner near the gas station. Ask them if they know what a stop sign means. Now point them to the backwards stop sign on the near corner by the fire hydrant. Ask if they know what kind of sign that is, even though they can't read it. Talk about other kinds of signs. Ask students to name some kinds of signs.

- Divide students into two teams. Each team appoints a recorder to report its answers. Each team tries to name as many kinds of signs as they can, including road signs, gas station signs, park signs, and warning signs. Teams then read their lists or write them on the board. The team that comes up with the most different kinds of signs wins.

- As a variation on the above activity, take the class on a field trip to the immediate area outside your school. Walk down the street with the students and ask them to point out all the different signs on each side of the street. You or an advanced student writes down the names of all the different signs.

WORKBOOK: Topic 6
See Teacher's Book page 25.

▶ CONTENT

Components: Dictionary pages 12-13, Transparency 6, Wall Chart 6, Content Reading Topic 6, Worksheet Topic 6, Cassette

- Present the content reading. **See pages xvii-xix for general techniques about presenting content readings**.

- Ask the following or similar questions:

  Is Mr. Clarke playing basketball?
  Where is this neighborhood?
  What's Mrs. Lopez doing?
  What's happening in the park?
  Where's the fire hydrant?

▶ **Adjective + noun**

> Nouns are naming words. Nouns name people, places, or things. Adjectives are describing words. Adjectives describe or tell something about nouns.

Write the adjectives from the first two paragraphs of the content reading in one column on the board: *beautiful, big, nice, tall, beautiful* (again), *pretty, quiet, clean, friendly*. Then write the nouns they describe or modify in another column on the board in a different order: *people, streets, blocks, houses, trees, yards, gardens, neighborhood,* and *flowers*. Have students look through the reading and circle the pairs of nouns and adjectives they find. Then invite students to come to the board and connect the adjective to the person, place, or thing it describes. Once they have connected all the adjectives and nouns as they appear in the content reading, ask students to be creative and connect some of these adjectives to other nouns: *beautiful trees, beautiful houses, nice gardens, clean neighborhood,* etc. Note that certain combinations of adjectives and nouns in these paragraphs won't make sense, such as *tall neighborhood, quiet flowers,* or *tall blocks*.

▶ **Present continuous.** Introduce the present continuous (*BE* + verb + *-ing*). The present continuous describes something that is happening now. Point to the first instance of the present continuous in the content reading: *Mr. Morse is riding his motorcycle.* Now ask students to point to or circle all the subsequent uses of the present continuous in the content reading.

▶ **Present continuous.** Ask students to make a list of the actions that are *not* happening in the picture. For example: *Paul and Brian are not riding a motorcycle. Mr. Clarke is not climbing a tree. Mrs. Lopez is not swimming in the swimming pool.*

WORKSHEET: Topic 6
See Teacher's Book page 25.

► CHANTS

Components: Dictionary pages 12-13, Content Chant Topic 6, Cassette

 CONTENT CHANT

Walk on the Sidewalk

Walk on the sidewalk,
not on the street.
Swim in the swimming pool. *

Stop at the stoplight.
Cross at the crosswalk.
Swim in the swimming pool. *

Drive in the driveway,
not on the sidewalk.
Swim in the swimming pool. *

Ride your bike,
but not on the sidewalk.
Swim in the swimming pool. *

Cross at the crosswalk.
Stop at the stoplight.
Swim in the swimming pool. *

- Present the content chant. **See pages xx-xxi for general techniques about presenting chants**.

- Before distributing Content Chant 6, establish the rhythm of the chant. Have the entire class repeat the line *Swim in the swimming pool*, and then clap. Do this three or four times. Then go around the class with one student at a time chanting the line and the entire class clapping afterwards. Continue until every student has chanted the line.

- Now distribute Content Chant 6 and begin the chant. Select one student to chant the first two lines of the chant. The entire class follows with the line *Swim in the swimming pool*, and then claps. Select another student to read the first two lines of the second stanza. Again, the entire class follows. Select other students to chant the first two lines of the remaining three stanzas.

- Explain that a stop light and a traffic light are similar, except that a traffic light usually has red, yellow, and green lights. Green means *go*, yellow means *slow*, and red means *stop*. A stop light only has one flashing red light. It means *stop, look for traffic, and then go if it's safe*. A stop light and a stop sign do the same thing.

- Explain that *bike* is a shorter word for bicycle. Ask students if they have bikes. Where do they ride their bikes? In the street? In the driveway? On the sidewalk? In the park? Ask students why it might not be safe to ride a bike in the street, on the sidewalk, or in the driveway.

► EXTENSION

Components: Dictionary pages 12-13, Transparency 6, Wall Chart 6

- Write on the board the adjectives that appear in the first two paragraphs of the content reading: *beautiful, big, nice, tall, pretty, quiet, clean,* and *friendly*. Ask students to list all the adjectives that are appropriate to describe each of the content words on the page. For example, almost all of them might be used to describe *street,* but only some of them could be used to describe the word *basketball*. When each student has completed a list, students exchange their lists with a partner.

- Ask students to brainstorm a list of nouns naming things in neighborhoods where they live. For example: *houses, apartments, community center, library*. Then help them add any appropriate adjectives to describe those nouns. For example: *small, crowded, noisy, large*.

- Divide the class into two teams. A student from Team 1 names a location in the Dictionary Illustration. A student from Team 2 has to tell how to get there from a second location. For example, using swimming pool and fire hydrant as prompts, a student might say *To get to the swimming pool from the fire hydrant, you have to walk on the sidewalk for one block, then cross the street at the crosswalk, then turn left.* If the student gives correct directions, Team 2 gets a point. Otherwise, Team 1 gets a point. Now teams switch roles. The next student from Team 1 names a location. The second student from Team 2 tells how to get there from the last place described (in this case, the swimming pool).

- Ask students how Saturday is different from other days of the week. Ask them if Saturday is different from Sunday for them. Have students write or talk about things they like to do on Saturday mornings. Have them talk about or write an essay about the things they would do if every day of the year was Saturday.

- Tell students to pretend that it is Saturday morning in their neighborhoods. Have students draw a picture or a street map of their neighborhoods. They should add people to their drawings or maps. Underneath their pictures, students should describe what each of the people is doing, using the present continuous. Encourage students to use both the full forms and the contracted forms of the present continuous. For example, *He is walking* or *He's walking*. Note that the full forms are more generally used in formal writing, but not in conversation.

► LITERATURE

Suggested Books

Fill It Up!: All About Service Stations
written and illustrated by Gail Gibbons.
HarperCollins, 1987. ISBN 0690044402

Playgrounds
written and illustrated by Gail Gibbons.
Holiday House, 1985. ISBN 0823405532
The information in these two books by Gail Gibbons expands upon the vocabulary and artwork featured in Topic 6, The Suburbs. Practical information about gas stations and playgrounds is conveyed in readable simple present tense and passive voice. The colorful illustrations with additional cartoon captions help explain the texts. Both books are effective when read aloud, especially to beginners. *Fill It Up!* is also useful for teaching Topic 16, The Southwest.

I Read Symbols
written by Tana Hoban; photographs by the author.
Mulberry Books, 1999. ISBN 0688166962
This wordless picture book is useful for generating language about traffic signs and traffic safety. Twenty-seven different common traffic signs appear in the book; the last two pages show each of the signs with its appropriate English-language label. Some of the signs seen in the Dictionary illustration are clearly featured in the photographs. As a follow-up, teachers may want to take students on a walk around the school, where they can identify signs and practice giving and receiving directions. The book is also useful in teaching Topic 56, Geometry.

Chicken Sunday
written by Patricia Polacco; illustrated by Edward Miller.
Paper Star, 1998. ISBN 0698116151
The author, a Russian-American, recalls the "Chicken Sundays" of the African-American family that took her in as a child. Her story tells of the events leading up to one very special Easter Sunday. This book weaves together an ingenious story of interracial and intercultural friendship. While some paraphrasing of the story may be necessary for beginning and intermediate students, the warm folk-art illustrations convey a rich impression of life in a familial suburban context.

WORKBOOK: Topic 6

On this page, students fill in the blanks in the sentences based on the pictures.

WORKSHEET: Topic 6

In A, students write complete sentences to answer the questions based on the pictures. In B, students unscramble the sentences. To do this, students need to understand how to place adjectives before the nouns they describe.

► **CONTENT**
....
Places in the country

► **LANGUAGE**
....
Adjectives for colors *(blue, green, red, white, yellow):* The barn is red.

There + BE (there is/there's/there are): *There are no cars on the road.*

Prepositions of place *(across, behind, inside, next to, outside, from, into, over):* There is hay inside the silo.

Present continuous: *Arthur Sampson is driving his tractor.*

CONTENT WORDS

1. farm
2. barn
3. silo
4. path
5. fence
6. chicken coop
7. orchard
8. pasture
9. pond
10. woods
11. hills
12. field
13. road
14. stream
15. bridge
16. airplane
17. train
18. truck
19. tractor
20. wagon

CONTENT READING

The Country

There are many farms in the country. This is the Sampsons' farm. It's a beautiful farm. The farmhouse is yellow. The barn is red. The pastures are green. The sky is blue and the clouds are white.

The barn is next to the house. There's a path from the house to the barn. There's a horse inside the barn and there are two cows outside the barn. The silo is behind the barn. There is hay inside the silo.

The chicken coop is next to the barn. There's a fence around the chicken coop. Some chickens are inside the chicken coop and some are not. But all the chickens are inside the fence.

Jeannette Sampson is feeding the chickens. Arthur Sampson is driving his tractor. His children are sitting in the wagon. Dave Sampson is driving the truck across the bridge. The bridge goes over a beautiful stream.

Jane Sampson is outside the house. She's waving to Dave. Billy Sampson is in the apple orchard. He's picking apples from a tree. His brother George is watching.

The pasture is behind the orchard. There's a fence around the pasture. There are sheep in the pasture. They are inside the fence. They are near the pond. The pond is in front of the woods.

An airplane is flying over the field and a train is going into the hills. There are no cars on the road. It is quiet in the country.

►WORDS

Components: Dictionary pages 14-15, Transparency 7, Wall Chart 7, Workbook page 7, Word and Picture Cards Topic 7, Cassette

- Present the content words. **See pages xiv-xvi for general techniques about presenting content words.**

- Display the wall chart and have students look at the picture. Divide students into three groups. Group 1 looks at the portion of the picture that includes the house, barn, and silo. Group 2 looks at the portion of the picture in front of the barn. Group 3 looks at the portion of the picture behind the house. Each group describes the scene in its area of the picture. The groups write down or circle all the content words that appear in that area.

- Draw two columns on the board. Label Column 1 *Things People Make*. Label Column 2 *Natural Things*. Explain that natural things are things that people don't make, like the sky and the oceans. Woods and streams are natural things. Distribute one word and picture card to each student. Have each student read the card, and then place it on the board in the appropriate column. (Note: Although pastures, ponds, orchards, fields, and streams can sometimes be man-made, they are considered natural things for the purposes of this activity. However, if students can present a good case that they are man-made, allow them to do so.)

- Divide the class into two teams. Give each team a set of word and picture cards to spread out randomly on a flat surface. The teams then have five minutes to sort their cards into three categories: Man-Made Things (bridges, buildings), Green and Natural Things (woods, streams), or Vehicles/Things That Move (tractors, etc.). The first group to sort their cards correctly into these three categories wins.

- Ask students to point to, name, or write down the different animals shown in the picture. There are two cows, five sheep, a horse, and more than a dozen chickens in the picture. If students do not know the names of the animals, invite them to say the names in their own languages. Write the names of the animals in English in one column, then write each animal's name in a different language in a second column, and in a third language in a third column. Continue making columns for as many languages as are spoken in your classroom.

WORKBOOK: Topic 7
See Teacher's Book page 29.

►CONTENT

Components: Dictionary pages 14-15, Transparency 7, Wall Chart 7, Content Reading Topic 7, Worksheet Topic 7, Cassette

- Present the content reading. **See pages xvii-xix for general techniques about presenting content readings.**

- Ask the following or similar questions:
    What color is the barn?
    Where's the chicken coop?
    What's inside the barn?
    Who's waving to Dave?
    What is Billy Sampson doing?

► **Adjectives for colors.** Write the words *blue, green, red, white* and *yellow* on the board. Ask students to point to or make lists of all the items in the picture that are each of these colors. Ask students to name other colors. For example: *What color is the truck?* Point to other objects in your classroom to introduce colors that do not appear in the picture.

► **Prepositions of place *inside* and *outside*.** Introduce the terms *inside* and *outside*. Put a pencil in a box. Close the box to demonstrate that the pencil is inside the box. Now open the box and take the pencil out of the box. Close the box again to demonstrate that the pencil is outside of the box. Have each student name an object that can have other objects inside or outside of it, such as a bookbag, a box, a desk drawer, a room, etc. Make the list as long as you can.

► **Prepositions of place *inside* and *outside*.** Divide students into two teams. Tell each team to put one thing inside another. Then put the two things inside a third thing, and so on. For example, a team might put a piece of paper inside a book, the book inside a bookbag, the bookbag inside a coat, and the coat inside a box. Then they might put the box and all its contents in a drawer or a closet. The team that puts the most things inside other things wins.

► **Present continuous.** Introduce the present continuous (*BE* + verb + *-ing*). Point to the first instance of the present continuous in the content reading: *Jeannette Sampson is feeding the chickens.* Now ask students to circle other present continuous sentences in the reading.

WORKSHEET: Topic 7
See Teacher's Book page 29.

▶ CHANTS

Components: Dictionary pages 14-15, Content Chant Topic 7, Cassette

 ## CONTENT CHANT

I Like the Country

I like the country.

    So do I.

I like the white clouds
in the bright blue sky,
the big red barns,
and the cows going moo,
and the little red rooster going
cock-a-doodle-doo.

    I love the country.
    I really do.
    I like the green hills,
    and the orchards, too.
    The ponds and the pastures,
    the woods and the streams.
    I see the country
    in my dreams.

- Present the content chant. **See pages xx-xxi for general techniques about presenting chants**.

- Before distributing Content Chant 7, establish the rhythm of the chant. Divide the class into two groups. Group 1 chants *I like the country.* Group 2 responds *So do I.* Have each group chant in turn, quickening the pace and increasing the volume each time. Then switch roles.

- Before distributing Content Chant 7, select one student to come to the front of the class and point to the appropriate part of the picture whenever the chant mentions a content word. For example, when the class chants *the white clouds*, the student at the front points to the white clouds in the picture. When the class chants *the big red barns*, the student points to the red barn. Select another student to come to the front of the class for the last stanza. A third student can do the sound effects when the class chants these lines: *and the cows going moo/and the little red rooster going cock-a-doodle-doo.*

- Distribute Content Chant 7, and begin the chant. Group 1 chants the lines at the left margin and Group 2 chants all the indented lines. Be sure that the individual students in the activity above are performing their actions while Groups 1 and 2 are chanting.

> **Language Note:** Explain that a rooster is a male chicken. Also explain that "going" in the context used in the chant is another word for "saying." (See notes for Extension.)

▶ EXTENSION

Components: Dictionary pages 14-15, Transparency 7, Wall Chart 7

- Talk with students about farms and farming. Ask them what kind of farm the picture looks like. Is it a big farm or a small farm? Does the farm produce milk, vegetables, fruit, meat? Ask students how this farm compares to farms in their home countries. Would they like to live on a farm? Why or why not? Do they know people who live on farms in the United States or other countries?

- Review the use of the word *going* meaning *saying* or *making a noise* as used in the phrase *the rooster goes cock-a-doodle-doo.* Explain that this is how we describe these animal noises in English. Write down the names of several animals in one column on the board. In the column next to the animal names, write the English words for the sounds these animals make. Then make sentences such as *A rooster goes cock-a-doodle-doo, A cow goes moo, A horse goes neigh, A sheep goes baaah,* etc. Now ask students to describe the noises these animals make in their own language. For example, the Spanish word for a rooster's sound is *qui-quiri-qui.* Add columns for the language(s) spoken in your classroom.

- Divide the class into two teams. A student from Team 1 pantomimes an action that people do on a farm or in the country, such as feeding the chickens or picking apples. A student from Team 2 describes what the other student is doing in the present continuous: *He's feeding the chickens,* or *She's milking a cow.* If the student guesses correctly, Team 2 gets a point. Then teams switch roles.

- Pair students. Student A talks about or makes a list of things he/she likes to do inside the house. Student B makes a list of things he/she likes to do outside the house. Students then exchange their lists and review their partner's choices. They put a checkmark (✔) next to the things they also like to do, and a crossmark (✗) next to the things they don't like to do. They also add things they like to do at the end of their partner's list. The students should then exchange papers again, and the partner should review the additional choices and add checks or X's next to them.

► LITERATURE

Suggested Books

Extra Cheese, Please!: Mozzarella's Journey from Cow to Pizza

written by Cris Peterson; photographs by Alvis Upitis.
Boyds Mills Press, 1994. ISBN 1563971771

This book introduces students to dairy farming in a way that they can well understand—it shows where the cheese in their pizza comes from. The author, a dairy farmer herself, describes the care and feeding of dairy cattle, and the process of making cheese from milking to manufacturing. The simple text and informative photographs make it appropriate for reading aloud and for generating factual questions based on Topic 7, The Country. This is a good complement to Gail Gibbons' *The Milk Makers* and it is a useful content connection to health and science. The book is also appropriate for Topic 13, The Midwest.

The Milk Makers

written and illustrated by Gail Gibbons.
Aladdin Paperbacks, 1987. ISBN 0689711166

This Reading Rainbow selection tells the story of milk production from the cow to the supermarket. The engaging pictures include numerous diagrams, which help to explain the process. There are only three or four lines of text per picture. The text provides an excellent script for discussion, questions, and answers. Furthermore, the clear pictures and brief text reinforce and extend the basic vocabulary in this topic. *The Milk Makers* can be used with all age and proficiency levels, and it works well in conjunction with *Extra Cheese, Please!* by Cris Peterson.

Kele's Secret

written by Tololwa M. Mollel; illustrated by Catharine Stock.
Lodestar Books Dutton, 1997. ISBN 0525675000

This is the story of Kele the hen and the young boy Yoanes who must track down her secret nest of eggs. It is a charming introduction to rural life in Africa, and as such, it can serve as a point of entry for students from Africa to share their home culture. Some of the language in the story may require teacher guidance. This book is recommended for intermediate and advanced students.

Town & Country

written by Alice Provensen;
illustrated by Martin Provensen.
Browndeer Press, 1994. ISBN 0152001824

In this journey of discovery, life in a busy city is compared to life in the countryside (see Topic 5, The City). Much of the detailed text is presented in the second person. This language structure provides opportunities for expanding vocabulary, as well as modeling and building grammar. The illustrations can be related to numerous Dictionary topics. The visuals can be useful especially for connecting this topic to Topic 9, People at Work.

WORKBOOK: Topic 7

On this page, students write the words for each numbered item in the picture.

WORKSHEET: Topic 7

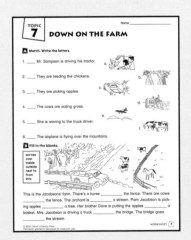

In A, students write the letters for the pictures that correspond to each sentence. In B, they choose prepositions from the word box to fill in the blanks in the paragraph.

8 THE HOSPITAL

Health workers and
medical items

► **LANGUAGE**

Present continuous: *The nurse
is helping him.*

Future with *going to*: *She's
going to see her parents today.*

CONTENT WORDS

1. patient
2. doctor
3. examination table
4. bandage
5. stethoscope
6. thermometer
7. medicine
8. X ray
9. nurse
10. crutches
11. cast
12. wheelchair
13. bed
14. pillow
15. blanket
16. ambulance
17. paramedic
18. stretcher

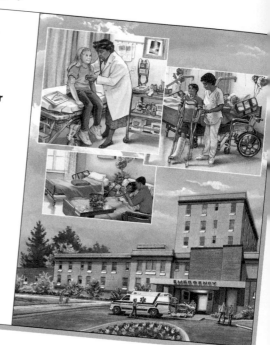

 CONTENT READING

The Hospital

The hospital is a busy place. There is a doctor and a patient in the emergency room. The doctor is listening to the patient's heart with a stethoscope. The patient is sitting on the examination table. She has a bandage on her arm. The doctor is going to look at the patient's X ray. Then, the doctor is going to take the girl's temperature with the thermometer. There are many bottles of medicine in the emergency room.

In another room, there are three patients. One patient is walking with crutches. The nurse is helping him. He has a broken leg. His leg is in a cast. He probably isn't going to play football this year.

There is a girl in the bed. Her wheelchair is next to her bed. She's under the blanket. Her head is on the pillow, but she isn't going to sleep. She's going to see her parents today.

There's a boy in the other bed. He's resting, but he isn't sleeping, either. He's watching TV.

There's a new baby in the next room. The baby's mother and father are holding their baby. They're going to take their baby home tomorrow. They are feeling very happy.

There's an ambulance outside the emergency entrance of the hospital. The paramedic is bringing a patient inside on a stretcher. The doctors are going to help the patient.

▶ WORDS

Components: Dictionary pages 16-17, Transparency 8, Wall Chart 8, Workbook page 8, Word and Picture Cards Topic 8, Cassette

- Present the content words. **See pages xiv-xvi for general techniques about presenting content words.**

  > **Language Note:** Point out the silent "e" at the end of many of the content words: *nurse*, *table*, *bandage*, *stethoscope*, *medicine*, and *ambulance*.

- Display the wall chart and have students look at the picture. Divide students into four groups. Group 1 looks at the top left panel. Group 2 looks at the top right panel. Group 3 looks at the middle panel. Group 4 looks at the main panel in the bottom half of the picture. Each group describes what is happening in its portion of the picture. The groups write down or circle all the content words that appear in those areas.

- Draw two columns on the board. Label Column 1 *People*. Label Column 2 *Medical Equipment or Supplies*. Distribute one word and picture card to each student. Have each student read the card, then place it on the board in the appropriate column. (Note: Blankets and pillows aren't medical supplies strictly speaking, but may be considered so for this activity.)

- Draw four columns on the board. Label the columns as follows:

  Column 1: People in the hospital

  Column 2: Things to help you get well

  Column 3: Things to find out why you are sick

  Column 4: Things to lie on or sit on

  Select four students to be judges for each of the four categories. These four students stand at the board, each one directly under or near his/her appropriate column. Now distribute all the word and picture cards (except *pillow* and *blanket*) to the rest of the class. Students join one of the four groups according to the appropriate category for their word and picture card. For example, a student with the card for *paramedic* stands next to Column 1. A student with the card for *X ray* stands next to Column 3. The category judge tells the student whether his/her word belongs in that category or not.

> **WORKBOOK:** Topic 8
> See Teacher's Book page 33.

▶ CONTENT

Components: Dictionary pages 16-17, Transparency 8, Wall Chart 8, Content Reading Topic 8, Worksheet Topic 8, Cassette

- Present the content reading. **See pages xvii-xix for general techniques about presenting content readings.**

- Ask the following or similar questions:

  Does the girl have a cast on her arm?
  Is the nurse taking the boy's temperature?
  Where is the X ray?
  Why is the boy walking with crutches?
  What is the paramedic doing?
  Who is the girl in the bed going to see?

▶ **Present continuous**

> We use the present continuous for an action that is happening now.

- Divide the class into three teams. A student from Team 1 pantomimes an action that someone is doing in any of the scenes in the wall chart. Students from Teams 2 and 3 try to guess the action. The first student who guesses the action correctly shouts out a sentence using the present continuous such as *She's taking the patient's temperature*, or *He's walking on crutches*. That students' team gets the point and then another student from the winning team pantomimes an action for students from the other two teams to guess. In order to score the point, the action must be described correctly and the correct form of the present continuous must be used. Once students have pantomimed all of the actions associated with the wall chart, encourage them to pantomime other actions they associate with being in the hospital.

▶ **Future with *going to***

> We use *going to* to express things that will happen in the near future.

- Introduce the future with *going to*. Ask individual students to say or write a sentence about something they or someone else is going to do tomorrow. For example: *I'm going to eat breakfast. Kim is going to talk to her teacher.* Encourage students to use full and contracted forms. Pair students. Student A in each pair tells how he/she feels. Student B in each pair tells the class what Student A is going to do. For example, if Student A says *My head hurts*, Student B says *She's going to lie down*. If Student A says *I feel great*, then Student B might say *He's going to walk five miles*. Students may also respond with negative sentences. For example, if Student A says *I have a stomachache*, Student B might respond *He's not going to eat 25 hot dogs today*.

> **WORKBOOK:** Topic 8
> See Teacher's Book page 33.

Components: Dictionary pages 16-17, Content Chant Topic 8, Cassette

CONTENT CHANT

Kenny's on Crutches

Kenny's on crutches.
Cathy's in a cast.
Willie's in a wheelchair,
moving fast.

Sally's on a stretcher.
Bobby's in a bed.
The nurse has a blanket
and a pillow for his head.

Andy's in an ambulance.
So is Pete.
They were driving too fast
on a busy street

Mommy had a baby.
I'm happy as can be.
Now I've got a little brother
and he looks like me.

- Present the content chant. **See pages xx-xxi for general techniques about presenting chants.**

- Before distributing Content Chant 8, explain to students that *on crutches* means walking with crutches. Also explain that *happy* as can be means very, very happy. Somebody who is "happy as can be" could not be happier. Ask students to talk about a time when they were *happy* as can be.

- Now distribute Content Chant 8. Divide the class into four groups with each group chanting one stanza. Have students repeat until they are comfortable with the language of the chant. Then, each group can chant its lines in the order of the chant.

- Select students to play the roles of the people in the chant. Select one student to pretend to be Kenny. He should walk as if on crutches. Another student should pretend to be Cathy by holding her arm in a sling. A third student should pretend to be Willie, sitting in a wheelchair and riding quickly. Select additional students to pretend they are Sally on the stretcher, Bobby in a bed, the nurse with a blanket, Andy and Pete in the ambulance, and Mommy with her new baby. These students stand next to the respective group that is chanting the action they are pantomiming.

► EXTENSION

Components: Dictionary pages 16-17, Transparency 8, Wall Chart 8

- Talk to students about hospitals. Ask them if they have ever been in a hospital. What happened to them? Did the doctors and nurses at the hospital help them? Did they like the hospital? Why or why not? Did they get crutches, a bandage? Did they take medicine? Did the doctor take X rays? Did the nurse use the stethoscope? Ask them if the hospital in the wall chart looks like hospitals in their country. How are they the same? How are they different?

- In the United States, when you go to see the doctor, he or she often puts a tongue depressor in your mouth and asks you to *Open wide and say aaahhh.* Ask students if this has happened to them. What do doctors in their countries say?

- Talk about things parents do when they have a new baby. One of the first things they do is give the baby a name. Ask students to think of names for babies. The names could be in English or in the native languages of the students. Write several suggestions from each student on the board. Then have the class vote on their two favorite names, one for a baby girl and one for a baby boy.

- Direct students' attention to the word *emergency* at the bottom of the picture. Ask students if they know the meaning of the word. If not, explain that an emergency is a very important situation in which somebody's life or health is in danger. An emergency can't wait. Ask students to talk about what to do in an emergency. Ambulances use their sirens during an emergency. Who else has sirens? What other kinds of emergencies are there?

- Ask each student to name a medical problem that would require a trip to the hospital emergency room, such as breaking an arm, having a painful stomachache, or swallowing bad medicine. Write all the answers on the board. The class then discusses the medical problems, deciding if they are real emergencies or problems that can wait.

► LITERATURE

Suggested Books

Tubes in My Ears: My Trip to the Hospital
written by Virginia Dooley; illustrated by Miriam Katin.
Mondo Publishing, 1996. ISBN 1572551186
Little Luke has been getting ear infections for some time. Eventually, his doctor decides that Luke needs a minor operation on his ears. This book describes Luke's experience in the hospital, from admission to discharge. Both the text and the pictures are clear and easy to follow. As a read-aloud, this book opens the way to classroom discussion about hospitals using the vocabulary, illustrations, and teaching suggestions for this topic. The information provides many starting points for questions and answers. As a follow-up to reading this selection, teachers may want to invite a person from the medical profession to talk to the class.

Emergency!
written and illustrated by Gail Gibbons.
Holiday House, 1995. ISBN 0823412016
This book, like many of the author's books, communicates practical information in a simple, readable style with descriptive illustrations. The brightly-colored art depicts emergency situations from the civic (downed power lines) to the personal (medical problem), and emphasizes the unique vehicles and equipment that allow rescue personnel to do their job effectively. Illustrated notes on policing, firefighting, and rescue operations can be found at the back of the book. These notes may also be useful for generating discussion for Topic 9, People at Work.

The Body Atlas
written and illustrated by Mark Crocker.
Oxford University Press, 1994. ISBN 019520963X
In addition to learning words that describe hospitals, students need to learn words that will help them describe their aches, pains, and body parts when they are sick or injured. This book is an exploration of anatomy that provides students with a detailed reference for this new vocabulary. Topics range from everyday phenomena (e.g., why people sometimes feel sleepy after a meal) to more complex topics (e.g., the principles of the immune system). The language is scientific and will require teacher guidance. A glossary at the back of the book will be helpful to more advanced students. This book is also useful in teaching Topic 30, Parts of the Body.

WORKBOOK: Topic 8

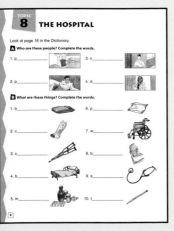

In A, students fill in the words for people in the hospital. In B, they fill in the words for things in the hospital. In both A and B, the first letter of each word is given as a clue.

WORKSHEET: Topic 8

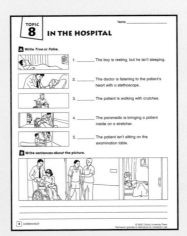

In the first exercise, students write *True* or *False* next to each sentence, based on the picture. In the second exercise, students write sentences about the picture.

▶ **CONTENT**
....
Occupations

▶ **LANGUAGE**
....
Habitual present: *Mechanics fix cars.*

Present continuous: *The messenger is riding a bicycle.*

CONTENT WORDS

1. construction worker
2. electrician
3. carpenter
4. mail carrier
5. firefighter
6. police officer
7. mechanic
8. messenger
9. musician
10. painter
11. computer operator
12. writer
13. dentist
14. dental assistant
15. hairdresser
16. plumber
17. pharmacist
18. salesperson

CONTENT READING

People at Work

Many people work in the city.

The mechanic is looking at the car. Mechanics fix cars. He's trying to fix the car. The police officer is directing traffic.

The messenger is riding a bicycle. Messengers deliver papers and packages to people.

The construction worker, the electrician, and the carpenter are working in the new building. The construction worker builds buildings. The electrician works with wires and electricity. The carpenter makes things with wood.

The painter is painting the bench. Sometimes, the painter works inside buildings and paints walls and ceilings.

The firefighter and the mail carrier work in the city, too. The firefighter stops fires. The mail carrier delivers the mail.

There's a musician on the street. He's playing music.

There are many people working inside the glass building. The computer operator puts information into the computer. Sometimes, he gets information from the computer. The writer writes books. The dentist fixes teeth and the dental assistant helps the dentist. The hairdresser cuts hair. The plumber fixes water pipes. The pharmacist and the salesperson are working in the drug store. The pharmacist prepares medicine. The salesperson sells things to shoppers.

These people are working hard. They like their jobs.

► WORDS

Components: Dictionary pages 18-19, Transparency 9, Wall Chart 9, Workbook page 9, Word and Picture Cards Topic 9, Cassette

- Present the content words. **See pages xiv-xvi for general techniques about presenting content words.**

- Draw three columns on the board. Label Column 1 *Outside*, Column 2 *Inside*, and Column 3 *Outside/Inside*. Distribute the word and picture cards to the class. Individual students group themselves into one of the three groups according to the appropriate category for their cards. For example, a student who has a card for *dental assistant* stands next to Column 2. A student with a card for *construction worker* stands next to Column 3 because the construction worker can work outside or inside.

- Display the wall chart for Topic 5, "The City." Explain that many of the people at work in Topic 9 could work in the city. Have individual students hold up their word and picture card workers from Topic 9 and show where their workers might work in "The City" wall chart. For example, a computer operator might work in the hotel, in the post office, or in the office building. A police officer might work in the police station. Encourage students to name all the possible places the workers could work.

- Talk to students about people at work. Ask each student what his or her mother and/or father do. Introduce the word *job*. Do students' parents do any of the jobs in the picture? What kind of jobs do the students want to have when they grow up? What do they want to be?

> **Language Note:** Often in English we add *-er* to the end of an action word (a verb) to describe a person who performs that action: a painter paints, a writer writes, and a firefighter fights fires.

- Direct students' attention to the *-er* at the end of words like *worker, carpenter, carrier, firefighter, officer, messenger, painter, writer, hairdresser*, and *plumber*. Explain that in English some words ending in *-er* indicate someone who performs an action. Write the following verbs on the board: *buy, sell, drive, bake, print, sing, dance, farm, photograph*, and *report*. Ask students what they might call a person who does these actions. Ask student if they can think of other actions and other types of workers.

WORKBOOK: Topic 9
See Teacher's Book page 37.

► CONTENT

Components: Dictionary pages 18-19, Transparency 9, Wall Chart 9, Content Reading Topic 9, Worksheet Topic 9, Cassette

- Present the content reading. **See pages xvii-xix for general techniques about presenting content readings.**

- Ask the following or similar questions:

  Does an electrician work with wires?
  Where's the painter?
  What is the mechanic doing?
  Who fixes teeth?
  Who fixes water pipes?
  What does a salesperson do?
  Does a writer paint or write?

► **Habitual present**

> We use the habitual present to talk about repeated activities or events, and habits. The forms of the habitual present are those of the simple present. For example: *I run five miles every day. He plays the piano. She collects stamps. I fix cars.* The habitual present is very often used to describe what somebody does for a living.

Distribute one word and picture card to each student. Have each student, in turn, read the card aloud, and then explain what that person does from the person's point of view. For example: *I'm a mechanic. I fix cars.* or *I'm a pharmacist. I prepare medicine.*

► **Present continuous**

> We use the present continuous to describe an activity or process that is happening now at the moment of speaking. Note that when talking about their jobs people often switch between the habitual present (what they do every day or regularly) and the present continuous (what they are doing at the moment of speaking).

Divide the class into two teams. A student from Team 1 pantomimes an action that somebody does at work. A student from Team 2 tries to guess the action, using the present continuous and naming the job. For example, if a student pantomimes delivering mail, the other student says *She's delivering the mail. She's a mail carrier.* If the student correctly names the job and describes the action, his/her team gets the point and then the next student from that team pantomimes an action. Continue until all students have pantomimed or guessed an action.

WORKBOOK: Topic 9
See Teacher's Book page 37.

► CHANTS

Components: Dictionary pages 18-19, Content Chant Topic 9, Cassette

 ## CONTENT CHANT

She's a Carpenter

She's a carpenter.
She makes things.

He's a construction worker.
He builds things.

She's a salesperson.
She sells things.

He's a messenger.
He delivers things.

She's a mechanic.
She fixes things.

He's a plumber.
He fixes sinks.

She's a hairdresser.
She fixes hair.

He's a dentist.
He fixes teeth.

- Present the content chant. **See pages xx-xxi for general techniques about presenting chants.**

- Before distributing Content Chant 9, divide the class into groups and have each group repeatedly chant one of the job names. For example, Group 1 chants *carpenter* repeatedly and pantomimes the actions of a carpenter. Group 2 repeatedly chants *construction worker* and pantomimes those actions. Continue with the rest of the job names in the chant. All the groups chant their words in turn.

- Distribute Content Chant 9. Select individual students or groups to chant each two-line grouping. For example, Student A or Group 1 chants *She's a carpenter. She makes things.* Student B or Group 2 chants *He's a construction worker. He builds things.* Select one student to point to the pictures of the people in the chant as their professions are mentioned.

- Repeat the chant, but change the lines to the first person. For example, Student A chants *I'm a carpenter. I make things.*

- Invite students to write their own verses of the chant, either in the first person or the third person. For example: *He's a writer. He writes books. I'm a dental assistant. I help the dentist.*

Language Note: Be sure to point out the contracted form of *BE* in the simple present and check to see if students are actually pronouncing the *m* sound in *I'm* and the *s* sound in *she's* or *he's.*

► EXTENSION

Components: Dictionary pages 18-19, Transparency 9, Wall Chart 9

- Talk with students about jobs normally associated with men and jobs associated with women. Elicit student discussion on questions such as *Can a woman be a construction worker? Can a man be a dental assistant?* Ask them if it is the same in their cultures. Encourage students to be open to nontraditional jobs for women and men.

- Explain that in the United States, the typical workweek is 40 hours. People generally work from 9 A.M. to 5 P.M. and take a lunch break around noon. *Rush hour* (which is not really an hour) is from 7 to 9 A.M. and 5 to 7 P.M. The streets are busy and buses and subways are crowded during rush hour. Ask students about when people work in their native countries. What time do people start work? What time do they come home? When is rush hour? Which days of the week do people work?

- Ask students to write or talk about the kinds of work they would like to do. Encourage them to discuss why they like a particular kind of work. Do they like to help people? Do they like to work with machines? Do they like to work outside?

- Have students conduct simple interviews, individually or as a class, with school personnel or parents. Questions about the person's profession could include: *What do you do? How many hours do you work? What is your favorite part of the job? How did you learn to do your job? What tools or materials do you use?* Interviews can be taped for listening practice, or answers can be written.

▶ LITERATURE

Suggested Books

I Got Community
written by Melrose Cooper; photographs by Dale Gottlieb.
Henry Holt & Company, Inc., 1995. ISBN 0805031790
In this illustrated rhyming book, different narrators from different backgrounds celebrate the people who make their community great. Among those celebrated are a baby-sitter, a good neighbor, a shopkeeper, and a policewoman—all useful tie-ins to the topic. The repetition of numerous language patterns in the rhyming lines makes this an excellent teaching tool.

Worksong
written by Gary Paulsen; illustrated by Ruth Wright Paulsen.
Harcourt Brace, 1997. ISBN 0152009809
In this ode to the everyday working person, simple rhymes and beautiful paintings depict people at work, from carpenters and farmers to nurses and street cleaners. There are only a few words on each page; many of them are words about people and places that are introduced in Unit 1, People and Places. Teachers can use this book to prompt students to talk about the kinds of work their family or friends have done, or the kinds of work they have seen on television. This book also works well with topics involving school or work.

Fire! Fire! Said Mrs. McGuire
written by Bill Martin, Jr.; illustrated by Richard Egielski.
Harcourt Brace, 1996. ISBN 0152275622
The strong, detailed pictures add humor and interest to this modern retelling of an old nursery rhyme. The rhyme is constructed as a series of questions and answers initiated by Mrs. McGuire, who is a television newscaster in this version. This book can be a starting point for students to invent their own rhyming patterns using the content words in this topic.

Town & Country
written by Alice Provensen; illustrated by Martin Provensen.
Browndeer Press, 1994. ISBN 0152001824
In this journey of discovery, life in a busy city is compared to life in the countryside (see Topic 5, The City and Topic 7, The Country). Much of the detailed text is presented in the second person. This language structure provides opportunities for expanding vocabulary, as well as modeling and building grammar. The visuals are especially useful for talking about people in various occupations. The illustrations can be related to numerous other Dictionary topics.

WORKBOOK: Topic 9

In both A and B, students match words to the corresponding pictures. Exercise A involves workers that have two words, so students need to connect one word to another before connecting to the picture.

WORKSHEET: Topic 9

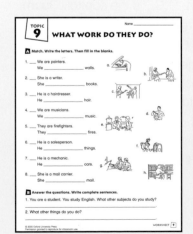

In A, students write letters to match the sentences to the pictures, then fill in the correct form of the verb in the sentence that describes what each worker does. In B, they answer the questions with personal information.

▶ **CONTENT**

Political maps and compass directions

▶ **LANGUAGE**

Comparative and superlative adjectives: *Canada and China are larger than the U.S., but Russia is the largest country in the world.*

Compound sentences with but: *Montana is a very large state, but Texas is larger than Montana.*

CONTENT WORDS

AL Alabama	MD Maryland	SC South Carolina
AK Alaska	MA Massachusetts	SD South Dakota
AZ Arizona	MI Michigan	TN Tennessee
AR Arkansas	MN Minnesota	TX Texas
CA California	MS Mississippi	UT Utah
CO Colorado	MO Missouri	VT Vermont
CT Connecticut	MT Montana	VA Virginia
DE Delaware	NE Nebraska	WA Washington
DC District of Columbia	NV Nevada	WV West Virginia
FL Florida	NH New Hampshire	WI Wisconsin
GA Georgia	NJ New Jersey	WY Wyoming
HI Hawaii	NM New Mexico	GU Guam
ID Idaho	NY New York	AS American Samoa
IL Illinois	NC North Carolina	VI U.S. Virgin Islands
IN Indiana	ND North Dakota	PR Puerto Rico
IA Iowa	OH Ohio	
KS Kansas	OK Oklahoma	
KY Kentucky	OR Oregon	
LA Louisiana	PA Pennsylvania	
ME Maine	RI Rhode Island	

U.S. Territories

 CONTENT READING

The United States

The United States of America is one of the largest countries in the world. It has more than 3 million square miles (9 million square kilometers) of land. Canada and China are larger than the U.S., but Russia is the largest country in the world.

There are 50 states in the U.S. The District of Columbia, or Washington, D.C., is the capital. Guam, American Samoa, the Virgin Islands, and Puerto Rico are four U.S. territories.

Montana is a very large state, but Texas is larger than Montana. The largest state is Alaska. Alaska is very far north. It is next to Canada.

There are many small states in the Northeast. Vermont and New Hampshire are small states, but Connecticut is smaller. Rhode Island is the smallest state in America.

California and Arizona are in the West. Florida is in the Southeast. Hawaii is in the Pacific Ocean. It's very far south. All of these states are warm. California is usually warmer than Florida.

What states do you know?

►WORDS

Components: Dictionary pages 20-21, Transparency 10, Wall Chart 10, Workbook page 10, Word and Picture Cards Topic 10, Cassette

- Present the content words. **See pages xiv-xvi for general techniques about presenting content words.**

- Display the wall chart and have students look at the picture. Ask students to locate their home state on the map. Ask students to identify the state's abbreviation. Then point to neighboring states and ask if students know the names of these states (without looking at the key on page 20).

  Language Note: Practice irregular pronunciation of state names with students. For example, the last syllable of *Arkansas* is pronounced *saw*. The middle *c* in *Connecticut* is silent. The *s* in *Illinois* is silent, too. The *h*, *e*, and *s* in *Rhode Island* are all silent. The *h* in *Utah* is silent. Point out also the silent final *e* in *Delaware*, *Maine*, and *New Hampshire*.

- Assign each student one or two state abbreviations from the alphabetical list in Dictionary Topic 10. Have the student find the state(s) on the map. Then have each student name all the states that border or neighbor those states.

- Help students draw a very large map of the U.S. on chart paper, showing the state borders. (The map can be labeled or left blank depending on the difficulty level desired.) Divide the class into two teams. Hand out half a set of the word cards to each team. Students take turns placing the cards on the appropriate locations on the map. Set a time limit for each student in a team to place a card. If the student places it correctly within the set amount of time, the team wins one point and the next student from the same team takes a turn to place the next card. If the student does not place it correctly, or the time runs out, the other team takes a turn. Play until all the states are labeled.

- Explain that the map in Dictionary Topic 10 is a map of the *contiguous* United States (sometimes referred to as the *Continental U.S.*). The contiguous U.S. is also sometimes called the *lower 48 states*. Two smaller boxes on the map show Alaska and Hawaii. Explain that these two states are very far from the other 48 states. Alaska is north and west of Canada. Hawaii is in the Pacific Ocean and very far south.

- Point to the Pacific Ocean and the Atlantic Ocean on the wall chart or on a world map. Show the relationship of the United States to these oceans. Explain that the territories Guam and American Samoa are in the Pacific Ocean and that the territories Puerto Rico and the U.S. Virgin Islands are in the Atlantic Ocean.

WORKBOOK: Topic 10
See Teacher's Book page 41.

►CONTENT

Components: Dictionary pages 20-21, Transparency 10, Wall Chart 10, Content Reading Topic 10, Worksheet Topic 10, Cassette

- Present the content reading. **See pages xvii-xix for general techniques about presenting content readings.**

- Ask the following or similar questions:

  Is the United States the largest country in the world?
  Is Vermont in the Northeast?
  Is California in the Northeast or in the West?
  How many states are in the U.S.?
  What is the capital of the United States?
  What is the largest state in the United States?

- Point to the compass rose on the map and explain the cardinal directions *north, south, east,* and *west.* Ask students to find North and South Dakota, North and South Carolina, and Virginia and West Virginia on the map. Ask individual students to explain why the states are named the way they are.

- Ask each student to write down a description of a state by naming the state (or states) to its north, south, east, and west. Non-writers can be paired with writers. Collect the papers, mix them, and redistribute them so that no student receives his or her own paper. Then ask each student, in turn, to read the description aloud and identify the state. For example, if the student reads the description *This state is north of Kansas, south of South Dakota, east of Wyoming and Colorado, and west of Iowa and Missouri,* the state would be identified as Nebraska. Continue until every student has read a description and identified a state.

- ► **Comparative and superlative adjectives.** Divide the class into two teams. A student from Team 1 names a state. A student from Team 2 names a state that is larger and a state that is smaller. For example, if a student from Team 1 says *California,* a student from Team 2 might say *Iowa is smaller than California, and Texas is larger than California.* Continue the game until all students have participated.

- ► **Compound sentences with *but.*** Have students find sentences in the content reading that use the word *but.* Using one of them as an example, point out the two full sentences within it. The word *but* is used to combine the two related sentences. Have students underline the two sentences in each compound sentence in the content reading.

- Ask each student to name a city in another state. Refer to a more detailed wall map of the U.S. or an atlas to help students find the locations of these cities.

WORKSHEET: Topic 10
See Teacher's Book page 41.

► CHANTS

Components: Dictionary pages 20-21, Content Chant Topic 10, Word and Picture Cards Topic 10, Cassette

 ## CONTENT CHANT

Riddle Chant

There are fifty states in the U.S.A.,
fifty states from sea to sea.
There are four states that start with A,
but not one state that starts with B.

There are three states that start with C.
There is one state that starts with D.
Which are the states that start with C?
Which is the state that starts with D?

There are two states that start with S.
There are two states that start with T.
Can you name the states that start with S?
Can you name the states that start with T?

There are fifty states in the U.S.A.,
plus Washington, D.C.
Fifty states in the U.S.A.,
but none of them starts with B.

- Present the content chant. **See pages xx-xxi for general techniques about presenting chants.**

- Before distributing the chant, have students practice with small chunks of the language. Form five groups, which chant the following. Group 1: *Four states start with A — A,A,A,A.* Group 2: *Three states start with C — C,C,C,*.* Group 3: *One state starts with D — D,* * *.* Group 4: *Two states start with S — S,S, * *.* Group 5: *Two states start with T — T,T, * *.* Have the groups practice individually and then simultaneously, increasing the volume and speed.

- Now distribute Content Chant 10. Form five groups. Four of the groups each chant one stanza aloud. Distribute pre-sorted word and picture cards to the fifth group. Whenever the students in this group hear a letter in the chant, they hold up the word card for a state that begins with that letter. For example, when Group 1 chants *There are four states that start with A*, Group 5 holds up a card for one of the several states that begins with the letter A, such as *Alabama*. Groups can switch roles until every group has had a chance to find and show the word cards.

- Ask students to name the four states that start with A, the three that start with C, the one that starts with D, the two that start with S, and the two that start with T.

- Have students invent new stanzas by substituting new letters. *There are three states that start with O. Which are the states that start with O?* The lines do not have to rhyme. Ask students to name the states that start with the letters they chose.

► EXTENSION

Components: Dictionary pages 12-13, Transparency 10, Wall Chart 10

- Introduce the standard abbreviations for the 50 states and the District of Columbia. Explain that these abbreviations are sometimes used instead of the two-digit postal abbreviations shown in Dictionary Topic 10. They are as follows: *Ala., Alaska, Ariz., Ark., Calif., Colo., Conn., Del., D.C., Fla., Ga., Hawaii, Idaho, Ill., Ind., Iowa, Kans., Ky., La., Maine, Md., Mass., Mich., Minn., Miss., Mo., Mont., Nebr., Nev., N.H., N.J., N.Mex., N.Y., N.C., N.Dak., Ohio, Okla., Ore., Pa., R.I., S.C., S.Dak., Tenn., Tex., Utah, Vt., Va., Wash., W.Va., Wis., Wyo.* Ask students to identify which of the standard abbreviations are the same as the postal abbreviations and which are different. Ask students why they might use a postal abbreviation and why they might use a standard abbreviation. Also ask students why they think certain states in the list of standard abbreviations are not abbreviated.

- Have students work in groups doing a research project. Assign to each group one of the states on the dictionary page that has a picture on it relating to that state (for example, the picture of the person skiing on the state of Colorado, the potatoes shown on Idaho, or the flamingo and alligator on Florida). Have students research information relating to the picture shown on their assigned state. They can use resources such as encyclopedias, the Internet, or other students who have been to those states. Each group writes a report and presents their information to the class orally.

- Divide the class into four groups. Assign one of the states beginning with *New* (New York, New Jersey, New Mexico, New Hampshire) to each group. Ask students why each state was named with the word *New*. Ask them if they know where "Old" Mexico, York, Hampshire, and Jersey were. Have each group find the original places, using atlases of the world, almanacs, or encyclopedias. Individual students from each group may present the group's findings to the class.

- Have students look at the boundaries between the states on the wall chart. Point out that some of the lines are straight and some of them are curvy or crooked. Ask students why they think that might be. For additional help, turn to an atlas or a physical map that might show geographic features like rivers, mountains, and other natural barriers between states.

- Have students cut up an old map of the U.S. along state borders. Then they can mount the state pieces on heavy paper and trim along the borders to make long-lasting puzzle pieces. Invent games that involve rejoining the pieces of the country.

► LITERATURE

Suggested Books

America: My Land, Your Land, Our Land
written by W. Nikola-Lisa; illustrated by 14 different artists.
Lee & Low Books, Inc., 1997. ISBN 1880000377
Fourteen artists contribute to this book's presentation of America as a country of vastly different landscapes and cultures that cohere into a united whole. The double-page scenes and simple text are well-suited to a straightforward presentation of opposites and adjectives. Teachers may also want to refer to the individual parts of the country and their landscapes as presented in the topics of Unit 2, The U.S. and Its Neighbors. This is a good book for beginners to use as an introduction to the diversity of the United States.

It Happened in America: True Stories from the Fifty States
written by Lila Perl; illustrated by Ib Ohlsson.
Henry Holt, 1996. ISBN 0805047077
Each chapter of this informative book profiles a state of the U.S. (including the District of Columbia) and an important historical incident or unusual occurence that took place there. The anecdotes are often humorous, sometimes serious, but always interesting. The stories in this collection can be matched to the regions of the country as they are introduced in Topics 11-17. This colorful history is more suitable for intermediate and advanced language learners, but beginning students can benefit from read-aloud sessions of the less complicated anecdotes.

Maps and Globes
written by Jack Knowlton; illustrated by Harriett Barton.
HarperTrophy, 1986. ISBN 0064460495
This Reading Rainbow selection presents a brief history of mapmaking, gives examples of many types of maps, and introduces key vocabulary for map-reading and geography. The large-print text presents the essential vocabulary, usually in italics, and the illustrations clearly show those words in context. Many of the illustrations have interesting, anecdotal captions that can be used to add greater interest. Since the text, grammar patterns, and illustrations are quite simple, it is an excellent resource that will help ESL students to grasp some rather difficult concepts. The book is also appropriate for Topic 18, Canada and Mexico.

The Young Oxford Companion to Maps and Mapmaking
written by Rebecca Stefoff.
Oxford University Press, 1995. ISBN 0195080424
This encyclopedic book describes everything about maps and mapmaking, from A to Z. The articles, most of which are accompanied by illustrations, cover such topics as cartography terms, the applications of mapmaking, types of maps, and biographies of geographers and explorers. This is an excellent classroom reference in which students can find many articles that explain the vocabulary in Units 2, 3, and 7. It is most appropriate for advanced students.

This Land Is Your Land
written by Woody Guthrie; illustrated by Kathy Jakobsen.
Little Brown & Co., 1998. ISBN 0316392154
The words to Woody Guthrie's folk song are beautifully illustrated in this book. Words and art take the reader across the entire country. This is an ideal book to use for a group reading time, with students reading the text aloud and singing the song together.

WORKBOOK: Topic 10

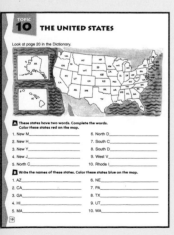

In A, students fill in the second word for each state. The first letter is given as a clue. Then, students color these states red on the map. In B, they write state names based on the abbreviations given. Then, they color these states blue on the map.

WORKSHEET: Topic 10

In A, students choose comparatives and superlatives from the word box to fill in the sentences comparing the states. In B, they write their own sentences using comparatives and superlatives. They compare a state in A to the state in which they live.

▶ **CONTENT**
....
States, features, and
landmarks in the Northeast

▶ **LANGUAGE**
....
Verb + infinitive: *Traders try
to buy stocks at low prices.*

Habitual present: *They work
in studios.*

Adverb *too*: *A trader is a
businessperson, too.*

CONTENT WORDS

1. stock market
2. stocks and bonds
3. businessperson
4. newspaper
5. magazine
6. buy
7. sell
8. headline
9. advertisement
10. studio
11. newscaster
12. television
13. radio
14. telephone
15. satellite
16. Statue of Liberty
17. Liberty Bell
18. The White House

GREETINGS FROM THE NORTHEAST!

CONTENT READING

The Northeast

The states in the Northeast are Maine, New Hampshire, Vermont, Massachusetts, Rhode Island, Connecticut, New York, New Jersey, Delaware, Pennsylvania, and Maryland. The District of Columbia, or Washington, D.C., is in the Northeast, too. Washington, D.C. is the capital of the United States.

The finance industry is in the Northeast. Banking is one part of the finance industry. A banker is a businessperson. The stock market is another part of the finance industry. Traders buy and sell stocks and bonds in the stock market. A trader is a businessperson, too. Stocks are shares, or parts, of a company. Traders try to buy stocks at low prices. Then, they try to sell the stocks at high prices.

The communications industry is in the Northeast, too. Newspapers, magazines, television, radio, telephones, and satellites are part of the communications industry. People in this industry need to communicate information quickly. Newspapers report interesting stories with big headlines. There are also many advertisements in newspapers. Television and radio newscasters tell people about the day's important events. They work in studios.

Some of America's greatest landmarks are in the Northeast. The Statue of Liberty is in New York City. The Liberty Bell is in Philadelphia, Pennsylvania. The White House is in Washington, D.C. The U.S. President lives and works in the White House.

▶ WORDS

Components: Dictionary pages 22-23, Transparency 11, Wall Chart 11, Workbook page 11, Word and Picture Cards Topic 11, Cassette

- Present the content words. **See pages xiv-xvi for general techniques about presenting content words.**

  > **Language Note:** The words *magazine*, *headline*, *telephone*, and *White House* have a silent *e*. We use the words *businessperson* for a man or a woman, *businessman* just for men, and *business-woman* just for women.

- Display the wall chart and have students look at the picture. Compare the bottom left picture of the Northeast with the map of the entire United States in Dictionary Topic 10. Point out and name the northeastern states on the U.S. map.

- Draw three columns on the board, one for each category of content words. Label the columns *The Finance Industry*, *The Communications Industry*, and *Landmarks*. Select three students to be the category judges and stand next to each column. Now distribute the word and picture cards to the rest of the class. Have individual students hold up their word and picture cards and group themselves near one of the three categories listed on the board. If students are not sure where to stand, have them ask the category judges. For example, a student with the *stock market* card stands next to Column 1, *The Finance Industry*.

- Have the class make labels for the parts of the wall chart which correspond to the categories they were using in the above activity. The top left picture on the chart should be labeled *The Finance Industry*, the top right picture should be labeled *The Communications Industry*, and the lower right picture should be labeled *Landmarks*. Have students place their word cards on the appropriate section of the wall chart.

- Draw a word web on the board like the one below and have students write the names of their favorite magazines, newspapers, and radio and television stations.

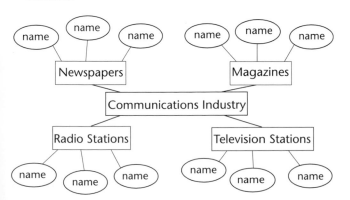

WORKBOOK: Topic 11
See Teacher's Book page 45.

▶ CONTENT

Components: Dictionary pages 22-23, Transparency 11, Wall Chart 11, Content Reading Topic 11, Worksheet Topic 11, Cassette

- Present the content reading. **See pages xvii-xix for general techniques about presenting content readings.**

- Ask the following or similar questions:

  Is New York in the Northeast?
  Is the capital of the United States in the Northeast or in the Northwest?
  Where is the Statue of Liberty?
  What do traders try to do?
  Where do newscasters work?

  > **Content Note:** The Northeast can be divided into the New England states and the Mid-Atlantic states. The states north and east of New York (Connecticut, Rhode Island, Massachusetts, Vermont, New Hampshire, and Maine) are often referred to as New England, because they were among the first states settled by English colonists. New York, New Jersey, Pennsylvania, Maryland, and Delaware are often called the Mid-Atlantic states.

- Point to any one of the outlined states in the bottom left picture of the Northeast. Ask students to name the state you are pointing to, without looking at the map in Dictionary Topic 10. Continue until students are familiar with all the states of the Northeast.

▶ **Habitual present.** List the professions found in the reading (trader, banker, newscaster). Pair students. The first student chooses one word from the list. The second student tells one thing that person does, using the habitual present. *Traders buy and sell stocks. Newscasters tell people about important events. A banker works in a bank.* To extend this activity, review and add to the list some professions from Topic 9.

▶ **Verb + infinitive**

  > Certain verbs such as *try*, *want*, *need*, *hope*, *like*, *plan*, and *promise* can be followed by an infinitive form of another verb. An infinitive is the word *to* plus the simple form of a verb (*to go*, *to eat*, etc.). For example: *Traders try to buy stocks at low prices.*

  Ask students in turn to pantomime somebody *trying to* do something but not being able to do it, such as climbing a wall or carrying a heavy object. The other students guess what the student is trying to do. Demonstrate how to make a sentence with *try* plus the infinitive forms of the verbs that were pantomimed. Then have students find examples of sentences in the reading with *try, need,* and *have.* Have them work in pairs to make up some of their own sentences.

WORKSHEET: Topic 11
See Teacher's Book page 45.

▶ CHANTS

Components: Dictionary pages 22-23, Content Chant Topic 11, Cassette

 CONTENT CHANT

Buy the Newspaper

Buy the newspaper.
Look at the headlines.
Turn on the radio.
Listen to the news.

Look at the headlines.
Read the newspaper.
Turn on the television.
Listen to the news.

Turn on the television.
Listen to the newscaster.
Watch the stock market.
Listen to the news.

Watch the stock market.
Listen to the newscaster.
    Buy? Sell?
    What should I do?

Read the newspaper.
Listen to the radio.
Turn on the television.
Watch the news!

- Present the content chant. **See pages xx-xxi for general techniques about presenting chants.**

- Before distributing the chant, have students establish the rhythm by chanting *Listen to the news* repeatedly. Have students increase their volume and speed until they are comfortable with the rhythm.

- Now distribute Content Chant 11. Divide the class into five groups. Have each group chant a stanza. As students chant the lines *Listen to the news* or *Watch the news*, the entire class joins in.

- Invite students to make up their own stanzas to this chant. Have them use the imperative forms of the verbs *buy*, *watch*, *listen*, *read*, *turn on*, and *look at* (the imperative form of *look* is almost always followed by *at*) with the nouns *newspaper*, *magazine*, *television*, *radio*, *headlines*, and *advertisement*. For example: *Buy the magazine*, *look at the advertisements*, *listen to the radio*, *turn on the news*.

> **Language Note:** Explain that *turn on* is a two-word verb that is used for electrical and electronic appliances. The opposite is *turn off*. In English, we often put the direct object noun or pronoun between the two words of two-word verbs such as *turn on* and *turn off*. For example: *turn the television off*, or *turn it off*; *turn the lights on* or *turn them on*.

▶ EXTENSION

Components: Dictionary pages 22-23, Transparency 11, Wall Chart 11

- Divide the class into three groups. Assign one of the landmarks from the wall chart to each group. Have each group research the history and importance of its landmark, using almanacs, encyclopedias, history books, or the Internet. Each group presents their findings to the class.

- Explain that each of the states in the U.S. has a capital city. Assign each state from this section to a student or group of students and ask them to find the name of the state's capital.

- Bring in old newspapers and magazines and distribute them. Ask students to identify headlines and advertisements. Ask them to cut out one car advertisement, one food advertisement, one airplane or travel advertisement, and some other kind of advertisement from their magazines. Then, have them cut out headlines of different sizes. Students can use them to make collages of advertisements, headlines, or combinations of both.

- Create a class newspaper. Talk about some of the things that have happened in your school or your classroom over the past week or month. Divide students into five or six groups. Each group writes a short newspaper article about an event that happened in your class or school. Groups can write articles about news, sports, finance, etc. Each group also draws a picture to accompany its article. Have the groups think of headlines that summarize their articles and write them in big letters at the top of the page. Students can select a name for the newspaper, such as *The Greenville School Gazette*, or the *Carysburg Times*. As a class, the students decide what should be on each page. Lay out the newspaper according to what the class decides. Then photocopy the pages and distribute the newspaper to the entire class.

- **Game: Telephone.** Have students sit in a line or a circle. Think of a sentence. For example: *Sam Butler buys and sells stocks and bonds*. Write the sentence down on a piece of paper, but keep it to yourself. Now whisper the sentence to the first student in the line or circle and then say *Pass it on*. The first student should whisper the same sentence to the second student, and repeat *Pass it on*. Students continue until the last student hears the sentence. Then the last student says the sentence he or she heard. Write the sentence on the board, and then write the original sentence above it. Compare the two sentences. Usually they are completely different.

►LITERATURE

Suggested Books

The White House
written by Patricia Ryon Quiri.
Franklin Watts, Inc., 1996. ISBN 0531202216
This short book tells almost everything one needs to know about the White House—its history, layout, and importance. Children can even find out how to e-mail the president and visit the White House. Although the book contains a great deal of information for its small size, the text is very clear and portions of it can be read aloud. This book is also useful for teaching Topic 28, The U.S. Government.

The Story of the Statue of Liberty
written by Betsy Maestro; illustrated by Giulio Maestro.
Mulberry Books, 1989. ISBN 0688087469
The story of the Statue of Liberty begins with French sculptor August Bartholdi's bold idea to create a statue commemorating the friendship between France and the United States. Bartholdi's show of imagination in planning this famous symbol of international friendship and his determination to carry out his plan are described in full. The vivid illustrations and straightforward text make this book a good reference for all students. A timeline and fun facts about the statue appear at the end of the book. To extend the Dictionary topic, teachers can have students design their landmarks or write about landmarks in their own communities.

The Story of Communications
written by Anita Ganeri.
Oxford University Press, 1998. ISBN 0195214110
The Northeast is a communications center, but it is only one of many centers in a communications sprawl that circles the globe. How did this communications explosion occur? This book traces the development of long-distance communication from early methods such as fire signals, drums, and semaphore to radio, television, satellites, and computers. This book is heavily illustrated, so language should be easier for students to acquire. It is an excellent source for reports and reference. Teachers may also wish to refer to it when they introduce technology in Topic 17, The West Coast and Pacific, or in Topic 60, Computers and Calculators.

The Story of Writing and Printing
written by Anita Ganeri.
Oxford University Press, 1996. ISBN 0195212568
This well-written, comprehensive book covers alphabets, the rise of newspapers, and the development of writing technology from quills to fountain pens to IBM's first word processor in 1964. The text is thoroughly illustrated. Teachers will find this book especially helpful when extending the topic. Student-generated newspapers and word-processing games are some excellent follow-up activities.

The Story of Money
written by Betsy C. Maestro; illustrated by Giulio Maestro.
Mulberry Books, 1995. ISBN 0688133045
This "story" is an easy-to-read book about the history of money from early trade and barter systems to modern day currency and the electronic transfer of funds. This book offers an extension of students' understanding of the making and use of money. Students will find the section on money in the Dictionary Appendix also useful for identifying American currency

WORKBOOK: Topic 11

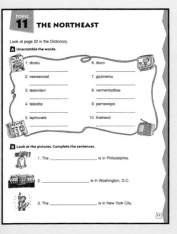

In the first exercise, students unscramble ten of the content words. In the second exercise, they look at the pictures and fill in the sentences about the landmarks.

WORKSHEET: Topic 11

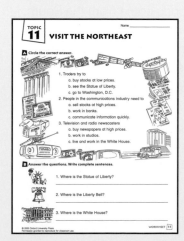

Exercise A is a multiple choice activity. Students pick the correct ending of each sentence from three choices. In B, they answer the questions. Both exercises require students to use information contained in the content reading.

12 THE SOUTH

CONTENT

States, features, and landmarks in the South

The food processing and manufacturing industries

LANGUAGE

Logical connector *such as* + **noun phrase:** *Goods are products such as furniture and clothing.*

Habitual present: *Workers make sugar from sugarcane.*

CONTENT WORDS

1. sugarcane
2. cotton
3. rice
4. crop
5. sugar
6. factory
7. worker
8. assembly line
9. lumber
10. cloth
11. thread
12. furniture
13. raw materials
14. goods
15. port
16. plantation
17. Mississippi River
18. Kennedy Space Center

CONTENT READING

The South

The states in the South are Virginia, West Virginia, Kentucky, Arkansas, Tennessee, North Carolina, South Carolina, Georgia, Alabama, Mississippi, Louisiana, and Florida. The South has good soil and warm weather. Crops such as sugarcane, cotton, and rice grow well in the South.

Many manufactured goods come from the South. Goods are products such as furniture and clothing. Workers make goods from raw materials such as lumber, rice, cotton, and sugarcane.

The South has a lot of factories and workers. The workers make goods with the raw materials. For example, workers make sugar from sugarcane. Then, they send the sugar to places such as restaurants and supermarkets. People put sugar in their coffee or on their breakfast cereal.

In furniture factories, workers make chairs with lumber, cloth, and thread. They work on an assembly line. Each worker does one job many times. One worker builds a chair with lumber. Another worker puts cloth on the chair. Another worker sews the cloth with thread. Then, the factory sends the chairs to furniture stores.

The South has many famous landmarks such as the historic plantations near the Mississippi River or the Kennedy Space Center in Florida. The historic city of New Orleans is one of the most important ports in the United States.

▶ WORDS

Components: Dictionary pages 24-25, Transparency 12, Wall Chart 12, Workbook page 12, Word and Picture Cards Topic 12, Cassette

- Present the content words. **See pages xiv-xvi for general techniques about presenting content words.**

- Display the wall chart and have students look at the picture. Compare the bottom left picture of the South with the map of the entire United States in Dictionary Topic 10. Point out and name the southern states on the U.S. map.

  > **Language Note:** Point out the silent *e* in the words *sugarcane*, *rice*, *assembly line*, *furniture*, and *Space*. Explain that the *s* in sugar is pronounced like *sh*.

- Bring to class real examples of some of the Topic 12 content words such as a sugar packet, a box of rice cereal, some uncooked rice, cotton fabric, and thread. Have students handle the items and identify them. Students ask and answer: *What's this? It's _____*. Ask students which word in Topic 12 refers to all of these items (*goods*). They are all goods because they have been manufactured from raw materials (cotton crops, rice grains, sugarcane, etc.).

- Distribute one word and picture card to each student. Draw three columns on the board. Label the first column *Food Processing*, the second *Manufacturing*, and the third *Landmarks*. Now ask students, in turn, to come to the front of the class, read their cards aloud, and place them in the appropriate column. For example, the student with the *furniture* card should place the card in the *Manufacturing* column.

- Ask each student, in turn, to name a piece of furniture in the classroom. There may be more students than different pieces of furniture, so allow students to point to different desks, different chairs, etc.

- Play a modified version of the game of "20 Questions." Hand out the picture cards. Students take turns being "it." The other students try to guess which picture card that person has. Students can only ask *Yes/No* questions. Encourage students to ask broad questions such as *Is it a crop?* or *Is it in a factory?* The student who guesses the correct answer then becomes "it." This game can also be played with teams.

- Introduce a mnemonic device to teach the spelling of *Mississippi*. Break up the letters of the word and say them in a rhythmic manner: M-ISS-ISS-IPP-I. Ask how many *i*'s there are in the word *Mississippi*. Then introduce students to this English play on words: Bet students that you can spell *Mississippi* with one *i*. When they don't believe you, cover one eye with your hand and spell the word aloud.

WORKBOOK: Topic 12
See Teacher's Book page 49.

▶ CONTENT

Components: Dictionary pages 24-25, Transparency 12, Wall Chart 12, Content Reading Topic 12, Worksheet Topic 12, Cassette

- Present the content reading. **See pages xvii-xix for general techniques about presenting content readings.**

- Ask the following or similar questions:

  > *Is Oregon in the South?*
  > *Is lumber a raw material?*
  > *Are furniture and clothing goods?*
  > *Which crops grow well in the South?*
  > *What do workers make from raw materials?*
  > *What state is New Orleans in?*

- ▶ **Logical connector *such as* + noun phrase.** Model sentences with *such as* + noun phrase. For example: *The classroom has many pieces of furniture such as tables, chairs, and desks.* Ask students to circle, underline, or otherwise identify all the sentences using *such as* in the content reading. Have students say or write their own sentences using *such as*. If students need help, offer some additional examples.

- Point to any one of the outlined states in the bottom left picture of the South. Ask students to name the state you are pointing to without looking at the map in Dictionary Topic 10. Now point to another state and have other students name the state. Continue until students are familiar with all the states in the South.

- Have students look at the wall chart and point to the appropriate picture in the top part of the illustration as you read the following sentences:

  > *Farmers grow crops such as sugarcane.*
  > *Machines cut the sugarcane and put it on trucks.*
  > *Machines wash the sugarcane at the factory.*
  > *Machines turn the sugarcane into sugar.*
  > *Workers put big bags of sugar into trucks.*
  > *Someone opens a packet of sugar and pours it into the coffee.*

  After students have done this activity as a class, have them copy these sentences onto a piece of paper and cut them into separate sentence strips. Have students take turns ordering these sentence strips and reading them aloud in the correct sequence. Repeat the activity with the middle picture on the wall chart, but this time have the students create their own sentence strips to describe the process of making furniture out of wood.

- Ask students to name some famous cities and features of any of the states in the South. For example, Orlando, Florida is famous because the Walt Disney World theme park is located there. Create a list and then have students make sentences based on the list.

WORKSHEET: Topic 12
See Teacher's Book page 49.

► CHANTS

Components: Dictionary pages 24-25, Content Chant Topic 12, Cassette

 CONTENT CHANT

The South

The South *
    Alabama
The South *
    Mississippi
The South *
    Louisiana

Cotton, rice, and sugarcane

The South *
    Georgia peaches
The South *
    Florida oranges
The South *
    Louisiana catfish

Cotton, rice, and sugarcane

The South *
    raw materials
The South *
    factory workers
The South *
    assembly lines

Cotton, rice, and sugarcane

- Present the content chant. **See pages xx-xxi for general techniques about presenting chants.**

- Before distributing Content Chant 12, explain that Georgia is famous for its peaches and Florida is famous for its oranges. If possible, bring in a few Georgia peaches or Florida oranges and a few peaches and oranges from other states. Cut them up so that each student may taste both kinds and compare.

- Have students practice with chunks of the language from the chant. Divide the class into three groups. The Group 1 students are the Georgia peaches. They repeatedly chant in a light sing-song manner *Georgia peaches, Georgia peaches*. The Group 2 students are the Florida oranges. They are more robust and they chant more loudly *Florida oranges, Florida oranges*. The Group 3 students are the Louisiana catfish. Explain that a catfish is a fish that has long whiskers like a cat's. For fun, Group 3 can chant *Louisiana catfish, meow!* Each group chants their lines first in turn, and then, simultaneously.

- Now distribute Content Chant 12. Divide the class into two groups. Group 1 chants the line *The South* and claps. Group 2 chants all the indented lines in the chant. The entire class whispers the line *Cotton, rice, and sugarcane* every time it occurs.

► EXTENSION

Components: Dictionary pages 24-25, Transparency 12, Wall Chart 12

- Explain that each of the states in the U.S. has a capital city. Assign each state from this section to a student or group of students. Have them find the name of the state's capital.

- Visit the cafeteria to show students how everybody in the cafeteria works together to make lunch for students. Different people in the cafeteria do different jobs, such as cooking the meals, carrying trays from the kitchen to the serving table, serving the food, preparing dessert, or washing lunch trays. Ask students to describe how jobs are done in the cafeteria compared with how they are done on an assembly line. Are they the same or different?

- Create a class assembly line. Ask students to put together a book of word and picture cards. Photocopy the word and picture cards. Stack all the photocopies on one student's desk. The first student cuts each page into cards and passes the cards to the next student. The second student punches holes in the top left-hand corner of all the cards. The third student puts all the cards in order. The fourth student puts a ring or string through all the holes. The fifth student folds a cover and puts it around the cards. The sixth student puts a price tag on the cover. Invent as many steps as you like.

- Divide the class into three groups. Assign one of the landmarks from the wall chart to each group. Have each group research the history and importance of its landmark, using almanacs, encyclopedias, history books, or the Internet. Each group should present their findings to the class.

- Divide the class into groups and ask them to chant the first four lines from the content chant using the names of the states they learned about in Dictionary Topic 11. For example:

    The Northeast*
        Maine
    The Northeast*
        Vermont
    The Northeast*
        New York

Each group takes turns performing these lines with as many different state names as they can remember. As students study each new topic in this unit, this same chant can be used to practice the names of states in each region.

► LITERATURE

Suggested Books

Harvest Year
written by Cris Peterson; photographs by Alvis Upitis.
Boyds Mills Press, 1996. ISBN 1563975718
Harvest Year is a useful visual reference for all of Unit 2, The U.S. and Its Neighbors. It shows the harvests that take place in America throughout the year, from pineapples and carrots in January to shrimp and pecans in December. Each double-page spread contains a mini-lesson in language and social studies; each includes the month of the year, the crop, and a map showing the states where each harvest takes place. Numerous captioned photographs add visual interest to the information. The simple language can be first read aloud and then assigned to partners or individuals. This book also works well with Topic 10, The United States.

The Cuban American Family Album
written by Dorothy Hoobler and Thomas Hoobler, with an introduction by Oscar Hijuelos.
Oxford University Press, 1998. ISBN 0195124251
This book from the series *The American Family Albums* presents the stories of one of the most influential immigrant groups in the South: the Cubans. The book is designed like an album, or scrapbook, containing period photographs and other memorabilia including diary entries, letters, and newspaper clippings. Many ESL students will identify with this immigrant group, who made a rich cultural and economic contribution to America, in general, and to Florida, in particular. Teachers will find this book to be a valuable resource on Southern culture. Direct instruction will be necessary. The book is recommended for intermediate and advanced students.

Drylongso
written by Virginia Hamilton; illustrated by Jerry Pinkney.
Harcourt Brace & Company, 1997. ISBN 0152015876
Virginia Hamilton's *Drylongso* is a moving, mythical story about the South during the drought of 1975. "Drylongso," an African colloquialism meaning "drought," is the name of the story's protagonist, who enters the life of a family suffering from the lack of rain. The story gives students an understanding of the struggles associated with growing up in the agricultural South and the struggles associated with food processing. The text is presented in chapter format with many full-page illustrations. It provides many opportunities to introduce students to colloquialisms, dialogue, similes, and metaphors. Teachers can use this book with advanced ESL students paired with mainstream students.

WORKBOOK: Topic 12

Students label the pictures for *Crops, Places,* and *Goods* in A. In B, the first letter of each numbered word is given and students complete the words depicted in the manufacturing scenes.

WORKSHEET: Topic 12

In A, students draw lines to connect the raw materials to the goods. Then, they complete the sentences. In B, they use their knowledge of the content reading to fill in the blanks. The pictures are cues for the answers.

13 THE MIDWEST

▶ **CONTENT**

States, features, and landmarks in the Midwest

The agriculture and dairy farming industries

▶ **LANGUAGE**

Future with *will*: *Bakeries will make bread with the flour.*

Present continuous: *These farmers are getting milk from the cows.*

Quantity expressions *some of, many*: *Some of the grain will become flour.*

CONTENT WORDS

1. dairy barn
2. cattle
3. farmhouse
4. plant
5. harvest
6. plow
7. combine
8. hay
9. wheat
10. soybeans
11. corn
12. grain
13. grain elevator
14. Great Lakes
15. Great Plains
16. Mount Rushmore

COME TO THE MIDWEST!

CONTENT READING

The Midwest

The states in the Midwest are North Dakota, South Dakota, Nebraska, Kansas, Wisconsin, Iowa, Missouri, Minnesota, Illinois, Indiana, Michigan, and Ohio.

The Midwest is in the middle of the United States. The Great Lakes are in the Midwest. The Great Plains are in the Midwest, too. The Great Plains are very flat.

Some of the farmers in the Midwest have dairy farms. A dairy farm has a farmhouse and a dairy barn. The farmers keep cattle, or cows, in the dairy barn. These farmers are getting milk from the cows. They will send the milk to a dairy processing plant. Then, some of the milk will become cheese or yogurt. Some of the milk will go to supermarkets.

Some of the farmers in the Midwest grow grain, like wheat and corn. Many farmers also grow soybeans. They turn the soil with plows. Then, they plant the seeds. These farmers are harvesting the grain with a combine. They will take the grain to a grain elevator. They will keep the hay for the cows. Some of the grain will become flour. Bakeries will make bread with the flour.

The Midwest has some famous landmarks. Mount Rushmore is a mountain in South Dakota. It has a very large carving of four famous American presidents. They are George Washington, Thomas Jefferson, Theodore Roosevelt, and Abraham Lincoln.

▶ WORDS

Components: Dictionary pages 26-27, Transparency 13, Wall Chart 13, Workbook page 13, Word and Picture Cards Topic 13, Cassette

- Present the content words. **See pages xiv-xvi for general techniques about presenting content words.**

> **Language Note**: The word *plow* is shown as a noun in the Dictionary, but this word can also be a verb. We use a *plow* to *plow* fields. When we plow fields, we break up the soil into small chunks, turn it over, and make it ready for planting crops.
>
> The words *cattle*, *wheat*, and *corn* are noncount nouns. This means that they don't have a plural form and we don't use *a* or *one* before them. We can say *some cattle*, *some wheat* or *a field of wheat*. The word *grain* can be used as a noncount noun (*some grain*) and also as a count noun (*a grain of rice*).

- Display the wall chart and have students look at the picture. Compare the bottom left picture of the Midwest with the map of the entire United States in Dictionary Topic 10. Point out and name the midwestern states on the U.S. map.

- Bring to class real examples of some of the content words (or items related to the words) such as milk, cheese, yogurt, corn, cereal, and bread. Help students to match some of the words to related products. For example, bread is made from wheat, corn puffs are made from corn, and cheese and yogurt are made from milk.

- Distribute the picture cards to the class and divide the class into two teams. Write the names of three categories on the board: *Food Products*, *Things on a Farm*, and *Things in the Midwest*. A student from Team 1 calls out a card, such as *dairy barn*. A student from Team 2 categorizes that word as *Things on a Farm*. Team 2 scores one point and a student from Team 2 calls out a word.

WORKBOOK: Topic 13
See Teacher's Book page 53.

▶ CONTENT

Components: Dictionary pages 26-27, Transparency 13, Wall Chart 13, Content Reading Topic 13, Worksheet Topic 13, Cassette

- Present the content reading. **See pages xvii-xix for general techniques about presenting content readings.**

- Ask the following or similar questions:

  Are Michigan and Ohio in the Midwest?
  Is the Midwest in the middle of the United States?
  Where are the Great Plains?
  What do farmers have on a dairy farm?
  Where is Mount Rushmore?
  Whose faces are on Mount Rushmore?

▶ **Future with *will*.** Explain that *will* is used to talk about actions which happen in the future. Model sentences with *will*. For example: *Tomorrow, we will learn more about agriculture and dairy farming.* Ask students to circle, underline, or otherwise identify all the sentences in the content reading which use the future with *will*. Have students take turns reading these sentences aloud.

▶ **Future with *will*.** After listening to and reviewing the content reading several times, ask students to describe what will happen to the milk from a dairy barn. Encourage students to use the word *will* as often as possible to indicate what will become of the milk. For example: *The farmers will send the milk to a diary processing plant. Some of the milk will become cheese or yogurt. Some of the milk will go to supermarkets. Some of the milk will go to my house. I will drink some of the milk.* Encourage students to do the same activity with *grain*.

▶ **Quantity expressions *some of, many*.** Have students draw pictures of as many milk or dairy products as they can think of. Have them do the same for grain, corn, or wheat products. Then they can label their drawings. Put one example of each product on large chart paper under the categories *Dairy*, *Grain*, *Corn*, or *Wheat*. Individual students take turns telling if they like *some*, *many*, or *all* of the products in a category. For example: *I like some of the dairy products. I like cheese and milk.*

WORKSHEET: Topic 13
See Teacher's Book page 53.

►CHANTS

Components: Dictionary pages 26-27, Content Chant Topic 13, Cassette

 CONTENT CHANT

Plow the Field, Plant the Corn

Plow the field.
Plant the corn.
Harvest the corn.
Feed America.

> Corn muffins
> Cornbread
> Cornflakes
> Corn on the cob

Plow the field.
Plant the wheat.
Harvest the wheat.
Feed America.

> Whole wheat bread
> Whole wheat bagels
> Whole wheat muffins
> Whole wheat cereal

Corn on the cob,
Whole wheat bread.
Feed America.
Feed the world!

- Present the content chant. **See pages xx-xxi for general techniques about presenting chants.**

- Distribute Content Chant 13. Divide students into two groups. The first group chants the odd stanzas and the second group chants the even stanzas. The first group should try to sound like they are doing hard work. The second group should sound excited because they get to eat all the good things that come from the hard work: corn muffins, cereal, corn on the cob, etc.

> **Language Note:** Model the different pronunciations of *wh* in *whole* and *wheat*. The *wh* sounds like an *h* in *whole*, but it sounds like a *w* (or *wh* in some dialects) in *wheat*.

- Explain that the Midwest is sometimes called "America's breadbasket" because most of America's breads, muffins, cookies, and cereals come from the midwestern states. Bring in a package of bread or a box of cereal. Ask students to find where the bread or cereal was made. See if that state is one of the midwestern states.

►EXTENSION

Components: Dictionary pages 26-27, Transparency 13, Wall Chart 13

- Explain that each of the states in the U.S. has a capital city. Assign each state from this section to a student or group of students. Have them find the name of the state's capital.

- Ask students what they know about farming. Some students may have lived on a farm. Ask them to describe or imagine daily life on a farm. Ask students if they would like to live on a farm and why or why not. If students haven't lived on a farm, they can find information about farm life by pairing with mainstream students or by looking in encyclopedias.

- Introduce the names of the Great Lakes and explain that this chain of lakes in North America forms the largest group of lakes in the world. The top-left lake on the map in the Dictionary illustration is Lake Superior, the largest and deepest of the Great Lakes. On the middle left is Lake Michigan, and on the middle right is Lake Huron. On the bottom is Lake Erie, which is the shallowest, and on the far-right is Lake Ontario, which is the smallest. Introduce the acronym "HOMES," which helps students to remember the names of the Great Lakes by their initial letters.

- Point out that Michigan is shaped like a hand inside a mitten. Have students look at a map of the U.S. (or the wall chart for Dictionary Topic 10) and describe other interesting state shapes, or aspects of state shapes that help them to remember which states they are. (See Topic 10, Extension, for a puzzle activity with the states. These puzzle pieces can also be used to study state shapes.)

- Divide the class into two groups. Assign one of the landmarks from the wall chart to each group. (The second landmark is the St. Louis Arch.) Have each group research the history and importance of its landmark, using almanacs, encyclopedias, history books, or the Internet. Each group should present their findings to the class.

- Distribute Content Chant 12. Have students look at the first stanza, which describes the states in the South. Divide the class into groups and ask them to chant the first stanza using the names of the states in the Midwest.

► LITERATURE

Suggested Books

The German American Family Album
written by Dorothy Hoobler and Thomas Hoobler, with an introduction by Werner Klemperer
Oxford University Press, 1998. ISBN 0195124227

The Scandinavian American Family Album
written by Dorothy Hoobler and Thomas Hoobler, with an introduction by Hubert Humphrey.
Oxford University Press, 1998. ISBN 0195124243
These two books from the series *The American Family Albums* tell the heroic stories of the two largest immigrant groups in the Midwest. Students will identify with these immigrant groups who left behind an "old country" to adopt and contribute to the diversity of the United States. Teachers will find these books to be a valuable resource on the Midwest, then and now. Direct instruction is necessary. These books are recommended for intermediate and advanced students.

Extra Cheese, Please!: Mozzarella's Journey from Cow to Pizza
written by Cris Peterson; photographs by Alvis Upitis.
Boyds Mills Press, 1994. ISBN 1563971771
This book introduces students to one of the chief industries of the Midwest: dairy farming. The author, a dairy farmer herself, describes the care and feeding of dairy cattle, and the process of making cheese from milking to manufacturing. The simple text and the informative photographs make it appropriate for reading aloud and for generating factual questions based on the content words and Dictionary Illustration. This is a good complement to Gail Gibbons' *The Milk Makers* (see Topic 7, The Country) and it is a useful content connection to health and science.

The House on Maple Street
written by Bonnie Pryor; illustrated by Beth Peck.
Mulberry Books, 1992. ISBN 0688120318
This historical fiction explores life in the Midwest, in the past and in the present. Two girls who live at 107 Maple Street look out from their front porch and see their neighborhood as it looked three hundred years ago. Teachers may find that reading the story aloud would be most beneficial to students. Post-reading activities could include discussing the book in sequence (past, present, and future). This book is thematically mature enough for older students yet it is grammatically simple enough for younger ones. This book can also be used with Topic 25, Westward Expansion.

WORKBOOK: Topic 13

The first exercise is a word search of the content words listed in the word box. In the word search, the words appear horizontally and vertically. Words do not appear backwards or diagonally. In the second exercise, students fill in the blanks.

WORKSHEET: Topic 13

Exercise A is a multiple choice activity. To choose correctly, students must understand the content reading, and recognize the appropriate tense for the sentence. In B, students use the word *will* and choose a verb from the word box to fill in the sentences. In C, students use *will* to describe what they will do.

THE WEST

▶ **CONTENT**
....

States, features, and landmarks in the West

The mining and ranching industries

▶ **LANGUAGE**
....

Present perfect: *Ranchers have lived in the West since the 1800s.*

CONTENT WORDS

1. open pit
2. mine
3. ore
4. minerals
5. ranch
6. livestock
7. corral
8. cowgirl
9. cowboy
10. buffalo
11. herd
12. graze
13. Rocky Mountains
14. peak
15. Continental Divide
16. rodeo
17. Yellowstone National Park
18. Old Faithful

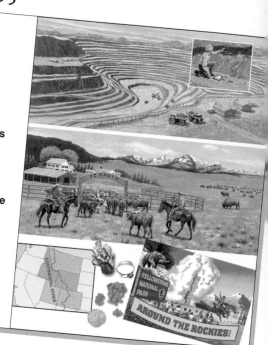

CONTENT READING

The West

The states in the West are Idaho, Montana, Wyoming, Utah, and Colorado. Some people call them the Rocky Mountain States because the Rocky Mountains are in these states. The Rocky Mountains have some of the highest mountain peaks in the U.S. The Continental Divide is in the Rocky Mountains, too. Rivers east of this line flow east. Rivers west of the Continental Divide flow west.

The Rocky Mountains have many minerals. Copper and silver are minerals. Ore is rock with minerals in it. People have looked for ore and minerals in the West for many years. They have dug open pits and they have made mines. People have used the minerals to make jewelry and coins.

Ranchers have lived in the West since the 1800s. They have built ranches and corrals. They have raised horses, cows, and other livestock on their ranches.

Herds of buffalo have roamed in the West for a long time, too. The buffalo have grazed on the grass for thousands of years.

Today, you can still see some of the old West. You can see cowboys and cowgirls at rodeos. You can see buffalo, bears, and geysers at Yellowstone National Park. The most famous geyser is Old Faithful. It has erupted every hour for more than 100 years.

▶ WORDS

Components: Dictionary pages 28-29, Transparency 14, Wall Chart 14, Workbook page 14, Word and Picture Cards Topic 14, Cassette

- Present the content words. **See pages xiv-xvi for general techniques about presenting content words.**

    Language Note: The words *ore, livestock,* and *buffalo* are noncount nouns, meaning they have don't have a plural form and we don't use *a* or *one* before these words. We can say *some ore,* and *some livestock.* We can say *a herd of buffalo. Livestock* refers to horses, cows, chicken, and other animals found on farms and ranches.

    There is a silent *e* in *mine, ore, livestock, Divide,* and *Yellowstone.* Note the stress on the first syllable in *RO-de-o* and on the second syllable in *cor-RAL.*

- Display the wall chart and have students look at the picture. Compare the bottom left picture of the West with the map of the entire United States in Dictionary Topic 10. Point out and name the western states on the U.S. map.

- Divide the class into two groups. Distribute a set of word cards to Group 1 and a set of picture cards to Group 2. Draw three large circles on the board or on chart paper. Label the circles *Mining, Ranching,* and *Landmarks.* Students in Group 1 put their word cards inside the appropriate circle. Students in Group 2 observe the placement of Group 1's word cards, make any necessary corrections, and place the appropriate picture card next to each word card in each of the circles. For example, a student from Group 1 puts the word card for *ore* in the circle labeled *Mining.* A Student from Group 2 with the picture card for *ore* checks that the word card is in the appropriate circle and puts the picture card next to the word card.

- Write the following capital letter combinations on large index cards:

    Y N P, O F, C D, R M

    Display the cards one-by-one and challenge students to call out the content words that begin with these letters (*Yellowstone National Park, Old Faithful, Continental Divide, Rocky Mountains*).

WORKBOOK: Topic 14
See Teacher's Book page 57.

▶ CONTENT

Components: Dictionary pages 28-29, Transparency 14, Wall Chart 14, Content Reading Topic 14, Worksheet Topic 14, Cassette

- Present the content reading. **See pages xvii-xix for general techniques about presenting content readings.**

- Ask the following or similar questions:

    Is Idaho a Rocky Mountain state?
    Do people find jewelry in mines?
    How long have ranchers lived in the West?
    Where is Old Faithful?
    What does Old Faithful do?
    What kinds of animals live in Yellowstone Park?

- Introduce the content reading by displaying some western-style clothing (or pictures of clothing) such as a shirt with fringes, cowboy boots, or a cowboy hat. Invite students to identify these clothes on the wall chart and to describe the clothes.

- Display several objects made of gold, silver, copper, or other precious metals (coins, jewelry, pots and pans, etc.). Explain that the metals used to make these items come from mines in the ground. Talk about the different kinds of metals. Bring in a newspaper that lists the prices of precious metals. Usually, they are listed by the ounce. Show how much an ounce is by using a scale, or displaying a common packaged food. Show how little metal there is in an ounce, and how much an ounce of the metal is worth. Ask students whether they would dig in a mine to find these metals.

▶ **Present perfect**

    The present perfect uses *have/has* plus the past participle. We use the present perfect to express past action that may still be ongoing or that is not yet completed.

Model some sample sentences using the present perfect: *We have practiced English for ten minutes this morning.* Ask students to identify all the sentences in the content reading which use the present perfect.

▶ **Present perfect.** Have students create sentences about the West using the present perfect. Encourage students to talk about their own experiences or their classmate's experiences using affirmative forms (*have/has* + past participle) or negative forms (*have/has not* or *have/has never* + past participle) of the present perfect. The class votes on whether each student's statement is true or false. For example:

I <u>have lived</u> in Utah for more than one year.

Kim <u>has never eaten</u> buffalo meat.

WORKSHEET: Topic 14
See Teacher's Book page 57.

Components: Dictionary pages 28-29, Content Chant Topic 14, Cassette

Components: Dictionary pages 28-29, Transparency 14, Wall Chart 14

 ## CONTENT CHANT

Cowboy, Cow

Cowboy, cow, buffalo, buffalo
Cowboy, cow, buffalo herd
Cowboy, cow, buffalo, buffalo
Buffalo grazing, near the corral.

Look at the cowboy on his horse.
Look at the cowboy near the corral.
Look at the cowboy, look at the cows.
Look at the buffalo near the corral.

Cowgirl, cow, buffalo, buffalo
Cowgirl, cow, buffalo herd
Cowgirl, cow, buffalo, buffalo
Buffalo grazing, near the corral.

Look at the cowgirl on her horse.
Look at the cowgirl near the corral.
Look at the cowgirl, look at the cows.
Look at the buffalo near the corral.

- Present the content chant. **See pages xx-xxi for general techniques about presenting chants.**

- Before distributing Content Chant 14, establish the rhythm by having students chant small chunks of the language from the chant. Divide the class into three groups: a group of boys, a group of girls, and a mixed group of boys and girls. The first group chants *Cowboy, cow*. The second group chants *buffalo, buffalo*. The third group chants *Cowgirl, cow*. The second group again chants *buffalo, buffalo*. Repeat until a steady rhythm is achieved. The second group should try to chant in a low, deep voice, imitating the big heavy buffalo.

- Distribute Content Chant 14. Divide the class into two groups, a group of boys and a group of girls. Four students should remain ungrouped. The boys chant the first stanza and the fourth stanza as loudly and deeply as possible. The girls chant the second and third stanzas in sweet, light voices. All grouped students should pantomime riding a horse as they chant. The four ungrouped students should pantomime the buffalo grazing on grass or hay.

- Explain that each of the states in the U.S. has a capital city. Assign each state from this section to a student or group of students. Have them find the name of the state's capital.

- Introduce the song "Home on the Range," a song sung originally by American cowboys and known to most Americans. Talk about the meaning of the song, and why cowboys might especially like it. Explain or show a picture of the word *antelope* (a fast-running animal from Asia or Africa with horns). Give some examples of discouraging words (*can't, hopeless*, etc.).

> Oh, give me a home
> where the buffalo roam,
> and the deer and the antelope play
> where seldom is heard
> a discouraging word
> and the skies are not cloudy all day.
>
> Home, home on the range,
> where the deer and the antelope play
> where seldom is heard
> a discouraging word,
> and the skies are not cloudy all day.

- Ask students to talk about some famous cowboys or cowgirls. They may know some famous names such as "Billy the Kid," "Wild Bill" Hickok, Annie Oakley, or Calamity Jane. Have groups research the history of some of these larger-than-life figures in encyclopedias, in history books, or on the Internet. Each group presents their findings to the class.

- Encourage students to see a Western movie and talk about it in class. What do they think of cowboys and cowgirls? Would they like to be a cowboy or cowgirl?

- Divide the class into five groups. Assign to each of the five groups one of the following popular U.S. National Parks: Yellowstone (in Wyoming and part of Montana), Bryce Canyon (in Utah), Rocky Mountain (in Colorado), Glacier (in Montana), and Grand Teton (in Wyoming). Information about each park may be available in almanacs, in encyclopedias, or on the Internet. Groups could also write to the National Park Service for additional information. Have the groups write reports on the parks when they have gathered their information.

- Distribute Content Chant 12. Have students look at the first stanza, which describes the states in the South. Divide the class into groups and ask them to chant the first stanza using the names of states in the West.

► LITERATURE

Suggested Books

Cowboys
written and illustrated by Glen Rounds.
Holiday House, 1993. ISBN 0823410617
This book about cowboys (and by extension, cowgirls) follows a cowboy through the course of one day. Each double-page illustration contains a simple sentence or phrase that can be used to spotlight specific language (compound predicates, prepositions of time, conjunctions, etc.). The humorous and lively illustrations will encourage students to discuss action in sequence. This is an excellent book for beginners.

The West: An Illustrated History for Children
written by Dayton Duncan, with an introduction by Stephen Ives and Ken Burns.
Little Brown & Co., 1996. ISBN 0316196320
This is one of three companion volumes to the PBS documentary, *The West*. (The video is available through most public broadcast stations and at local libraries.) It tells the story of the pioneers who pushed the boundaries of American settlement. This book gives Topic 14, The West, historical perspective and contains many photographs that show the first miners. Students can compare and contrast these images with the Dictionary illustration. If the video is available, students can read passages of the book in conjunction with the video for greater comprehension.

Let's Go Rock Collecting
written by Roma Gans; illustrated by Holly Keller.
HarperCollins Juvenile Books, 1997. ISBN 0064451704
"Ore" and "minerals" are two of the types of rock shown in *Let's Go Rock Collecting*. The text, labels, and illustrations identify many types of rocks, their structures, and origins. This book can be a starting point and guidebook for "mining" expeditions around the schoolyard or neighborhood. It also works well for teaching Topic 52, The Earth and Its Landforms.

WORKBOOK: Topic 14

In A, students label the numbered items in the picture with words from the word box. In B, students use the pictures as a guide and fill in the words for landmarks of the west. The first letter is given for each word.

WORKSHEET: Topic 14

In A, students use *have* and choose verbs from the word box to fill in the present perfect. In B, students answer the questions with personal information. They start each answer with *Yes, I have* or *No, I haven't* and continue the sentences using the present perfect.

▶ **CONTENT**

States, features, and landmarks in the Northwest

The logging, fishing, and canning industries

▶ **LANGUAGE**

Habitual present: *Lumberjacks cut down the trees with chain saws.*

Compound words: *There is a lot of sawdust at sawmills.*

 ## CONTENT WORDS

1. forest
2. logging
3. lumberjack
4. chain saw
5. redwood
6. pine
7. timber
8. sawmill
9. wood
10. sawdust
11. fish
12. cannery
13. boat
14. net
15. rainfall
16. Puget Sound
17. Space Needle
18. Alaska Pipeline

CONTENT READING

The Northwest

The states in the Northwest are Alaska, Washington, and Oregon. These three states border the Pacific Ocean.

The Northwest has many forests. Redwood forests have redwood trees. Pine forests have pine trees.

Logging is an important industry in the Northwest. Lumberjacks cut down the trees with chain saws. They drive logging trucks into the forests and take the timber to sawmills. Workers at the sawmills cut the timber into boards. There is a lot of sawdust at sawmills. People use wood to build houses and furniture.

Fishing is an important industry in the Northwest, too. Fishermen take their boats into Puget Sound and the Pacific Ocean to catch fish. They catch hundreds of fish in their fishing nets. The fishermen take the fish to a fish cannery. Cannery workers clean the fish and pack them into cans.

The northern part of Alaska has a lot of oil. The Alaska Pipeline carries the oil across Alaska. The oil pipeline is 800 miles long. People in the U.S. use the oil for gasoline. They also heat their houses with oil.

The Northwest has a lot of rainfall, but sometimes it's sunny. On sunny days, you can go to the top of the Space Needle in Seattle. It's a very tall landmark. From the top, you can see for miles and miles.

▶ WORDS

Components: Dictionary pages 30-31, Transparency 15, Wall Chart 15, Workbook page 15, Word and Picture Cards Topic 15, Cassette

- Present the content words. **See pages xiv-xvi for general techniques about presenting content words.**

  > **Language Note:** *Timber*, *wood*, *fish*, and *rainfall* are noncount nouns. These nouns don't have a plural form and we don't use *a* or *one* before these words. (However, we can say *some wood*.) We use singular verb forms with these noncount nouns. For example: *The rainfall is a very big problem.* ("Rainfall" refers to the total amount of rain in a particular area.)

- Display the wall chart and have students look at the picture. Compare the bottom left picture of the Northwest with the map of the entire United States in Dictionary Topic 10. Point out and name the northwestern states on the U.S. map.

▶ **Compound words**

  > Compound words are two words which together function as a single word. Compound words can appear as one word or two separate words. The plural is added to last part of the compound word. Examples of compound words are *lumberjack*, *chain saw*, *redwood*, *fish cannery*, *sawmill*, and *sawdust*.

  Write the word *chalkboard* on the board. Ask students to underline the two words which make up this compound word. Now have the students look at the Dictionary illustration and find other examples of compound words.

- Have students write each word of the compound words on separate index cards. For example: *red* and *wood*, *chain* and *saw*, *rain* and *fall*. Collect the index cards and distribute them to all of the students. Have students circulate and ask each other questions to find each of the two words in all of the compound words.

- Divide the class into two teams. Distribute one set of word cards to each team. Each team uses their word cards to construct "odd man out," or category word groupings, for students on the other team. In each grouping there is one card that does not go with the others. For example, Team 1 puts the following grouping of word cards on the board: *fish*, *boat*, *cannery*, *lumberjack*. In this case *lumberjack* does not belong, because the other three are all about the fishing industry. Have the teams explain their groupings if there is disagreement about which word does not belong. There may be more than one interpretation. Encourage discussion.

WORKBOOK: Topic 15
See Teacher's Book page 61.

▶ CONTENT

Components: Dictionary pages 30-31, Transparency 15, Wall Chart 15, Content Reading Topic 15, Worksheet Topic 15, Cassette

- Present the content reading. **See pages xvii-xix for general techniques about presenting content readings.**

- Ask the following or similar questions:

  > *Do the states in the Northwest border the Pacific Ocean?*
  > *Which states are in the Northwest?*
  > *Where is there a lot of oil?*
  > *What do fish cannery workers do?*
  > *What do people do with oil?*
  > *Is Utah in the Northwest or in the Northeast?*

▶ **Habitual present**

  > The habitual present is the present tense used to describe habitual or repeated activities, such as things we do every day.

  Divide the class into small groups. Have each group look at either the top picture or the middle picture of the wall chart. Have groups make up stories about the people and their jobs in each picture. Encourage students to use the habitual present in their stories. Encourage them to give the people names as if they were real people they knew. For example: *John, Donald, Kenji, and Raymond are fishermen. They catch fish in Puget Sound. They bring their fish to the fish cannery. Edward and Jane work at the fish cannery. They clean 500 fish every day.* Have the groups present their stories to the class.

▶ **Compound words.** Introduce some other compound words that students might be familiar with. For example: *shoelace*, *wristwatch*, *fingernail*, *doorbell*, *windshield*, *snowstorm*, etc. Write them on the board. Ask students if they know the meanings of these words. If they do not, ask them if they know the meanings of the parts of these compound words. Then see if they can figure out the meanings of the compound words.

▶ **Compound words.** Invite students to invent some compound words of their own. Have each student write a new compound word on the board. Let the other students guess what the word might mean. Ask them if they think this would be a good word for the English language to have.

WORKSHEET: Topic 15
See Teacher's Book page 61.

► CHANTS

Components: Dictionary pages 30-31, Content Chant Topic 15, Cassette

 ## CONTENT CHANT

Redwood Forest

Redwood forest
Tall trees
Strong trees
Old trees

Strong lumberjacks
pick up a chain saw,
cut down the trees,
redwood trees.

Strong lumberjacks
cut down the trees,
take them to the sawmill,
turn them into lumber.

Strong lumberjacks
Strong trees
Redwood forest
Tall trees

Puget Sound, full of fish.
Young fishermen in their boats
throw their nets in the cold water.
Catch the fish, fresh fish!

Cannery workers clean the fish.
Cannery workers cut the fish.
Cannery workers put them into cans.
Canned fish, canned fish!

- Present the content chant. **See pages xx-xxi for general techniques about presenting chants.**

- Before you distribute the chant, establish the rhythm by having students chant phrases from the chant. Divide the class into four groups. The first group repeatedly chants *tall trees*. The second group chants *strong trees*. The third group chants *old trees*. The fourth group chants *Redwood trees*. Then the groups chant simultaneously and loudly.

- Now distribute Content Chant 15. Each of the four groups pantomimes its lines. Students in Group 1 are the trees. They put their arms out like trees. Group 1 chants the first stanza and the last three lines of the fourth stanza. Group 2 students are the big, strong lumberjacks. They chant the second and third stanzas and the first line of the fourth stanza. They act out picking up the chain saw, cutting down the trees, taking the trees to the sawmill, and turning them into lumber. Group 3 students are the fishermen, and they pantomime throwing their nets in the ocean and catching fish as they chant the fifth stanza. Group 4 students are the cannery workers and they chant and pantomime the words in the last stanza.

► EXTENSION

Components: Dictionary pages 30-31, Transparency 15, Wall Chart 15

- Explain that each of the states in the U.S. has a capital city. Assign each state from this section to a student or group of students. Have them find the name of the state's capital.

- Listen to and introduce the words for the song "This Land Is Your Land" written by Woody Guthrie. Talk about the meaning of the song, and explain any words students might not understand. (See page 41, Literature.)

- To help students understand the size of the Alaska Pipeline, display a political map of Alaska. Have students locate Prudhoe Bay and Valdez. Remind them that the pipeline between these two cities is 800 miles long. Now display a map of your state or region. Have students use the map scale on the map of your region to determine 800 miles. Now have them measure 800 miles from your home city in any given direction. To give students a sense of the size of the pipe used in the Alaska Pipeline, cut a 12.5-foot length of string. Make a giant circle on the floor with the string. This is the size of the pipe. Some of the smaller students in your class may be able to lie down completely inside this circle.

- Introduce Paul Bunyan, the mythical character who could chop down the tallest trees in the forest. Have students go to the school library and find books about Paul Bunyan.

- Distribute Content Chant 12. Have students look at the first stanza, which describes the states in the South. Divide the class into groups and ask them to chant the first four lines using the names of the states in the Northwest.

► LITERATURE

Suggested Books

Uncle Daney's Way
by Jessie Haas.
Beech Tree Books, 1997. ISBN 0688154913
Uncle Daney is a disabled lumberjack who comes to live with his nephew Cole and Cole's family after a logging accident. Uncle Daney and Cole form a strong bond as they try to devise a way to keep Uncle Daney's old horse Nip, who is taxing the family finances. This book contains a wealth of information about growing up in the country. Advanced learners will benefit most from reading and discussing this short novel.

My Father's Boat
written by Sherry Garland; illustrated by Ted Rand.
Scholastic, 1998. ISBN 0590478672
My Father's Boat is a story of familial love told by a school-age, Vietnamese-American boy who goes fishing with his father. As they fish, the boy's father tells the boy about his grandfather, who fished the China Sea, and the lessons that he learned from their time together. The beautiful illustrations help reinforce the vocabulary of this topic. The spare, lyrical text is clear and unintimidating, so that beginning and intermediate readers should be able to master it in two or three read-aloud sessions.

Fishes
written and illustrated by Brian Wildsmith.
Oxford University Press, 1987. ISBN 0192721518
This book contains brilliant, exuberant paintings of fish, accompanied by traditional and inventive collective nouns such as "a stream of minnows" and "a hover of trout." The text extends students' familiarity with names and features of creatures in the natural world as it entertains them with its wordplay. This book is also useful for teaching Topic 42, Fish.

WORKBOOK: Topic 15

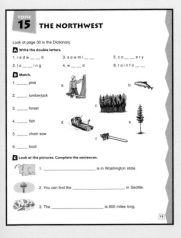

For each word in A, students fill in the missing double letters. In B, they write the letters to match the pictures to the words. In C, they look at the pictures and complete the sentences.

WORKSHEET: Topic 15

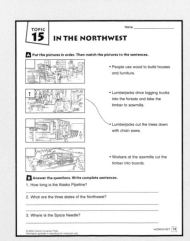

In the first exercise, students number the pictures of the steps of the logging process in the order in which they occur. Then, they match each picture to the sentence describing it. In the second exercise, students answer the questions based on the content reading.

16 THE SOUTHWEST

▶ **CONTENT**

States, features, and landmarks in the Southwest

Natural resources

▶ **LANGUAGE**

So...that (***so*** + **adjective/adverb** + ***that*** + **result clause**): *It is so beautiful that millions of people visit it every year.*

CONTENT WORDS

1. well
2. oil
3. natural gas
4. drill
5. refinery
6. pipeline
7. tank
8. gasoline
9. water storage
10. dam
11. reservoir
12. irrigation canal
13. hydroelectric plant
14. electricity
15. Grand Canyon
16. cactus

CONTENT READING

The Southwest

The states in the Southwest are Nevada, Arizona, New Mexico, Texas, and Oklahoma. The Southwest has many natural resources. People cannot make natural resources. They exist in nature. We have to use them carefully.

Oil and natural gas are natural resources. People heat their houses with oil and natural gas. These resources are so valuable that people spend a lot of money looking for them. People use drills to dig deep wells in the ground. If they find oil, the wells pump it into a pipeline. The pipeline goes to an oil refinery. Sometimes the wells pump so much oil that people have to put it in tanks. The refineries make gasoline from the oil.

Water is another natural resource. It is so important that people have to protect it. In some parts of the Southwest, it is so dry that only cactuses can grow. There is so little water that people have to build reservoirs, dams, and irrigation canals for water storage. Irrigation canals carry water to farmers' crops. Dams hold water in a reservoir. Hydroelectric plants next to the dams make electricity from the power of the falling water. People use electricity in their homes for lights, TVs, and refrigerators.

The Grand Canyon is in the Southwest, too. It is so beautiful that millions of people visit it every year.

▶ WORDS

Components: Dictionary pages 32-33, Transparency 16, Wall Chart 16, Workbook page 16, Word and Picture Cards Topic 16, Cassette

- Present the content words. **See pages xiv-xvi for general techniques about presenting content words.**

- Display the wall chart and have students look at the picture. Compare the bottom left picture of the Southwest with the map of the entire United States in Dictionary Topic 10. Point out and name the southwestern states on the U.S. map.

  Language Note: There is a silent *e* in *pipeline* and *gasoline*. Note also the different pronunciations between the last four letters of the two words.

- Review the sound of the letter *l* in final position in a word (*oil*) and in the middle of a word (*pipeline*). Write the letter *l* on the board. Then, pronounce each of the content words in Topic 16. Have students raise their hands each time they hear a word with an *l* sound and repeat that word after you. Now, pair students and have them look at the content words. Student A pronounces each of the words in the left column on the page. Student B makes a list of each of those words which has an *l* sound in it. Then, Student B pronounces each of the words in the right column on the page, and Student A writes down all the *l* words that he or she hears. Students A and B then check their work together.

- Distribute one word and picture card to each student. Draw three columns on the board. Label the first column *Oil and Gas*. Label the second column *Water*. Label the third column *Landmarks*. Now ask students, in turn, to come to the front of the class, read his or her card aloud, and place it in the appropriate column on the board. For example, the student with the *refinery* card should place the card in the *Oil and Gas* column.

- Point to the picture of a gasoline pump. Ask students why people need gas. Have students name a brand of gasoline from a local gas station. Ask them what they think a gallon of gas costs. Then tell them what it does cost. Ask them if they think that is a fair amount. Should it be more or less?

- Point to the picture of the cactus. Ask students if they have ever seen a cactus. Where did they see it? What was the weather like there? Was it cold and rainy or warm and dry? What does that tell them about the cactus plant? Ask students if a cactus plant could live in their area.

WORKBOOK: Topic 16
See Teacher's Book page 65.

▶ CONTENT

Components: Dictionary pages 32-33, Transparency 16, Wall Chart 16, Content Reading Topic 16, Worksheet Topic 16, Cassette

- Present the content reading. **See pages xvii-xix for general techniques about presenting content readings.**

- Ask the following or similar questions:

  Is Alaska in the Southwest?
  Is water a natural resource?
  Are there many natural resources in the Southwest?
  What do irrigation canals do?
  How do hydroelectric plants make electricity?

▶ *So* + **adjective/adverb** + *that* + **result clause**

  We use [*so* + adjective/adverb + *that* + result clause] in these sentences. Adjectives (*tall*) or adverbs (*slowly*) are descriptive words. In sentences with *so...that*, the descriptive word affects the result clause. For example: *He is so tall that he can touch the basket.* (*He can touch the basket* is the result of being so tall.)

Introduce sentences with *so...that*. Demonstrate how to construct this kind of sentence. Ask students to circle, underline, or otherwise identify all the instances of sentences with *so...that* in the content reading.

▶ *So* + **adjective/adverb** + *that* + **result clause.** Divide the class into two teams. A student from Team 1 says a descriptive word (an adjective or an adverb). A student from Team 2 uses that word in a sentence with *so...that*. For example, if the student from Team 1 says *slow*, the student from Team 2 might say *My sister is so slow that a turtle is faster.* Team 2 scores a point for a correct sentence and the next student from Team 2 takes a turn. Encourage students to be funny and imaginative.

- Turn out the lights in your classroom and turn off all of the electric devices. Ask students what is missing from the classroom (electricity). Now turn the lights on again. Ask students to think of things you need electricity to do. Ask each student, in turn, to come to the chalkboard and write one action that requires electricity, such as listening to the radio, playing video games, or working on the computer.

WORKSHEET: Topic 16
See Teacher's Book page 65.

►CHANTS

Components: Dictionary pages 32-33, Content Chant Topic 16, Cassette

 ## CONTENT CHANT

How to Get Rich in Texas

Go to Texas.
Buy a drill.
Take your drill and
dig a well.

Dig a well
and find oil.
Pump that oil out. *

Pump that oil, ship that oil.
Send it through the pipeline.
Send it through the pipeline.

Send it through the pipeline
or store it in a tank.
Put your money in a great big bank.

Drill for oil.
It's not hard.
I found some
in my backyard.

Drill for oil.
It's not hard.
You might find some
in your backyard.

- Present the content chant. **See pages xx-xxi for general techniques about presenting chants.**

- Before you distribute the chant, have students practice with small chunks of the language from the chant. Have the entire class chant repeatedly *Send it through the pipeline*. Increase the volume and the speed of the chanting. Now divide the class into two groups. The first group chants *Pump that oil*. The second group quickly follows with *Ship that oil*. Then, the entire class chants *Send it through the pipeline, send it through the pipeline*.

- Now distribute Content Chant 16. Assign individual students to chant one stanza each. The entire class should clap at the * prompt. Ask students to pantomime the actions as they chant each stanza.

- When students are familiar with the chant, distribute the word or picture cards for *oil, well, drill, tank,* and *pipeline* to one group or pair of students. Assign these students the task of holding up word and picture cards each time they hear the appropriate words in the chant.

►EXTENSION

Components: Dictionary page 32-33, Wall Chart 16, Transparency 16

- Explain that each of the states in the U.S. has a capital city. Assign each state from this section to a student or group of students. Have them find the name of the state's capital.

- Point to the short, wide portion of Oklahoma. Explain that this part of Oklahoma is called "the panhandle." Ask students if they can explain why that is. Now point to the outline of Texas and ask students if they can see a panhandle there. After they recognize the Texas panhandle, ask students to study the map of the U.S. to find other states that have a panhandle (Idaho and Florida).

- Point to the perfect cross between the states of Utah, Colorado, Arizona, and New Mexico. Introduce the term *Four Corners states*. Show students that these four states all meet at one point. That point is called *the Four Corners*, and those four states are called the *Four Corners states*. It is the only place where the four states meet. Ask students to study the United States map to find places where three states meet at the same point.

- Point to the picture of the Route 66 highway sign. Explain to students that Route 66 was a much-traveled road between Chicago and Los Angeles. Millions of people drove Route 66 from the cold Midwest to sunny, warm Los Angeles. Today, fewer people drive Route 66. There are bigger and more direct highways now. Bring in a road map of the entire United States. Divide students into two or three groups. Have each group choose a highway route from Chicago to Los Angeles. Each group should write down its route as though it were giving directions. For example: *Take U.S. 55 South to St. Louis. Then take U.S. 44 West to Oklahoma City. Then Take U.S. 40 West to Barstow, California. Then take U.S. 15 South to Pasadena. Then take U.S. 10 West to Los Angeles.*

- Ask students to work in groups to research and report on different aspects of the Grand Canyon. Research topics could include location and size, types of rock in the main canyon and in the smaller canyons, animal and plant life, tourism in the canyon (including number of tourists, where they are from, and the best and worst times to visit), or the Grand Canyon National Park. Encourage all groups to use resources such as books, magazines, the Internet, and multimedia sources from the local library.

- Distribute Content Chant 12. Have students look at the first stanza, which describes the states in the South. Divide the class into groups and ask them to chant the first stanza using the names of the states in the Southwest.

LITERATURE

Suggested Books

I'm in Charge of Celebrations
written by Byrd Baylor; illustrated by Peter Parnall.
Aladdin Paperbacks, 1995. ISBN 0689806205
The "celebrations" of this book's title are a young girl's celebrations of the natural world's beauty as manifested in the plants, animals, and landscape of the Southwestern desert. For ESL students, this is an excellent read-aloud story to accompany the study of the geography in this region. Teachers may wish to create breaks in the reading so students can comment on the pictures and act out what is going on. The reading can be further enhanced by creating a word bank of desert words that appear in the book. It is also useful for teaching Topic 52, The Earth and Its Landforms.

This Big Sky
written by Pat Mora; illustrated by Steve Jenkins.
Scholastic, 1999. ISBN 0590371215
This Big Sky is a collection of fourteen poems by Latina poet Pat Mora that evoke the beauty of the American Southwest. Many of the poems will give students practice in recognizing and learning certain repetitive language patterns (past tense, relative clauses, prepositions, etc.) and vocabulary. Individual poems and illustrations provide clear models for students to create their own pictures and poems about the Southwest.

The Mud Family
written by Betsy James; illustrated by Paul Morin.
Oxford University Press, 1998. ISBN 0195124790
The Anasazi Indians lived and grew maize in the American Southwest long before the arrival of Europeans. This picture book tells the story of Sosi, an Anasazi girl who creates an imaginary family out of dried mud when lack of rainfall makes her real family tense and temperamental. When Sosi's family is ready to leave the land in desperation, Sosi engages her "mud family" in one last rain dance. This book's simple prose and rich oil paintings on feathers and burlap convey a strong sense of the geography of the American Southwest. Together, the story and illustrations create a unique physical and historical setting for universal emotions. This book is also useful in teaching Topic 19, The Native Americans.

Ali, Child of the Desert
written by Jonathan London; illustrated by Ted Lewin.
Lothrop Lee & Shepard, 1997. ISBN 0688125603
While traveling across the Sahara Desert on their way to the Moroccan market, Ali and his father are separated during a sandstorm. This book tells the story of Ali's adventure alone in the desert before he is reunited with his father. Students are encouraged to compare and contrast the harsh landscape of North Africa with America's dry and dusty Southwest. This is a mature story and may require some teacher direction. A short glossary of important Arabic words and greetings is provided at the end of the book. The story can be read aloud or retold in the teacher's own words.

Fill It Up!: All About Service Stations
written and illustrated by Gail Gibbons.
HarperCollins, 1987. ISBN 0690044402
The information in this book is an adjunct to this topic's focus on managing natural resources. It conveys practical information in a readable simple present tense and passive voice. The colorful illustrations with additional cartoon captions help explain the text. The book is an effective read aloud for beginners of all ages. It is also useful for teaching Topic 6, The Suburbs.

WORKBOOK: Topic 16

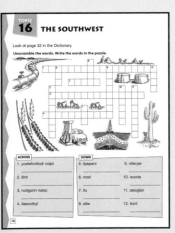

This page contains a crossword puzzle. The clues are the content words, scrambled. As students fill in each word in the puzzle, they will get more clues as to the order of the letters of the other words.

WORKSHEET: Topic 16

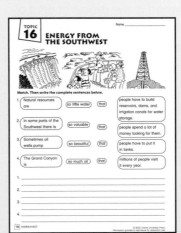

On this page, students are given four sentences with *so...that*. The sentences are broken into parts to help students see the structure of the sentences. Students match the four parts of each sentence and write the complete sentences on the lines provided.

▶ **CONTENT**

States, features, and landmarks on the West Coast

The technology, tourism, and entertainment industries

▶ **LANGUAGE**

Correlative conjunctions ***both...and:*** *Both California and Hawaii border the Pacific Ocean.*

CONTENT WORDS

1. filmmaking
2. actor
3. actress
4. director
5. script
6. camera
7. set
8. fiber optics
9. laser
10. microchip
11. resort
12. tourist
13. surfing
14. freeway
15. shopping mall
16. Golden Gate Bridge

CONTENT READING

The West Coast and Pacific

Both California and Hawaii border the Pacific Ocean. California is one of the largest states in America. Hawaii is a group of islands in the Pacific Ocean.

Both filmmaking and technology are important industries in California. The film industry is in southern California. Hollywood is the movie capital of the world. The director is the boss on a movie set. Actors and actresses read the scripts. Camera operators run the cameras.

The technology industry is in northern California. People work with both fiber optics and lasers in northern California. Microchips come from Silicon Valley. It's in northern California, too. Microchips are important parts of computers.

The tourism industry is very important in Hawaii. Hawaii has beautiful beaches and luxury resorts.

Tourists enjoy both surfing and swimming. Some people just sit on the beaches.

San Francisco is the largest city in northern California. The Golden Gate Bridge is in San Francisco. Los Angeles is the largest city in southern California. There are a lot of freeways and shopping malls in both northern and southern California. There are a lot of cars, too.

▶ WORDS

Components: Dictionary pages 34-35, Transparency 17, Wall Chart 17, Workbook page 17, Word and Picture Cards Topic 17, Cassette

- Present the content words. **See pages xiv-xvi for general techniques about presenting content words.**

- Display the wall chart and have students look at the picture. Compare the bottom left picture of California and Hawaii with the map of the entire United States in Dictionary Topic 10. Point out California and Hawaii on the U.S. map.

- Distribute one word and picture card to each student. Ask students, in turn, to read their cards aloud, and then to say whether their card describes a person, place, thing, or action. For example, the student with the *script* card should say that the card describes a thing. The student with the *surfing* card should say that the card describes an action.

- Divide the class into groups. Give each group a set of word and picture cards. Using groups of cards (for example, all the cards relating to movies, or all the cards relating to tourism), ask students to rank their word and picture cards from 1 (not very important or valuable) to 5 (very important or valuable). Each group draws a rank ladder graphic organizer (see below) on chart paper and puts their word and picture cards on each of the steps in the rank ladder in the order they wish. Compare the rank ladders of each group. Students in each group tell why they ranked a particular card as they did. For example, a student might rank *script* as 5 and say, *Writing the movie is very important.* Another group might rank *actress* as 5 and say, *The most important thing about a movie is the actress.* Have groups discuss the differences in their rankings.

5
4
3
2
1

- Point to the picture of the freeway. Ask students if they know any other words for roads. Some examples might include *highway, expressway, parkway, roadway, thruway, interstate,* and *turnpike.* Discuss some of the differences between these roads. Ask students to name some of the freeways, highways, parkways, or expressways nearby.

WORKBOOK: Topic 17
See Teacher's Book page 69.

▶ CONTENT

Components: Dictionary pages 34-35, Transparency 17, Wall Chart 17, Content Reading Topic 17, Worksheet Topic 17, Cassette

- Present the content reading. **See pages xvii-xix for general techniques about presenting content readings.**

- Ask the following or similar questions:

  Is Hawaii the largest state in America?
  Is the Golden Gate Bridge in Hollywood?
  Where is the film industry?
  Where do microchips come from?
  What industry is very important in Hawaii?
  What is the largest city in southern California?

- Divide the class into four groups. Assign one of the picture groupings on the wall chart to each group. First, the groups label their pictures (for example, *Southern California* or *Hollywood* for the top left picture, *Silicon Valley* or *Northern California* for the top right picture, *Hawaii* for the beach scene and *Postcard from the Pacific* for the lower right picture). Then ask students in each group to make up a story about what is happening in their section. Encourage students to give the people names, and describe the action. For example: *Tim and Tamara are acting in a movie about the 16th century.* For the postcard, have students talk about various things in California as if they sent the postcard. For example: *We loved the great shopping malls! The Golden Gate Bridge is beautiful.* The groups present their stories to the whole class and the class votes for the most interesting stories.

▶ **Correlative conjunctions *both...and***

> The conjunctions *both...and* are used to link two things, concepts, or people together. Note that when two subjects are connected by *both* and *and*, they use the plural verb form: *Both California and Hawaii* <u>border</u> *the Pacific Ocean.*

Introduce correlative conjunctions by making statements about students in the class. For example: *Both Jimmy and Daria are wearing glasses. Both Michiko and Alessandra are absent today.* Ask students to circle, underline, or otherwise identify all of the sentences in the content reading that use *both...and.*

▶ **Correlative conjunctions *both...and.*** Pair students. Student A names two things that are related, such as shoes and socks, or peanut butter and jelly. Student B says or writes a sentence using the two items with *both...and.* For example: *You should wear both shoes and socks in the winter* or *Both peanut butter and jelly are very sticky.* Have students write their sentences on the board.

WORKSHEET: Topic 17
See Teacher's Book page 69.

CHANTS

Components: Dictionary pages 34-35, Content Chant Topic 17, Cassette

CONTENT CHANT

San Francisco, California

San Francisco, California.
Tourists riding cable cars.
Climbing hills in San Francisco.
Golden Gate Bridge, Wow!

San Jose, California.
Microchips, fiber optics.
Lots of cars in California.
Freeways and shopping malls.

Hollywood, California.
Lots of actors out of work.
Actresses, waiting on tables.
Lots of actors working out.

Hawaii, lots of tourists.
Spending money here and there.
Hawaii, Pacific Ocean.
Surfing, swimming everywhere.

- Present the content chant. **See pages xx-xxi for general techniques about presenting chants.**

- Have students practice phrases from the chant. Divide the class into groups. Each group repeatedly chants one of the following: *cable cars*, *Golden Gate*, *microchips*, *fiber optics*, *shopping malls*. Then one group starts and each group joins in until all are chanting simultaneously.

- Distribute Content Chant 17. Have the entire class read through each stanza. Then assign each student one line. The entire class joins in for *WOW!* Do the chant repeatedly, with students switching lines each time.

- Explain that San Jose is a city in northern California. Hollywood is a city in southern California that is part of the Los Angeles area. Display a detailed map of California and show students where the cities in the chant are. Show them the freeways that connect these cities with each other and with other parts of California and the U.S.

- Explain that *out of work* means without a job. *Waiting on tables* means working as a waiter or waitress in a restaurant. *Working out* means exercising. Actors and actresses often work as waiters and waitresses because they can work at night. That means they can try to become actors during the day. Many actors and actresses work out because they want to look their best.

EXTENSION

Components: Dictionary pages 34-35, Transparency 17, Wall Chart 17

- Explain that each of the states in the U.S. has a capital city. Assign each state from this section to a student or group of students. Have them find the name of the state's capital.

- Discuss students' favorite movies, actors, and actresses. Make a list on the board of five or six of the class' favorite movies, actors, and actresses. Now talk about the Academy Awards, or the Oscars, Hollywood's annual awards ceremony for the year's best movies, actors, and actresses. Ask students to pick one of the movies on the board as the best movie. Then ask them to choose a best actor and best actress. Students should write each of their selections on a separate piece of paper. Collect all the pieces of paper and tally the winners in each category (but don't reveal them). Now select three students to reveal the results. Each student announcing the winner should say ...*and the Oscar goes to*....

- Pair students. Have students make a list of all the states that border the Pacific Ocean. Then, have them make a list of all the states that border the Atlantic Ocean. Finally, have students make a list of states that border the Gulf of Mexico and a list of states that border the Great Lakes. Now have students exchange papers with their partners, who should check the lists for accuracy.

- Have students describe how they would spend a great day at the shopping mall. What would they do? What stores would they shop in? Who would they go with?

- Make movies with small groups of students using a video camera or movie camera. (Note: Teachers without access to film equipment can make this a pretend activity.) Each group collaborates to write a script that tells a story. Each group has a director and a student to operate the camera. The script should contain at least one speaking role for the remaining students, who are the actors and actresses. Show students how to write a script with lines for each character. After each group has written its script, have the group act out the story. The director yells *Action!* and the camera operator starts the camera. Then the actors begin saying their lines. If the actors make a mistake, the director might yell *Cut!* and have the actors start again from the beginning. Or, if the actors perform well, the director waits until the end of the scene and yells *Cut, print*. Have each group perform its movie in front of the entire class.

LITERATURE

Suggested Books

The Japanese American Family Album
written by Dorothy Hoobler and Thomas Hoobler, with an introduction by George Takei.
Oxford University Press, 1998. ISBN 0195124235
The first Japanese Americans immigrated to Hawaii and then California before settling throughout the U.S. This book documents how they adapted and flourished, even in the face of adversity and prejudice. Like the other books in this series, this book is designed like an album, or scrapbook, filled with photos, diary excerpts, and newspaper clippings. Follow-up activities can include having students create scrapbooks about their own immigrant experiences.

The Young Oxford Book of the Movies
written by David Parkinson.
Oxford University Press, 1997. ISBN 0195212444
This comprehensive book discusses the history of moviemaking from silent films to today's blockbusters, with a special focus on Hollywood, America's moviemaking center. This book will give students many opportunities to build upon the language they learn in Topic 17, The West Coast and Pacific with its detailed information about the production, distribution, and marketing of movies. A wealth of photos, posters, and movie stills will remind students of movies that they've seen here or in their home country. Like most books about this popular subject, *The Young Oxford Book of the Movies* provides an excellent prompt for independent speaking and class discussion.

Cybermama: An Extraordinary Voyage to the Center of Cyberspace
written by Alexandre Jardin.
DK Publishing, 1997. ISBN 0789418061
Set in the 21st Century, this futuristic tale about a group of children who enter a computer's memory through a virtual transporter is an unusual way to introduce students to the technical world of computers. The stunning graphics and progressive design may present problems for some ESL students, but this adventurous book is worth the effort. The fantastic photographs and illustrations will encourage students to talk about technology and how it has impacted on their lives. (Recent immigrants to America may have interesting stories to share about the technological differences between their former country and America.) The illustrations can be used for story starters, predicting, and generating *Wh-* questions. This book is also useful for teaching Topic 60, Computers and Calculators.

WORKBOOK: Topic 17

In A, students fill in the missing vowels from the content words. In B, they write the letters to match each picture to a word.

WORKSHEET: Topic 17

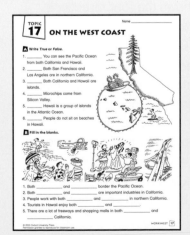

Both exercises on this page are based on the content reading. Exercise A is a true/false activity. In B, students fill in the blanks.

CONTENT WORDS

1. compass rose
2. legend
3. latitude
4. longitude
5. national border
6. province
7. state
8. capital
9. money
10. totem pole
11. pyramid
12. silver

▶ **CONTENT**

Features and landmarks of Canada and Mexico

Maps

▶ **LANGUAGE**

Expression *stand for*: *On these maps, a thick red line stands for a national border.*

Prepositional phrases in initial sentence position: *On the map of Mexico, dotted lines stand for borders between states.*

Modal *can*: *You can find totem poles in Canada.*

CONTENT READING

Canada and Mexico

Canada and Mexico are neighbors of the United States. Canada is north of the United States. It's above the U.S. in the top map. Mexico is south of the United States. It's below the U.S. in the bottom map.

Maps are drawings of parts of the Earth. They show information about places. Almost every map has a compass rose. It shows the four directions: north, south, east, and west.

The colors, lines, and shapes on maps are symbols. Every symbol stands for a different thing. The map legend explains the symbols. On the maps of Canada and Mexico, green stands for land and blue stands for water. Brown stands for mountains. The Sierra Madres are mountains in Mexico. The Rocky Mountains are mountains in Canada.

On these maps, a thick red line stands for a national border. This is a border between two

countries. The red star stands for a national capital. Ottawa is the capital of Canada. Mexico City is the capital of Mexico. On the map of Canada, dotted lines stand for borders between provinces. On the map of Mexico, dotted lines stand for borders between states.

Some maps show longitude and latitude lines. These lines help us find places on a map. Longitude lines go up and down, or north and south. Latitude lines go from side to side, or east and west.

These maps show other symbols, too. The symbols stand for things you can find in each country. You can find totem poles in Canada. You can find pyramids and silver in Mexico. The maps also show the money and flag for each country.

▶ WORDS

Components: Dictionary pages 36-37, Transparency 18, Wall Chart 18, Workbook page 18, Word and Picture Cards Topic 18, Cassette

- Present the content words. **See pages xiv-xvi for general techniques about presenting content words.**

  > **Language Note**: Point out the silent *e* in the words *rose*, *latitude*, *longitude*, *province*, *state*, and *pole*. Explain that *longitude* has a soft *g* sound (as in the *g* sound in *lounge*) and is not pronounced like the *g* sound in *long* or *longer*.

- Display the wall chart and have students look at the picture. Compare the two pictures with the map of the entire United States in Dictionary Topic 10. Explain that this topic deals with the countries directly above and below the United States: Canada and Mexico.

- Draw a large Venn diagram (similar to the example below) on chart paper. Distribute two sets of picture cards to the students. Ask students to put their picture cards in the appropriate place on the diagram. For example, *totem pole* belongs in Canada, *silver* belongs in Mexico and *national border* belongs in Canada and Mexico. Have students say the appropriate words for each picture card and discuss any disagreements which might arise.

- Point to the compass rose. Ask students if they know why it is there. Ask students if they know what the letters N, S, E, and W mean. Identify the four directions on a map. Have students point up, down, to the right, or to the left as you name the directions.

- Using a compass, locate the north side of the classroom. Then label the four walls of the classroom. Write the letters N, S, E, and W on separate pieces of paper and post each one on the corresponding side of the room. Select one student to come to the front of the room and call out "marching orders" to the rest of the class. The student directs the class to walk, skip, or jump one, two, or three steps to the north, south, east, or west. Allow several students to take turns as the leader.

- Ask students to compare the flags of Canada and Mexico to the U.S. flag. Ask them to draw a picture of the U.S. flag and the flag of their native country. If possible, display a chart of flags of the world. Collect the pictures and redistribute them randomly. Students guess the name of the country from the picture of the flag and the name of the student who drew it. If students are all from the same country, encourage them to select another country's flag for this activity.

> **WORKBOOK:** Topic 18
> See Teacher's Book page 73.

▶ CONTENT

Components: Dictionary pages 36-37, Transparency 18, Wall Chart 18, Content Reading Topic 18, Worksheet Topic 18, Cassette

- Present the content reading. **See pages xvii-xix for general techniques about presenting content readings.**

- Ask the following or similar questions:

  Is Mexico north of the United States?
  Are there totem poles in Canada?
  What is the capital of Mexico?
  What does a map legend show?
  What does the color brown stand for on the map?
  What are the directions on the compass rose?

- ▶ **Expression *stand for***

  > The expression *stand for* means to represent or symbolize something. A star on the map *stands for,* or symbolizes, the capital of the country.

  Draw a picture of a traffic light with the top red light illuminated. Ask students what that color stands for (*Stop*). Draw a picture of a dog inside a circle with a diagonal line through it. Ask students what that symbol stands for (*No dogs*, or *No pets*). Now ask students to circle, underline, or otherwise identify in the content reading all the sentences that contain the expression *stands for.* Ask students to think of some other symbols they see all the time that stand for something else. They should draw their symbols on one side of a piece of paper and write what the symbols stand for on the back of the same page. Collect all the papers and hold each one up, one at a time. Ask other students if they know what each symbol stands for.

- Draw two columns on the board. In the first column, write *On the map of Mexico*. In the second column, write *On the map of Canada*. Invite students, in turn, to contribute phrases that will complete these sentences. For example: *On the map of Mexico, the red star stands for Mexico City* or *On the map of Canada, there is a picture of a moose*. Allow students to contribute sentences from the content reading if necessary, but encourage them to try to contribute new sentences if possible. They need not limit themselves to the vocabulary of this topic.

> **WORKSHEET:** Topic 18
> See Teacher's Book page 73.

▶ CHANTS

Components: Dictionary pages 36-37, Content Chant Topic 18, Cassette

 CONTENT CHANT

Canada and Mexico

Canada is north of the U.S.A.
Canadians come here every day.
They come to work. They come to play.
Canadians come here every day.
Americans go there every day.
They go to work. They go to play.

Mexico is south of the U.S.A.
Mexicans come here every day.
They come to visit. They come to stay.
Mexicans come here every day.
Americans go there every day.
They go to visit. They go to stay.

Canada is cold.
Mexico's not.
Canada is chilly.
Mexico is hot.

Canada has polar bears,
Mexico does not,
'cause Canada's cold
and Mexico's hot.

- Present the content chant. **See pages xx-xxi for general techniques about presenting chants.**

- Have students practice some of the language from the chant and add some expressions. Divide students into two groups. Group 1 chants *Canada is north. Brrr, It's chilly* as they mime being really cold. Group 2 chants *Mexico is south. Whew! It's hot* as they mime being really hot.

- Distribute Content Chant 18. Assign individual students to chant two-line groupings of the chant. Have the entire class chant the third stanza.

- Write the words *Mexico and Canada* in one column on the board. In the next column, write the words *Mexicans and Canadians*. Explain that the word for somebody from Mexico is *Mexican*. A person from Canada is *Canadian*. Write the names of the countries your students come from, and add other countries. Ask students if they know the words used to describe people from those countries.

- Have the entire class chant just the first two lines of the first two stanzas. Then, ask students to invent their own versions of these lines using the names of their own countries. For example: *Japan is west of the U.S.A. Japanese come here every day.* Have the students practice the entire chant again with some of these variations included.

▶ EXTENSION

Components: Dictionary pages 36-37, Transparency 18, Wall Chart 18

- Assign a geographic direction to each of the four walls of the classroom. Write the letters N, S, E, and W on separate pieces of paper and post each one on the corresponding wall. Select three students. Blindfold two of them and place them at opposite ends of the classroom. Turn the blindfolded students around a few times so that they don't remember what direction they face. The third student now gives directions so that the blindfolded students will meet each other. For example: *Elio, you are facing south. Take four steps north and stop. Marina, you are facing north. Take three steps south, then two steps west. Then stop and hold out your hands. Elio, now you take two steps east.* Continue until the two students touch hands. Then choose three new students to play the game.

- **Game: Geography.** One student names a country, city, state, or province. Each successive student must name another place that starts with the last letter of the previous country. For example, if Student A says *Mexico*, then Student B names a place that starts with *O*. If Student B says *Oregon*, Student C names a place that starts with *N*. If a student cannot think of a place that starts with the appropriate letter, or name a place that was named before, that student is out of the game. Continue the game until only one student remains. That student is the winner.

- Display a world atlas. Show students the longitude and latitude lines that run through every country in the world. Explain that latitude and longitude are measured in degrees. Degrees of latitude increase in each direction from the equator. Degrees of longitude increase in each direction from the prime meridian, which runs through England, Spain, and Western Africa. Draw a diagram on the board to aid in the explanation. Los Angeles is 34 degrees north of the equator and approximately 118 degrees west of the Prime Meridian. Written in geographic notation, that is 34°N, 118°W. New York City is 40 degrees north of the equator and 74 degrees west of the prime meridian, or 40°N, 74°W. Have students work in groups. Each group chooses a different city or country and then finds the (approximate) latitude and longitude of their city or country. The groups share the information with the entire class.

- Divide the class into two groups. Assign Canada to one group and Mexico to the other group. Group 1 finds the names of the Canadian provinces and the capitals of each province. Group 2 finds the names of the Mexican states and the capitals of each state. Encourage groups to research the information in an atlas, an encyclopedia, or on the internet. Have each group present its findings to the class.

► LITERATURE

Suggested Books

Amelia's Road

written by Linda Jacobs Altman;
illustrated by Enrique O. Sanchez.
Lee & Low Books, 1995. ISBN 188000027X
Amelia Martinez's family are migrant farmworkers from
Mexico. Amelia longs for a home of her own, and her story
conveys the sense of what it is like to work and move all
the time. Many ESL students will likely sympathize with
this unsentimental portrait of a girl making the best of a
bad situation. Each of the fresco-like, full-page
illustrations is accompanied by simple, repetitive text that
introduces students to many high-utility words. Since part
of the story poignantly covers Amelia's school experience,
this book is also appropriate for Topic 2, The School.

The Mexican American Family Album

written by Dorothy Hoobler and Thomas Hoobler, with an
introduction by Henry G. Cisneros.
Oxford University Press, 1998. ISBN 019512426X
This overview of Chicano history and family life is
conveyed through personal observations, memoirs, and
stories. It records the struggle of these immigrants to gain
acceptance in their adopted country, as well as their
subsequent contribution to American food, music, art,
and literature. A look at life in Mexico is featured in the
first half of the book and is well-suited for extending Topic
18, Canada and Mexico. The text is dense, but the
photographs and captions can be used independently to
expand students' understanding of the features,
landmarks, and culture of Mexico. This book is also
appropriate for Topic 21, The Spanish Missions.

O Canada

written and illustrated by Ted Harrison.
Ticknor & Fields, 1993. ISBN 0395660750
This province-by-province celebration of the people and
places of Canada features brief introductions to each
province accompanied by lush landscape art. Teachers
may want to read each province description in connection
with the Dictionary illustration. Some of the text may need
to be paraphrased since it is slightly advanced, but with
guidance, most ESL students should be able to read
along. Students can also spot many of the icons in the
Dictionary illustration in this book's illustrations. This
book can be used effectively in conjunction with *It
Happened in America* from Topic 10, The United States.

Maps and Globes

written by Jack Knowlton; illustrated by Harriett Barton.
HarperTrophy, 1986. ISBN 0064460495
This Reading Rainbow selection presents a brief history of
mapmaking, gives examples of many types of maps, and
introduces key vocabulary for map-reading and
geography. The large-print text presents the essential
vocabulary, usually in italics, and the illustrations clearly
show those words in context. Many of the illustrations
have interesting, anecdotal captions that can be used to
add greater interest. Since the text, grammar patterns,
and illustrations are quite simple, it is an excellent
resource that will help both younger and older ESL
students to grasp some rather difficult concepts. This
book is also appropriate for Topic 10, The United States.

WORKBOOK: Topic 18

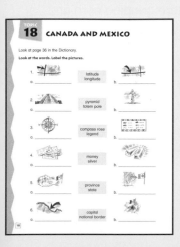

For each number on this
page, students have a
choice of two words with
which to label the two
pictures. This exercise
helps students to
distinguish between the
two closely-related words
in each pair.

WORKSHEET: Topic 18

In A, students fill in the
blanks to explain the
symbols in the map and
the letters of the compass
rose. In B, they complete
the sentences based on
the content reading.

▶ **CONTENT**

The Native American groups inhabiting North America before European exploration

▶ **LANGUAGE**

Simple past: *They made boats, houses, and masks from wood.*

CONTENT WORDS

1. ceremony
2. mask
3. tepee
4. chief
5. tribe
6. bow
7. arrow
8. spear
9. hide
10. cliff dwelling
11. pictograph
12. loom
13. weave
14. pottery
15. longhouse
16. hunt
17. gather
18. grind
19. basket
20. wampum

CONTENT READING

The Native Americans

Most people in the United States came from another country, but not the Native Americans. They lived in North America before the European explorers came. The explorers called them Indians. Today, we call them Native Americans.

The Native Americans in the Pacific Northwest lived along the Pacific Ocean. They made boats, houses, and masks from wood. They had dance ceremonies on special days. They wore animal masks and danced at these ceremonies.

The Native Americans in the Great Plains lived in tepees. The men hunted for animals with spears and bows and arrows. The women dried the animal hides in the sun. They made clothes and tepees from the hides.

The Native Americans in the Southwest lived in cliff dwellings. They drew pictographs about their lives on the walls of the cliff dwellings. They made pottery and beautiful baskets. They used looms to weave blankets.

The Native Americans in the East lived in wooden longhouses. Many people in the same family lived together in one longhouse. The men hunted for animals. The women's jobs were grinding corn and gathering fruits and nuts. They made belts from wampum.

Many Native Americans still live in tribes today. The leader of the tribe is the chief.

▶ WORDS

Components: Dictionary pages 38-39, Transparency 19, Wall Chart 19, Workbook page 19, Word and Picture Cards Topic 19, Cassette

- Present the content words. **See pages xiv-xvi for general techniques about presenting content words.**

  Language Note: Point out that the word *hide* can be a noun, meaning the skin of a large animal. It can also be a verb, with a very different meaning: to put or keep something or someone out of sight.

  Content Note: Wampum was used as a form of money as well as a record of tribal history.

- To introduce the topic, display a set of Native American objects or artifacts similar to those on the dictionary page (for example, silver or turquoise jewelry, a drum, a dreamcatcher, moccasins, a feathered headband). Name the objects and have students locate any of them that are in the picture. Name the objects for the students and ask them to tell you what they know about them.

- Use a drum to explain the concept of syllables. Tell students that syllables are like drum beats. Each drum beat stands for a syllable. Words have one or more syllables. Beat the drum once and model a one-syllable word from the list, such as *mask*. Then beat the drum twice, and model the two-syllable word *tepee*. Model the word *ceremony* and beat the drum four times. Divide the class into two teams. Distribute one set of the word and picture cards to each team. A student from Team 1 reads his/her word and picture card and a student from Team 2 beats the drum the appropriate number of times for the number of syllables in that word. For example, the student from Team 1 pronounces *longhouse* and the student from Team 2 beats the drum twice. Team 1 gets a point for correct pronunciation and Team 2 gets a point for the correct number of syllables. Next, a student from Team 2 takes a turn. Continue until all students have had a chance to pronounce their word and to beat the drum.

- Distribute the picture cards, leaving out the card for *ceremony*. Make four columns on the board. Label the columns *Homes*, *Things*, *Actions*, and *People*. Have individual students hold up their picture cards, say the correct word for their pictures, and then come to the front of the room and place their picture cards under the appropriate column on the board. For example, a student holds up the picture card for *tepee*, says *tepee*, and places the card under *Homes*. Continue until all students have had a turn.

WORKBOOK: Topic 19
See Teacher's Book page 77.

▶ CONTENT

Components: Dictionary pages 38-39, Transparency 19, Wall Chart 19, Content Reading Topic 19, Worksheet Topic 19, Cassette

- Present the content reading. **See pages xvii-xix for general techniques about presenting content readings.**

- Ask the following or similar questions:

  Did the Native Americans come from another country?
  Do Native Americans still live in tribes today?
  Where did the Native Americans in the Pacific Northwest live?
  Which Native Americans lived in cliff dwellings?
  What is the leader of the tribe called?
  What did the Native Americans in the Southwest make?

▶ **Simple past**

> We form the simple past by adding *-d* or *-ed* to regular verb forms. Irregular verbs have special forms for the simple past. The irregular verbs in the content reading and their simple past forms are: *come/came, make/made, have/had, draw/drew.* The irregular past of *be* is *was/were.*

Divide the class into four groups. Assign each group one panel of the wall chart. The groups label their panels. For example, Group 1 labels its panel *The Pacific Northwest*. Group 2 labels its panel *The Great Plains*. Each group selects a "chief." Students in each group role-play being Native Americans from that area telling the chief about their ancestors. Students describe the scene and the actions in their panels using statements in the simple past. For example: *We made houses from wood.* Each chief writes down the group's descriptions and then reads them to the class.

▶ **Simple past**

> We form *Yes/No* questions in the simple past with [*Did* + subject + the simple form of the main verb]. For example: *Did he walk?* We form *Wh-* questions with [*Wh-* question word + *did* + subject + simple form of main verb]. For example: *Where did they live?/What did they draw?*

After each chief from the above activity has presented his or her group's descriptions to the class, the rest of the students ask the chief questions using the simple past. For example: *Did you live in longhouses?* or *What were the women's jobs?* The chiefs answer all the questions that they can about their group. If they can't answer a question based on the information in the wall chart panel, they write down the question and research the answer later with their group. Give chiefs the opportunity to answer these difficult questions at a later time (see Extension in this topic, page 76).

WORKSHEET: Topic 19
See Teacher's Book page 77.

►CHANTS

Components: Dictionary pages 38-39, Content Chant Topic 19, Cassette

 ## CONTENT CHANT

Bow and Arrow

Bow and arrow.
Hunt the deer.
Shoot the deer.
Kill the deer.

Take the hide.
Dry it in the sun.
Wear the deerskin.
Thank the deer.

Take the hide.
Make a tepee.
Wear the deerskin.
Thank the deer.

Gather nuts.
Grind the corn.
Kill the buffalo.
Kill the deer.

Eat the meat.
Wear the hide.
Thank the buffalo.
Thank the deer.

- Present the content chant. **See pages xx-xxi for general techniques about presenting chants.**

- Before practicing the chant, explain that Native Americans hunted for deer and buffalo. Many tribes had great respect for the animals they had to kill. They "thanked" the buffalo and deer for dying so that the tribe could have food. They tried to use every part of the animal, not just the meat. They made tepees and clothes from the animals' hides.

- Before distributing the chant, divide the class into two groups and have them practice with lines from the chant. Group 1 chants and pantomimes *Kill the deer* (loudly), *Thank the deer* (softly). Group 2 chants and pantomimes *Kill the buffalo* (loudly), *Thank the buffalo* (softly).

- Now distribute Content Chant 19. Divide the class into five groups. Each group chants one stanza repeatedly until the group is comfortable with the words. The entire class joins in each time on *Kill the deer, Thank the deer, Kill the buffalo,* and *Thank the buffalo.* Encourage students to pantomime the actions as they chant each stanza. If possible, use the drum from earlier in this topic. Select one student to beat the drum to the words (by syllable) as the entire class chants.

►EXTENSION

Components: Dictionary pages 38-39, Transparency 19, Wall Chart 19

- Have students talk about, write about, or draw the kinds of dwellings they have seen in their neighborhood or surrounding area (such as apartments, houses, mobile homes, or adobe huts). The dwellings can be ones they have lived in. The students should mention the location of the homes, the materials used to build them, the size and shape of the rooms, etc. Ask them to compare and contrast these homes with tepees and longhouses.

- Have students tell the stories of their lives by drawing pictographs on paper. They should write their names on the papers, but no other words, just pictures. Collect all the papers and then redistribute them randomly. Have each student look at a paper and try to figure out the story from the pictographs. Each student tries to "translate" the pictograph story into words. Then the student who drew the pictographs tells the story.

- Make masks from empty plastic gallon water or milk bottles. Cut off the bottom half, leaving the handle for the nose. Cover with papier-mâché and paint. Tie a string or a piece of elastic around the back. After students have created their masks, divide them into groups and have each group come up with a dance. Groups can invent dances that they hope will bring rain, good luck in the hunt, or good crops. Students can perform the dances for the class.

- Have students write or talk about the earliest natives in the countries where they come from. They may do research in textbooks, encyclopedias, or on the Internet. They should talk about the kinds of clothes their early ancestors wore, the dwellings they lived in, the foods they ate, the ceremonies they performed, and the goods they produced. If possible, students can bring in examples of artifacts that tell about their culture's history.

- Review the difficult questions that the chiefs and their groups researched in the Content section (see page 75). Groups can do research in encyclopedias, on the Internet, or with their mainstream peers. Have each chief present the information to the entire class.

- Learn more about Native American tribes still living in the U.S. by arranging a field trip to a local community, or an Indian museum. Bring the wall chart or word/picture cards so students can identify some of the objects whose names they have learned.

- As students research various Native American tribes, they may become familiar with tribe names such as the Apache, Seminole, Iroquois, Inca, Maya, and Hopi. As students learn these names, write them on chart paper. Once there is a group of about ten names, have students chant each of the names repeatedly in succession. Use the drum to help students' pronunciation.

► LITERATURE

Suggested Books

The House on Maple Street
written by Bonnie Pryor; illustrated by Beth Peck.
Mulberry Books, 1992. ISBN 0688120318
This historical fiction depicts life in the Midwest in the past and in the present. Two girls who live at 107 Maple Street look out from their front porch and see their neighborhood as it looked three hundred years ago. Teachers may find that reading the story aloud is most beneficial to students. Post-reading activities could include discussing the book in sequence (past, present, and future). This book is thematically mature enough for older students while being grammatically simple enough for younger ones. This title can also be used with Topic 25, Westward Expansion, and Topic 13, The Midwest.

The First Americans (A History of US, Book 1)
written by Joy Hakim.
Oxford University Press Children's Books, 1993.
ISBN 0195077466
Joy Hakim's popular history series for young people, *A History of US*, is an excellent resource for teachers and ESL students alike. This first volume contains a great deal of information that relates to this topic. Its clear writing, fascinating illustrations, and sidebars of interesting stories and facts make it useful for reference and for reading aloud. The lively text will encourage discussion and the numerous illustrations will serve as detailed elaborations of the topic's content words.

The Girl Who Loved Wild Horses
written and illustrated by Paul Goble.
Simon & Schuster, 1986. ISBN 0689716966
Based on a Native American legend, this Caldecott Medal-winning book tells the story of a girl who loves horses so much that she eventually becomes one. The tale is told in simple words using the past tense. The author also makes extensive use of descriptive phrases and similes. Detailed illustrations reflect the life of the Plains Indians and add to the visual information conveyed in the Dictionary illustration. To extend the reading, teachers can use the illustrations as prompts for student-generated art.

Brother Eagle, Sister Sky: A Message from Chief Seattle
adapted and illustrated by Susan Jeffers.
Dial Books for Young Readers, 1991. ISBN 0803709692
Beautiful and dignified art frames this adaptation of Chief Seattle's famous message to the Commissioner of Indian Affairs in 1850. The poetic language captures the Chief's spiritual outlook on nature and his fears of man's effect on nature. The imaginative language may require some guidance when read aloud with beginner and intermediate students. Teachers may also refer to this book for Topic 48, Our Environment.

The Mud Family
written by Betsy James; illustrated by Paul Morin.
Oxford University Press, 1998. ISBN 0195124790
The Anasazi Indians lived and grew maize in the American Southwest long before the arrival of Europeans. This picture book tells the story of Sosi, an Anasazi girl who makes an imaginary family out of dried mud when the lack of rainfall creates tension in her real family. As Sosi's family, in desperation, is ready to leave the land, Sosi engages her "mud family" in one last rain dance. This book's simple prose and rich paintings rendered with feathers and burlap convey a strong sense of the geography of the American Southwest.

WORKBOOK: Topic 19

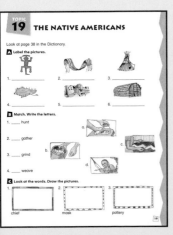

In the first activity, students label the pictures. In the second activity, they match the pictures to the words by writing the letters. In the third activity, they draw pictures of the three words given.

WORKSHEET: Topic 19

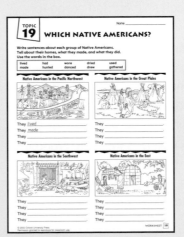

On this page, students write sentences about the four groups of Native Americans using the verbs in the word box. The words *lived* and *made* can be used for all four sets of descriptions.

20 EXPLORATION AND DISCOVERY

CONTENT

The explorations of Leif Eriksson, Christopher Columbus, and Ponce de León

LANGUAGE

Common nouns and proper nouns: *Many European explorers came after Columbus.*

Past continuous: *They were looking for wood.*

Compound sentences with but: *Each one followed a different route, but they all came on ships.*

CONTENT WORDS

1. route
2. Vikings
3. Leif Eriksson
4. mast
5. rope
6. knot
7. cargo
8. crew
9. oar
10. sailor
11. prow
12. wave
13. Christopher Columbus
14. Niña
15. Pinta
16. Santa Maria
17. sail
18. jewelry
19. native
20. Ponce de León

 CONTENT READING

Exploration and Discovery

Many European explorers came to the New World. Each one followed a different route, but they all came on ships.

Each ship had large sails and a tall mast. The sailors pulled on ropes and tied knots for the sails, but sometimes they rowed with oars. The ship's prow cut through the waves. Each ship carried cargo for food and trade.

Leif Eriksson was the first European explorer. He and his crew of Vikings came to the New World around the year 1000. They were looking for wood. They sailed to Iceland and Greenland first. Then, they sailed to Newfoundland.

Christopher Columbus sailed to the New World in 1492. He was looking for a new route to India. He left Spain with three ships. They were the Niña, the Pinta, and the Santa Maria. He didn't find India, but he found new islands in the Atlantic Ocean. Those islands are now called the Bahamas. Columbus gave the natives beads and jewelry. The natives gave Columbus gold.

Many European explorers came after Columbus. Most of them were looking for gold. Ponce de León wasn't looking for gold. He was looking for the Fountain of Youth. He wanted to drink the water from the Fountain of Youth and live forever. He never found the Fountain of Youth, but he discovered a new land in 1513. He called it Florida.

▶ WORDS

Components: Dictionary pages 40-41, Transparency 20, Wall Chart 20, Workbook page 20, Word and Picture Cards Topic 20, Cassette

- Present the content words. **See pages xiv-xvi for general techniques about presenting content words.**

  > **Content Note:** Although Ponce de León is credited with finding North America when he landed at Florida, what he was actually looking for was the Fountain of Youth. The Fountain of Youth was an Indian legend about a natural spring that had the power to cure illness and make the old young. The Fountain of Youth did not exist, but many explorers of the time believed that it did.
  >
  > When we refer to the "New World," we are referring to that part of the world unknown to Europeans in the era of exploration. The New World was comprised of the Americas and surrounding islands.

▶ Common nouns and proper nouns

  > Common nouns refer to general objects, such as *prow*, etc. Proper nouns refer to names of specific people, places, or things, such as *Leif Eriksson*, etc. Proper nouns almost always begin with a capital letter.

  Divide the class into small groups and give each group a set of word and picture cards. Ask each group to divide the cards into two piles: one for common nouns, another for proper nouns. Have groups exchange their piles of cards and check for accuracy.

- Ask students to turn to Dictionary Topic 20 and point to Leif Eriksson, Christopher Columbus, and Ponce de León. Ask students if they know who these men are. Explain that they were all *explorers* and that *to explore* means to travel in search of something. Have students identify each explorer on the wall chart. Ask students the word for *explore* or *explorers* in their native language(s) and have all students share their words with the class. Then discuss what each explorer was attempting to find.

- Choose three students to come to the front of the class to be explorers. Then hand out one word and picture card to each student. Tell the first explorer to go around the class and collect cards that are parts of a boat or ship. Next, ask the second explorer to collect cards that are people. Then ask the third explorer to collect all the other cards. Have the three explorers display their "cargo" to the class.

- Draw three columns and label them *Parts of a Boat or Ship*, *People*, and *Other*. Invite the three explorers from the previous activity to place each of their cards in the appropriate column.

WORKBOOK: Topic 20
  See Teacher's Book page 81.

▶ CONTENT

Components: Dictionary pages 40-41, Transparency 20, Wall Chart 20, Content Reading Topic 20, Worksheet Topic 20, Cassette

- Present the content reading. **See pages xvii-xix for general techniques about presenting content readings.**

- Ask the following or similar questions:

  > *Did all the European explorers come on ships?*
  > *When did Columbus come to the New World?*
  > *What did the ships carry?*
  > *What were the names of Columbus' three ships?*
  > *Who was the first European explorer?*
  > *What was Ponce de León looking for?*
  > *What did Ponce de León discover?*

- Before reading the content reading, gauge students' prior knowledge by asking who discovered America and when. Write all answers on the board and discuss. Then introduce the mnemonic device *In fourteen hundred and ninety-two, Columbus sailed the ocean blue.*

▶ Past continuous

  > The past continuous is used to describe an action in progress at a specific time in the past. We form the past continuous with the simple past of *BE* + the verb + *-ing* (*was/were* + verb + *-ing*).

  Demonstrate how to form the past continuous. Ask students to circle or underline all the sentences in the content reading that contain the past continuous.

▶ **Past continuous.** Write the following statements in one column on the board:

  > *He was looking for a new route to India.*
  > *He was looking for the Fountain of Youth.*
  > *He was sailing with the Vikings.*

  Then write the names of the three explorers in another column on the board. Ask students to draw lines between the explorer and the statement that describes him.

▶ **Past continuous.** Divide students into small groups. Have one student in each group pantomime an activity. It can be an activity performed by one of the European explorers, such as sailing, but it does not have to be. When the student is finished, have another student ask questions using the past continuous. Example:

  Student A pantomimes giving jewelry to natives.

  Student B: *Was he eating?*

  Student C: *No. He was giving jewelry to the natives.*

WORKSHEET: Topic 20
  See Teacher's Book page 81.

► CHANTS

Components: Dictionary pages 40-41, Content Chant Topic 20, Cassette

 ## CONTENT CHANT

Columbus Sailed Across the Sea

Columbus sailed
across the sea
without a phone,
without TV.

No fax, no e-mail, no PC
when Columbus sailed
across the sea.

When he woke up
in the middle of the night,
the moon and stars
were his only light.

Without an engine,
only a sail,
it wasn't easy,
but he didn't fail.

The crew was fine.
The masts were strong.
On his three little ships,
the journey was long.

Columbus sailed
into history
without a phone,
without TV.

We give Columbus
the highest score,
though he didn't find
what he was looking for.

- Present the content chant. **See pages xx-xxi for general techniques about presenting chants.**

- Before distributing the chant, have students practice small chunks of the language. Divide the class into two groups. Group 1 chants *without a phone, without TV.* Group 2 chants *No fax, no e-mail, no PC.* First the groups chant in turn and then simultaneously, starting in a whisper and chanting louder and faster.

- Now distribute Content Chant 20. Select one student to be Columbus. This student pantomimes the actions of the chant as the rest of the class chants it. Then, divide the class into groups or pairs to chant the individual stanzas. Students can take turns being Columbus.

- Have students identify the rhyming words (*sea, TV, PC, history; night, light; sail, fail; strong, long; score, for*). Invite the class to give other examples that rhyme with these words. Encourage students to keep these lists of words in their notebooks or in a word bank.

► EXTENSION

Components: Dictionary pages 40-41, Transparency 20, Wall Chart 20

- Ask students to talk about the explorer(s) in their family. *Who was the first person in your family to come to this country? Why did your family come here? What was your family looking for?*

- Have students trace the world map in Appendix G. Then have them label the city they are in, and the city or country they came from. Then have them draw the route their family took to this country.

- Draw a very large map of the world on the board or on chart paper. Have each student find on the map the city or country he or she comes from. Students can write the name of their home cities or countries on the map.

- Tell students to pretend they are leaving this country forever and looking for a new land. Have them make a list of the things they would bring with them on this journey and why.

- Ask students what age they would be if they could drink from a Fountain of Youth and be one age forever. Why would they choose that age? What age would they *not* want to be forever? Students may draw pictures or write a short composition about their ideas.

- Ask students to identify where each of the explorers came from and went to on the map. Divide students into three groups: Newfoundland, the Bahamas, and Florida. Students may choose to be in any of the three groups. Each group then adopts a place as their research project and must find and report on three facts about the place. Students can use an encyclopedia, the Internet, or other students as resources. Students in any group who have been to the group's research place can be encouraged to give an "eyewitness account" of their visit there.

- Pair students with mainstream classmates. Have the students interview the mainstream students about what places they would go sailing or exploring.

- Brainstorm the names of other explorers with the class. The students may know the names of other explorers from their home countries. Write all the names on the board. Then have each student choose a new explorer and look up information about that explorer in an encyclopedia.

► LITERATURE

Suggested Books

Encounter
written by Jane Yolen; illustrated by David Shannon.
Harcourt Brace, 1996. ISBN 015201389X
This book recreates what a young Taino Indian boy from the West Indies saw and thought when Columbus landed on his island in 1492. The story's poetic language may require teacher guidance, but the expressive illustrations will help students to comprehend the central tension between the natives and the European explorers. For an extension activity, students can adopt the persona of the boy and tell the story in their own words.

A Picture Book of Christopher Columbus
written by David Adler;
illustrated by John and Alexandra Wallner.
Holiday House, 1992. ISBN 082340949X
A Picture Book of Christopher Columbus relates the life of Christopher Columbus from birth to death in simple sentences and syntax. Much of the vocabulary from this topic is used and should therefore be familiar to students. This is a good book for both read-along sessions and individualized reading, especially for beginners.

Viking
written by Susan Margeson;
illustrated by Peter Anderson.
Alfred A. Knopf Books for Young Readers, 1994. ISBN 0679860029
This story of the Vikings—their ships, weapons, heroes, and myths—is encyclopedic. Teachers and students will find it useful as a resource. The many photographs and illustrations provide an extended understanding of the Dictionary illustration. Many of the photographs can be matched to the word and picture cards to promote language learning.

The Discovery of the Americas
written and illustrated by Betsy and Giulio Maestro.
Mulberry Books, 1992. ISBN 0688115128

Exploration and Conquest
written and illustrated by Betsy and Giulio Maestro.
Mulberry Books, 1997. ISBN 0688154743
As companion volumes, these two books provide a rich context for this topic. *The Discovery of the Americas* covers the early migrations and explorations of the Americas through the 16th century, while *Exploration and Conquest* discusses further exploration and the effects of European influence on the Americas up to 1620. Although the text may be too difficult for beginning and intermediate students, teachers can use the many illustrations and the easy-to-read historical tables at the end of each book to reinforce the textual information about the events and their chronology.

Follow the Dream
written and illustrated by Peter Sis.
Dragonfly, 1996. ISBN 0679880887
This simply-told biography follows the life of Christopher Columbus from childhood to his first voyage of exploration. Its rich, imaginative illustrations convey a strong sense of Columbus' 15th century world. Although the language may need to be paraphrased or read with frequent stops to check understanding, most learners should be able to master it. The rendering of a ship's log at the end of the book serves as a useful picture diary. Students can use it as a model to write and illustrate their own "ship's log."

WORKBOOK: Topic 20

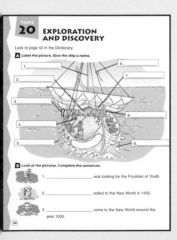

In A, students label the parts of the ship and write its name on the prow. In B, they complete the sentences with the names of the explorers in the pictures.

WORKSHEET: Topic 20

To do this puzzle, students complete the sentences and write the words in the boxes. In each sentence they circle *was* or *were*. If the puzzle is done correctly, the word *discovery* will be highlighted in the box. Students fill in this word at the bottom of the page.

▶ **CONTENT**
....
Daily life in and around the Spanish missions

▶ **LANGUAGE**
....
Passive voice, simple past:
Many of the buildings were made of adobe.

Spanish words in English:
adobe, patio, San Francisco, pueblo

CONTENT WORDS

1. pueblo
2. fort
3. trading post
4. adobe
5. gate
6. arch
7. patio
8. fountain
9. cross
10. bell
11. candles
12. missionary
13. teach
14. Spanish soldiers
15. ride
16. sword

CONTENT READING

The Spanish Missions

Spanish missionaries came to North America in the 16th century. They built missions in Florida, Texas, New Mexico, Arizona, and California. The missionaries taught the Native Americans about Christianity.

Most missions were built around a square open area, or patio, with a fountain. The patio was surrounded by buildings. Many of the buildings were made of adobe. Some of the buildings had arches, walkways, and gates.

The main building at the mission was the church. There was a cross and a bell on top of the church. The cross is a symbol of the Christian religion. The bell was rung to call people to church.

Some Native Americans lived at the mission with the missionaries. They made adobe, candles, tools, and clothing. More Native Americans lived nearby in pueblos.

Other people lived near the mission, too. Some people lived at trading posts. Food and clothing were bought and sold at the trading posts. Spanish soldiers lived in forts. They went riding to and from the mission. They were armed with swords.

Many missions are still here today. People don't live in missions anymore, but the buildings are still standing. Now they are museums.

▶ WORDS

Components: Dictionary pages 42-43, Transparency 21, Wall Chart 21, Workbook page 21, Word and Picture Cards Topic 21, Cassette

- Present the content words. **See pages xiv-xvi for general techniques about presenting content words.**

- Distribute the word cards. Have students look at the wall chart to determine where the picture for their word appears. Does it appear inside the mission, outside the mission or both inside and outside? For example, *pueblo* and *fort* are outside the mission. *Bell*, *gate*, and *patio* are inside the mission. *Missionary* can be either inside or outside the mission. Draw a large Venn diagram on chart paper like the example below. Ask students to write their words in the appropriate regions.

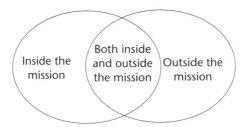

- Divide the class into groups. Ask each group to count the number of arches, crosses, bells, trees, and people in the wall chart. A reporter from each group reports the results to the class. If the results of the groups are different, encourage the students to discuss. Note that not all of the arches are exactly alike. Some of the arches have decorative columns.

- Explain that adobe is clay mixed with straw and dried by the sun. Adobe was used to make buildings in the missions. Have students find everything in the picture that is made of adobe.

- ▶ **Spanish words in English.** Point to the place names in the inset map on the wall chart. Write the following words on the board: *Saint Augustine, San Francisco, San Diego, Santa Fe*. Ask students if they notice anything similar about these names. Explain that *San, Santa,* and *Santo* are Spanish words for *Saint*. Ask students to name other places that start with *San, Santo, Santa,* or *Saint (St.)*. Examples might include *Santa Barbara, St. John's, San Jose, Santo Domingo*. Give some examples of Spanish words that have entered the English language, such as *patio, adobe,* and *pueblo*. Then have students brainstorm a list of other words they may know in English that are of Spanish origin.

WORKBOOK: Topic 21
See Teacher's Book page 85.

▶ CONTENT

Components: Dictionary pages 42-43, Transparency 21, Wall Chart 21, Content Reading Topic 21, Worksheet Topic 21, Cassette

- Present the content reading. **See pages xvii-xix for general techniques about presenting content readings.**

- Ask the following or similar questions:

  Were most missions built around a patio?
  Do people live in the missions today?
  Where were missions built by Spanish missionaries?
  When did the Spanish missionaries come to America?
  Where did the Spanish soldiers live?
  Why was the bell rung in a mission?

- ▶ **Passive voice, simple past**

  We use the passive voice when we don't know who is performing the action of a sentence or when the doer of the action is not important. The passive voice is used with the simple present tense. For example: *Spanish is spoken here.* We also use the passive voice with the simple past tense. For example: *Our school was built in 1965.* The passive voice in the simple past is formed with the simple past of *BE* plus the past participle of the main verb [*was/were* + past participle]. Many of the verbs in the content reading have irregular past participles. They are: *built, bought, made, rung, sold,* and *taught*. The regular past participles are *surrounded* and *armed*.

  Explain the use of the passive voice in the simple past and have students underline all instances of this in the content reading.

  Invite students to make up their own sentences using the passive voice in the simple past. Ask them to make a list of the things that happened this week. For example: *My homework was stolen. The bell was rung seven times in one minute.* Have students read their sentences aloud to the class.

- ▶ **Passive voice, simple past.** Divide the class into groups. Have each group describe the wall chart in their own words. Encourage students to use the passive voice in the simple past as much as possible. For example: *The candles were carried by Native Americans. People were taught by the missionaries.*

- Divide the class into groups. Have each group prepare a dramatization of daily life in and around the mission. In each group, there should be missionaries, Spanish soldiers, Native American candlemakers, Native Americans being taught, and a trading post owner. Groups present their dramatizations to the class. The presentations can be descriptive dramatizations or dialogues about daily lives in and around the mission.

WORKSHEET: Topic 21
See Teacher's Book page 85.

►CHANTS

Components: Dictionary pages 42-43, Content Chant Topic 21, Cassette

 ## CONTENT CHANT

**Light the Candles,
Listen to the Bells**

Light the candles.
Listen to the bells.

Light the candles.
Look at the cross.

Light the candles.
Listen to the bells.
Look at the cross
on top of the church.

Walk through the patio.
Stop at the fountain.
Listen to the fountain.
Listen to the bells.

Light the candles.
Listen to the bells.
Look at the cross
on top of the church.

- Present the content chant. **See pages xx-xxi for general techniques about presenting chants.**

- Before distributing Content Chant 21, have students practice with small chunks of language from the chant. Divide the class into two groups. Group 1 chants the words *Listen, listen, listen, listen* in a four-beat rhythm. Group 2 chants the words *bong, bong, bong, bong* to sound like mission bells in a four beat rhythm. The two groups chant individually first and then simultaneously.

- Now have students practice two lines from the chant. Divide the class into three groups. Group 1 chants *Light the candles*. Group 2 chants *Listen to the bells*. Group 3 chants *bong, bong, bong, bong* in imitation of the mission bells.

- Distribute Content Chant 21. Divide the class into six groups. The first five groups take turns chanting the stanzas. Group 6 echoes *bong, bong, bong, bong* softly as the other groups chant their lines.

- Now have individual students chant various lines of this chant. Select one student to read any line that starts with the word *Light*. Select another student to read lines starting with *Listen*. Other students may read lines beginning with *Look*, *Walk*, or *Stop*.

►EXTENSION

Components: Dictionary pages 42-43, Transparency 21, Wall Chart 21

- Bring in several copies of detailed road maps of California. Divide the class into groups, one group per map. Ask each group to search the maps for names of missions in California and write them down on a separate sheet of paper. There are 21 missions in California, mostly along the coast, although they may not all be labeled on each map. Have students try to find all of them. Mission names include San Juan Capistrano, San Luis Rey, San Luis Obispo, and San Carlos.

- Assign one student to each of the 21 California missions. Have each student research the person for whom the mission is named. Some information may be available on the Internet. Students can also look up information in biographical dictionaries or encyclopedias. Students could also research Father Junipero Serra, who implemented the mission system.

- Point out to students that the influence of the Spanish language on English is strong. Not only are there many Spanish words that are now in the English language, but there are also many Spanish place names in each of the states where Spanish missions were located. Have students look at current state maps or road maps of Florida, Texas, New Mexico, and California and make lists of all the Spanish names they can find for cities, towns, rivers, parks and roads.

- Explain that *Spaniards* are people from Spain. *Italians* are people from Italy. *Peruvians* are people from Peru. Ask students to say where they come from and to give the word that describes them as a native of that place. (A good almanac should have the correct nationality names for every country in the world.) In addition, ask students about names for residents of various U.S. states (*Floridian*, *New Yorker*, *Texan*, *Michigander*, etc.) or cities (Los Angeleno, Bostonian, San Franciscan, Portlander, etc.).

- Divide the class into two teams. Ask each team to make a list of reasons why they would ring a bell, or why a bell might be rung. Ideas might include: time for dinner, school is starting, school is ending, etc. Reporters from each team write down the team's list. After a set time period, one member of each team reads the list aloud.

► LITERATURE

Suggested Books

A Mission for the People: The Story of La Purisima
written and illustrated by Mary Ann Fraser.
Henry Holt & Company, Inc., 1998. ISBN 0805050507
On December 8, 1787, Spanish missionaries arrived in what is now Santa Barbara, California, where they built a mission called La Purisima. This book begins with the history of the land before the missionaries arrived and continues through the settling of the mission. The clear text and dramatic illustrations add depth and necessary background to the content. Teachers will find the sidebars that define and illustrate words in the story helpful. These words may be used as a word bank or reproduced and cut up to make additional word cards.

Whispers Along the Mission Trail
written and illustrated by Gail Faber and Michele Lasagna.
Magpie Publications, 1986. ISBN 0936480033
This journey along the mission trails begins with Columbus's conquest of the New World in 1492. The reader meets the Native Americans, the Spanish conquistadors, and the missionaries who were a part of this period in United States history 500 years ago. The book is well-documented with maps of the routes, illustrations from the period, and photographs of the missions. A helpful summary, called "Backtracking," presents the content in short, clear language. Each chapter also contains a series of questions for further discussion, which are useful as students learn the content reading. Small sections may be assigned to advanced readers. For beginner and intermediate students, the photographs may be matched with the word and picture cards.

The Mexican American Family Album
by Dorothy and Thomas Hoobler;
with an introduction by Henry G. Cisneros
Oxford University Press Children's Books,
1998. ISBN 019512426X
This overview of Chicano history and family life is conveyed through personal observations, memoirs, and stories. It records the struggle of these immigrants to gain acceptance in their adopted country, as well as their subsequent contribution to American art, food, music, and literature. The text is heavy, but the photographs and captions can be used independently to expand students' understanding of the features, landmarks, and culture that followed the Spanish conquest. This book also can be used with Topic 18, Canada and Mexico.

Spanish Pioneers of the Southwest
written by Joan Anderson; photographs by George Ancona.
E P Dutton, 1989. ISBN 0525672648
This outstanding photo essay by George Ancona recreates how early Spanish settlers lived in the Southwest circa 1750. It follows one family as they conduct their daily routine in and around their hacienda. The photographs in this text can be linked directly to the Dictionary illustration and the content words.

WORKBOOK: Topic 21

Students match the pictures to the words in A by writing the letters. In B, they unscramble eight of the content words.

WORKSHEET: Topic 21

In A, students match the verbs to their past participles, which are scrambled in the second column. In B, they choose *was* or *were* for each sentence and use the unscrambled words above to create passive voice sentences.

22 COLONIAL LIFE

▶ **CONTENT**
....
The life of the pilgrims in
colonial America

▶ **LANGUAGE**
....
Simple past: *Apprentices
learned their jobs from the
workers./The cobbler made
shoes.*

Compound words: *The
courthouse was for the
government.*

CONTENT WORDS

1. Pilgrims
2. Thanksgiving
3. town meeting
4. shore
5. bay
6. cape
7. harbor
8. common
9. stockade
10. meetinghouse
11. courthouse
12. inn
13. mill
14. blacksmith
15. apprentice
16. tobacco

CONTENT READING

Colonial Life

The Pilgrims were the first English settlers. They came to America from England in 1620. They settled the first colony on the eastern shore of North America. The Pilgrims built their towns near bays on the Atlantic Ocean. Capes, or curved pieces of land, made the bays safe harbors for the Pilgrims' ships.

Most early colonial towns looked alike. The Pilgrims often built stockades around their towns. The stockades protected the people and their animals. The towns usually had an open area in the middle. This was called the common. Sometimes, the Pilgrims built a meetinghouse, a courthouse, and an inn near the common. The meetinghouse was for church services and town meetings. The courthouse was for the government. The inn was for visitors.

Pilgrims worked in other buildings near the common. The blacksmith made iron pots and pans.

The cobbler made shoes. The silversmith made silver knives, forks, and spoons. Many workers had a young helper, or apprentice. Apprentices learned their jobs from the workers.

Farmers grew tobacco, corn, wheat, and other crops in the fields. The miller ground the grain into flour at the mill.

The Pilgrims celebrated their first year in the New World in 1621. They made a big dinner and they called it Thanksgiving. They invited the Native Americans to dinner and thanked them for their help. Thanksgiving is still an important American holiday.

▶ WORDS

Components: Dictionary pages 44-45, Transparency 22, Wall Chart 22, Workbook page 22, Word and Picture Cards Topic 22, Cassette

- Present the content words. **See pages xiv-xvi for general techniques about presenting content words.**

- Display the wall chart and have students look at the picture. Ask students to describe the village. Where is this village? Does it look like a village from this country? Does it look like a village from the countries the students come from? Is this a present-day village or one from the past? What things are the same as villages of today? What things are different?

- Display a calendar. Turn to November. Ask students if they know the important holiday that occurs in November. Have students tell what they know about the holiday and the people who started it. Write the correct responses on the board.

▶ **Compound words**

> Compound words are two words which together function as a single word. Compound words can be written as one word or two separate words. The plural is added to the last part of the compound word. Examples of compound words are *Thanksgiving*, *town meeting*, *meetinghouse*, *courthouse*, and *blacksmith*.

Point out the compound words to the students on the Dictionary page. Explain that the compound word *blacksmith* refers to a person who makes things out of iron. Ask students if they can guess what a silversmith does, or what a goldsmith or a tinsmith does. Encourage students to add these compound words to their word banks. Make a list of all these compound words on the board and have students write each word of the compound words on index cards. For example: *silver* and *smith*, *meeting* and *house*. Collect the index cards and distribute them to all the students. Have students circulate and ask each other questions to find each of the two words in all of the compound words.

- Make three large signs: one with the word *People*, another with the word *Places*, and the third with the word *Things*. Select three individual students to come to the front of the room and hold each of the signs. Distribute the picture cards to the rest of the students. Each student, in turn, looks at his or her picture cards, says the word for that card, and joins the student holding the appropriate category sign for that card. For example, if a student has the picture card *bay*, he or she says *bay* and stands with the student holding up the sign *Places*.

WORKBOOK: Topic 22
See Teacher's Book page 89.

▶ CONTENT

Components: Dictionary pages 44-45, Transparency 22, Wall Chart 22, Content Reading Topic 22, Worksheet Topic 22, Cassette

- Present the content reading. **See pages xvii-xix for general techniques about presenting content readings.**

- Ask the following or similar questions:

  Were the Pilgrims the first English settlers?
  Did most early colonial towns look alike?
  Why did the Pilgrims build stockades?
  When did the Pilgrims come to America?
  Where did the Pilgrims settle their first colony?
  How did the Pilgrims celebrate their first year in the New World?

- Make three columns on the board. Label column 1 *In a Colonial Town*. Label column 2 *In Our Town*. Label column 3 *In a Colonial Town and Our Town*. Ask each student to write a statement on a piece of paper that refers to a colonial town, to your own town, or to both. For example: *There are buildings* (column 3) or *There's a supermarket* (column 2). Collect all the papers. Ask students to take turns coming to the front of the class, choosing a paper, reading it aloud, and putting it in the correct column. Afterwards, have students judge whether the papers are in the correct columns.

- Select one student to think of a kind of building, such as a house, a meetinghouse, a church, an inn, or a mill. The remaining students take turns asking the first student *Yes/No* questions in order to guess the type of building. For example: *Do people live in this building?* The student who guesses correctly thinks of a new kind of building.

▶ **Simple past**

> We form the simple past by adding *-d* or *-ed* to regular verb forms. Irregular verbs have special forms for the simple past. The irregular verbs in the content reading and their simple past forms are: *BE/was* and *were*, *build/built*, *make/made*, *have/had*, *grow/grew*, *grind/ground*.

Tell students that in the content reading there are a number of examples of both regular simple past forms (for example, *settled*, *thanked*) and irregular simple past forms (for example, *were*, *came*). Divide the class into two teams. Each team has five minutes to count the number of regular and irregular simple past forms in the content reading and to make two lists: one of regular forms and one of irregular forms. The team with the most correct answers wins. There are nine occurrences of regular forms: *settled*, *looked*, *protected*, *worked*, *learned*, *celebrated*, *called*, *invited*, *thanked*. There are 17 occurrences of irregular forms: *were*, *came* (3), *built* (5), *made* (2), *had* (3), *was*, *grew*, *ground*.

WORKSHEET: Topic 22
See Teacher's Book page 89.

►CHANTS

Components: Dictionary pages 44-45, Content Chant Topic 22, Cassette

 ## CONTENT CHANT

Town Meeting

Town meeting, meetinghouse,
courthouse, inn *

Town meeting, meetinghouse,
courthouse, inn *

The Pilgrims are meeting.
    Where are they meeting?
They're meeting in the meetinghouse,
next to the inn.

    Where's the inn?
It's next to the courthouse.
    Where's the courthouse?
It's next to the inn.

Town meeting, meetinghouse,
courthouse, inn *

Town meeting, meetinghouse,
courthouse, inn *

- Present the content chant. **See pages xx-xxi for general techniques about presenting chants.**

- Before distributing Content Chant 22, have students practice with small chunks of the language from the chant. Divide the class into two groups. Tap out a four beat rhythm with a ruler or with your hand on the desk. Group 1 chants the words *town meeting, meeting house* and Group 2 chants the words *courthouse, inn.* Group 2 claps at the clap cue (*). Have the groups chant their lines individually and then together.

- Now distribute Content Chant 22. Divide the class into four groups. Group 1 chants all occurrences of the line *Town meeting, meetinghouse.* Group 2 chants all occurrences of the line *courthouse, inn* (and claps after *inn*). Group 3 chants all of the questions in stanzas 3 and 4. Group 4 responds with all of the statements in those stanzas. Have students point to the appropriate objects on the wall chart as they chant their lines.

- Now select individual students to take each of the parts of the four groups in the above activity.

►EXTENSION

Components: Dictionary pages 44-45, Transparency 22, Wall Chart 22

- Talk about the meaning of Thanksgiving. Have students research the first Thanksgiving. Pair students with mainstream students and have them interview the mainstream students about their favorite part of Thanksgiving.

- Plan a class Thanksgiving. Ask students if they know the traditional Thanksgiving dishes. Record all the students' answers on the board. Review the list, and ask the class to decide which five or six dishes they would like to have at the class Thanksgiving. (Other dishes can also be added to the list.) Now divide the class into five or six groups. Assign one dish to each group. Have students draw a picture of what the dish is supposed to look like, or bring in cooking magazines and have them cut out pictures of the dish. Students can look through magazines or cookbooks and copy down recipes for the dishes underneath their pictures. When every group has finished, collect all the pictures and organize them into a class Thanksgiving collage.

- Arrange a class "town meeting." Appoint one student to act as the head of the town meeting. Invite other students to raise issues or suggest ideas at the meeting. For example, a student might have a good idea of a new way to arrange the desks, an idea for a new bulletin board project, or a suggestion for rotating class jobs. After each student raises an issue, the other "townspeople" take turns discussing it. If a problem is raised, encourage other students to help come up with possible solutions. After the meeting, groups of students may sit down and write down what happened at the meeting, or a class list can be created on chart paper showing the issues and possible solutions.

- Ask students to imagine they are going to settle a new colony in another part of the world. Tell them they can only bring one large suitcase with them. Have them make a list of the things they would put in the suitcase and explain why they would bring each item. Later, students may read their lists in front of the class.

► LITERATURE

Suggested Books

Molly's Pilgrim
written and illustrated by Barbara Cohen.
Yearling Books, 1983. ISBN 0440410576
Barbara Cohen's story *Molly's Pilgrim* is about a Russian-Jewish girl who emigrates to America with her family. At school, Molly's classmates taunt her constantly about her Old World looks and manners. Molly feels unwelcome and ashamed of her differences until her class studies Thanksgiving and she discovers how her family is much like the early pilgrims. Newcomers to this country certainly will identify with Molly's predicament. This is an entertaining, thoughtful read-aloud that is especially relevant when the topic is introduced near Thanksgiving.

Sarah Morton's Day: A Day in the Life of a Pilgrim Girl
written by Kate Waters; photographs by Russ Kendall.
Scholastic Professional Books, 1993. ISBN 0590474006

Samuel Eaton's Day: A Day in the Life of a Pilgrim Boy
written by Kate Waters; illustrated by Russ Kendall.
Scholastic Professional Books, 1996. ISBN 0590480537
Each of these companion photo-essays recreates a day in the life of a young child in Colonial America during the 1620s. Both stories are told in the first person in an approximation of the spoken language of the time. The photographs endeavor to be as realistic as possible in their evocation of life in Plymouth, Massachusetts. The text is simple enough for beginners to follow with help, and the photos are interesting enough for all students to enjoy. These books are excellent supplements to the topic.

Making Thirteen Colonies (A History of US, Book 2)
by Joy Hakim.
Oxford University Press Children's Books, 1994.
ISBN 0195095073
This second volume of the series *A History of US* (see Topic 19) begins with the founding of Jamestown in 1607 and ends just before the Revolutionary War. Each page of this lively account is filled with period illustrations, maps, and sidebars that can be selected for short reading passages. Often the author invites the readers to imagine themselves in the place of the colonists. These passages are particularly useful for role-playing in class.

Ox-Cart Man
written by Donald Hall; illustrated by Barbara Cooney.
Viking Press, 1983. ISBN 0140504419
This historical fiction, which won the Caldecott Medal and was selected by Reading Rainbow, captures the feeling of life among the early settlers. The story unfolds against the background of the seasons. The numerous compound sentences with high-frequency past tense verbs make this book useful for introducing both compound sentences and the past tense. Many of the content words in this topic and unit can be found in the illustrations.

WORKBOOK: Topic 22

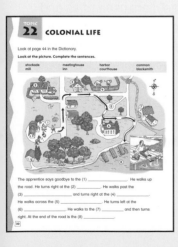

On this page, students follow the path of the apprentice. At each numbered spot on his path, they fill in a word in the paragraph, choosing from the words in the word box.

WORKSHEET: Topic 22

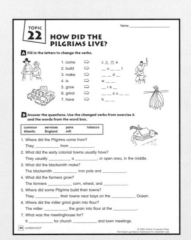

In A, students fill in the missing letters to form the past tense of the words listed. In B, they complete the sentences. For each sentence, they choose one word from the word box, plus one of the verbs they completed in A.

23 THE REVOLUTIONARY WAR

▶ **CONTENT**

The events leading up to and including the Revolutionary War

Weapons used in battle

▶ **LANGUAGE**

Adverbial clauses and phrases of time with *when*, *before*, and *after*: When England charged a tax on tea, the American colonists were angry./After the war, America was a free country.

CONTENT WORDS

1. tea
2. crate
3. disguise
4. tomahawk
5. Paul Revere
6. Old North Church
7. steeple
8. lantern
9. sky
10. battle
11. redcoat
12. Continental soldier
13. minutemen
14. rifle
15. bayonet
16. musket
17. cannon
18. cannonball
19. powder horn
20. load

CONTENT READING

The Revolutionary War

The Boston Tea Party, Paul Revere's Ride, and the Battle of Bunker Hill were three important events of the Revolutionary War.

The Boston Tea Party took place in 1773. When England charged a tax on tea, the American colonists were angry. They didn't want to pay the tax. One night, the colonists put on disguises. They dressed like Mohawk Indians and they carried tomahawks. They went onto the English ships in the harbor. After they broke open the crates, they threw all the tea into the harbor. Then, nobody could buy the tea or pay the tax. The Boston Tea Party led to the Revolutionary War.

Paul Revere made his famous ride in April 1775. A colonist hung two lanterns in the steeple of the Old North Church. This signal in the night sky meant that the British soldiers were coming in ships. When

Revere saw the two lanterns, he rode all night and warned the colonists. The Revolutionary War began the next day.

The Battle of Bunker Hill took place in June 1775. The British soldiers, or redcoats, fought the American minutemen and the Continental soldiers at the Battle of Bunker Hill. The soldiers used rifles and muskets. Some of the rifles had knives, or bayonets, on the end. When the soldiers loaded their weapons with gunpowder, they used powder horns. Before they fired their cannons, they loaded cannonballs. The Battle of Bunker Hill was one of the most important battles of the Revolutionary War.

Before the Revolutionary War, the American colonies were part of England. After the war, America was a free country.

▶ WORDS

Components: Dictionary pages 46-47, Transparency 23, Wall Chart 23, Workbook page 23, Word and Picture Cards Topic 23, Cassette

- Present the content words. **See pages xiv-xvi for general techniques about presenting content words.**

  > **Language Note:** Point out the pronunciation of the letters *le* in words like *steeple*, *battle*, and *rifle*. Ask students to think of other words that end in *le* with this pronunciation such as *little*, *eagle*, *table*, *terrible*, *cattle*, *staple*, *temple*, *shuffle*, *candle*, *simple*, etc.

- Introduce the term *weapon*. Explain to students that a weapon is something people use to attack others with or to defend themselves with. For example, a gun is a type of weapon. Weapons are used in war. Write the word *weapons* on the board. Have the class look at the Dictionary page and tell which words and pictures are weapons. Have one student write each of these words on the board as individual students identify each of the weapons on the page (rifle, bayonet, musket, cannon, and tomahawk). You may need to explain to the class that a cannon is a weapon, but a cannonball is not.

- Divide the class into two teams and play the "Answer and Question" game. Distribute a set of word and picture cards to all the members on each team. Students on each team, in turn, give the answer (the word on their card) and a corresponding student on the other team asks a question about that word. For example, a student from Team 1 holds up the picture card for tea and says *tea*. In response, a student from Team 2 asks *What do we drink?* or *What is a hot drink?* Score one point for each correct answer and question.

- **Game: War.** Make one copy of the word and picture cards for every two students. Pair students and give each pair of students a set of word and picture cards. One student shuffles the cards several times. Then the other student deals the cards. Each student receives ten cards. Students keep their cards secret from their partners. Each student puts a card face-up on the table. If only one student puts a weapon card down, he wins the other student's card. If neither student puts a weapon card down, or if both students put a weapon card down, each student puts a second card on top of the first card. Students continue putting cards down until only one student puts down a weapon card. Then that student wins all the cards on the table. The game continues until one student has won all of the other student's cards.

> **WORKBOOK: Topic 23**
> See Teacher's Book page 93.

▶ CONTENT

Components: Dictionary pages 46-47, Transparency 23, Wall Chart 23, Content Reading Topic 23, Worksheet Topic 23, Cassette

- Present the content reading. **See pages xvii-xix for general techniques about presenting content readings.**

- Ask the following or similar questions:

  Did England charge a tax on tea?
  When was the Boston Tea Party?
  Was America a free country after the war?
  When was Paul Revere's famous ride?
  When was the Battle of Bunker Hill?
  Why were the American colonists angry?

- Write the following sentences on the board:

  America was a free country.
  England started to charge taxes on tea.
  Paul Revere rode all night.
  The American colonists wore disguises.
  Paul Revere saw the lanterns in the steeple of the Old North Church.
  The American colonists threw the tea into the ocean.
  The minutemen and the redcoats fought at the Battle of Bunker Hill.
  They went onto the English ships.

  Tell students that the sentences are not in the correct order. Select two or three students to come to the board and number them in the correct order. Have the rest of the students copy the sentences in their notebooks or on a piece of paper in the correct order. Encourage discussions about the order of events.

- ▶ **Adverbial clauses and phrases of time**

  > Clauses contain a verb (*before he came*). Phrases don't contain a verb (*after dinner*). Adverbial clauses or phrases are used in complex sentences. They begin with a time word (*When, Before, After,* and also *While*) and they depend on the main clause to complete their meaning. For example: *After the war, America was a free country.*

  Point out an adverbial clause or phrase in the content reading and ask students to underline as many clauses or phrases beginning with *when, before*, or *after* as they can find.

- ▶ **Adverbial clauses and phrases of time.** Draw three columns on the board. In column 1, write *Before I go to school....* In column 2, write *When I get to school....* In column 3 write *After school is over....* Students, in turn, finish one of the sentences with an activity that they do before, during, or after school. For example: *I brush my teeth* (column 1), *I see my friends* (column 2), and *I go home and do my homework* (column 3).

> **WORKSHEET: Topic 23**
> See Teacher's Book page 93.

▶ CHANTS

Components: Dictionary pages 46-47, Content Chant Topic 23, Cassette

 CONTENT CHANT

Cannonball, Cannon

Cannonball, cannon
Continental soldier

Redcoat, minuteman
bayonet. Hey!

Load the rifle.
Shoot the rifle.
Fire the cannonball.
Light up the sky!

Cannonball, cannon
Continental soldier

Musket
powder horn
bayonet. Hey!

Pick up the powder horn.
Load the musket.
Shoot the musket.
Light up the sky!

- Present the content chant. **See pages xx-xxi for general techniques about presenting chants.**

- Before distributing the chant, have students practice with chunks of the language from the chant. Establish a four-beat rhythm as students march around the room while chanting. Divide the class into two groups. Group 1 chants *Cannonball, cannon, Continental soldier.* Group 2 chants *Hey, Hey, Hey, Hey.* Both groups keep up the marching rhythm as they chant.

- Distribute Content Chant 23. Divide the class into five groups. Group 1 chants all occurrences of *Cannonball, cannon, Continental soldier* (stanzas 1 and 3). Each of the other four groups chants one of the other stanzas. The entire class chants the word *Hey!* in stanzas 2 and 5. The entire class chants the last line in a triumphant, slightly slower, more deliberate rhythm: *Light - up - the - SKY!*

- Once the class is comfortable with the words of the chant, select individual students to play the roles of the cannon, the bayonet, the rifle, and the musket. When the class chants, these students do not chant the words *cannon, rifle* or *musket.* Instead, each of the four students makes the sound of the weapon when the word appears. The *cannon* student makes the sound of a cannon going off. The *rifle* and the *musket* students take aim and make the sounds of these guns being shot whenever these words appear in the chant.

▶ EXTENSION

Components: Dictionary pages 46-47, Transparency 23, Wall Chart 23

- Pair students. Each student writes half of a sentence on an index card or a piece of paper. The sentence should begin with *When.* Students then exchange cards and finish their partner's sentence. For example, if the first student writes *When my father comes home,* the second student could write *he starts cooking dinner.*

- Write the following phrase on the board: *No taxation without representation.* Explain that the American colonists paid taxes (on tea, sugar, etc.), but they couldn't vote. Ask students if they think this is fair. Talk with students about things that are taxed in your area. Explain different kinds of taxes (property tax, sales tax, income tax, tolls, etc.). Ask students if they think all of these taxes are fair. Why or why not?

- Introduce the concept of a time line. Explain that a time line puts important events in chronological order. Begin a class time line of American history on a long sheet of paper or on the board. (You may want to continue this time line in later topics in this unit.) Write down the date 1773 at the far left end of the time line. Ask students what happened in 1773 (the Boston Tea Party). Make an entry for the Boston Tea Party below 1773 on the time line. Now ask students what happened in 1775. Make two entries for 1775, one for Paul Revere's Ride, and one for the Battle of Bunker Hill. Tell students to copy the time line in their notebooks so that they can refer to it in later topics.

- Divide the class into four groups. Assign the year 1770 to one group, 1771 to the second group, 1772 to the third group, and 1774 to the fourth group. Each group will research what happened in America during those years. Encourage students from each group to look in history books, almanacs, and encyclopedias for things that happened in each year. When each group has finished its research, the group collaborates on one or two entries to add to the class time line. One student reads the entries aloud while another adds them to the time line.

- Tell students to imagine they are minutemen or Continental soldiers at the Battle of Bunker Hill. Ask them to write a letter or postcard to someone back home about their experience. Alternatively, have students imagine they are colonists who wore disguises at the Boston Tea Party and are back home telling their friends and family about what they did.

► LITERATURE

Suggested Books

The Oxford Book of Children's Verse in America
edited by Donald Hall.
Oxford University Press, 1990. ISBN 0195067614
This traditional anthology is a comprehensive collection of poems written for children by American poets. This volume contains poems for every occasion and theme, including several with vocabulary and situations relevant to this topic and Topic 24, A Nation is Born ("John Quincy Adams," "Excelsior," "Tales of a Wayside Inn").

From Colonies to Country (A History of US, Book 3)
by Joy Hakim.
Oxford University Press Children's Books, 1993.
ISBN 0195077504
The third volume of Joy Hakim's award-winning series *A History of US* describes the events leading up to the war for American independence and the war itself. Like the previous volumes in the series, this volume features an engaging storytelling format supplemented by many period illustrations, maps, and sidebars. Interesting facts and stories abound! A Chronology of Events time line is particularly helpful for demonstrating the historical context of this topic. The book's easy-to-use format makes it perfect for the occasional checking of facts and for read-along sessions. Students will benefit from the extensive support that it lends to the Dictionary topic.

Paul Revere's Ride
written by Henry Wadsworth Longfellow;
illustrated by Ted Rand.
Puffin, 1996. ISBN 0140556125
In this book, Henry Wadsworth Longfellow's classic poetic tribute to Revolutionary War hero Paul Revere is accompanied by beautiful paintings that capture the drama of that famous ride. The text of the original poem should not be too difficult for young students, and many of the content words for this topic can be found within it. This more detailed depiction of Paul Revere's midnight ride also usefully extends the Dictionary illustration.

And Then What Happened, Paul Revere?
written by Jean Fritz; illustrated by Margot Tomes.
PaperStar, 1996. ISBN 0698113519
This imaginative retelling of the story of American patriot Paul Revere is a more lighthearted complement to *Paul Revere's Ride*. The informal, often humorous language serves to model language that students can use in their own conversations. The author's detailed treatment of Paul Revere's ride and narrow escape also lends itself to dramatization and role play. This is an excellent biography to read aloud to intermediate and advanced students.

WORKBOOK: Topic 23

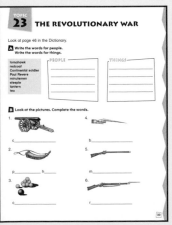

In A, students sort the listed words into two groups by rewriting the words in two new lists, one labeled *People* and the other labeled *Things*. In B, they label the pictures. The first letter of each is given as a clue.

WORKSHEET: Topic 23

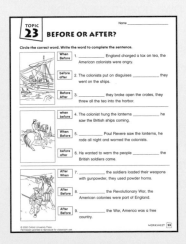

For each picture on this page, there are three sentences. Each sentence is missing the word *before*, *after*, or *when*. Students fill in the correct words, choosing between the two words in each word box.

24 A NATION IS BORN

CONTENT
....
People and events connected with the Declaration of Independence

LANGUAGE
....
Adverbial clauses of purpose with *so (that)*: *They declared independence from England so that the thirteen colonies could form their own government.*

Simple past: *He wrote the Declaration of Independence.*

Roman numerals I–X

CONTENT WORDS

1. Declaration of Independence
2. founding fathers
3. printing press
4. printer
5. pamphlet
6. draw
7. cartoon
8. Benjamin Franklin
9. write
10. quill
11. signature
12. Thomas Jefferson
13. John Adams
14. John Hancock
15. King George III
16. Independence Hall

CONTENT READING

A Nation Is Born

Many important colonists helped the United States become a separate nation. They were called the "founding fathers."

America's founding fathers met in Independence Hall in Philadelphia on July 4, 1776. They declared independence from England so that the thirteen colonies could form their own government. The United States of America was born.

Thomas Jefferson was one of the founding fathers. He wrote the Declaration of Independence. It is one of the most important documents in U.S. history.

John Hancock was another founding father. He wrote his signature at the end of the declaration with a quill pen. Hancock wrote his name in big letters so King George III could read it without his glasses.

Benjamin Franklin and John Adams were founding fathers, too. They also signed the Declaration of Independence. Then, they took it to a printer. The printer printed many copies on a printing press so that a lot of people could read it.

Printers also printed political drawings, cartoons, and pamphlets for the people. Benjamin Franklin drew a famous cartoon of a snake cut into pieces. He wrote the words "Unite or Die" under the picture so that people could understand the importance of becoming one nation.

►WORDS

Components: Dictionary pages 48-49, Transparency 24, Wall Chart 24, Workbook page 24, Word and Picture Cards Topic 24, Cassette

- Present the content words. **See pages xiv-xvi for general techniques about presenting content words.**

- Distribute the word and picture cards. Ask students with word and picture cards showing people to come to the front of the room. Each student, in turn, reads the name on the card and pretends to be that person. Then the student writes his or her new name on the board. The student with the founding father card can stand with the rest of the founding fathers.

- ► **Roman numerals I-X.** Draw two columns on the board. Label one column *Roman Numerals* and list the roman numerals I, II, III, IV, V, VI, VII, VII, IX, X. Label the other column *Arabic Numbers* and list the numbers 1-10. Explain that the Roman numeral III after King George stands for and is spoken as *the Third*. King George I and King George II were the *first* and *second* before him. Ask students what the name of the next King George would be after *King George the Third*. Then, have students practice recognizing the Roman numerals and matching them with the Arabic numbers. Ask students if they know any other people who have III in their names. Explain that in the U.S., it is more common to use *Jr.* for the second person with the same name and not II. Ask students if they know anyone who has Jr. in their name. They might mention Martin Luther King, Jr. or Ken Griffey, Jr.

- Explain the importance of the word *signature*. Tell students that a signature is a very special way to write their own names. When we write our signature or sign something, it means that we promise something, give our word about something, or say that we believe something. A signature is important in legal documents, just like John Hancock's signature on the Declaration of Independence. Tell students that people try to make their signatures unique so that no one can write their names like they can. Have students practice writing their signatures in various ways until they discover a signature that they like. Then collect all the student signatures, redistribute them, and ask students to match the various students with their special signatures.

WORKBOOK: Topic 24
See Teacher's Book page 97.

►CONTENT

Components: Dictionary pages 48-49, Transparency 24, Wall Chart 24, Content Reading Topic 24, Worksheet Topic 24, Cassette

- Present the content reading. **See pages xvii-xix for general techniques about presenting content readings.**

- Ask the following or similar questions:

  Did the founding fathers help the thirteen colonies form their own government?
  When did the founding fathers meet in Independence Hall?
  Who wrote the Declaration of Independence?
  Who were some of the people who signed the Declaration of Independence?
  Why did John Hancock make his signature so large?

- ► **Adverbial clauses of purpose with *so* (*that*)**

  Adverbial clauses with *so* (*that*) are clauses of purpose. They introduce and describe the purpose of an action. For example: *They declared independence from England so that the thirteen colonies could form their own government.* The word *that* is optional and usually not used in conversational English. For example: *He lent me five dollars so I could get a sandwich.*

  Introduce adverbial clauses with *so* (*that*) by writing the following questions on the board:

  Why did the founding fathers declare independence?
  Why did John Hancock write his signature in big letters?
  Why do you go to English class?
  Why do you wear shoes?

  Have students answer the questions using the adverbial clause alone (not a complete sentence): *So (that) King George wouldn't rule the thirteen colonies.* Or, students could use the adverbial clause in a complete sentence: *The founding fathers declared independence so (that) King George wouldn't rule the thirteen colonies.* Then pair students and have them take turns asking and answering *Why* questions with adverbial clauses of purpose. For example: *Why do you wear shoes? So that I won't hurt my feet,* or *I wear shoes so I won't hurt my feet.*

- Ask students to explain in their own words what *Unite or Die* means on Benjamin Franklin's cartoon. Ask what the letters stand for. Show students some current examples of political cartoons. Explain that these cartoons are funny, but their purpose is very serious. Their purpose is to make people aware of political problems. Ask students to draw their own cartoon based on the words *Unite or Die*. Or, have students draw cartoons illustrating slogans they think are important.

WORKSHEET: Topic 24
See Teacher's Book page 97.

► CHANTS

Components: Dictionary pages 48-49, Content Chant Topic 24, Cassette

 ## CONTENT CHANT

Printer, Printing Press

Printer, printing press
Pamphlet, quill
Start the printing press.

    * I will.

Printer, printing press
Pamphlet, quill
Read the pamphlet.

    * I will.

Look at the signature.
    Thomas Jefferson

Look at the signature.
    Benjamin Franklin

Look at the signatures.
    John Hancock
    John Adams

    * We're free!
No more kings, no more queens
Good-bye, George the Third.
We're free!

No more kings, no more queens
Good-bye, George the Third.
We're free!

- Present the content chant. **See pages xx-xxi for general techniques about presenting chants.**

- Before distributing the chant, have students practice with small chunks of the language from the chant. Divide the class into two groups. In a call and response rhythm, Group 1 chants *Look at the signature*; Group 2 chants in response *Thomas Jefferson*. Group 1 chants *Look at the signature* and Group 2 chants *Benjamin Franklin*. Group 1 chants *Look at the signatures* and Group 2 responds *John Hancock, John Adams*. Have the class practice these lines until they are comfortable with the words and the rhythm.

- Distribute Content Chant 24. Keep the same groups as before. Have students pantomime the lines as they chant. This time Group 1 chants all the lines that are flush left and Group 2 chants all the indented response lines. Remember to have students clap where indicated. Then, the entire class loudly chants the last two stanzas beginning with *We're free!* and ending with *We're free!*

► EXTENSION

Components: Dictionary pages 48-49, Transparency 24, Wall Chart 24

- Talk with students about the creation of documents in colonial times and today. How did people create documents in 1776? How do they do it now? How did they make copies in 1776? How do they do it now? Where did people get information in 1776? Where do they get information now?

- Write the following date on the board: July 4, 1776. Ask students if they notice anything important about that date. Show them another way of writing the date: 7/4/76. Explain that in the United States, unlike the rest of the world, people write the month before the date followed by the year. Introduce the abbreviations for the months: Jan., Feb., Mar., Apr., May, June, July, Aug., Sept., Oct., Nov., Dec.

- Pair students. Each student writes a date in day/month/year format on one side of a card. Students then exchange cards and write the date out in long form on the other side of the card. Students then exchange cards again and check to see that their partners wrote the correct long form version of the date.

- Explain that a time line puts important events in chronological order. (See Extension, Topic 23 for information about how to begin a time line, or continue your time line from previous topics.) Write down the date 1776 at the left end of the time line, or to the right of the other dates already on the time line. Ask students what happened in 1776. Make an entry for 1776 listing the students' responses. Tell students to copy the time line in their notebooks so that they can refer to it in later topics.

- Ask students to research the important people in their own countries' histories. They may ask their parents, look up information in textbooks, or use the Internet. Some students may be able to write a short history of how their country started. Students can read their histories to the entire class.

► LITERATURE

Suggested Books

The New Nation (A History of US, Book 4)
by Joy Hakim.
Oxford University Press Children's Books, 1994.
ISBN 0195077520
This volume in *A History of US* covers the period from Washington's inauguration through the first half century of the United States. The chronology, bibliography, and index make this a useful teaching reference. The many photographs, maps, and illustrations provide additional content support for students. Advanced students can transfer much of the information gathered here to their mainstream history units.

Will You Sign Here, John Hancock?
written by Jean Fritz; illustrated by Trina Hyman and Margot Tomes.
PaperStar, 1997. ISBN 069811440X
Jean Fritz has an inimitable way of conveying events in an amusing, interesting, and historically accurate fashion. True-to-form, *Will You Sign Here, John Hancock?* is an entertaining life story of the man most famous for his signature on the Declaration of Independence. (A whole page is devoted to explaining the signature seen in the Dictionary illustration.) Many of the colloquialisms in the storytelling can enrich student understanding of English, although some guidance may be necessary.

A More Perfect Union: The Story of Our Constitution
written by Betsy Maestro; illustrated by Giulio Maestro.
Lothrop Lee & Shepard, 1987. ISBN 0688068405
A More Perfect Union is the story of the founding fathers and what they accomplished at Independence Hall: the drafting and ratification of the U.S. Constitution. Many of the illustrations in this book have a one-to-one correspondence to what students see in the Dictionary illustration. This book also can be used with Topic 28, U.S. Government.

A Picture Book of Benjamin Franklin
written and illustrated by David A. Adler, John Wallner, and Alexandra Wallner.
Holiday House, 1991. ISBN 0823408825
In this book from David Adler's series of picture-book biographies, the author condenses a famous life into clear prose without sacrificing information or readability. The book functions like a low-level reader, but still retains a high interest level for older students. There are only a few lines of text per page. A chronology is included for summary and review.

WORKBOOK: Topic 24

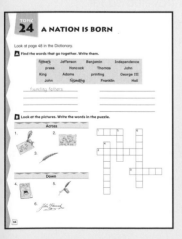

In A, students look through the group of words to find pairs of words that make full names or compound words. Then, they write these words on the spaces provided. In B, they complete the crossword puzzle using the picture clues.

WORKSHEET: Topic 24

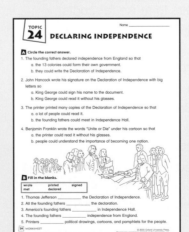

In A, students choose the best answer to complete each sentence, based on their knowledge of the content reading. In B, they choose words from the word box to fill in the blanks in each sentence.

▶ **CONTENT**
....
Pioneer life during the period of westward expansion

▶ **LANGUAGE**
....
Adverbial clauses of reason with *because*: *Many wagons traveled together in wagon trains because it was safer that way.*

Prepositions of place (*across, along, through, onto, into, on, in, under, over, by*): *The pioneers drove the wagons along trails and over mountain passes.*

Compound words: *They rode on flatboats, steamboats, rafts, and canoes on rivers and canals.*

 CONTENT WORDS

1. flatboat
2. steamboat
3. raft
4. canoe
5. canal
6. pioneer
7. wagon train
8. covered wagon
9. oxen
10. pass
11. trail
12. supplies
13. barrel
14. journal
15. homestead
16. cabin
17. stagecoach
18. campsite
19. trapper
20. pelt

Westward Expansion

 CONTENT READING

Westward Expansion

Many Americans moved across the country between 1770 and 1853. They wanted to go west because the West had a lot of land and very few people.

Hunters and trappers went west. They trapped animals like bears, beavers, and foxes because they could sell the animals' pelts to make fur coats. Hunters and trappers didn't build many houses because they didn't stay in one place for very long. They usually slept in campsites under the stars.

The pioneers followed the trappers. They went west with their families. Some pioneers traveled by water. They rode on flatboats, steamboats, rafts, and canoes on rivers and canals.

Other pioneers traveled by land. They put all their supplies into boxes and barrels. They put them onto stagecoaches and covered wagons. Horses and oxen pulled the wagons. The pioneers drove the wagons along trails and over mountain passes. Many wagons traveled together in wagon trains because it was safer that way.

The first pioneers built cabins, barns, and fences. They were proud of their new homesteads because they had worked so hard and traveled so far.

The pioneers' lives were hard and dangerous. Many of the pioneers wrote their thoughts and stories in journals. Today, we can read their journals and learn about pioneer life.

▶ WORDS

Components: Dictionary pages 50-51, Transparency 25, Wall Chart 25, Workbook page 25, Word and Picture Cards Topic 25, Cassette

- Present the content words. **See pages xiv-xvi for general techniques about presenting content words.**

- If students don't already know the meaning of the words *north, south, east,* and *west,* write the words on the board and indicate their directions. Assemble all students at one end of the classroom (preferably the east end). Distribute the word and picture cards that show forms of transportation (*flatboat, steamboat, raft, canoe, wagon train, covered wagon, oxen,* and *stagecoach*) so that half the students have word cards and the other half have the matching picture cards. Students compare cards with their neighbors and each student forms a pair with the student who has the matching card. When a match is made, the pair makes the "trip" across the classroom from east to west. Ask each pair to name the form of transportation they used to go west.

- Continue the above game. When all students have reached the other side of the classroom, distribute the word and picture cards showing food or shelter (*supplies, barrel, homestead, cabin, campsite*). Have students again compare their cards to make pairs. Help the students in each pair to form sentences or phrases about their food or shelter. For example: *We put our supplies on the stagecoach. We built a cabin.*

- Divide the class into two teams. Put the following word and picture cards in a bag or box so that students can't see them: *canal, flatboat, steamboat, oxen, raft, canoe, wagon train, covered wagon, pass, trail,* and *stagecoach.* A student from Team 1 asks a student from Team 2, *How did you come?* The Team 2 student picks a word and picture card from the box and, depending on the card, says *I came by land* or *I came by water.* Then the student shows Team 1 the card. If the response is correct, Team 2 gets a point. Otherwise, Team 1 gets a point. Then, a student from Team 2 gets a turn to ask the question. Continue the game until all students have asked or answered the question.

- ▶ **Compound words.** (See also Topic 22, page 86.) Point out the compound words *flatboat, steamboat, stagecoach, campsite, wagon train,* and *covered wagon.* Ask students to write each part of the compound word on separate index cards. Then have them find the matching half from among their classmates.

> **WORKBOOK: Topic 25**
> See Teacher's Book page 101.

▶ CONTENT

Components: Dictionary pages 50-51, Transparency 25, Wall Chart 25, Content Reading Topic 25, Worksheet Topic 25, Cassette

- Present the content reading. **See pages xvii-xix for general techniques about presenting content readings.**

- Ask the following or similar questions:

  Did the pioneers follow the trappers?
  Were the lives of the pioneers hard?
  When was westward expansion in the United States?
  How did the pioneers travel?
  What did the hunters and trappers do with the animal pelts?
  How can we learn more about the pioneer's lives?

- Ask students what the dates and lines in the map on the wall chart mean. Explain that in 1770, the United States ended at the first line from the right. In 1803, the United States ended at the second line from the right. And, in 1853, the United States reached from the Atlantic to the Pacific Ocean. Ask students about the people who lived in the areas on the map before those areas became part of the United States. Refer to Topic 19 for more information about who settled these areas long before the pioneers came.

- ▶ **Adverbial clauses of reason with *because***

  > Adverbial clauses of reason tell the reason for an action or a situation in the main clause. These clauses answer the question *Why* about the main clause.

  Ask students *Why* questions about the content reading. For example: *Why did hunters and trappers trap animals?* Have students answer the questions using either adverbial clauses of reason alone (*Because they could sell the animals' pelts to make fur coats*) or in complete sentences (*The hunters and trappers trapped animals because they could sell the animals' pelts to make fur coats*). After reviewing these types of questions in the content reading, pair students and have them ask and answer questions like this about their lives. For example: *Why did you bring an umbrella today? I brought an umbrella because it's raining,* or *Because it's raining.*

- ▶ **Prepositions of place.** Divide the class into two teams. Students have ten minutes to write as many sentences as possible about the content reading using prepositions. For example: *The pioneers rode <u>in</u> canoes. They rode <u>on</u> flatboats. They rode <u>over</u> mountains.* Students read their sentences to the class. The team with the most sentences using prepositions correctly is the winner.

> **WORKSHEET: Topic 25**
> See Teacher's Book page 101.

► CHANTS

Components: Dictionary pages 50-51, Content Chant Topic 25, Cassette

CONTENT CHANT

Pioneers, Packing Up

Pioneers
packing up,
moving west,
following a dream.

> How did they come?

They came by water:
>> flatboat,
>> steamboat,
>> raft, canoe.

> How did they come?

They came by land:
>> stagecoach,
>> wagon train,
>> covered wagon.

Pioneers,
they came by land.
Pioneers,
they came by sea.
Pioneers,
moving west.
Pioneers,
following a dream.

- Present the content chant. **See pages xx-xxi for general techniques about presenting chants.**
- Before distributing the chant, have students practice with small chunks of the language from the chant. Divide the class into two groups. Group 1 chants *They came by water: flatboat, steamboat, raft, canoe.* They pantomime traveling west by water. Group 2 chants *They came by land: stagecoach, wagon train, covered wagon* as they pantomime traveling west by land.
- Distribute Content Chant 25. Divide the class into three groups. Group 1 chants all of the stanzas that are not indented. Group 2 chants the question *How did they come?* Group 3 repeatedly chants quietly in a steady undertone, *Pioneers, packing up.* Have all students pantomime the words as they chant.
- This chant can also be read as a poem. Select individual students to read each line. For example:

Student A: Pioneers

Student B: packing up,

Student C: moving west,

Student D: following a dream.

► EXTENSION

Components: Dictionary pages 50-51, Transparency 25, Wall Chart 25

- Draw a large map of the United States on the board. Copy the dates and boundaries to create three sections as shown in the wall chart. Divide the class into three groups, one for each section of the map. Have them write the names of all the states in their section on the map. Encourage them to use atlases, wall maps, or the map of the U.S. in Topic 10 for reference.
- Keep the same groups as in the above activity. Explain that some pieces of land were parts of the U.S., but did not become states until much later. For example, South Dakota was U.S. land by 1803, but it did not become a state until 1889. Ask each group to research the date when each state officially became part of the United States. Have each group write the date next to each state on their section of the map. Date information should be available in encyclopedias, almanacs, in other general reference books, and on the Internet.
- Explain that a time line puts important events in chronological order. (See Extension, Topic 23 for information about how to begin a time line, or continue your time line from previous topics.) Write down the date 1787 at the left end of the time line (or to the right of the other dates already on the time line). Have each group enter on the time line statehood dates for the states in the group's section. Have each student in the group enter at least one date. If more than one state entered the union in the same year (for example, 1787, 1788, 1959), make one entry listing all the states that joined the U.S. that year.
- Have students imagine they are pioneers writing in their journals about a trip west. Ask them to write a short entry for every day of their journey, which may last up to a month. They may choose to travel by land or by water.
- Talk with students about forms of transportation during the period of westward expansion and in modern times. How did people go across the country then and how do they go now? How long did a journey take in those times, and how long does it take now? Would they prefer to travel during the period of westward expansion or today? What is the longest journey they have ever taken? How did they travel?
- Ask students to talk about pioneers in their own families. Who were the first people in their families to come to a new land? When did they do it? What was life like for them? Students write and illustrate their stories and then present them to the entire class.

► LITERATURE

Suggested Books

Trouble for Lucy

written by Carla Stevens; illustrated by Ronald Himler.
Houghton Mifflin Company, 1987. ISBN 0899195237
Based on the records of pioneers who traveled the Oregon Trail in 1843, this short, easy-to-read book enables students to understand what the journey westward was like for a young girl. The story documents Lucy's experiences and feelings as she travels west with her family. Lucy's feelings may resonate with newcomers to this country, or anyone who has made a similar trip to a new home. This book adds depth and content to the topic's illustration.

The Sweetwater Run: The Story of Buffalo Bill Cody and the Pony Express

written and illustrated by Andrew Glass.
Yearling, 1998. ISBN 0440411866
This book skillfully blends fact and fiction to tell the tale of the teenage Buffalo Bill Cody, who gets his first opportunity to deliver a message for the Pony Express. The story is told as the first person reminiscence of the older Buffalo Bill, who is looking back on this pivotal moment of his life. The book's structure gives students the opportunity to study sequence and the use of past tense. Students can also predict what the story will be about after a first look at the dramatic western-style illustrations. Teachers can then read the story aloud and compare and contrast the students' predictions with the actual content. An illustrated map of the Pony Express route and biographical facts add further context to the subject.

Wagon Wheels

written by Barbara Brenner; illustrated by Don Bolognese.
HarperTrophy, 1995. ISBN 0064440524
This "I Can Read Book" tells the story of a widowed African-American man and his sons who leave the South to settle in the West on land offered by the Homestead Act of 1862. This period of American migration is probably unfamiliar to many second-language students, but many students may identify with characters who have chosen to uproot themselves in search of a better life. Teachers may want to read this book aloud in sections, stopping occasionally to review the action and themes, and to relate them to the Dictionary illustration. This book is recommended primarily for intermediate and advanced students.

The Amazing, Impossible Erie Canal

written and illustrated by Cheryl Harness.
Simon & Schuster Books for Young Readers, 1995. ISBN 02742616
The ground was broken for the Erie Canal on July 4, 1817. By 1825, the Atlantic Ocean would be linked by water to Lake Erie. Many historians attribute the beginning of westward expansion to this development. In this informative book, the author weds historical information about the planning and construction of the canal with maps and illustrations that convey what this "amazing" event was like, especially for small town Americans. Students should be able to spot many of the topic's content words in the text and pictures.

WORKBOOK: Topic 25

For each word in A, there are two picture choices. Students circle the correct picture. In B, they write the words to label the pictures. The first letter for each is given.

WORKSHEET: Topic 25

The wagon wheel on this page contains eight sentences. Using *because* (shown in the center of the wheel), the sentences can be combined to make four longer sentences from the content reading. Students write the four new sentences on the spaces provided.

▶ **CONTENT**
....
The lives of the people who migrated west during the California gold rush of 1848

▶ **LANGUAGE**
....
Direct object gerunds (verb + gerund): *The headlines started appearing in the New York papers in 1848: "Gold!"*

CONTENT WORDS

1. gold
2. Sutter's Mill
3. prospector
4. pan
5. dig
6. dirt
7. shovel
8. pick
9. tent
10. hammer
11. nail
12. Levi Strauss
13. mule
14. clipper ship
15. across
16. around

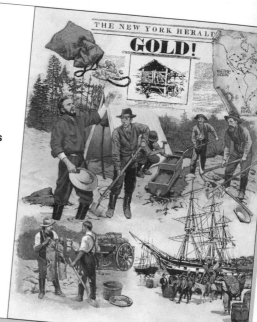

 ## CONTENT READING

The Gold Rush

The headlines started appearing in the New York papers in 1848: "Gold!" Prospectors were digging in the dirt with shovels and picks at Sutter's Mill in California, and they were finding big pieces of gold.

Soon, a lot of people began dreaming of gold. They started traveling to California. Some people rode across the country in wagons or stagecoaches. Other people sailed on clipper ships around the tip of South America.

In California, the prospectors bought a piece of land and some mules and started looking for gold. After they put up their tents they began digging in the dirt and panning in the streams for gold. Some people found gold in their pans. Some didn't. But more and more prospectors kept coming.

Soon, there were a lot of people in California. Some people got rich from gold. Others got rich from selling supplies, like hammers and nails, to the prospectors. Traders like Levi Strauss started selling clothes to gold diggers. Levi Strauss made and sold the first pair of jeans. His jeans were stronger than other pants. They lasted longer. The prospectors began wearing Levi's jeans. People all over the world wear them now.

▶ WORDS

Components: Dictionary pages 52-53, Transparency 26, Wall Chart 26, Workbook page 26, Word and Picture Cards Topic 26, Cassette

- Present the content words. **See pages xiv-xvi for general techniques about presenting content words.**

   Language Note: Explain that the content word *pan* is shown as a noun (a naming word) in the Dictionary, but it can also be a verb (an action word). A pan is a container, usually made of metal, for holding liquids or for cooking. *Panning* means washing something (usually gravel) in a pan in order to find gold or another metal in the gravel. Many prospectors panned for gold during the gold rush.

- Write the word *metal* on the board. Explain that most metals are shiny. Tell students that gold, silver, aluminum, tin, and copper are different kinds of metal. Ask students to identify classroom objects containing various metals. For example, parts of desks and doors may be made of metal. Now ask students to name the content words that name objects with metal in them. Record correct answers on the board: *gold, pan, shovel, pick, hammer, nail, clipper ship.*

- Ask students what the most valuable substance is. They may say gold, silver, or diamonds. Ask them questions such as *Why is gold so valuable? Can you find gold everywhere?* Ask them to name some things made of gold. List the items on the board. Display or point to several other items that are made of gold or gold-plated. Have students name the items.

- Write the word *Tools* on the board. Explain that tools are objects people use to help them work. Ask students to name those content words that are tools. List students' answers on the board. *Shovel, pick, hammer,* and *nail* are all tools. Next to the word *Tools,* write the word *Uses.* Now ask students if they know what you use each tool for. Write correct answers next to each tool. For example: *You use a shovel to dig.*

- Explain that a mule is the offspring of a male donkey and a female horse. Mules are smaller than horses. They can pull heavy wagons, but they can't run as fast as horses. Ask students to think of situations when they might use a mule and situations when they might use a horse.

WORKBOOK: Topic 26
See Teacher's Book page 105.

▶ CONTENT

Components: Dictionary pages 52-53, Transparency 26, Wall Chart 26, Content Reading Topic 26, Worksheet Topic 26, Cassette

- Present the content reading. **See pages xvii-xix for general techniques about presenting content readings.**

- Ask the following or similar questions:

   Were prospectors looking for gold?
   Did anyone get rich from gold?
   When did the gold rush start?
   Why did people start traveling to California?
   What did people do to try to find gold?
   Who made and sold the first pair of jeans?

   Content Note: The California football team the "San Francisco 49ers" is named for the thousands of people who came to San Francisco in 1849 during the gold rush.

▶ **Direct object gerunds (verb + gerund)**

   A gerund is a verb form [verb + *-ing*] that is used in place of a noun or pronoun to name a situation or an action. Sometimes a gerund can be the direct object in a sentence. Direct object gerunds follow the main verb in a sentence. For example: *Soon a lot of people began dreaming of gold.*

Introduce direct object gerunds by pointing out the first sentence in the content reading: *The headlines started appearing in the New York papers in 1848: "Gold!"* Ask students to look for sentences in the reading that follow the pattern of verb + gerund. Students underline the verbs *started, began,* or *kept* and circle the direct object gerund following each verb (*appearing, dreaming, traveling,* etc.). Students then exchange their papers with their neighbors, who check to see if they have found all the sentences.

▶ **Direct object gerunds (verb + gerund).** Divide the class into two teams. A student from Team 1 pantomimes an activity, then stops and does nothing for a few seconds, and then pantomimes a different activity. A student from Team 2 describes these actions using direct object gerunds. For example, if the Student from Team 1 pantomimes eating, then stops, and then pantomimes dancing, the student from Team 2 says, *He started eating. Then he stopped eating. Then he started dancing.* Continue until all students from both teams have had a turn to pantomime and describe.

WORKSHEET: Topic 26
See Teacher's Book page 105.

► CHANTS

Components: Dictionary pages 52-53, Content Chant Topic 26, Cassette

 ## CONTENT CHANT

California Gold

Sail on a clipper ship.
Ride on a mule.
Go to California.
Look for gold.

Go to California,
Northern California.
Pick up a shovel.
Dig for gold.

Go to California.
Walk to a stream.
Pick up a pan.
Pan for gold.

Sail on a clipper ship.
Ride on a mule.
Go to California.
Look for gold!

- Present the content chant. **See pages xx-xxi for general techniques about presenting chants.**

- Before distributing the chant, have students practice with small chunks of the language from the chant. Have the entire class chant the lines *Look for gold*, *Dig for gold*, and *Pan for gold*. Then divide the class into three groups, with each group chanting one of these lines, first in turn, and then simultaneously.

- Distribute Content Chant 26. Divide the class into four groups, with each group chanting one stanza. The entire class should join in for the last line of each stanza. Encourage students to pantomime the actions of their stanza as they chant. Another variation is to have five groups, with the first four groups chanting one stanza each and the fifth group chanting softly and repeatedly *Look for gold* underneath the stanzas.

- Once students are comfortable with the rhythm of the chant, invite them to make up their own four-line verses, ending with the line *Look for gold*. For example: *Go across the country. Sleep in a tent. Buy some jeans. Look for gold.*

► EXTENSION

Components: Dictionary pages 52-53, Transparency 26, Wall Chart 26

- Bring in a copy of a newspaper, but paste a new headline across the top that says: *Prospectors Find Gold in _____* (fill in the name of a state that's far from your class). Ask students what they would do. Would they go there and dig for gold? Would they sleep in a tent? Would they try to sell tools to the prospectors?

- Have students act out a scene about looking for gold. Select one student to be the prospector. This person leaves the classroom. Choose another student to be a piece of gold. That person sits at the back of the room. Choose other students to be different obstacles in the prospector's way. For example, various students might pretend to be a big log, a very deep hole, a big rock, a river, a lake, or an angry bear. All the students playing obstacles sit between the piece of gold and the front of the classroom. Now invite the prospector back in. Point out that there is a piece of gold in the classroom (indicate the student at the back of the room), but that there are many obstacles on the way. As the prospector goes up to each student playing an obstacle, the student identifies and pantomimes the obstacle, and the prospector tells how he or she will get around it. For example, a student might block the prospector's path and say: *I'm a big log*. The prospector might say, *I'm going around the big log* and walk around the obstacle. When gold is finally found, the prospector can say *Gold! I found gold!*

- Explain that a time line puts important events in chronological order. (See Extension, Topic 23 for information about how to begin a time line, or continue your time line from previous topics.) Write down the date 1848 at the left end of the time line (or to the right of the other dates already on the time line). Have students write an entry for "Gold at Sutter's Mill" for the year 1848. Have them research in history books, almanacs, or encyclopedias things that occurred in 1849, 1850, and 1851. If an important event occurred in those years, students may write time line entries for each of those years.

- Ask students if they are wearing Levi's jeans. If any students are, ask them why they wear Levi's jeans. If they are wearing other kinds of jeans, ask them why they are wearing that brand. Ask questions like the following: *Why do you like to wear jeans? Are jeans stronger than other pants? Are they more comfortable? What do you think people wore before jeans?*

► LITERATURE

Suggested Books

Liberty for All? (A History of US, Book Five)
by Joy Hakim.
Oxford University Press Children's Books, 1994.
ISBN 0195077547
This fifth volume of *A History of US* focuses on American life immediately preceding the Civil War. (See Topics 19, 22, 23, and 24 for descriptions of other books in the series.) The section on the gold rush provides valuable primary source material (photographs, maps, period art) that is a useful supplement to the Dictionary illustration and teaching notes. The writing is suitable primarily for more advanced students, but much of it can be paraphrased for beginners when discussing the illustrations. Sections of this volume may also be used with Topic 21, The Spanish Missions, and Topic 25, Westward Expansion.

The California Gold Rush: West with the Forty-Niners
by Elizabeth Van Steenwyk.
Franklin Watts, Inc., 1991. ISBN 0531200329
Except for the Civil War, the gold rush may have been the greatest cause of change in America during the mid-to-late 19th Century. This chapter book unfolds both the drama and history of America's rush to the hills of California. Chapter 3, "Life in the Diggings," is an especially good complement to the Dictionary illustration of the prospector panning, cradling, and mining gold. Many of the book's illustrations are rich in examples of the topic's content words.

Chang's Paper Pony
written by Eleanor B. Coerr; illustrated by Carolyn Croll and Deborah Ray.
HarperCollins Children's Books, 1993. ISBN 0064441636
Many thousands of Chinese immigrants came to America between 1850 and 1864. Some of them became workers for the miners who went west seeking gold. Young Chang is one of these immigrants. This easy-reader tells how he earned a pony panning for gold with his friend Big Pete. This book works well when read aloud, but it can also be read independently since it is composed of short, simple sentences. Chinese-speaking ESL students who are unfamiliar with the role of Chinese immigrants in the gold rush may especially appreciate this book's insight into the topic.

WORKBOOK: Topic 26

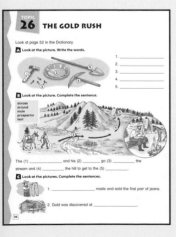

In A, students write the words for each numbered portion of the picture. In B, they trace the path of the prospector and choose words from the word box to fill in the word for each numbered point on the path. In C, they complete the sentences based on the pictures.

WORKSHEET: Topic 26

In A, students read the sentences and draw two routes on the map to show how people traveled to California for gold. In B, they unscramble the sentences. In C, they write their own sentences about the gold rush. For each sentence, they choose one word from each word box.

▶ **CONTENT**

People and events of the Civil War

▶ **LANGUAGE**

Simple past: *They wore blue uniforms.*

Emphatic *own* (possessive adjective + *own*): *They created their own government, elected their own president, and made their own flag.*

Appositives: *The U.S. President, Abraham Lincoln, wanted to keep the southern states in the Union.*

CONTENT WORDS

1. Union
2. Yankee
3. Confederacy
4. Rebel
5. Abraham Lincoln
6. Emancipation Proclamation
7. slave
8. flag
9. knapsack
10. canteen
11. ammunition
12. uniform
13. cemetery
14. surrender
15. Ulysses S. Grant
16. Robert E. Lee

BULL RUN 1861
GETTYSBURG 1863
APPOMATTOX 1865

CONTENT READING

The Civil War

The Civil War was one of the most important events in American history. It divided the United States.

Before 1860, all the states were in the Union. But in 1860, eleven states in the South left the Union and started a new country. They called it the Confederacy. They created their own government, elected their own president, and made their own flag.

The states in the North didn't want to divide the country. The U.S. President, Abraham Lincoln, wanted to keep the southern states in the Union. He wanted to keep the country together. So, the Union and the Confederacy went to war.

The soldiers wore uniforms. They carried knapsacks and canteens. They had ammunition for their weapons, too. The Union's soldiers were the Yankees. They wore blue uniforms. The Confederacy's soldiers were the Rebels. They wore gray uniforms.

The first big battle of the Civil War was Bull Run in 1861. The Rebels won. They also won many other early battles.

In January 1863, Abraham Lincoln wrote the Emancipation Proclamation. It declared freedom for the slaves in the rebellious states. Many people in the Confederacy had slaves. They didn't like Lincoln's proclamation.

The Yankees won a big battle at Gettysburg in July 1863. They fought part of this battle in a cemetery. The Union won more battles after that. In 1865, the Rebel general, Robert E. Lee, surrendered to the Union general, Ulysses S. Grant, at Appomattox Courthouse. The war was over. The United States was one country again.

► WORDS

Components: Dictionary pages 54-55, Transparency 27, Wall Chart 27, Workbook page 27, Word and Picture Cards Topic 27, Cassette

- Present the content words. **See pages xiv-xvi for general techniques about presenting content words.**

   Language Note: Explain that the word *surrender* means to give up, or to agree to stop fighting. Ask students if they think it is okay to surrender. If they were in a war, would they want to surrender?

   Content Note: The Civil War is also referred to as "the War Between the States."

   Explain that *slaves* were people who were considered property of another person or household. Slaves were forced to work for no money and to obey their owners and do whatever their owners wanted them to do. A slave is not a free person. Abraham Lincoln freed the slaves in the South.

- Make two columns on the board. Label one column *People*. Label the other column *Not People*. Now distribute the word and picture cards. Have each student read a card and say whether it is a person or not a person. Then each student writes the word in the correct column on the board. The *People* column should contain the words *Yankee, Rebel, Abraham Lincoln, slave, Ulysses S. Grant,* and *Robert E. Lee.*

- Talk to students about uniforms. Ask them what a uniform is. Ask them why people wear uniforms. Perhaps your school has a uniform. Ask them who else wears uniforms: sports teams, waiters, nurses, mailmen, etc. Ask them if their parents have to wear uniforms at their jobs.

- Ask students if they know who Abraham Lincoln is and if they know where they have seen his picture before. Display a penny and have students look at their own pennies, if they have some. Ask students to tell you whose face is on the penny. Now, display a five dollar bill and ask students to say whose picture is on this bill. Ask students why they think Lincoln is on the penny and the five dollar bill.

WORKBOOK: Topic 27
See Teacher's Book page 109.

► CONTENT

Components: Dictionary pages 54-55, Transparency 27, Wall Chart 27, Content Reading Topic 27, Worksheet Topic 27, Cassette

- Present the content reading. **See pages xvii-xix for general techniques about presenting content readings.**

- Ask the following or similar questions:

   When did the Southern states start the Confederacy?
   Did Abraham Lincoln want to divide the country?
   Who won the battle at Bull Run?
   Who surrendered at Appomattox Courthouse?
   What did the Emancipation Proclamation do?
   Did people in the Confederacy like the Emancipation Proclamation? Why or why not?

- Write the seven sentences below in a list. Have students rewrite them in the correct sequence in their notebooks. Have one student work at the board. Encourage the class to discuss any disputes.

   Eleven states in the South started the Confederacy.
   Abraham Lincoln freed the slaves.
   The Rebels and the Yankees started a war.
   The Yankees won at Gettysburg.
   Robert E. Lee surrendered at Appomattox.
   All the states were in the Union.
   The Rebels won at Bull Run.

- Make a comparison chart like the example below. Have groups copy the chart and use it to compare the Union and the Confederacy with regard to their regions, the color of their uniforms, their famous generals, and how they referred to their soldiers, their flags, and the war. Have each group present its information to the class.

Union	Confederacy
Their Regions	
The Color of Their Uniforms	

► Emphatic *own*

We use [possessive adjective + *own*] to make the ownership stated by the possessive adjective more emphatic. For example: *They created their own government.* Possessive adjectives in English are *my, his, her, its, their, our, your.*

Introduce possessive adjectives with *own*. Model the sentence from the reading. Then write the following sentence on the board: *Every soldier had his own uniform, knapsack, and canteen.* Now ask students to write and illustrate sentences about things that belong only to them or only to someone in their family. For example: *I have my own bike. My mother has her own car.* Have students present their sentences and their drawings to the class.

WORKSHEET: Topic 27
See Teacher's Book page 109.

► CHANTS

Components: Dictionary pages 54-55, Content Chant Topic 27, Cassette

CONTENT CHANT

Civil War, A Nation Divided

Civil War,
a nation divided.
North against South,
Civil War.

Yankees against Rebels,
blue against gray.
Brother fought brother,
Civil War.

Who won the war?
    The North won the war.

Who lost the war?
    The South lost the war.

Mothers lost sons,
sisters lost brothers,
children lost fathers,
in the Civil War.

    "A house divided
    against itself"
A nation divided
by the Civil War.

- Present the content chant. **See pages xx-xxi for general techniques about presenting chants.**

- Before presenting the chant, explain the two meanings of *lose* in the chant. In the first case, it means to fail to win a war or contest. In the second case, it means the death of loved ones. Ask students if they know any other meanings of the word "lose."

- Explain that the words *A house divided against itself* means that the country was split in half. The nation was fighting itself. Divide the class into two groups. Group 1 chants *A house divided against itself* and Group 2 chants *A nation divided by the Civil War.* Have the groups chant individually and then simultaneously until they are comfortable with the words.

    Content Note: The line in the chant comes from a quote by President Lincoln: "A house divided against itself cannot stand."

- Distribute Content Chant 27. Divide the class into two teams, North and South. The entire class chants the entire chant, except that only the North team chants when the words *North, Yankee,* or *blue* appear in the chant; only the South team chants when the words *South, Rebel,* or *gray* appear in the chant.

► EXTENSION

Components: Dictionary pages 54-55, Transparency 27, Wall Chart 27

- Draw this Venn diagram:

Divide the class into two teams. A student from Team 1 names a U.S. state. A student from Team 2 says whether that state was in the Union, the Confederacy, or not a state at the time of the Civil War (such as Nevada, Oklahoma, or Alaska). The student from Team 2 then writes the abbreviated name of the state in the appropriate part of the Venn diagram. Then, the teams switch roles. For help with state abbreviations, refer students to Topic 10, The United States.

- Bring in examples of the U.S. flag and of the Confederate flag (either actual flags or colored pictures from encyclopedias or textbooks). Ask students if they know what the stars and stripes mean on each flag. Explain that the 13 stripes on the U.S. flag stand for the original 13 U.S. colonies, and the 50 stars stand for the 50 states in the U.S. today. Explain that there were fewer stars on the U.S. flag during the Civil War. The 11 stars on the Confederate flag stand for the 11 states of the Confederacy. Ask students to draw the flags from their countries. If they know what the different colors, shapes, and symbols on their flags mean, they may also explain this information.

- Explain that a time line puts important events in chronological order. (See Extension, Topic 23 for information about how to begin a time line, or continue your time line from previous topics.) Write down the date 1861 at the left end of the time line (or to the right of the other dates already on the time line). Have students write an entry for the beginning of the Civil War in 1860, Bull Run in 1861, Gettysburg in 1863, and Appomattox and the end of the Civil War in 1865. Then divide the class into two groups. One group prepares a time line entry for 1862; the other group prepares a time line entry for 1864. Each group can research their year in history books, almanacs, or encyclopedias.

- If there are any students in your class from countries that have had more recent civil wars, invite them to talk about their experiences with the class, if they feel comfortable.

- Ask students if they notice anything about the people—sons, brothers, and fathers—who were "lost" in the Civil War. They were all men. Ask students why that was. Do they think women should also fight in wars? Why or why not?

► LITERATURE

Suggested Books

The Drinking Gourd: A Story of the Underground Railroad
written by F. N. Monjo; illustrated by Fred Brenner.
HarperCollins Children's Books, 1993. ISBN 0064440427
This suspenseful book follows a boy named Tommy and his family on the Underground Railroad as they help a fugitive slave family reach freedom. The simple dialogue is suitable for reading aloud and dramatization, and the full-color illustrations (revised from the original 1970 edition) can be used to invent new dialogue or stories.

Lincoln: A Photobiography
by Russell Freedman.
Clarion Books, 1989. ISBN 0395518482
This Newberry Medal winner surveys the life of one of the most important men in American history, Abraham Lincoln, through an entertaining mix of photographs, prints, and commentary. Because the text is slightly demanding, teachers may wish to divide the class into cooperative learning groups when presenting the material. Fortunately, the many vivid photographs will help students to decode the story. This book is an excellent elaboration of the topic and will give students a better idea of Lincoln's role not only in the Civil War, but also in 19th Century American history.

War, Terrible War (A History of US, Book Six)
by Joy Hakim.
Oxford University Press Children's Books, 1994.
ISBN 0195077563
The "terrible war" referred to in the title of this sixth volume of *A History of US* is the Civil War. This volume of the popular history series depicts the effects of the war on the lives of all Americans. Joy Hakim's prose places the reader in the middle of the events, but the level of the language may require teachers to provide extra guidance. This volume is especially helpful for expanding on the historical events depicted in the Dictionary illustration.

Nettie's Trip South
written by Ann Turner; illustrated by Ron Himmler.
Aladdin Paperbacks, 1995. ISBN 0689801173
Nettie is a young girl from the North who encounters the brutal realities of slavery on her first visit to the South. Disturbed by what she has seen, she recounts her impressions in a letter home to a friend. Teachers may wish to compile a word bank containing the unfamiliar words that Nettie uses to express her feelings. Another useful extension activity suggested by the story's structure is to use Nettie's letter as an instructional model for letter-writing activities.

WORKBOOK: Topic 27

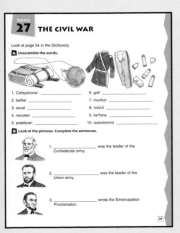

In A, students unscramble ten of the content words. In B, they fill in the names based on the pictures.

WORKSHEET: Topic 27

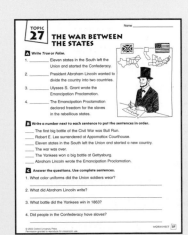

Students do the activities on this page based on the information in the content reading. In A, students write *True* or *False* for each sentence. In B, they write numbers to put the sentences in the order in which the events occurred. In C, they answer the questions.

▶ **CONTENT**

How the government of the United States works

▶ **LANGUAGE**

Passive voice, simple present:
One branch is called the executive branch. It is governed by the President.

CONTENT WORDS

1. Constitution
2. Bill of Rights
3. citizens
4. candidate
5. vote
6. ballot
7. executive branch
8. President
9. Oval Office
10. Great Seal
11. legislative branch
12. Senate
13. House of Representatives
14. Congress
15. judicial branch
16. Supreme Court

CONTENT READING

U.S. Government

The Constitution is the United States' most important document. It lists the rights and powers of the U.S. government. The first ten additions, or amendments, to the Constitution are called the Bill of Rights. The Bill of Rights describes the rights and powers of the people, and it lists things that the U.S. government may not do.

The U.S. government has three divisions, or branches. One branch is called the executive branch. It is governed by the President. The President works in the Oval Office in the White House. The President uses the Great Seal on important documents.

Another branch is called the legislative branch. The legislative branch is divided into two groups. They are the Senate and the House of Representatives. Together, these two groups are called Congress. Congress makes the rules for everyone in the U.S.

The third branch is called the judicial branch, or the Supreme Court. It is governed by nine judges. These judges are not elected. They are appointed by the President and approved by Congress.

The President and members of Congress are elected by the citizens of the U.S. The candidates' names are listed on a ballot. People go into a voting booth and vote for a candidate. The candidate with the most votes wins the election and then helps govern the country.

▶ WORDS

Components: Dictionary pages 56-57, Transparency 28, Wall Chart 28, Workbook page 28, Word and Picture Cards Topic 28, Cassette

- Present the content words. **See pages xiv-xvi for general techniques about presenting content words.**

    > **Language Note:** The words *Congress, Senate, House of Representatives*, and *Supreme Court* can refer to both people and places. These words are always capitalized when referring to these specific institutions of the United States government. The word *President* is also always capitalized when it refers to the head of the United States government.

- Distribute two sets of word and picture cards and divide the class into two teams. Set a time limit for students to answer the following questions about the word and picture cards. The team that answers each question first gets a point.

    1. *Name the word card that refers to an action word (a verb).*
    2. *Name the word cards that refer to important historical documents.*
    3. *Name the three word cards that refer to branches of the U.S. government.*
    4. *Name the word that is a circle.*
    5. *Name the four word cards that can refer to both people and places.*
    6. *Name the word that people use in order to vote.*

- Draw three columns on the board. Label them *Executive Branch, Legislative Branch* and *Judicial Branch.* Ask students to identify these three branches on the wall chart and tell which words belong in each of the columns on the board.

- Have students look at the three buildings in the wall chart: the White House, the Capitol building, and the Supreme Court building. Ask students if they can figure out from the wall chart who works in each of these buildings. Explain to students that these buildings are in Washington, D.C., the capital of the United States. Point out the difference between the *capital* of a country and the U.S. *Capitol* building.

> **WORKBOOK:** Topic 28
> See Teacher's Book page 113.

▶ CONTENT

Components: Dictionary pages 56-57, Transparency 28, Wall Chart 28, Content Reading Topic 28, Worksheet Topic 28, Cassette

- Present the content reading. **See pages xvii-xix for general techniques about presenting content readings.**

- Ask the following or similar questions:

    Is the Constitution the United States' most important document? Why or why not?
    What are the three branches of the United States Government?
    Which two groups are part of Congress?
    Which members of the government are elected by the citizens of the United States? Which are appointed and not elected?

▶ **Passive voice, simple present**

> The passive voice, simple present consists of the simple present of *BE* plus the past participle of the action verb. The passive voice is used to shift attention to the object of the verb, rather than the subject. For example: *The Supreme Court judges are appointed by the President.* The object (*The Supreme Court judges*) goes in the subject position at the beginning of the sentence and the subject, or doer of the action (*the President*), goes in a prepositional phrase [*by* + agent] at the end. Many passive sentences do not contain a [*by* + agent] phrase, as the agent is unknown or unimportant for the meaning of the sentence. For example: *The candidates' names are listed on a ballot.*

Work with sentence strips to change active voice sentences to passive statements with *by.* Start with strips showing the active voice sentences below.

The President / governs / the executive branch.

Nine judges / govern / the Supreme Court.

The President / appoints / the Supreme Court judges.

Congress / approves / the Supreme Court justices.

The citizens of the U.S. / elect / the President and members of Congress.

Separate the first sentence into three parts by cutting at the slashes. Show students that if you begin with *The executive branch*, you need to replace *governs* with *is governed by.* Write these new words on a card, and construct the sentence *The executive branch is governed by the President.* Then divide students into groups to practice with the other sentences. For each one, they will need to make a new card to replace the verb. When students have completed the sentence strips, ask them to find these and other passive voice sentences in the content reading. Students read the sentences, write them on the board, and underline the passive forms of the verbs.

> **WORKSHEET:** Topic 28
> See Teacher's Book page 113.

► CHANTS

Components: Dictionary pages 56-57, Content Chant Topic 28, Cassette

 ## CONTENT CHANT

Don't Forget to Vote

Senate *
House of Representatives
Congress *
Legislative branch

Senate *
House of Representatives
Congress *
Don't forget to vote.

Here comes the President.
Stand up!
Executive branch
Oval Office

Here comes the President.
Stand up!
Don't forget to vote.
Don't forget to vote.

Judicial branch
Supreme Court
Nine judges, here they come!
Count them, count them one by one.
Nine judges, here they come!

(repeat first and second stanzas)

- Present the content chant. **See pages xx-xxi for general techniques about presenting chants.**
- Before distributing the chant, have students practice with small chunks of language from the chant. The entire class chants *Don't forget to vote.* They chant in a whisper and gradually increase their loudness and speed.
- Divide the class into three groups. Group 1 is Congress, the largest group. They chant *Legislative branch.* Group 2, the Executive Branch, chants *Executive branch.* One student from this group is the President. Group 3 students (nine of them, if your group size is big enough) are the Supreme Court judges. They chant *Judicial branch.* The groups first chant in turn and then simultaneously.
- Distribute Content Chant 28. Keep the same groups as above. Group 1 chants the first two stanzas and the last two stanzas. Group 2 chants the third and fourth stanzas as the student President walks back and forth in front of the group. The students in Group 2 stand as they chant the lines *Stand up.* Group 3 chants the fifth stanza as they slowly walk in a straight line one by one.

► EXTENSION

Components: Dictionary pages 56-57, Transparency 28, Wall Chart 28

- Ask students the name of the President of the United States. Ask them if they can name any past presidents of the United States. Ask them to name either of the two senators in their state and at least one representative. If they don't know the answers to these questions, encourage them look up the answers in an almanac or on the Internet.
- Ask students to talk about the leaders and government in the country they come from. Does their country have a president? Do people vote in their country?
- Ask students if they know what it means to be a citizen. *Is everybody in the U.S. a citizen? What makes a person a citizen?*
- Elect a class president. Explain the process of nomination: somebody must nominate you, or make a suggestion that you become a candidate; you cannot nominate yourself. Accept nominations from the students in the class. After all the nominations have been made, invite the nominees to talk about why they would be good class presidents. Other students ask them questions, and decide on their candidates based on their answers to those questions. Limit the number of candidates to five. Conduct a primary election. Hand out secret ballots to every student (including the candidates) with the names of all the candidates on them. Explain that the ballots are secret because they do not write their names. Students circle their choice for president and hand in their ballots. Count all the ballots. The candidates with the two highest vote totals run against each other in a second election. Invite each candidate to make another speech about what why they would be good class presidents. Then hand out secret ballots with just the two candidates' names on them. Students circle their choice and hand in their ballots. Count the ballots again. The winner is the candidate who receives the most votes.
- As a class, create a school Constitution and Bill of Rights. Remind students that the Constitution lists the powers that the government (or the school) has, and the Bill of Rights lists the rights that the people have and that the government (or the school) does not have. For example, the school has the power to set class schedules, to give homework, or to schedule tests. The school does not have the right to decide who a student's friends are, or to tell a student what he or she can eat for lunch. Some rights of the school or the student will depend on the particular school or state the school is in. For example, students may or may not have the right to dress as they want to, depending on the dress code of the school. Write the ideas of the class on the board; then transfer them to a large piece of official-looking paper. Students can help with the writing.

► LITERATURE

Suggested Books

**A More Perfect Union: The Story of
Our Constitution**
written by Betsy Maestro; illustrated by Giulio Maestro.
Lothrop Lee & Shepard, 1987. ISBN 0688068405
A More Perfect Union is the story of the founding fathers
and what they accomplished at Independence Hall: the
drafting and ratification of the Constitution. The Table of
Dates and Interesting Facts at the end of the book offers
additional content and language support for this topic.

**We the People: The Constitution of the United
States of America**
written and illustrated by Peter Spier.
Doubleday Books, 1991. ISBN 0385419031
The award-winning author Peter Spier brings an
innovative approach to the subject of the Constitution. In
the first and last pages of his book, he presents the history
of the Constitution and a reproduction of the document. In
between, he interprets in commentary and illustrations
what each phrase of the Preamble to the Constitution can
mean in our everyday life. For second-language teachers
the book provides an opportunity to practice language
through student discussion about the pictures. Many of
the scenes can be matched with the Dictionary illustration
using the word and picture cards.

The White House
written by Patricia Ryon Quiri.
Franklin Watts, 1996. ISBN 0531202216
This short book tells almost everything one needs to know
about the White House—its history, layout, and
importance. Children can even find out how to e-mail the
president and visit the White House. Although the book
contains a great deal of information for its small size, the
text is very clear and lends itself to reading aloud.

**The Young Oxford Companion to the
United States Government (3 Volumes)**

**The Young Oxford Companion to the
Presidency of the United States**
by Richard M. Pious.
Oxford University Press Children's Books, 1993.
ISBN 0195077997

**The Young Oxford Companion to the
Congress of the United States**
by Donald A. Ritchie.
Oxford University Press Children's Books, 1993.
ISBN 0195077776

**The Young Oxford Companion to the
Supreme Court of the United States**
by John J. Patrick.
Oxford University Press Children's Books, 1993.
ISBN 0195078772
Taken together, these three volumes represent a
comprehensive overview of the United States government.
Each volume is dedicated to one of the three branches of
government. Teachers can pick and choose from the more
than 200 alphabetically-arranged articles in each book to
support the topic. These books feature excerpts from
primary sources such as memoirs, oral histories,
newspaper articles, cartoons, hearings, and debates. They
are also good for reference and for reading. Most of the
entries can be adapted to a variety of language levels.

WORKBOOK: Topic 28

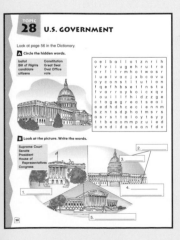

Activity A is a word
search. The listed words
appear horizontally,
vertically, or diagonally,
but not backwards. In
activity B, students label
the picture using words
from the word box.

WORKSHEET: Topic 28

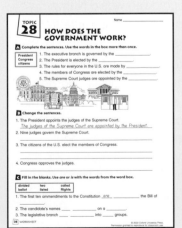

In A, students choose
between *President*,
Congress, or *citizens* for
each sentence. In B, they
change the sentences to
use the passive voice. In
C, they write *are* or *is* in
each sentence and choose
verbs from the word box
to complete the sentences
using the passive voice.

▶ **CONTENT**

Famous men and women who shaped the history of our country

▶ **LANGUAGE**

Verb + infinitive of purpose:
Frederick Douglass fought to end slavery.

CONTENT WORDS

1. Pocahontas (1595-1617)
2. George Washington (1731-1799)
3. Sequoya (1760-1843)
4. Sacajawea (1787-1812)
5. Frederick Douglass (1817-1895)
6. Harriet Tubman (1820-1913)
7. Clara Barton (1821-1912)
8. Thomas Edison (1847-1931)
9. Alexander Graham Bell (1847-1922)
10. Susan B. Anthony (1820-1906)
11. Henry Ford (1863-1947)
12. Helen Keller (1880-1968)
13. Eleanor Roosevelt (1884-1962)
14. Margaret Mead (1901-1978)
15. Cesar Chavez (1927-1993)
16. Martin Luther King, Jr. (1929-1968)

CONTENT READING

People in U.S. History

Many people were important in the history of the United States. These are just a few of them.

Pocahontas was a Native American princess. She worked to keep peace between the Native Americans and the first colonists. George Washington was America's first president. He helped the colonists to create the new nation. Sacajawea was a Native American guide. She helped Lewis and Clark to explore the American West.

Some people worked to make our country better. Frederick Douglass fought to end slavery. Harriet Tubman helped slaves to escape to freedom. Clara Barton started the American Red Cross. Helen Keller fought to improve conditions for blind and deaf people. Susan B. Anthony helped women to win the right to vote. Martin Luther King, Jr. led the civil rights movement. Cesar Chavez fought to improve conditions for farm workers. Margaret Mead worked to teach people about other cultures. Eleanor Roosevelt fought to improve people's basic human rights.

Some people worked to make life easier. Sequoya invented an alphabet for the Cherokee Native Americans and taught them to read and write. Thomas Edison invented the lightbulb. Alexander Graham Bell invented the telephone. Henry Ford built a factory to make cars.

These people helped to make the United States a great country.

▶ WORDS

Components: Dictionary pages 58-59, Transparency 29, Wall Chart 29, Workbook page 29, Word and Picture Cards Topic 29, Cassette

- Present the content words. **See pages xiv-xvi for general techniques about presenting content words.**

- Have students in groups look at the names and dates of the famous people on the word and picture cards. First explain that some of these people had only one name. Then explain that the numbers under the names show the date they were born and the date that they died. For example, Pocahontas was born in 1595 and she died in 1617. If we want to know her age when she died, we subtract the first number from the second number. For example: 1617 - 1595 = 22. She was only 22 when she died. Have students find out how old some of the people were when they died.

- Tell students that we can list famous people in several different ways: *alphabetical order* (by the first letter of their last name or of their only name), *gender* (whether they were men or women), *chronological order* (according to who was born first, second, etc.), and *age* when they died (from the youngest to the oldest). Introduce students to the graphic organizers below. Divide students into groups and help each group create one of the graphic organizers. Each group uses its organizer to sort their word and picture cards. Note that the rank order ladder starts from the bottom and goes up.

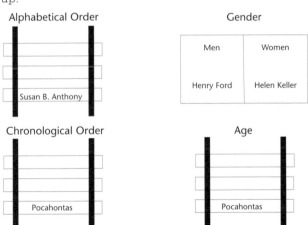

- Have students look at the wall chart to find clues about what made some of the people in the picture famous. For example: the lightbulb by Thomas Edison, and the early version of the telephone by Alexander Graham Bell. Ask students to identify the other clues (the map behind Sacajawea, the automobile in front of Henry Ford, the alphabet next to Sequoya, the colonial flag behind George Washington, and the grapes behind Cesar Chavez) and to try to figure out what the clues tell them about these people.

> **WORKBOOK:** Topic 29
> See Teacher's Book page 117.

▶ CONTENT

Components: Dictionary pages 58-59, Transparency 29, Wall Chart 29, Content Reading Topic 29, Worksheet Topic 29, Cassette

- Present the content reading. **See pages xvii-xix for general techniques about presenting Content Readings.**

- Ask the following or similar questions:

  Were men and women both important in the history of the United States?
  Which two people fought against slavery?
  Who led the civil rights movement?
  Who fought to improve conditions for farm workers?
  What did Harriet Tubman do?

- Divide the class into two teams. A student from Team 1 gives the name of a famous person. A student from Team 2 gives the dates of birth and death of that person and tells one reason why that person was famous. Then teams reverse roles. A team scores one point if all of the information about each person is correct.

▶ **Verb + infinitive**

> Infinitives [*to* + the simple form of a verb] can follow certain other verbs. Sometimes an infinitive following a verb shows someone's purpose. It answers the question *why*. For example: *Margaret Mead worked to teach people about other cultures.* (Why did she work? To teach people.)

Point out the pattern of verb + infinitive with the verbs *work, help,* and *fight* in the content reading. Have students underline all the examples of this pattern in the reading and then ask them to read these sentences aloud. Now have students look at the wall chart. Ask individual students to describe various people in the wall chart and tell, in their own words, what these people did. Encourage students to use the verbs *work, help,* and *fight* + infinitive of purpose. For example: *Cesar Chavez worked to improve the lives of farm workers.*

- Have students look very closely at the faces of the people in the wall chart. Ask them to speculate on what these people were like. For example, was Cesar Chavez rich? Did Henry Ford help poor people? Was Helen Keller kind? Ask students to think about which of these people they want to be like and why. Have students share their thoughts with their classmates.

> **WORKSHEET:** Topic 29
> See Teacher's Book page 117.

► CHANTS

Components: Dictionary pages 58-59, Content Chant Topic 29, Cassette

 CONTENT CHANT

Human Rights

Human rights
Equal rights

Women's rights
The right to vote

> Susan B. Anthony
> Equal rights
> Women's rights
> The right to vote

Farm workers' rights
Fair pay

> Cesar Chavez
> Farm workers' rights

Black and white
Equal rights

> Martin Luther King
> Civil rights

Who helped the women?
> Susan B. Anthony

Who helped the African-Americans?
> Martin Luther King

Who helped the farm workers?
> Cesar Chavez

Equal rights
Human rights

- Present the content chant. **See pages xx-xxi for general techniques about presenting chants.**

- Before distributing the chant, have students practice with small chunks of the language. Each of three groups chants in turn, and then simultaneously, one of the following lines: *Human rights, Equal rights,* or *Women's rights.*

- Now distribute Content Chant 29. First, have the class practice the chant. Then, select three students to chant the words about Susan B. Anthony, Cesar Chavez and Martin Luther King. Have each of these students also call out their person's name in answer to the lines beginning with *Who helped.*

- Pair students and have them write a two-line chant using different people from the picture. For example, *Who helped the blind and deaf? Helen Keller.* One student writes the question; the other student writes the answer. Then, have each pair chant their question and answer, one after the other.

► EXTENSION

Components: Dictionary pages 58-59, Transparency 29, Wall Chart 29

- Have individual students select one person from the picture and do more in-depth research about that person. Encourage students to use history books, encyclopedias, the Internet, or other reference materials. When they finish, they can present their reports to the class.

- Have students make a class encyclopedia of "Famous People in U.S. History" using their researched reports from the above activity. First, students double-check their reports for accuracy and spelling with a classmate. Then, working as a whole group, they alphabetize the order of presentation of the famous people in their encyclopedia and put consecutive page numbers on the pages. Now introduce students to the concept of making an *index,* an alphabetized list of names and other important words and the pages upon which they appear. Have students alphabetically list their famous people's names in the index and the pages upon which they appear. Have them also list one or more things about the person so that others can look up a word in the index and find the information. For example, a student might list Henry Ford's name in the index and also *factory* and *cars.* Once the class has completed their index, have them practice using it to check its accuracy. When the entire encyclopedia is finished, have students bind it and make a cover. Display the encyclopedia in the school, or invite students to give a presentation to another classroom about their book and how it is used.

- Have each student select one important event from the life of the famous person they have researched and create a time line entry for a specific year. Explain the concept of a time line (see Extension, Topic 23) and create a time line with these 16 entries. Include the birth and death dates for each of the 16 famous people. (If you created a time line for a previous topic, add these 16 new entries to the time line. For example: *1789: George Washington becomes first U.S. president.*)

- Have each student select one person that they would like to interview from the list of famous people. Students write three questions they would like to ask the famous person. For example, a student might like to ask George Washington: 1) *Did you want to be President?* 2) *Were you scared?* 3) *Who helped you become President?* Students can present their questions to the class and other students can answer the questions as they think the famous person might answer them.

► LITERATURE

Suggested Books

There are many biographies appropriate for ESL students, including encyclopedia entries, that present the lives of people in U.S. history. The following is a list that may supplement books that are already a part of classroom and school libraries.

The Oxford Children's Book of Famous People
Oxford University Press Children's Books, 1994. ISBN 019910171X
This fully-illustrated book contains summaries of the lives of a thousand men and women who have shaped our world. These stories are about politicians, scientists, explorers, musicians, artists, and sports heroes. Teachers may pick and choose the entries to supplement this topic and add interest to many of the other topics in the Dictionary. An occupational, thematic, and chronological index is also included.

Eleanor
written and illustrated by Barbara Cooney.
Viking Children's Books, 1996. ISBN 0670861596
The focus of this now-classic book is not the adult Eleanor Roosevelt, but the young girl. In this true story, young Eleanor outgrows her fears and gains self-confidence despite her social awkwardness and plain looks. The book is beautifully illustrated and can be read aloud by the teacher or independently by the students. It is recommended as a springboard for students to talk and write about their own lives and what they hope to achieve when they grow up.

I Have a Dream
by Martin Luther King, Jr. and Coretta Scott King.
Scholastic Trade, 1997. ISBN 0590205161
On August 28, 1963, Dr. Martin Luther King delivered his famous "I Have a Dream" speech. In this beautiful book, fifteen artists have created illustrations that correspond to a short passage of the speech. Each passage and illustration can be taught separately so that students can learn the language and study the content. Many illustrations can be related to the content words and illustrations in Units 1, 2, and 3.

Picture Book Biographies
written and illustrated by David Adler.
Holiday House.
The following books are recommended because of their unique ability to present an entire lifetime in clear, simple prose appropriate for beginner and advanced students. These books are useful because of their repetitive language patterns and their specific content. A chronology appears at the end of each book.

A Picture Book of. . .

Abraham Lincoln (also available in Spanish) ISBN 0823408019

Benjamin Franklin ISBN 0823408825

Christopher Columbus (also available in Spanish) ISBN 082340949X

Eleanor Roosevelt ISBN 0823411575

Frederick Douglass ISBN 0823412059

George Washington ISBN 0823408000

Harriet Tubman ISBN 082341065X

Helen Keller ISBN 0823408477

Martin Luther King, Jr. (also available in Spanish) ISBN 0823411877

Patrick Henry ISBN 0823411443

Paul Revere ISBN 0823412946

Thomas Alva Edison ISBN 0823412466

Thomas Jefferson ISBN 0823408817

WORKBOOK: Topic 29

In A, students sort the names of important people in U.S. history. They rewrite the names to make a list of women and a list of men. In B, they draw the faces and write the names of another important woman and man in history.

WORKSHEET: Topic 29

On this page, students match the men and women in history to the sentences telling the important things they did. They write the letter for each picture next to the sentence.

30 PARTS OF THE BODY

▶ **CONTENT**

The parts of the body

▶ **LANGUAGE**

Modal *have to*: *Sam has to use many parts of his body.*

Conjunction *or (else)*: *Sam has to bend his knees, or (else) he will fall.*

CONTENT WORDS

1. head
2. hair
3. eye
4. ear
5. nose
6. mouth
7. teeth
8. chin
9. neck
10. shoulder
11. arm
12. elbow
13. wrist
14. hand
15. finger
16. thumb
17. chest
18. leg
19. knee
20. ankle
21. foot
22. toe

CONTENT READING

Parts of the Body

Sam is going surfing today. Surfing is fun, but it is also hard work.

Sam has to use many parts of his body. Sam listens to the ocean with his ears. He feels the wind in his hair. He smells the salty air with his nose. He watches the waves with his eyes.

Sam walks into the ocean with his surfboard. He has to hold his surfboard with two hands, or it will float away. He has to watch the ocean, or else he won't see the best wave.

Finally, Sam sees a big wave. Now, he has to get ready. He puts his chest on the surfboard. He has to keep his head up, or else the wave will go past him. He has to keep his mouth closed, or else he will swallow water.

The wave comes to Sam. He puts one foot on the surfboard. Then, he puts his other foot on the board. He stands up. He can feel the surfboard with his toes.

Sam has to bend his knees, or else he will fall. He has to put his arms out for balance. He doesn't fall! He rides the wave!

► WORDS

Components: Dictionary pages 60-61, Transparency 30, Wall Chart 30, Workbook page 30, Word and Picture Cards Topic 30, Cassette

- Present the content words. **See pages xiv-xvi for general techniques about presenting content words.**

    Language Note: The word *teeth* is an irregular plural for the singular *tooth*. The word *foot* takes the irregular plural *feet*. The word *hair* is generally used as a noncount noun. However, we sometimes use the singular *a hair* to refer to a single strand of hair, in which case the plural is *hairs*. All of the other content words have regular plurals (the letter -*s* added to the singular form) with the exception of *body* (*bodies*).

- Display the wall chart and have students look at the picture. Divide the class into two groups. One group identifies all the content words relating to Sam's head. The other group identifies all the content words which are found below Sam's neck. Each group makes a list of its content words or pastes its content words appropriately on the wall chart.

- Introduce the rhyming song "Head, Shoulder, Knees, and Toes":

    Head, shoulders, knees, and toes, knees and toes,
    Head, shoulders, knees, and toes, knees and toes,
    Eyes and ears and mouth and nose,
    Head, shoulders, knees, and toes, knees and toes.

As students sing, they touch the corresponding parts of their bodies. When students know the song well, try varying the tempo.

    Culture Note: Be aware of particular cultural beliefs that involve touching the body. For example, in some cultures, such as Thai culture, touching the top of someone's head is taboo.

- Talk about how many of each body part we have (one head, two eyes, etc.). Now write the numbers 1, 2, and 10 in three columns on the board. Ask students, in turn, to write the name of a body part in the appropriate column on the board according to how many a person has. For example, *head* would go in the 1 column, *fingers* in the 10 column. Continue until all students have written a body part. If you have an advanced class, encourage students to come up with a number for each of the content words that do not fit in any of the three columns (*hair* and *teeth*). List them in a fourth column called *Other* or *More Than 10*.

WORKBOOK: Topic 30
See Teacher's Book page 121.

► CONTENT

Components: Dictionary pages 60-61, Transparency 30, Wall Chart 30, Content Reading Topic 30, Worksheet Topic 30, Cassette

- Present the content reading. **See pages xvii-xix for general techniques about presenting content readings.**

- Ask the following or similar questions:

    What is Sam doing?
    What does Sam do with his ears?
    How does Sam smell the salty air?
    How does Sam hold his surfboard?
    Why does Sam have to keep his mouth closed?
    What will happen if Sam doesn't bend his knees?

- ▶ **Modal *have to***

    A modal is an auxiliary verb, or a helping verb. It is followed by the simple form of the main verb. The modal *have to* (or *has to*) expresses necessity.

    Ask students to underline all the uses of *have to* and *has to* in the content reading. Then ask students to read these sentences aloud.

- ▶ **Modal *have to*.** Ask individual students to write a sentence on the board expressing necessity using the modal *have to*. For example: *I have to take out the trash*, or *I have to go to sleep at 9 o'clock*. Have students write their names next to their sentences. Now ask students questions about their classmates. For example: *Nancy, what does Joe have to do?* Nancy answers *He has to take out the trash*. Keep the students' sentences on the board for the activity below.

- ▶ **Conjunction *or* (*else*)**

    The conjunction *or* or *or else* can introduce a consequence or result of a person failing to do something. For example: *Joe has to see his grandmother on Tuesday, or (else) she will be sad.*

    Have students underline all instances of *or* and *or else* in the content reading. Then, ask students to look at their sentences on the board from the activity above and add *or* or *or else* plus the consequences of the first action. For example: *I have to go to bed at 9 o'clock or else I will be tired the next day*. If your class is advanced, have students add clauses with *or (else)* to their classmates' sentences rather than their own sentences.

WORKSHEET: Topic 30
See Teacher's Book page 121.

► CHANTS

Components: Dictionary pages 60-61, Content Chant Topic 30, Cassette

 ## CONTENT CHANT

His Feet Are Big

His feet are big.
His legs are long.
His arms are strong.
He's a basketball player. * *

Her waist is small.
Her neck is long.
Her toes are strong.
She's a dancer. * * *

His legs are short.
His arms aren't long.
His ankles, knees, and back are strong.
He's a jockey. * * *

Her eyes are good.
Her arms are strong.
Her body is thin. Her legs are long.
She's a tennis player. * *

- Present the content chant. **See pages xx-xxi for general techniques about presenting chants.**

- Before distributing the chant, have students practice small chunks of the language from the chant. Divide the class into two groups. Group 1 chants *His feet are big. His legs are long. His arms are strong.* Group 2 chants *Big feet. Long legs. Strong arms.* Group 1 continues with the other lines in the chant, such as *Her waist is small, Her neck is long,* etc. Group 2 continues to give the shortened versions of the line (adjective + noun) such as: *Small waist, Long neck,* etc.

- Distribute Content Chant 30. Divide the class into four groups, one for each stanza. First, have each group, in turn, chant the words *basketball player, dancer, jockey, tennis player.* Then, have each group chant their stanza. Select one student in each group to pantomime the actions of either a basketball player, a dancer, a jockey, or a tennis player. The other students in the groups point to the various body parts mentioned (*feet, legs, waist*) as they chant.

► EXTENSION

Components: Dictionary pages 60-61, Transparency 30, Wall Chart 30, Word and Picture Cards Topic 30

- Put the word and picture cards in a pile on the desk. Ask individual students to come to the front of the class and pick two cards at random. Each student reads his or her card aloud, and attempts to touch the body part shown on the first card with the body part shown on the second card. For example, if the two words on the cards are *chin* and *ankle,* the student tries to touch her chin with her ankle. Encourage students to be creative in the ways they control their bodies. In some cases, such as *ear* and *teeth,* the activity will be impossible, but students will have fun trying.

- Introduce the terms *left* and *right.* Present this way to distinguish between the two: Tell students to put their hands out in front of them, with their palms facing down and thumbs out. In this position, the thumb and the first finger of the left hand makes an L. *L* is for *left.*

- **Game: Simon Says.** One student plays the role of Simon and gives commands to the rest of the class. The other students do whatever Simon says, as long as the command is preceded by the words *Simon says.* If Simon gives a command, but does not first say *Simon says,* any student who performs the command is eliminated. When only one student remains in the game, the student wins, and becomes *Simon* in a new game. Example: *Simon says touch your left knee.* (Students who touch their right knees or any other body parts other than their left knees are eliminated from the game.) *Simon says touch your ear.* (Students touch one of their ears.) *Touch your ankle.* (Students who touch their ankles are eliminated from the game because Simon did not say *Simon says.*)

- Have students write or talk about a physical activity they like, such as riding a bike or playing a sport. Students write or say which parts of their bodies they *have to* use to perform this activity. Encourage them to use clauses introduced with *or (else)* to describe what will happen if they don't do the things they have to do. For example: *I ride my bike every day. I have to hold the handlebars with my hands or else I'll fall. I have to pedal with my legs or else I won't go anywhere.*

- Teach the Hokey Pokey. Students form a large circle as they sing the song and mime the actions.

    Put your right hand in, put your right hand out.
    Put your right hand in, and shake it all about.
    Do the Hokey Pokey and turn yourself around,
    That's what it's all about. (*)

Continue the words and actions, substituting other body parts for the words *right hand.*

► LITERATURE

Suggested Books

Looking at the Body!

written by David Suzuki; illustrated by Barbara Hehner.
John Wiley & Sons, 1991. ISBN 0471540528
This book is a treasury of simple, engaging activities about the different parts of the body and how they work. The materials required to perform the experiments are readily available and the directions are numbered and written in easy-to-read sentences. Each of the nine chapters begins with a brief introduction and includes several sections of remarkable facts. The language of the introductions is simple, concise, and interesting. Since the activities can be performed with minimal direct instruction, they are suitable for pairing ESL students with their mainstream classmates.

Hairs/Pelitos

written by Sandra Cisneros; illustrated by Terry Ybanez.
English/Spanish. Dragonfly, 1997. ISBN 0679890076
Human diversity is captured in this simple presentation of different kinds of hair. Excerpted from Sandra Cisneros's best-selling *The House on Mango Street*, this book is ideal for reading aloud. Each page has only one line of text (in English at the top and Spanish at the bottom). Important language patterns such as possessive pronouns, compound sentences, and prepositions of place are found throughout the text. This book is especially recommended for beginners as a springboard to talk and write about their own bodies.

The Visual Dictionary of the Human Body

written by Deni Brown.
Dorling Kindersley, 1991. ISBN 1879431181
This book explains in greater detail the aspects of the human body as presented in the Dictionary illustration. Each two-page spread features a different body part (head, eye, ear, skin, hair, etc.) with a short, introductory paragraph, full-color photographs, and clear labels. The content words can be matched to the entries to encourage further discussion of body parts and their functions. This book also works well with Topic 31, Inside the Human Body.

The Body Atlas

by Mark Crocker.
Oxford University Press Children's Books, 1994. ISBN 019520963X
This book, a collection of maps of the human body, is an excellent reference for this topic. Every page is fully illustrated and all illustrations are explained. Topics range from everyday phenomena (why people sometimes feel sleepy after a meal) to complex and rare ailments (Munchausen's syndrome). The language is scientific and will require direct instruction and paraphrasing. The glossary of key terms is very helpful for advanced students. The book can also be used with Topic 8, The Hospital, and Topic 31, Inside the Human Body.

WORKBOOK: Topic 30

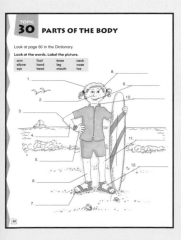

On this page, students label the parts of the body of the surfer, using the words from the word box.

WORKSHEET: Topic 30

In A, students match to complete the sentences that contain *or else*. In B, students fill in the blanks with verbs from the word box, based on the pictures.

31 INSIDE THE HUMAN BODY

▶ **CONTENT**

The functions of the human body

▶ **LANGUAGE**

Wh- questions with *what*:
What does the heart do?

Possessive adjective *your*:
The skull protects your brain.

CONTENT WORDS

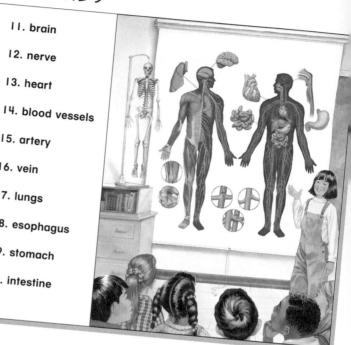

1. skeleton	11. brain
2. bone	12. nerve
3. skull	13. heart
4. jaw	14. blood vessels
5. spine	15. artery
6. muscle	16. vein
7. joint	17. lungs
8. cartilage	18. esophagus
9. ligament	19. stomach
10. tendon	20. intestine

CONTENT READING

Inside the Human Body

There are a lot of different, important parts inside your body.

What do the bones do? The bones protect and support your body. The bones all fit together to make your skeleton.

The skull protects your brain. The jaw is part of the skull. The spine supports your skull. The spine is in your back. Some people call it "the backbone." There are many small bones in your spine.

What do the joints do? The joints connect your bones. Ligaments and cartilage are parts of the joints. The joints help us move.

What do the muscles and the tendons do? The muscles move your bones. The tendons are like stretchy bands. They attach the muscles to the bones.

What does the brain do? The brain controls your body. It sends messages to the other parts of the body through the nerves.

What does the heart do? The heart pumps blood through your blood vessels. There are two kinds of blood vessels: arteries and veins. Arteries take blood from your heart to all the parts of your body. Veins bring the blood back to your heart.

What do the lungs do? The lungs take in air. You breathe with your lungs.

What does the esophagus do? It brings the food from your mouth to your stomach. Then, the food goes into your intestines.

All these different parts of your body work together to keep you alive.

▶ WORDS

Components: Dictionary pages 62-63, Transparency 31, Wall Chart 31, Workbook page 31, Word and Picture Cards Topic 31, Cassette

- Present the content words. **See pages xiv-xvi for general techniques about presenting content words.**

    > **Language Note:** The word *cartilage* is a noncount noun. A noncount noun has only one form, which is neither singular nor plural. It does not take *a/an* before it. We can use the words *a lot of* and *much* before noncount nouns but not the word *many*. *Blood* is also a noncount noun.

- Distribute one word and picture card to each student. Ask students, in turn, to read the word on the card and to say whether the body has *one, two,* or *a lot of* these parts. For example, the student with the *spine* card says *The body has one spine.* The student with the *muscle* card says *The body has a lot of muscles.*

- Explain to students that the parts inside the human body are actually parts of systems. Introduce the following words and have students write them in their word banks. Demonstrate the word and picture cards for each system as you explain it. The *skeletal system* (*skeleton, bone, skull, jaw, spine, joint, cartilage, ligament*) supports the basic structure of the human body. The *muscular system* (*muscles, tendons*) helps various parts of our bodies to move. The *nervous system* (*brain, nerve*) is the center of our feelings and our senses. The *digestive system* (*esophagus, stomach*) takes the food we eat and turns it into energy for our bodies. *The circulatory system* (*heart, blood vessels, artery, vein*) moves blood through our bodies. The *respiratory system* (*lungs*) brings air into our bodies and helps us breathe. Now draw a word web on the board like the one below and have students place their cards in the appropriate place in the word web.

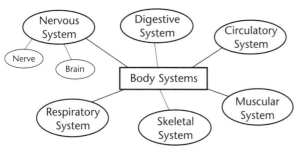

- Have students identify and point to each of the systems in the wall chart and the content words that belong in each system. For example, the skeletal system is on the left. The muscular and nervous systems are shown in the left body model. The circulatory, respiratory, and digestive systems are shown in the model on the right.

WORKBOOK: Topic 31
See Teacher's Book page 125.

▶ CONTENT

Components: Dictionary pages 62-63, Transparency 31, Wall Chart 31, Content Reading Topic 31, Worksheet Topic 31, Cassette

- Present the content reading. **See pages xvii-xix for general techniques about presenting content readings.**

- Ask the following or similar questions:

    What do the bones do?
    Where is the spine?
    What controls the body?
    What are the two kinds of blood vessels?
    How does blood travel?

▶ **Wh- questions with *what***

> *Wh-* questions are those which start with *What, Who, When, Where, Why,* and *How.* We use *Wh-* questions in English to ask for information, as opposed to *Yes/No* questions, which can be answered with a *Yes* or a *No.* The intonation of *Wh-* questions usually goes down at the end of the question (more like the voice at the end of a sentence), whereas intonation rises at the end of *Yes/No* questions.

Ask students to circle, underline, and read aloud all of the *Wh-* questions with *What* in the content reading. Point out to students that questions always have a question mark at the end of the question. Then, have individual students take turns asking each other *Wh-* questions with *what* and have other students answer them. Encourage students to ask and answer questions about the content reading or about other parts of the body. For example: *What do the ears do? They help us hear.*

- Pair students and have them each draw outlines of their partner's body on chart paper. Students work together using different color crayons to label their body outlines with as many of the systems and content words as possible. Students write their names on their own drawings and then exchange their drawings to check for accuracy. Hang the students' drawings around the room.

WORKSHEET: Topic 31
See Teacher's Book page 125.

► CHANTS

Components: Dictionary pages 62-63, Content Chant Topic 31, Cassette

 CONTENT CHANT

Brain - Think, Lungs - Breathe

Brain	think
Lungs	breathe
Esophagus	swallow
Heart	fall in love
Joint	move
Muscle	exercise
Stomach	growl
Heart	fall in love
Spine	straighten
Bone	break
Tendon	pull
Heart	fall in love
Brain	think
Lungs	breathe
Jaw	drop
Heart	fall in love

- Present the content chant. **See pages xx-xxi for general techniques about presenting chants.**

- Before distributing the chant, have students practice with small chunks of language from the chant. Divide the class into five groups. Each group chants the three body parts of each stanza quickly and repeatedly. Group 1 chants *brain, lungs, esophagus*. Group 2 chants *joint, muscle, stomach*. Group 3 chants *spine, bone, tendon*, and Group 4 chants *brain, lungs, jaw*. Group 5 repeatedly chants *heart*.

- Explain that *fall in love* means to have a feeling of love. We associate love with the heart. Point to the picture of the heart on Dictionary page 62. Now draw a picture of a Valentine's Day heart. Explain that the heart drawing represents love. Explain the line *Jaw-drop*. Gesture a jaw dropping. We use this expression to describe when someone is surprised.

- Distribute Content Chant 31. Divide the class into two groups. Group 1 chants the first word of each line. Group 2 chants the second word in each line. The entire class chants *Heart-fall in love* together softly and slowly at the last line of each stanza.

► EXTENSION

Components: Dictionary pages 62-63, Transparency 31, Wall Chart 31

- Pair students and show them how to take each other's pulse. Tell them to find the spot on the inside of the wrist where they can feel the number of beats. They should use their index fingers, not their thumbs. Once students find their partner's pulse, they should count (silently) the number of beats in exactly one minute, and write that number down. Have students report their answers to the class, and record them on the board next to each student's name.

- Have students work in the same pairs as in the above activity. This time Student A in each pair does some light exercise, such as 10 pushups or sit-ups, or running in place for one minute. Student B takes Student A's pulse immediately after the exercise and writes down the number of beats per minute. Students then switch roles. Have students report their answers, and record the new pulse numbers next to their old ones on the board. The new pulse numbers should be much higher than the numbers in the earlier activity. Talk to students about why this is. *What does the pulse measure? Why is it higher after exercise? What is the heart doing?*

- Pair students. Have them flex their biceps while their partners measure the muscles with a measuring tape and record the size of the biceps.

- Students select any three content words of their choice to research. Encourage students to use the library or the Internet to find out as much additional information about their three words as possible. Students write up their reports with pictures or drawings for visual aides and then present their findings to the class. Ask students to identify their sources. Compare the information of students who have chosen the same content words.

- Provide opportunities for students to explore the complexity of their bodies. Challenge students to roll their tongues or raise only one eyebrow. Ask students if any of them can flex their fingers in unusual ways. Have students try to rub their stomachs and pat their heads at the same time, or to close their eyes, put their hands out horizontally and stand on one foot. Encourage student inquiries and discussion.

► LITERATURE

Suggested Books

The Digestive System
written by Merce Parramon; illustrated by Marcel Socias.
Chelsea House Publications, 1994. ISBN 0791021262

How Our Muscles Work
written by Victoria Avila; illustrated by Marcel Socias.
Chelsea House Publications, 1995. ISBN 0791031500

How Our Blood Circulates
written by Merce Parramon; illustrated by Marcel Socias.
Chelsea House Publications, 1995. ISBN 0791021270

The Skeletal System
written by Eduard Arnau;
illustrated by Antonio Munoz Tenllado
Chelsea House Publications, 1995. ISBN 0791031519

The Respiratory System
written by Nuria Bosch Roca and Marta Serrano;
illustrated by Antonio Munoz Tenllado.
Chelsea House Publications, 1995. ISBN 0791031535
These five books are part of a series called "The Invisible World." Each title presents an in-depth look at one major system of the body. Aspects of the system are described in two-page spreads. Colorful drawings and models depict interior views of the human body and how the systems work. Numbered outline drawings are often included with the text to further clarify what happens in each system. Teachers may want to use these books for follow-up activities such as tracing outlines of students' bodies on large paper and having students draw in the organs and systems.

The Magic School Bus Inside the Human Body
written by Joanna Cole; illustrated by Bruce Degen.
Scholastic Trade, 1990. ISBN 0590414275
Join Ms. Frizzle as she and her fourth grade class take a tour of the digestive system, the arteries, the lungs, the heart, the brain, and the muscles. Like all of the Magic School Bus books, *The Magic School Bus Inside the Human Body* imparts a large amount of factual information as it entertains. The book is also very flexible for extension activities. To reinforce word acquisition, show an illustration and read the speech balloons as students use their word and picture cards to identify the body system that is described. The illustrations may also be used as a springboard for retelling, writing, and drawing.

The Heart: Our Circulatory System
written and photographed by Seymour Simon.
William Morrow & Co., 1996. ISBN 0688114075
This beautifully designed book uses computer-enhanced photographs to introduce the human heart and the circulatory system to readers. The enlarged images are unusual enough to prompt immediate discussion. Each two-page spread addresses a single topic (e.g., blood vessels, anatomy of the heart, strokes, blood vessels). The large-type text is direct and simple. Students will be able to identify most of the content words from the Dictionary in the pages of this book.

WORKBOOK: Topic 31

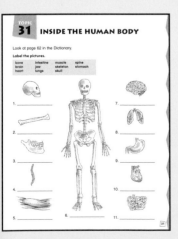

On this page, students label the organs and parts of the skeleton with words from the word box.

WORKSHEET: Topic 31

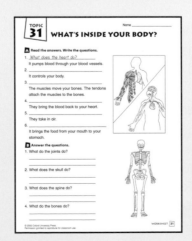

In A, students write appropriate questions about the functions of organs, based on the answers. In B, they write answers to the questions.

► **CONTENT**

The five senses

► **LANGUAGE**

Imperatives: *Look at the stars.*

Linking verb + adjective: *They look bright.*

Adverb *also*: *The sun is also bright.*

CONTENT WORDS

1. see
2. bright
3. dark
4. hear
5. loud
6. soft
7. smell
8. fragrant
9. foul
10. taste
11. sweet
12. sour
13. salty
14. touch
15. smooth
16. rough

CONTENT READING

The Senses

People have five senses. These are the sense of sight, the sense of hearing, the sense of smell, the sense of taste, and the sense of touch.

We use our sense of sight to see things. Look at the night sky. It looks dark. Look at the stars. They look bright. A closet is also dark. The sun is also bright.

We use our sense of hearing to hear things. Listen to the finger cymbals. They sound soft. Listen to the big cymbals. They sound loud. A whisper is also soft. Fireworks are also loud.

We use our sense of smell to smell things. Smell a flower. It smells fragrant. Smell garbage. It smells foul. Yuck!

We use our sense of taste to taste things. Taste a cookie. It tastes sweet. Taste a lemon. It tastes sour. Taste popcorn. It tastes salty.

We use our sense of touch to feel things. Touch a rock. It feels smooth outside. It feels rough inside. A mirror is also smooth. Sandpaper is also rough.

We use our senses every day. Sometimes, we use all five senses at the same time.

►WORDS

Components: Dictionary pages 64-65, Transparency 32, Wall Chart 32, Workbook page 32, Word and Picture Cards Topic 32, Cassette

- Present the content words. **See pages xiv-xvi for general techniques about presenting content words.**

- Draw five columns on the board and label each one with the name of one of the senses (*Sight, Hearing, Smell, Taste,* and *Touch*). Distribute the word and picture cards to the students and ask them to form groups based on which of the five senses their word and picture cards represent. For example, students with the word and picture cards for *see, bright,* and *dark* group themselves together in the *Sight* group. Students with the cards for *taste, sweet, sour,* and *salty* group themselves in the *Taste* group, etc. Use two or three sets of cards if the class is large. Have students in each group look at the wall chart, point out their assigned section of the chart (for example, *Sight*), place their word and picture cards in that panel, and then write their words in the appropriate column on the board.

- Direct students' attention to the words *see, hear, smell, taste,* and *touch* and have them name the parts of the body used for each sense (*eye, ear, nose, tongue,* and *fingers*). Refer students to Topic 30, Parts of the Body, if necessary. If appropriate to your students' language levels, have students write sentences that connect the part of the body to the sense. For example: *We see with our eyes.*

- Arrange students in the same groups as in the first activity above. For homework, have them plan to bring to class as many objects as possible representing their assigned sense. For example, the *Sight* group might bring in a kaleidoscope, photos, drawings, etc. The *Taste* group might bring in various foods (or pictures of foods) which represent *sweet, sour,* and *salty.* Help the groups organize their planning and the date for them to bring in their objects. On that date, have each group exhibit and label the objects. Then give all students the opportunity to look at and comment on each group's work.

- Ask students if they know the names of the things shown in the pictures. For example, the musical instrument used to demonstrate *loud* is the cymbals. Garbage is used to demonstrate *foul.* Ask students to name some of the other words.

WORKBOOK: Topic 32
See Teacher's Book page 129.

►CONTENT

Components: Dictionary pages 64-65, Transparency 32, Wall Chart 32, Content Reading Topic 32, Worksheet Topic 32, Cassette

- Present the content reading. **See pages xvii-xix for general techniques about presenting content readings.**

- Ask the following or similar questions:

    Can people use more than one sense at a time?
    How many senses do people have?
    What are the senses? Name them.
    What sense do we use to feel things?
    What sense are you using right now?
    Do people use the sense of sight to hear things or to see things?

► **Linking verb + adjective**

A linking verb is a type of intransitive verb. (Intransitive verbs do not take direct objects.) Some common linking verbs are *look, sound, smell, taste,* and *feel.* A linking verb is often used with an adjective. (*It looks dark.*) Linking verbs are usually stative verbs. (Stative verbs describe states or conditions, not actions.) Some linking verbs can also be action verbs. For example, *look* is a linking verb in *They look bright,* but *look* is an action verb in *Look at the stars.*

On the board, write an example from the content reading of a sentence with a linking verb (*The stars look bright* or *They look bright*). Then make a list on the board of the linking verbs in the reading, and another list of the adjectives used with them. Have students circle, underline, or read aloud all the instances they can find. Then divide the class into two teams. Team 1 names an object (*apple*). Team 2 describes the object with reference to one of the five senses using the linking verb + adjective pattern (*It tastes great* or *It smells nice*). Then teams switch roles. The team with the most appropriate answers in 15 minutes is the winner.

► **Imperatives.** Explain to students that we use imperative forms when we tell someone to do something. We can use the words *look* (*at*), *listen* (*to*), *smell, taste,* and *touch* to give commands involving the five senses. Give students examples from the content reading (*Taste a cookie*) and have them circle, underline, and read aloud all the instances of imperatives. Then divide the class into two teams. Team 1 names an object (*a rock*). Team 2 gives a command about the object involving one of the five senses (*Touch the rock*). Then teams switch roles. The team with the most appropriate imperatives in 15 minutes is the winner.

WORKSHEET: Topic 32
See Teacher's Book page 129.

► CHANTS

Components: Dictionary pages 64-65, Content Chant Topic 32, Cassette

CONTENT CHANT

The Senses Chant

Touch *
    smooth, rough

Don't touch the stove. It's hot! *

Taste *
    sweet, sour, salty

Taste the soup! It's wonderful.

See *
    bright, dark

Turn on the lights. I can't see a thing.

Hear *
    loud, soft

Speak up! * I can't hear you.

Smell *
    fragrant, foul

What's that smell?
    Phew!

- Present the content chant. **See pages xx-xxi for general techniques about presenting chants.**

- Before distributing the chant, have students practice with small chunks of language from the chant. Have the entire class chant the words *Touch, Taste, See, Hear, Speak up!,* and *Smell,* including the clap after each word. Students start chanting and clapping softly and slowly, and then increase the loudness and speed as they repeatedly chant these words.

- Introduce the meaning of the word *phew* to express something foul-smelling. Explain that *phew* (sometimes expressed as *pyew* or *p.u.*) is an informal expression not usually used in formal conversation.

- Distribute Content Chant 32. Divide students into two groups. Group 1 chants the first and the third lines of each stanza. Group 2 chants the second (indented) lines of each stanza.

- Invite students to make up their own verses to the chant by changing the last lines of each stanza. For example:

    Touch *
        smooth, rough
    Touch the mirror. It's smooth.
    Taste *
        sweet, sour, salty
    Taste the pie. It's yummy.

► EXTENSION

Components: Dictionary pages 64-65, Transparency 32, Wall Chart 32

- Introduce expressions such as *yum* or *yummy* (to express something that smells or tastes delicious) and *yuck, yucky,* or *icky* (to express something that smells or tastes bad). Elicit other words or expressions from students for something that looks, feels, smells, sounds, or tastes great (*cool, awesome, fantastic,* etc.) or for words or expressions for something that looks, feels, smells, sounds, or tastes awful (*gross, bad, disgusting, the pits,* etc.). Have students guess which are formal expressions and which are informal expressions. Ask students what people from their home countries say in these situations.

- Divide students into groups of five. Take a class field trip around the classroom or around the school. Ask each group to make lists of things they encounter with their five senses. The first student in each group makes a list of things he or she sees. The second student makes a list of things he or she hears. The third, fourth, and fifth students make lists of the things they feel, smell, and taste. (Note: Encourage the fifth student in each group to taste things such as water from the water fountain, or food from the cafeteria, etc.) When all the groups are finished, encourage them to share their experiences.

- Explain to students that they are going to have a race, but without using their senses of sight. First introduce additional imperatives such as *go, stop, walk, put your hand out, take a step, turn around, move,* etc. Now pair students. Blindfold Student A in each pair. Student B in each pair maneuvers Student A around the room to a specific spot (such as the door or the teacher's desk) by giving commands which Student A follows. (Remove sharp objects or anything that might cause an accident.) Then, Students A and B in each pair reverse roles. The first four pairs of students who reach the finish line fastest are the winners. After the activity, ask students if they felt they listened better (to the commands of their partner) because they couldn't use their own sense of sight.

- Explain that some people don't have all of their senses. Some people can't see. They are *blind.* Some people can't hear. They are *deaf.* Many deaf people are also *mute.* They can't speak. They use sign language. They talk with their hands. Explain that American Sign Language is a real language used by hearing-impaired people to communicate. Many hearing people also learn to sign so they can interpret for non-hearing people. Divide students into groups. Have the groups research American Sign Language in encyclopedias, on the Internet, or perhaps at a school for the deaf in your area. Ask each group to learn five signs in American Sign Language and demonstrate the signs and their meanings to the class.

LITERATURE

Suggested Books

The Science Book of the Senses
written by Neil Ardley.
Harcourt Brace, 1992. ISBN 0152006141
A simple, hands-on experiment can often teach students a concept faster than a written explanation. *The Science Book of the Senses* shows how the five senses work through simple experiments that students can perform in class or at home. Both teachers and students will appreciate this book's appealing design, colorful photographs, and easy-to-follow experiment instructions. The blocks of large type make locating important information easy, and most of the materials needed to perform the experiments can be found around the house or in the classroom.

Sound and Vision: The Sensory Systems
written by Jenny Bryan.
Dillon Press, 1994. ISBN 0875185916
Sound and Vision explains how the eyes and ears work, and why it is important to take proper care of them. The book highlights certain common eye and ear ailments and discusses remedies for them. The numerous photographs and diagrams augment and enrich the information. A glossary and bibliography are included. This book may also be used with Topic 8, The Hospital.

I See the Moon and the Moon Sees Me
written by Jonathan London; illustrated by Peter Fiore.
Puffin Books, 1998. ISBN 0140554874
Seeing is the focus of this easy-to-read illustrated rhyme. A boy has an adventurous day in the country, where he sees many things. The text is based on the childhood rhyme, "I see the moon and the moon sees me..." Each verse of the rhyme presents a different activity using this language pattern (for example, "I see the river and the river sees me"). The repetition of the text helps to build vocabulary and give students practice in forming first and third person sentences. For speaking and writing practice, students can form their own "seeing" sentences using this book as a model.

WORKBOOK: Topic 32

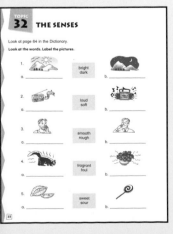

Each number on this page has two pictures and a pair of words which are opposites. Students choose which word matches which picture, and they write the words beneath the pictures.

WORKSHEET: Topic 32

In A, students fill in the imperative form of the sense verbs from the word box. In B, they complete the sentences and then write sentences telling what else can be described by the adjectives in the sentences.

33 FEELINGS

▶ **CONTENT**
....
Feelings and emotions

▶ **LANGUAGE**
....
BE + predicate adjective: *He is lonely.*

Intensifier (*really*, *very*) + adjective: *He's really hungry.*

CONTENT WORDS

1. sick	9. scared
2. tired	10. surprised
3. thirsty	11. proud
4. hot	12. sad
5. cold	13. happy
6. hungry	14. lonely
7. silly	15. excited
8. shy	16. angry

CONTENT READING

Feelings

Everyone is at the football game. The fans are happy. The cheerleader is very excited. One boy is sitting alone. He is lonely. One girl has a blanket around her shoulders. She's very cold. Her father is eating a sandwich. He's really hungry.

Some football players are sitting on the bench. Number 7 is sick. His head hurts. Number 10 is very tired. He can't run any more. Number 78 is thirsty. He's drinking water. Number 68 is really hot. He's sweating. Number 33 is fighting with another player. They're both really angry.

The football players win the game. Number 79 is very proud. He scored the last touchdown. Everyone celebrates on the street. They're having a parade.

The clowns are very silly. One clown is squirting water at a boy. The boy is surprised. His sister is scared. Another clown is losing his balloon. He's very sad.

One little boy is with his mother. He likes clowns, but he hides behind his mother's leg. He is really shy.

▶ WORDS

Components: Dictionary pages 66-67, Transparency 33, Wall Chart 33, Workbook page 33, Word and Picture Cards Topic 33, Cassette

- Present the content words. **See pages xiv-xvi for general techniques about presenting content words.**

  > **Language Note:** The word *feel* has several different meanings in English. In this context it refers to physical feelings that our bodies experience (*sick, tired,* etc. in Content Words 1-6) and it also refers to emotional states that we experience (*happy, sad,* etc. in Content Words 7-16). This is different from how the word *feel* is used in Topic 32, where it is used to describe the sense of touch (*The rock feels rough*).

- Explain the difference between physical feelings and emotional feelings. Ask students how they describe such differences in their first languages. Draw two columns on the board. Label one *Physical Feelings* and the other *Emotional Feelings*. Distribute the word and picture cards and ask students to place their cards in one of the appropriate columns.

- Distribute one word and picture card to each student. Have each student read his or her card aloud and pantomime the feeling expressed on the card.

- Divide the class into two teams and distribute two sets of word and picture cards. Students from each team, in turn, pantomime the feeling expressed on one of the cards, and students from the other team guess the word which describes that feeling. The team with the most accurate guesses is the winner.

- Divide the class into two groups and distribute two sets of word and picture cards. Individual students in the first group make a sentence about themselves using the feeling shown on their word and picture card. For example: *I'm sick.* Individual students in the second group give an appropriate response or appropriate advice. Then students in each group reverse roles. For example, one student says, *I'm sick* or *I feel sick.* The other student says *That's awful* or *Call a doctor.* If students have trouble with appropriate responses, use that as a basis of discussion.

WORKBOOK: Topic 33
  See Teacher's Book page 133.

▶ CONTENT

Components: Dictionary pages 66-67, Transparency 33, Wall Chart 33, Content Reading Topic 33, Worksheet Topic 33, Cassette

- Present the content reading. **See pages xvii-xix for general techniques about presenting content readings.**

- Ask the following or similar questions:

  Is Number 10 angry?
  Which football player is sick?
  Who is hot?
  Who is very tired?
  How does Number 79 feel?
  Why does the girl have a blanket around her shoulders?

- Have students look at the wall chart. Explain that the scene shows a typical Saturday afternoon at an American high school football game. The team is playing football and the fans are watching the game. The winners of the game have a parade after the game to celebrate. Ask students if they have ever seen an American football game. Find out how many students like football or would like to know more about it. Have students who know something about the game describe it for the class.

▶ **BE + predicate adjective.** Point to people in the picture and ask students at random how that person in the picture feels. For example, point to Number 10. Students say *He's tired.* Now have students express their own feelings and tell their classmates about them. Have all students form a circle. Student A whispers *I'm happy* in Student B's ear. Student B tells the class what Student A said. For example: *He's happy* or *Pedro is happy.* Now Student B whispers *I'm silly* in Student C's ear, and Student C reports to the class what Student B said.

▶ **Intensifier (*really, very*) + adjective**

  > Certain adverbs are called *intensifiers*. The intensifiers *really* and *very* increase the degree of intensity of the adjectives following them. For example: *After an hour, I was hungry. After four hours, I was really hungry.*

  Have students underline and read aloud all sentences with *very* or *really* in the content reading. Then, divide the class into two teams. Students in Team 1 pantomime one of the content words. Students in Team 2 guess the word and pantomime an intensified version of that word. Then team 1 students say the word with *very* or *really.* For example, Team 1 pantomimes *sick.* Team 2 says *sick* and pantomimes *very sick.* Team 1 says *very sick* or *really sick.* The teams then reverse roles.

WORKSHEET: Topic 33
  See Teacher's Book page 133.

▶ CHANTS

Components: Dictionary pages 66-67, Content Chant Topic 33, Cassette

 CONTENT CHANT

Feelings

I'm excited. *
We're winning. * *

I'm proud. *
We won! * *

I'm scared. *
We're losing. * *

I'm sad. *
They won! * *

He's angry. *
They lost. * *

She's surprised. *
We won! * *

They're sad. *
We're happy. *
We're proud. *
We won! * *

- Present the content chant. **See pages xx-xxi for general techniques about presenting chants.**

- Before distributing the chant, have students practice just the clapping indicated by * and ** in the chant. Divide the class into two groups. The first group claps once and then the second group claps twice. Repeat this clapping pattern until the rhythm increases in sound and speed.

- Now have the whole class practice words from the chant. Students chant the following words, clapping once after each word: *excited*, proud*, scared*, sad*, angry*, surprised*, happy**. Students chant all seven words with claps repeatedly.

- Distribute Content Chant 33. Divide the class into two groups. Group 1 chants the first lines of each stanza with the single clap. Group 2 chants the second lines of each stanza with the double claps. In the last stanza, Group 1 chants the first three lines and Group 2 chants the last line. Another variation is to have individual students chant each line of the chant. The entire class claps in rhythm as indicated by the clap cues. The entire class chants the last stanza in unison.

▶ EXTENSION

Components: Dictionary pages 66-67, Transparency 33, Wall Chart 33

- Have each student write an illustrated story about a particular time when they felt a certain emotion. Ask students to tell their stories and show their pictures to their classmates. Gather several pages of students' work and make various class books entitled *Our Feelings*. Put the books around the room and have students look through them at a later time.

- Ask students to discuss what they do when they feel sick. Encourage students to suggest cold remedies from their home countries. For example, chicken soup is recognized as a good remedy for sickness in the United States.

- Have a "Silliest Student" contest. Ask each student to do the silliest thing he or she can think of and perform it for the class. The rest of the class may rate each student's performance on a scale of 1 to 10. Write down the total of all the scores (or the average of all the scores) next to each student's name. When all of the students have performed a silly action, look at the total (or average) scores for each student and determine who is the silliest student.

- Ask all students to talk about the time in their lives when they were most excited. What happened to them? Why were they excited?

- Have students form a circle and sing and act out the song "If You're Happy and You Know It":

  If you're happy and you know it, clap your hands.**
  If you're happy and you know it, clap your hands.**
  If you're happy and you know it,
  and you really want to show it,
  If you're happy and you know it, clap your hands.**

Have students sing various other verses, substituting silly, proud, and excited. Then ask students to create their own verses and substitute another action for clap your hands. For example: *If you're scared and you know it, close your eyes.*

- Display a range of color swatches including the color black. Distribute them to students. Next, draw three faces: a happy face, a neutral face, and a sad face. Then have students place a color swatch above each face they think is represented by that color.

► LITERATURE

Suggested Books

Everybody Has Feelings/Todos Tenemos Sentimientos
written and photographed by Charles E. Avery.
Open Hand Publishing, Inc. 1992. ISBN 0940880342
This bilingual concept book isolates words for feelings in English and Spanish and weds them to a photographic essay that captures the many moods of children. This book can be used to supplement the introduction of the content words from this topic with additional words and photographs. Because of its simplicity, this book is highly recommended for beginners.

The Giving Tree
written and illustrated by Shel Silverstein.
Harpercollins Juvenile Books, 1986. ISBN 0060256656
Shel Silverstein's classic parable about unconditional love and the joy of giving is well-suited to the topic of feelings. The simple text and line drawings make it appropriate for young readers, but its universal themes make it appealing to all ages. For second-language learners especially, *The Giving Tree* presents a complex topic in easy-to-understand language.

How Humans Make Friends
written and illustrated by Loreen Leedy.
Holiday House, 1996. ISBN 0823412237
In this delightfully humorous title, an alien named Zork Tripork delivers an illustrated lecture to fellow aliens about a recent trip to Earth. Zork tries to explain how humans make friends, what friends talk about, and how friends can sometimes hurt one another's feelings. This complex subject is treated in a very lighthearted fashion. The illustrations resemble cartoon panels, and each is accompanied by a single sentence. In a witty way, *How Humans Make Friends* teaches students how to describe everyday feelings, and how to relate to other children.

WORKBOOK: Topic 33

On this page, students fill in the blanks with words from the word box, based on the explanations and pictures.

WORKSHEET: Topic 33

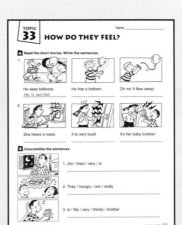

In A, students tell how the people pictured feel in each part of the short picture stories. In B, they unscramble the sentences.

34 EXPLORING SCIENCE

▶ **CONTENT**

Basic principles of the scientific method

▶ **LANGUAGE**

Modal *might*: *You might use a hand lens.*

Noun forms of specific verbs: *planning, observation, classification, measurement, experimentation, reporting*

Imperatives: *Plan your work.*

CONTENT WORDS

1. hand lens
2. microscope
3. tweezers
4. slide
5. cover glass
6. chart
7. data
8. collection
9. eyedropper
10. fire extinguisher
11. first aid kit
12. safety glasses
13. equipment
14. model
15. diagram
16. exhibit

CONTENT READING

Exploring Science

The boys and girls in the picture are using the scientific method. They are learning about the world around them. You can follow these steps and be a scientist, too.

To begin, ask yourself a question about the world around you. How will you answer that question? What will you do? Plan your work. Write your ideas on paper. Planning is the first step.

Next, observe. Look at things very closely. Observation is an important step. You might use a hand lens or a microscope. You use the microscope to look at very small things on slides. You might use tweezers to put a cover glass on top of the slide.

Classification is another step in the scientific method. You might classify a collection of plants. You sort them into different groups. For example, you might classify plants into three groups: plants with flowers, plants with cones, and plants without seeds. You might make a chart to record the data. The data is the information about each group.

Measurement is another step in the scientific method. You might measure length with a ruler. You might measure the volume of a liquid with a beaker or an eyedropper.

Experimentation is another step. You might experiment to test your idea. Some experiments use a lot of equipment. Some experiments are dangerous. Use safety glasses. You should have a fire extinguisher and a first aid kit in your classroom.

The last step is reporting. You might share your information with others in an exhibit, a model, or a diagram. Your report tells others the answers to your question.

▶ WORDS

Components: Dictionary pages 68-69, Transparency 34, Wall Chart 34, Workbook page 34, Word and Picture Cards Topic 34, Cassette

- Present the content words. **See pages xiv-xvi for general techniques about presenting content words.**

    > **Language Note:** Some people pronounce the first *a* in *data* like the *a* in *date* or *make*. Others pronounce it like the *a* in *add* or *sad*. The word *data* is most often used in American English as a noncount noun (a singular mass entity) with a singular verb form (*The data shows...*). It can also be used with a plural form (*The data show...*), but this usage is more common in British English.

- Bring to class actual examples of some content words on Dictionary page 68 (*hand lens, microscope*, etc.). Activate students' prior knowledge by having them tell how each item is used. If students don't know, let them guess. Encourage class discussion.

- Distribute the word and picture cards. Have students ask each other questions to find out which cards they have. Then, have them divide themselves into two category groups. One category group is *Equipment*, meaning something used in experiments (*hand lens, slide, first aid kit*, etc.). The other category group is *Things we might make or do* (*chart, data, model*, etc.). Have each group read aloud and display their cards after they have formed their groups.

- Display the wall chart and have students look at the picture. Explain that the first step in exploring science is *planning*. In the wall chart, two students are writing their questions and ideas down on paper. That is planning. Now draw six columns on the board and label them *Planning, Observation, Classification, Measurement, Experimentation* and *Reporting*. Write the words *questions* and *ideas* under *Planning*. Now, distribute word and picture cards to the students, and ask where their word and picture cards belong on the wall chart. Then, have students go to the board and write their word under the appropriate category. For example, the student with the *hand lens* card writes that word in the *Observation* column. Encourage discussion about these steps in the scientific method.

- Ask students what they think should be in a first aid kit in a science class (bandages, scissors, tape, burn cream, etc.). Divide the class into two groups. Students in each group draw individual pictures of items they want in their first aid kit. Then, the groups pantomime the use of the items. If possible, items from a real first aid kit can also be used to begin discussion or for pantomime.

> **WORKBOOK:** Topic 34
> See Teacher's Book page 137.

▶ CONTENT

Components: Dictionary pages 68-69, Transparency 34, Wall Chart 34, Content Reading Topic 34, Worksheet Topic 34, Cassette

- Present the content reading. **See pages xvii-xix for general techniques about presenting content readings.**

- Ask the following or similar questions:

    What are the six steps in the scientific method?
    Why might you use a microscope?
    Why might you make a chart?
    What does a beaker measure?
    Why is a fire extinguisher important in the science classroom?
    How do you share scientific information?

- ▶ **Noun forms of specific verbs.** For each of the verbs on the wall chart (*plan, observe, classify, measure, experiment, report*), point out to students the matching noun forms (*planning, observation, classification, measurement, experimentation, reporting*). The verb form describes the action and the noun form describes the process. Ask students to underline and read aloud sentences in the content reading using the noun forms of the words on the wall chart. Then ask the class as a whole to list the steps in the scientific method using the noun forms of these words.

- ▶ **Modal *might*.** Point out to students that the modal *might* is used with all subjects (*he might, they might*) and is generally used to make suggestions or express possibility. Have students circle and read all sentences in the content reading using *might*. Then have students describe the details involved in each of the steps or stages in the scientific method using *might*. For example: *In the observation stage, you might use a microscope.*

- Have individual students take turns pantomiming the various actions portrayed in the wall chart while other students guess the actions.

- Ask students why they think the scientific method is important. Explain that the scientific method is an organized way of thinking that allows scientists to get exact, factual information from their experiments. When scientists who use the scientific method write their final reports, their experiments can be duplicated by other people. Ask students if there are any scientific questions they might like to answer through experimentation. How would they do it? Encourage class discussion.

> **WORKSHEET:** Topic 34
> See Teacher's Book page 137.

► CHANTS

Components: Dictionary pages 68-69, Content Chant Topic 34, Cassette

 CONTENT CHANT

Put on Your Safety Glasses

Put on your safety glasses.
Pick up the tweezers.
Pick up a leaf.
Put it on the slide.
Look at it under the microscope.
Now turn it over.
Eeeeeeeek! Look at the little bug!

Observe, * classify,
measure very carefully.
Observe, * classify,
study the data.
Fill out the chart.

Observe, * classify,
measure very carefully.
Start a collection.
Start it today.
       Where's the little bug?
He ran away.

- Present the content chant. **See pages xx-xxi for general techniques about presenting chants.**

- Before distributing the chant, have students practice with small chunks of language from the chant. Divide the class into three groups. Group 1 chants *Observe * classify, measure very carefully.* Group 2 chants *safety glasses, tweezers, leaf, slide.* Group 3 chants *microscope, bug.* Each group chants in turn, and as they become more comfortable with the language, they chant their lines repeatedly and simultaneously.

- Distribute Content Chant 34. Divide the class into three groups. Have each group chant one stanza and pantomime their words as they chant. Select two individual students. One student chants the lines *Eeeeeeeek! Look at the little bug!* and *Where's the little bug?* The other student pantomimes the little bug running away in the last stanza.

- Have students substitute other words for the lines *Observe,* classify, measure very carefully.* Encourage students to use various words describing actions in the scientific method. For example: *Plan, * observe, classify very carefully* or *Classify * measure, experiment very carefully.* Remind students to clap (as indicated by the asterisk) and try to keep the rhythm of the chant.

► EXTENSION

Components: Dictionary pages 68-69, Transparency 34, Wall Chart 34

- Explain that there are many different areas of study in the field of science (biology, chemistry, physics, geology, astronomy). Divide the class into groups. Each group researches one of these sub-fields and finds out the following information: what the science is the study of; its real life uses (medicine, industry, new products, etc.); examples of famous people and famous achievements associated with it; and the type of study necessary to become this kind of scientist. Encourage students to use almanacs, encyclopedias, and the Internet. Each group reports its data to the class.

- Discuss careers in science with the students. Have students find out more about a career in one of the sciences and explain why they would or would not like to be that type of scientist. Discuss what people who work in these fields are called: *biologists, chemists,* etc.

- If possible, take the students on a field trip to a local laboratory, hospital, or other science facility and have students interview the scientists there about their jobs. Students present the information from their various interviews to the class.

- Invite a firefighter to the class to talk about fire safety and how to use a fire extinguisher, safety glasses, and a first aid kit. Have the class organize and practice a fire drill.

- If possible, pair students with mainstream partners to find out about as many simple science experiments as possible. Then, divide the class into groups. Each group performs one of the experiments using the scientific method and keeps a journal of the exact steps and measurements that they performed. They write their final report of their data in their journals. After each group has completed their experiment, they submit their journals. Check the journals for any problems. Then, redistribute the journals to other groups. Challenge them to follow the same steps to see if they can produce the same results.

►LITERATURE

Suggested Books

Science and Technology
Edited by Jill Bailey and Catherine Thompson.
Oxford University Press, 1993. ISBN 0199101434
This volume is an ideal starting point for presenting information on exploring science. It includes sections on science and materials, energy and the home, technology, and astronomy. This book is similar to the Dictionary in that it shows science at work in everyday situations and places, including the home and the classroom. The short selections may be chosen to isolate particular content words throughout Units 5, 6, 7, and 8.

Archibald Frisby
written and illustrated by Michael D. Chesworth.
Farrar Straus & Giroux, 1994. ISBN 03743030924.
Archibald is a boy who is obsessed with science and the way things work. In an effort to tame this overanalytical tendency, his mother sends him to camp. True to form, Archibald applies scientific concepts to the camp activities, opening the eyes of his fellow campers to the practical applications of science. In this fun book, scientific terms are skillfully fit into a rhyming text that builds vocabulary and familiarizes students with everyday expressions. Teachers will find that the detailed illustrations and comic rhymes will help students to increase their general knowledge of science while also making them aware of its utility in day-to-day living.

The Oxford Children's Book of Science
by Charles Taylor and Stephen Pople.
Scholastic Trade, 1998. ISBN 0590956205
The Oxford Children's Book of Science presents scientific information by focusing on large themes: forces and motion, the nature of energy, atoms and molecules, and the basis of life. The text, however, is very down-to-earth and specific, and the book is generously illustrated with colorful charts, photographs, and diagrams. Students, especially younger ones, will need some guidance for some of the scientific terminology, but this reference should be useful for this topic and others throughout Units 5, 6, 7, and 8.

WORKBOOK: Topic 34

In A, students label the three pictures. In B, they match the words and the pictures by writing the letters next to each word. In C, students fill in the missing vowels in the six content words.

WORKSHEET: Topic 34

In A, students match the sentences about the steps in the scientific process with the sentences that describe what that step could include. In B, they fill in the blanks with the noun forms of the verbs for the scientific processes.

35 LIVING ORGANISMS

▶ **CONTENT**
....

Living organisms: monerans, protists, fungi, plants, and animals

▶ **LANGUAGE**
....

Have as a main verb:
Monerans and protists have only one cell.

CONTENT WORDS

1. plants
2. cells
3. cell wall
4. cell membrane
5. nucleus
6. chromosome
7. cytoplasm
8. photosynthesis
9. monerans
10. protists
11. fungi
12. animals
13. vertebrates
14. invertebrates

CONTENT READING

Living Organisms

There are five kinds of living organisms: monerans, protists, fungi, plants, and animals. All living organisms are made of cells. All cells have cytoplasm and a cell membrane.

Protists and monerans have only one cell. They are very small. You can only see them under a microscope. Protist cells have chromosomes and a nucleus. An amoeba and a paramecium are two examples of protists. Moneran cells don't have chromosomes or a nucleus. Bacteria are examples of monerans.

Fungi can have one cell or many cells. Every cell of a fungus has a nucleus. Some of these cells have more than one nucleus. Bread mold and mushrooms are examples of fungi.

Plants and animals have many cells. Most plant cells have chromosomes, a nucleus, a cell

membrane, and a cell wall. The cell wall protects the cell. The cell membrane allows water into the cell. Trees and flowers are examples of plants. Some plant cells use water, air, and sunshine to make food. Making food in this way is called photosynthesis.

Every animal cell has chromosomes, a nucleus, and a cell membrane. Animal cells don't have cell walls.

There are two kinds of animals: vertebrates and invertebrates. Vertebrates have spines, or backbones. People, dogs, birds, and fish are examples of vertebrates. Invertebrates don't have backbones. Worms and spiders are examples of invertebrates.

►WORDS

Components: Dictionary pages 70-71, Transparency 35, Wall Chart 35, Workbook page 35, Word and Picture Cards Topic 35, Cassette

- Present the content words. **See pages xiv-xvi for general techniques about presenting content words.**

> **Language Note:** *Fungi* is pronounced either [fun-gi] with a hard *g* sound as in *good*, or [fun-ji] with a soft *g* sound as in *gentle*. The singular form of *fungi* is *fungus*, which is pronounced with a hard *g* sound. Some people do say *funguses* in American English, but that form of the plural is not generally used in science.
>
> The word *monerans* has the stress on the second syllable and is pronounced [muh-NIHR-uns].

- Distribute a set of word and picture cards to the class. Explain that all living things (or living organisms) are divided into five groups: *monerans, protists, fungi, animals,* and *plants.* They are all made up of *cells.* Draw two columns on the board and label them *Organisms* and *Cells.* Have students divide themselves into two groups by asking each other which cards they have. Students form one group if they have cards relating to the five organisms. Students form a second group if they have cards relating to various cells or parts of a cell. Once students are in their groups, they each read aloud the word on their card and the class discusses the appropriateness of the groupings. The cards are then placed in the appropriate columns.

- Draw two columns on the board or on chart paper. Label the columns *Plants* and *Animals.* Divide the class into two groups. Students in Group 1 look at the top part of the wall chart and name as many of the plants as they can. They say the words aloud and then write them in the appropriate column. Then they add as many additional names of plants as they can. Encourage them to think about plants they see every day, perhaps on their way to school. Group 2 students do the same thing, naming the animals in the bottom half of the wall chart and also adding as many animal names as they can in the appropriate column.

- Have the entire class look at the column on the board labeled *Animals.* Have students look at Dictionary page 70 to see specific examples of *vertebrates* (*dog, frog,* etc.) and specific examples of *invertebrates* (*worms, octopus,* etc.). Explain that vertebrates have backbones and invertebrates don't have backbones. Now draw two new columns on the board, label them *Vertebrates* and *Invertebrates,* and ask individual students to classify the animals listed in the *Animals* column as *Vertebrates* or *Invertebrates.* Encourage students to think of additional examples of animals in these two subcategories.

WORKBOOK: Topic 35
See Teacher's Book page 141.

►CONTENT

Components: Dictionary pages 70-71, Transparency 35, Wall Chart 35, Content Reading Topic 35, Worksheet Topic 35, Cassette

- Present the content reading. **See pages xvii-xix for general techniques about presenting content readings.**

- Ask the following or similar questions:

  What are the five types of living organisms?
  How many cells do protists and monerans have?
  How many cells do fungi have?
  What's the main difference between plant cells and animal cells?
  What's the difference between vertebrates and invertebrates?

- ► ***Have* as a main verb.** Tell students that when we talk about living organisms we talk about physical characteristics that they have or don't have. For example, we say that all cells *have* cytoplasm and a cell membrane, but some cells *don't have* cell walls. Have students underline and read aloud all sentences with *have/has* or *don't have* in the content reading. (Introduce *doesn't have* for singular subjects even though it doesn't occur in the content reading. For example: *A worm doesn't have a backbone.*) Now divide the class into two teams. Ask students to look at the wall chart and make up as many sentences as possible to describe the pictures using *have/has* or *don't have/doesn't have.* For example: *An octopus doesn't have a backbone. A tree has leaves. Dogs have tails.* Give the teams a time limit to write their sentences. Then students from each team read their sentences aloud. The team with the greatest number of sentences using the language point correctly is the winner.

- Divide the class into five groups. Assign each group one of the living organisms. Each group makes a poster describing the organism, the characteristics of its cells, and as many examples of the organism as possible. Have groups make diagrams or drawings of the organisms and label them on their posters. Then groups can present their posters to the whole class.

WORKSHEET: Topic 35
See Teacher's Book page 141.

Components: Dictionary pages 70-71, Content Chant Topic 35, Cassette

 CONTENT CHANT

Protists Have One Cell, Not Two

Protists have one cell, not two.
You can't see them. They can't see you.

Monerans * are very small.
You can't see monerans at all.
But you better be careful, you better take care,
'cause monerans * are everywhere!

"I'm a vertebrate," *
said the dog to the frog.
"Well, so am I," said the frog to the dog.
"Not me," said the octopus,
"no, not me,
but I'm just fine at the bottom of the sea."

- Present the content chant. **See pages xx-xxi for general techniques about presenting chants.**

- Before distributing the chant, have the students practice with small chunks of language from the chant. Divide the class into two groups. Group 1 repeatedly chants *Protists have one cell*. Group 2 repeatedly chants *Monerans* are very small* in a tiny voice. Groups chant in turn and then simultaneously.

- Distribute Content Chant 35. Divide the class into two groups. The groups chant the first and second stanzas in turn. Select three individual students to chant the solo lines in the third stanza. Student A pantomimes a dog and chants the first two lines. Student B pantomimes a frog and chants the third line. Student C pantomimes the octopus and chants the last three lines.

- Have students work in groups to make up their own words for the last stanza. For example:

*"I'm a vertebrate," ***
said the duck to the man.

"Well, so am I," said the man to the duck.

"Not me," said the spider,
"no, not me."

Components: Dictionary pages 70-71, Transparency 35, Wall Chart 35

- Have students build a papier-mâché or clay model of either a plant cell or an animal cell and label the parts. Display the model cells for other students to see.

- Have students form groups to research the period of growth and development of a plant or an animal. Groups write reports and make posters with diagrams to illustrate their findings. Encourage groups to use science books, encyclopedias, and the Internet. Ask the groups to report their findings to the class.

- Have students research the process of *photosynthesis* in science books and encyclopedias. Students can work together in groups of their choice. Each person in the group is responsible for one task in preparing the group's research for presentation. One person draws the picture or diagrams, another labels the parts in the process, another writes the report, and one or two others read the report or dramatize the process of *photosynthesis* to the rest of the class.

- Divide the class into groups. Have students in each group bring bread into class at the beginning of the week. Students keep the bread in plastic bags, and each day watch as the bread mold begins to grow. If possible, have students look at these fungi cells under a microscope. Students should keep a log or journal of the changes in the mold each day.

- Bring to class a microscope, some onions, and enough toothpicks for all the students in your class. Divide students into groups. Have one student from each group, in turn, take the thin layer between the slices of the onion, and place it on a slide. Students look at the layer's plant cells through the microscope and then draw and label the parts of the plant cell. Now ask students to rub a clean toothpick lightly on the inside of their cheek or mouth, and place the residue cells on the toothpick onto another slide. Have students draw and label the parts to these human animal cells.

► LITERATURE

Suggested Books

Crinkleroot's 25 Fish Every Child Should Know
written and illustrated by Jim Arnosky.
Simon and Schuster, 1993. ISBN 0027058441

Crinkleroot's 25 Birds Every Child Should Know
written and illustrated by Jim Arnosky.
Simon and Schuster, 1993. ISBN 002705859X

Crinkleroot's 25 Mammals Every Child Should Know
written and illustrated by Jim Arnosky.
Simon and Schuster, 1994. ISBN 002705845X

Crinkleroot's 25 More Animals Every Child Should Know
written and illustrated by Jim Arnosky.
Simon and Schuster, 1994. ISBN 0027058468

The four volumes in this series give students a basic introduction to fish, birds, mammals, and other assorted creatures. Each volume begins with general information about an animal group, followed by realistic illustrations of twenty-five animals chosen from that group. The jovial woodsman character, Crinkleroot, acts as a guide through each book and lends continuity to the series. These books are recommended for use by beginners in small groups or with partners. Students can match the names of the animals in these books to the pictures in the Dictionary illustration. These books can also be used with other topics in Unit 5.

Animal Seasons
written and illustrated by Brian Wildsmith.
Oxford University Press Children's Books, 1991. ISBN 0192721755
Charming illustrations take the reader on a journey through the seasons. The text characterizes each changing season by its effect on the lives and activities of plants, animals, and birds. The book is written in the simple present, so beginning readers should have little difficulty approaching it. The story and pictures present vocabulary that is introduced in this topic.

Biggest, Strongest, Fastest
written and illustrated by Steve Jenkins.
Houghton Mifflin Co., 1997. ISBN 0395861365
In this attractive book, comparative facts and figures about the animal world are illustrated with cut-paper collage art. As students read the simple text, they can identify familiar animals while they learn to use comparatives and superlatives. A chart on the last page shows the size, weight, and diet of each animal and where it lives. This book is also useful for Topics 42-46.

WORKBOOK: Topic 35

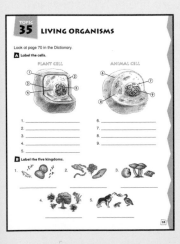

In the first activity, students label the parts of a plant cell and an animal cell. In the second activity, students label the pictures with the names of the five kingdoms.

WORKSHEET: Topic 35

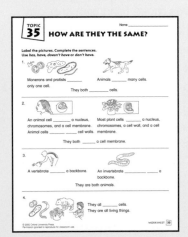

On this page, students fill in *has*, *have*, *doesn't have*, or *don't have* in the sentences which describe and compare the various living organisms.

36 PLANTS

▶ **CONTENT**
....
The different parts of various kinds of plants

▶ **LANGUAGE**
....
Stative verbs (*smell, have, be*): *Pecan trees have short, flat leaves.*

Action verbs (*make, carry*): *The plant's leaves make food with sunlight, air, and water.*

 ## CONTENT WORDS

1. nut	11. pinecone
2. seed	12. flower
3. tree	13. petal
4. trunk	14. stamen
5. limb	15. pistil
6. bark	16. pollen
7. leaf	17. bud
8. stem	18. stalk
9. branch	19. bulb
10. needle	20. root

CONTENT READING

Plants

Plants are living things. They have roots, stems, and leaves.

There are many kinds of leaves. Pecan trees have short, flat leaves. Pine trees have long, thin leaves, or needles. Pine needles are sharp.

Roots hold the plant in the soil. The roots also take in water. The plant's leaves make food with sunlight, air, and water. The stem carries food and water to all the parts of the plant. The trunk of a tree is a very big stem. The trunk has bark on the outside. The trunk carries food and water to the limbs, branches, and leaves of a tree.

Many plants start as seeds. A pecan tree starts as a small seed. The seed is inside a pecan nut. A pine tree also starts as a seed. Pine seeds are in pinecones. One pinecone has many seeds. Pinecones fall from pine trees onto the soil.

Other plants start as round bulbs. The lily plant starts as a bulb under the soil. The bulb keeps food for the new plant.

Some plants have buds and flowers. A bud has large petals. The petals open and the bud becomes a flower. Flowers smell good. The lily plant has a long stalk and beautiful flowers. Every flower has a pistil in the middle and stamens around the pistil. There is a powder on the stamens. The powder is pollen. Bees and other insects spread the pollen. The pollen helps make new flowers.

▶ WORDS

Components: Dictionary pages 72-73, Transparency 36, Wall Chart 36, Workbook page 36, Word and Picture Cards Topic 36, Cassette

- Present the content words. **See pages xiv-xvi for general techniques about presenting content words.**

  Language Note: The noun *stalk* has a silent *l* and is pronounced like the word *walk*. The words *pinecone* and *needle* have a silent *e*.

- Distribute the word and picture cards to all students. Then have students look at the wall chart to see how these parts of trees and flowering plants look in context. Draw a Venn Diagram like the example below on the board or on chart paper. Ask students to say their words aloud and then place their cards in the appropriate area of the diagram. If their cards relate only to trees, or only to flowering plants, students place their cards in those circles. If their cards relate to both trees and flowering plants, then students place them in the overlapping section in the center labeled *Trees and Flowering Plants*.

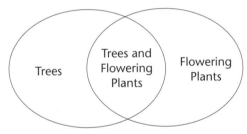

- Divide students into three groups and have each group look at one of the three sections in the Venn Diagram above. Ask each group to write a paragraph about that section using *have* and *don't have*. Group 1 writes a paragraph about what a tree has and doesn't have, Group 2 writes a paragraph about what flowering plants have and don't have, and Group 3 writes a paragraph about what both trees and flowering plants have and don't have. Each group reads the paragraph to the entire class.

- Pair students. Give each pair two real flowers, two dried flowers, or two pictures of flowers. Students label the parts of the flowers and exchange their work with their partners, who check for accuracy. Each pair then makes a large poster identifying both flowers and their parts. Pairs, in turn, present their posters to the entire class.

WORKBOOK: Topic 36
See Teacher's Book page 145.

▶ CONTENT

Components: Dictionary pages 72-73, Transparency 36, Wall Chart 36, Content Reading Topic 36, Worksheet Topic 36, Cassette

- Present the content reading. **See pages xvii-xix for general techniques about presenting content readings.**

- Ask the following or similar questions:

  What are the three main parts of all plants?
  What does the stem do?
  What do the roots do?
  What do the leaves do?
  What does a bulb do?
  What does pollen do?

▶ **Stative verbs versus action verbs**

  Stative verbs do not express actions. They are generally used to describe existing conditions and states. We use stative verbs to talk about possessions, descriptions, the five senses, emotions and ideas. Some examples of stative verbs are *be, have, contain, look like, resemble, seem, appear, smell, like, love, hate,* and *know*.

Explain to students that most verbs are action verbs, such as *make, carry,* or *start*. Some verbs are stative verbs such as *be, have, look like, smell,* or *feel*. Divide the class into two groups. Group 1 circles all the action verbs in the content reading and Group 2 draws a box around all the stative verbs in the content reading. Then each group, in turn, reads their sentences aloud while students in the other group mark their copies of the content reading with either a circle for the action verbs or a box for the stative verbs.

▶ **Stative verbs.** Divide students into three groups. Students in Group 1 bring to class as many different leaves as they can find. Students in Group 2 bring in as many different types of tree bark as they can find. Students in Group 3 bring in as many flowers as they can find. Groups 1 and 2 make rubbings of their leaves and their bark. Group 3 dries its flowers. Then each group writes sentences using as many stative verbs (such as *look like, smell, feel have, etc.*) as possible. The groups each make a poster of their work (including their sentences) and present it to the entire class.

WORKSHEET: Topic 36
See Teacher's Book page 145.

► CHANTS

Components: Dictionary pages 72-73, Content Chant Topic 36, Word and Picture Cards Topic 36, Cassette

 ## CONTENT CHANT

Plant Chant

Plant a bulb.
Watch it grow.
Strong roots
Long stem
Green leaves
Beautiful flowers
Soft petals
Tiger lily

Plant a seed.
Watch it grow.
Little pine tree, young branches
Little leaves, little needles
Young pine tree
Watch it grow.

Old pine tree
Strong trunk
Strong limbs
Brown bark
Green needles
Brown pinecones
Beautiful pine tree
Watch it grow.

- Present the content chant. **See pages xx-xxi for general techniques about present chants.**

- Before distributing the chant, have students practice with small chunks of the language from the chant. Divide the class into three groups, with each group repeatedly chanting one of the following lines: *Young pine tree, Watch it grow,* or *Old pine tree.* Groups chant in turn and then simultaneously.

- Distribute Content Chant 36. Divide the class into two groups. The students in Group 1 chant and pantomime the second stanza. They pretend to be the little pine trees and chant in a tiny voice. The students in Group 2 chant and pantomime the third stanza. They pretend to be the old, strong pine trees and chant in a big, booming voice.

- Now divide the class into three groups to chant and pantomime the entire chant. Each group chants one stanza. Once students are very comfortable with the lines of the chant, have individual students in each group chant one line each.

- For variation, have individual students hold up picture cards for the parts of the plants and trees as these words occur in the chant. For example, the student who chants *Strong roots* holds up the picture card for *root.*

► EXTENSION

Components: Dictionary pages 72-73, Transparency 36, Wall Chart 36

- Dampen some paper towels, place several lima beans in each one, and put them in small dishes or cups in a warm place. Divide the class into groups and assign a lima bean dish to each group. Groups observe and record in a journal the daily changes that take place in their lima beans.

- Demonstrate how to plant a seed, bulb, and/or cutting. Divide the students into groups. Distribute soil, water, cups, markers, and rulers, as well as seeds, bulbs, or cuttings. Have students in each group plant their seed, bulb, or cutting and then measure and record each plant's growth in their journals. At the end of two weeks, students collect all their findings and write a final report with illustrations of their data. Groups present their reports to the entire class.

- Bring an aloe vera plant (or a picture of one) to class. Tell students that we use the gel from the leaves of this plant for cosmetics and for treating skin burns. Explain to students that we use plants and flowers for a variety of things including food, perfume, medicine, and cosmetics. Divide the class into two groups, one for plants and one for flowers. Have each group do research on the various uses of plants or flowers. Encourage students to use encyclopedias, science books, and the Internet. Also, if possible, encourage students to go to health food stores, supermarkets, or drug stores to look at some of the labels on products. Have them find out whether plants or flowers have been used. Discuss in class.

- Pair students and take a walk around the school or elsewhere in the community where there are a lot of plants and flowers. Afterwards, have the paired students make a map illustrating the plants and/or flowers they saw on the walk. Different pairs may see different plants or flowers. Then, have one student in each pair list the way these plants affect their lives. Have the other student in each pair tell what it would be like if these plants or flowers were no longer in the areas. Students compare their lists and then together wriite two paragraphs decribing how they feel about these plants and flowers. Encourage students to share their work with the class, especially their illustrated maps.

► LITERATURE

Suggested Books

From Seed to Plant
written and illustrated by Gail Gibbons.
Holiday House, 1993. ISBN 0823410250
Gail Gibbons invites readers to wonder at the nature of growing plants. With clear, concise text and bright, detailed illustrations, this book offers basic information about the structure of plants and their life cycles—from seed to flower, from flower to fruit, and then to seed again. The book also includes instructions for growing bean plants. To extend instruction, teachers may want to bring in live plants or cut flowers so that students can compare them to the illustrations in this book and in the Dictionary. This book is especially useful for beginners and intermediate students.

Plants (Make It Work! Science Series)
written by Andrew Haslam, Claire Watts, Alexandra Parson, and Wendy Baker; photographs by Jon Barnes.
World Publications, 1997. ISBN 0716647044
This book contains a series of simple experiments students can perform to learn more about plants. Twenty topics range from collecting specimens to making natural dyes. The steps in the procedures are clearly written and accompanied by colorful photographs. The required materials are commonly available and appropriate for students to use independently. The text is succinct and reinforces classroom language. Intermediate and advanced students will be able to use the text with little direct instruction.

The Science Book of Things That Grow
written by Neil Ardley.
Gulliver Books, 1991. ISBN 0152005862
Like the other titles in Neil Ardley's "Science Book" series, *The Science Book of Things That Grow* is a down-to-earth science book full of interesting information and simple experiments. Each of the seventeen plant-related topics is presented in a one or two-page format. The expository text is simple and often accompanied by examples for clarification. The clear photographs and illustrations make it easy for students to replicate the experiments. Materials needed to perform the experiments are readily available in most classrooms and households.

How a Plant Grows
written and illustrated by Bobbie Kalman.
Crabtree Publishing Company, 1996. ISBN 0865057281
Beginning ESL students will appreciate this book because they will be able to read much of the text after learning the content words for this topic. The text is accompanied by numerous colorful illustrations, including many close-up photographs of plants. Three simple activities at the back of the book involving growing and observing plants are useful for extending the topic. A short glossary can serve as a review of important content words.

Poisonous Plants
written by Suzanne M. Coli; illustrated by Astrid M. Lenox.
Franklin Watts, 1992. ISBN 0531156478
Being able to identify that some plants are poisonous to eat or touch is important and practical. *Poisonous Plants* features no-nonsense descriptions of some of the plants found in North America. After working with this book, students will be able to identify the poisonous plants in their area. To extend the topic, teachers can role-play calling a poison control center or invite a health professional to talk to the class about dangerous plants and the appropriate antidotes to certain poisonous plants.

WORKBOOK: Topic 36

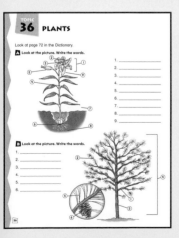

In A, students label the parts of the plant. In B, they label the parts of the tree.

WORKSHEET: Topic 36

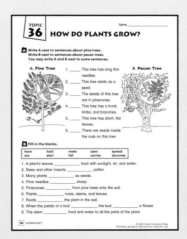

Activity A has six statements that are true for pine trees, pecan trees, or both. Students write the letter *A*, the letter *B*, or both letters next to each sentence that is true about the corresponding tree. In B, students choose words from the word box to fill in the sentences based on the content reading.

▶ **CONTENT**

Various kinds of vegetables

▶ **LANGUAGE**

Count and noncount nouns:
Mrs. Ruiz buys some celery and a pound of string beans.

Quantity expressions: *some...,*
a head of..., a pound of...,
a bag of...

CONTENT WORDS

1. lettuce
2. celery
3. cabbage
4. broccoli
5. cauliflower
6. carrot
7. onion
8. radish
9. peppers
10. lima beans
11. cucumber
12. string bean
13. potato
14. yam
15. mushroom
16. peas

CONTENT READING

Vegetables

Vegetables are plants, but they are food, too. We don't eat the whole plant. We only eat some parts of the plant. We eat the roots of carrot plants and radish plants. We eat the bulbs of onion plants. We eat the stalks of celery plants. We eat the flowers of broccoli and cauliflower plants. We also eat the leaves of cabbage and lettuce plants.

Mr. and Mrs. Pak own a vegetable market. Mrs. Ruiz is shopping at the market. She needs vegetables for her family. She looks at the broccoli and the cauliflower. The broccoli is big and thick. The cauliflower is very white. She buys a head of broccoli. Mrs. Ruiz sees the bright orange carrots and round onions. They are perfect for her dinner. She buys six carrots and ten onions.

Mrs. Ruiz's daughter Carla wants string beans and celery. The string beans are long and thin. The celery is very thick. Mrs. Ruiz buys some celery and a pound of string beans.

Mrs. Ruiz wants to make a salad. She still needs peppers, radishes, and cucumbers. She buys three peppers, two cucumbers, and a bag of radishes. Then she sees the lima beans and the peas. They are very green. Mrs. Ruiz buys a pound of peas and a pound of lima beans.

Mr. and Mrs. Pak help Mrs. Ruiz. Mrs. Pak chooses a head of lettuce for Mrs. Ruiz. Mr. Pak carries a head of cabbage for her.

Mrs. Ruiz and Carla love the fresh vegetables.

▶ WORDS

Components: Dictionary pages 74-75, Transparency 37, Wall Chart 37, Workbook page 37, Word and Picture Cards Topic 37, Cassette

- Present the content words. **See pages xiv-xvi for general techniques about presenting content words.**

- Distribute the word and picture cards. Have students ask each other *Yes/No* questions about which cards they have (for example: *Do you have a carrot?*). Based on their answers, they form themselves into two groups, one with green vegetables and one with non-green vegetables. Each group draws pictures of all their vegetables and labels each picture. The groups present their pictures to the class.

- Bring some real vegetables to class. Have the students open their Dictionaries to Topic 37, look at the content words, and compare the pictures to the real vegetables. Make a chart on the board like the example below and ask students to classify the vegetables by color, shape, and size. Check the appropriate characteristics in the chart for each vegetable.

Vegetable	green	red	orange	brown	white	long	round	large	small
1. lettuce	✓						✓	✓	
2. celery	✓					✓		✓	

- Use the vegetables for a paper bag surprise game. Keep all of them hidden from view. Place one in a bag, but don't let the class know which vegetable it is. Individual student volunteers put their hands into the bag to feel the vegetable. The student describes the shape of the vegetable that he or she feels, and the class guesses which vegetable it is. As the students guess each vegetable, lay the vegetable on a table so that each subsequent guess will become easier. The student who guesses the correct vegetable is the next to reach into the bag.

- Divide students into groups and help them conduct a poll of which vegetables they like, don't like, or have never tasted. Students record their data using a chart like the example below which subcategorizes the data for boys and girls. Each group then presents its data to the entire class. Help students combine their data and then make bar graphs to illustrate the combined data. Encourage students to discuss the results.

Vegetables	Like		Don't like		Never tasted	
	Boys	Girls	Boys	Girls	Boys	Girls
1. lettuce						
2. celery						

WORKBOOK: Topic 37
See Teacher's Book page 149.

▶ CONTENT

Components: Dictionary pages 74-75, Transparency 37, Wall Chart 37, Content Reading Topic 37, Worksheet Topic 37, Cassette

- Present the content reading. **See pages xvii-xix for general techniques about presenting content readings.**

- Ask the following or similar questions:

  Which part of celery plants do we eat?
  Do Mrs. Ruiz and Carla like vegetables?
  Which vegetable is white?
  How much broccoli does Mrs. Ruiz buy?
  How many carrots does Mrs. Ruiz buy?

- Review the Topic 36 content words *leaf, flower, stalk, bulb,* and *root.* Have students look at the picture cards for *carrot, radish, onion, celery, cabbage, lettuce, broccoli,* and *cauliflower.* For each vegetable, ask students to refer to the content reading and name what part of the plant we eat.

▶ **Count and noncount nouns, Quantity expressions**

> Count nouns have singular and plural forms. They can take *a/an* or a number before them. We can count them (*a carrot, two carrots*). Noncount nouns (*lettuce, celery, cabbage, broccoli,* and *cauliflower*) only have one form, which is neither singular nor plural. Noncount nouns cannot be counted. They are quantified by using quantity expressions such as *some, a head of, a pound of,* or *a bag of* (*two heads of lettuce, a pound of celery*). We can also use quantity expressions with plural count nouns (*a pound of string beans*).

Make two lists on the board, one of noncountable vegetables (*lettuce, celery, cabbage, broccoli,* and *cauliflower*) and one of countable vegetables (the rest of the content words). Then list the expressions *a pound of, a head of, a bag of, some.* Show students that you can use numbers to count the vegetables in the second list, but for the first list you cannot put numbers directly in front of the word. You need to use the words *a pound of, a head of, a bag of,* or *some* (or *two heads of, three pounds of,* etc.). Ask students to find examples in the content reading of the vegetables from each list and the quantity expressions or numbers used with them.

▶ **Count and noncount nouns, Quantity expressions.** Form two teams. Students from Team 1 say a quantity expression or a number. Students from Team 2 say an appropriate noun. For example, Team 1 says *three.* Team 2 says *carrots.* Then teams exchange roles.

▶ **Count and noncount nouns, Quantity expressions.** Have students role-play Mr. Pak, Mrs. Pak, Mrs. Ruiz, and Carla. Encourage students to use the quantity expressions and numbers of vegetables from the content reading.

WORKSHEET: Topic 37
See Teacher's Book page 149.

▶ CHANTS

Components: Dictionary pages 74-75, Content Chant Topic 37, Cassette

 CONTENT CHANT

Mushroom, Broccoli

Mushroom, broccoli,
cauliflower pie.
She hates broccoli.
  So do I.

String beans, celery,
cauliflower stew.
He hates broccoli.
  So will you.

Onions, lima beans,
yams. Hooray!
They eat broccoli every day.

I ate broccoli
in my dream.
I love broccoli * ice cream!

- Present the content chant. **See pages xx-xxi for general techniques about presenting chants.**

- Before distributing the chant, have students practice with small chunks of the language from the chant. Divide the class into three groups. Each group repeatedly chants the words *mushroom, broccoli,* or *cauliflower.* Groups first chant in turn and then simultaneously.

- Now distribute Content Chant 37. Have the entire class chant all the stanzas. Assign solo parts to a boy and girl and have them come to the front of the room. In the first stanza, the class points to the girl as they chant *She hates broccoli.* The girl makes a nasty face at the mention of the word *broccoli.* The boy chants loudly *So do I.* In the second stanza, the class points to the boy as they chant *He hates broccoli.* The boy mimes the appropriate facial gesture. The girl chants knowingly *So will you* and points to the class. The class points to the boy and girl as they chant the line in the third stanza *They eat broccoli every day.*

▶ EXTENSION

Components: Dictionary pages 74-75, Transparency 37, Wall Chart 37

- Display local newspaper ads or supermarket flyers for vegetables. Have students, working in pairs, make shopping lists of vegetables to buy using the content words and quantity expressions. Encourage students to use additional vegetable and quantity expressions. Refer students to Topic 58 (Measurement) and the Appendix (Money) as needed.

- Set up a vegetable market in the class. Have various students draw pictures of the vegetables and others draw pictures of the money to be used. (Refer to page 123 of the Dictionary Appendix for pictures of money.) Students take turns playing the role of the storekeeper. The storekeeper has to answer any questions about the vegetables that the customers (the other students) ask about the taste of a certain vegetable and its price. The storekeeper and customers can perform transactions using the money.

- Encourage students to talk about vegetables listed in the content words which they have never tasted. Then ask students to talk about vegetables they eat at home or have eaten in their countries which are not listed in the content words. Invite those students to describe these vegetables, and draw pictures of them to share with the class. If possible, ask students to bring in samples of the real vegetables.

- Have students make an inventory of the number of fresh, canned, and frozen vegetables in their homes. Also have them interview friends and family members about which of these vegetables they like best. Ask students to present their lists to the class and choose the most popular vegetables in their homes. Make a list on the board of the most popular vegetables.

- Using the information from the vegetable inventories compiled in the previous activity, have students make a combined vegetable list from all of the lists in the class. Then have students make vegetable alphabet books from *avocado* to *zucchini* with a picture and a one sentence description of each vegetable.

- Divide the class into groups. Have each group plan to make a vegetable salad. First they plan the ingredients of their salad. Then, they draw pictures of each of the separate vegetables (in the appropriate quantities) in their salad. If possible, students can make a salad with real ingredients. If not, they can cut out their drawings and paste them into a drawing of a bowl. The groups present their salads to the class and each group tells the class why its salad is the best. Then the entire class votes on which salad they think would be the most delicious.

► LITERATURE

Suggested Books

The Victory Garden Vegetable Alphabet Book
written by Jerry Pallotta and Bob Thomson;
illustrated by Edgar Stewart.
Charlesbridge Publishing, 1992. ISBN 0881064688
This book presents an alphabetical collection of garden vegetables, from asparagus to zuchetta. Each vegetable is accompanied by an illustration and a description of how it grows. These descriptions contain many action verbs in the past, present, and future that students can learn and practice. Teachers can introduce this book at the same time as the content words or as support for them. Even though this is an alphabet book, the art and text are sophisticated enough for older students.

How My Family Lives in America
written by Susan Kuklin; photographs by the author.
Simon & Schuster Children's Books, 1992.
ISBN 0027512398
Food and family life are the common themes in this photo essay. The author profiles three families and shows how each family's distinct heritage influences their adaptation to American life. The photographs are filled with examples of words that can be matched to the word and picture cards for this topic. Family recipes are also provided as a bonus.

Stone Soup
written by Ann McGovern;
illustrated by Winslow Pinney Pels
Scholastic Trade, 1987. ISBN 0590416022
In this classic tale, a weary traveler tricks an old lady into making a soup for him. After convincing her that he is able to make soup from a stone, he enlists her in his efforts to make some "stone soup." Many of the ingredients for the "stone soup" are the vegetable content words from this topic. The text is composed of short sentences in the simple past. This book is simple enough to read aloud to beginners and intermediate students.

WORKBOOK: Topic 37

In the code in activity A, each number corresponds to a letter. Students find the corresponding letter for each number to spell the names of eight vegetables. In B, students unscramble the names of six more vegetables and match them to the pictures.

WORKSHEET: Topic 37

In A, students choose from the word box to fill in the quantities of each vegetable that the woman in the picture is buying. In B, they make up their own shopping list, using the various phrases for quantities. In C, they list vegetables they like or don't like to eat.

▶ **CONTENT**
....
Various kinds of fruit

▶ **LANGUAGE**
....
Present continuous: *Henry Warner is looking at the melons.*

Stative verbs (*have, love, like, be, taste, smell*): *Anita loves bananas.*

Noncount nouns: *Fruit is delicious.*

 ## CONTENT WORDS

1. banana
2. pineapple
3. cantaloupe
4. watermelon
5. tomato
6. peach
7. cherry
8. avocado
9. pit
10. apple
11. pear
12. citrus
13. lemon
14. lime
15. orange
16. grapefruit
17. section
18. rind
19. strawberry
20. raspberry

CONTENT READING

Fruit

Some plants produce fruit. Fruit begins as a flower. It usually has a skin on the outside. It has juicy flesh and seeds on the inside. Fruit is delicious.

This supermarket has many kinds of fruit. Mr. Rodriguez and his daughter Anita are weighing bananas. Anita loves bananas. She eats two bananas every day. Mr. Rodriguez doesn't like bananas, but he buys them for Anita. He prefers pineapples. Bananas and pineapples are tropical fruit. They grow in very warm areas.

Henry Warner is looking at the melons. He likes watermelon and he loves cantaloupe. Cantaloupe is his favorite melon.

Mrs. Lee and her daughter Jennifer are thinking about cherries and peaches. Mrs. Lee loves peaches. Jennifer doesn't like peaches, but she likes cherries. Peaches, cherries, and avocadoes have

pits inside. Peach pits are big. Cherry pits are little. Avocado pits are the biggest.

Betty Wizmur is putting raspberries and strawberries on the table. Berries have tiny seeds. You can eat them. Betty doesn't like fruit. She sees fruit every day. She prefers vegetables.

Mike Koslov works in the fruit section, too. He is bringing more grapefruit. Grapefruit goes with the other citrus fruit: limes, lemons, and oranges. Citrus fruit has a thick rind outside and juicy sections inside. Mike likes apples and pears, but he doesn't like citrus fruit. Mike loves tomatoes. Many people think that tomatoes and avocadoes are vegetables, but they are really fruit.

► WORDS

Components: Dictionary pages 76-77, Transparency 38, Wall Chart 38, Workbook page 38, Word and Picture Cards Topic 38, Cassette

- Present the content words. **See pages xiv-xvi for general techniques about presenting content words.**

    Language Note: The plural form of *tomato* is *tomatoes* and the plural form of *avocado* is *avocados or avocadoes*. In the plural forms of *cherry, strawberry*, and *raspberry*, we change the final letter *y* to *i* and add *es: cherries, strawberries*, and *raspberries*. The *p* in *raspberry* is silent and the *s* is pronounced like a *z*.

- Give each of three groups a set of word and picture cards (omit *pit, citrus, section*, and *rind)*. Each group draws an outline of a salad bowl and arranges their picture cards in the salad bowl with the word cards next to each picture. Groups present their fruit salads to the entire class. The class votes on the best fruit salad.

- Bring some real fruit to class. Have students open their Dictionaries to Topic 38, look at the content words, and compare them to the real fruit. Make a chart on the board like the example below and ask students to classify the fruit by color, shape, size, and texture, and write the appropriate characteristics in the chart. Explain that *peach* is also a color and that *pear* can also be a shape (*pear-shaped*). Point out that the outsides and insides of many kinds of fruit can be different in color, shape, and texture.

Fruit	Color yellow/brown red/green/orange	Shape Round/long/ pear-shaped	Size small/ medium/ large	Texture smooth/ rough
1. banana	yellow	long	medium	smooth
2. pineapple	brown outside/ yellow inside	long	large	rough
3. cantaloupe	brown outside/ orange inside	round	medium	rough

- Help students conduct a poll of which fruit they like, don't like, or have never tasted. Students work in groups and record their data using a chart like the example below, which subcategorizes the data for boys and girls. Each group then presents their data to the class. Help students combine the data and to make bar graphs to illustrate the combined data. Encourage students to discuss the results.

Fruit	Like		Don't like		Never tasted	
	Boys	Girls	Boys	Girls	Boys	Girls
1. banana						
2. pineapple						

WORKBOOK: Topic 38
See Teacher's Book page 153.

► CONTENT

Components: Dictionary pages 76-77, Transparency 38, Wall Chart 38, Content Reading Topic 38, Worksheet Topic 38, Cassette

- Present the content reading. **See pages xvii-xix for general techniques about presenting content readings.**

- Ask the following or similar questions:

    Do all plants produce fruit?
    Name four kinds of citrus fruit.
    Which fruit has a thick rind outside and juicy sections inside?
    Do cherries have pits or seeds?
    Does Betty Wizmur like fruit? Why or why not?
    What is Mike Koslov doing?

► **Stative verbs**

    Language Note: Stative verbs do not express actions. They are generally used to describe existing conditions and states. We use stative verbs to talk about possessions, descriptions, the five senses, emotions, and ideas. Some examples of stative verbs are *be, have, contain, resemble, seem, appear, smell, like, love, prefer, hate*, and *know*.

    Explain to students that most verbs are action verbs such as *eat* and *put*. Some verbs are stative verbs such as *be, have, love, like, hate, prefer, smell*, and *feel*. Ask students to underline all the stative verbs in the content reading and then take turns reading their sentences aloud to the class.

► **Stative verbs**. Divide the class into two teams and play a game called *Name That Fruit*. Students from each team take turns being "it." The student who is "it" writes the name of a fruit on a piece of paper which only his or her teammates see. Students from the opposite team ask *Yes/No* questions with stative verbs to try to determine which fruit it is. For example: *Is it red? Does it have a pit? Does it feel rough?* Score one point for each fruit guessed correctly.

► **Stative verbs.** If possible, have students label and taste samples of real fruit. They can then write and illustrate a paragraph describing their favorite fruit and what they like about it. Ask students to underline all the stative verbs in their paragraphs.

- Have students look at the wall chart and role-play in groups of seven the roles of each of the characters in the content reading. Encourage students to use the information in the content reading in their role plays.

WORKSHEET: Topic 38
See Teacher's Book page 153.

►CHANTS

Components: Dictionary pages 76-77, Content Chant Topic 38, Cassette

 ## CONTENT CHANT

Please Have an Apple!

Please have an apple.
They're right over there.

> I don't want an apple.
> I want a pear.
> I don't want an apple,
> not today.

"An apple a day
keeps the doctor away."

> I don't care.
> I want a pear.

How about a peach?

> I don't want a peach.

How about strawberries? They're OK.

> But I ate all the strawberries yesterday!

- Present the content chant. **See pages xx-xxi for general techniques about presenting chants.**

- Before distributing the chant, have students practice with chunks of language from the chant. Divide the class into four groups. Each group chants in turn, and then simultaneously, one of the following: *an apple, a pear, a peach, strawberries.* Be sure that students are pronouncing the *n* sound in the word *an* and the final *z* sound of the plural in *strawberries.*

- Now distribute Content Chant 38. Explain to the class that the expression "An apple a day keeps the doctor away" means that if you eat an apple every day you will not get sick because apples are very good for you.

- Divide the class into two groups and have them chant alternating stanzas of the chant. Group 1 chants all of the unindented lines of the first voice, and Group 2 chants all of the indented lines.

- Now pair students and have them take turns doing the two voices of the chant.

►EXTENSION

Components: Dictionary pages 76-77, Transparency 38, Wall Chart 38

- Display local newspaper ads or supermarket flyers for fruit. Have students, working in pairs, make shopping lists of fruit to buy. The lists can include the content words plus any additional fruit for which students have learned the names. Encourage students to use quantity expressions which they may find in the ads, such as *some, a pound of, a bag of*, etc. These phrases can be used with both count and noncount nouns (see Topic 37). Refer students to Topic 58 (Measurement) and the Appendix (Money), as needed.

- Have a discussion about the poll students did in the Words section of this topic. Encourage students to talk about fruit listed in the content words which they have never tasted. Then ask students to talk about other fruit they eat at home or have eaten in their countries. Invite those students to describe the fruit, and draw pictures to share with the class. If possible, ask students to bring in samples of the real fruit.

- Set up a fruit market in the class. Have various students draw pictures of the fruit and other students draw the money to be used. Students take turns playing the role of the storekeeper(s), who answers questions about the fruit. The other students are the customers, who ask questions about the taste of the fruit or its price.

- Divide the class into groups. Have each group create plans for making a fruit salad. First, they plan the ingredients of their fruit salad. They plan the quantities and make lists of each fruit in the salad. If possible, then have students make a real fruit salad. Encourage students to include fruit from their various countries in addition to those listed in the content words. Have groups exchange their salads. Each group guesses or names the fruit in the other group's salads.

- Have individual students research the fruit listed in the content words, as well as fruit grown in other countries. Encourage students to use science books, encyclopedias, and the Internet to find out where their fruit grows and whether their fruit grows on a tree (like peaches), a bush (like raspberries), or a vine (like cantaloupes and tomatoes). Then have students work together to complete a chart like the one below. Students list their own names in the chart if they are from any of the countries where the fruit grows. Ask students to draw a picture of their fruit and put it in the *Fruit* column. Display the chart on the bulletin board.

Fruit	Country	Student	Tree	Bush	Vine
1. apple	United States		✓		
2. grapes	United States Italy	Tony			✓

► LITERATURE

Suggested Books

Cherry Tree
written by Ruskin Bond; illustrated by Allan Eitzen.
Boyds Mills Press, 1996. ISBN 1563976218
In the foothills of the Himalayas, a young Northern Indian girl plants a cherry pit. As the cherry pit grows into a strong, adult tree, the girl grows into a young woman. Teachers may want to read this gentle, metaphorical story aloud, stopping occasionally to ask questions about its meaning. Intermediate and advanced students can use the story in sequencing activities.

Fruits, Roots, and Fungi: Plants We Eat
written and illustrated by Isamu Sekido.
Lerner Publications Company, 1993. ISBN 0822539025
Nine common foods are shown in close-up, full-color photographs. The foods are introduced in a guessing game fashion that can be adapted by teachers into an effective language-learning game. Students can match the word and picture cards to the photographs. Then they can play guessing games to reinforce the language structures and vocabulary.

The Seasons of Arnold's Apple Tree
written and illustrated by Gail Gibbons.
Harcourt Brace, 1988. ISBN 0152712453
Arnold's secret place is a big apple tree. In each of the four seasons, he goes there to play. The simple grammar of this story links the basic vocabulary to the seasons. Beginning ESL students should have little difficulty reading this story. As a culminating activity, students will certainly enjoy following the four easy steps to make Arnold's apple pie.

Harvest Year
written by Cris Peterson; photographs by Alvis Upitis.
Boyds Mills Press, 1996. ISBN 1563975718
This book gives a month-by-month account of the many different harvests that occur in the United States throughout the year. It describes the ways in which and the times at which many of the fruits in this topic are harvested. Numerous captioned photographs add visual interest to the information. The simple language can be first read aloud and then assigned to partners or individuals. This book also works well with Topic 12, The South, and Topic 10, The United States.

WORKBOOK: Topic 38

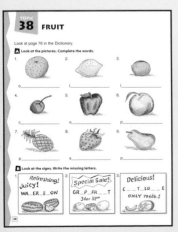

In A, students write the name for each fruit. The initial letters are given as clues. In B, they fill in the missing letters for each fruit pictured in the signs.

WORKSHEET: Topic 38

In A, students fill in the sentences to tell whether the people pictured like or don't like various fruit. Then, they match the sentences to the pictures. In B, they write sentences to describe what the people in the pictures are doing. In C, they write about which fruits they like or don't like.

39 SIMPLE ORGANISMS

▶ **CONTENT**

Single-celled organisms, worms, and sea creatures

▶ **LANGUAGE**

Modal *can*: *Starfish, sea urchins, and sand dollars can move, but they move slowly.*

Adjective clauses with *that*: *Protozoans are simple organisms that only have one cell.*

Compound words: *Roundworms and flatworms are two types of worms.*

CONTENT WORDS

1. amoeba
2. paramecium
3. protozoans
4. flatworm
5. roundworm
6. segmented worms
7. earthworm
8. leech
9. jellyfish
10. coral
11. starfish
12. sponge
13. sand dollar
14. sea urchin

Single-Celled Organisms

Worms

Sea Creatures

 CONTENT READING

Simple Organisms

Simple organisms are organisms that don't have many parts. Protozoans are simple organisms that only have one cell. They are single-celled organisms. The amoeba and the paramecium are protozoans. They live in water. They get their food and air from the water. You can only see them with a microscope.

Worms are another kind of simple organism, but they have more than one cell. Roundworms and flatworms are two types of worms. Segmented worms have bodies that have many identical sections. Leeches and earthworms are segmented worms. Leeches have three, four, or five segments, and they live in the water. Earthworms have about 150 segments, and they live in the earth.

Some simple organisms live in the sea. They are sea creatures. Jellyfish are sea creatures that look like umbrellas. They have soft bodies and move around. They eat any tiny sea animals that they can find. Corals and sponges are sea creatures that can't move around. They eat sea plants that live near them. Starfish, sea urchins, and sand dollars can move, but they move slowly. They eat animals that live at the bottom of the ocean.

▶ WORDS

Components: Dictionary pages 78-79, Transparency 39, Wall Chart 39, Workbook page 39, Word and Picture Cards Topic 39, Cassette

- Present the content words. **See pages xiv-xvi for general techniques about presenting content words.**

  > **Language Note:** The word *amoeba* is pronounced [a-MEE-ba]. The vowel *o* is not pronounced.

- Have students look at the wall chart as you point out the groupings of *Single-Celled Organisms*, *Worms*, and *Sea Creatures*. Now distribute the word and picture cards and ask students to walk around the room asking their fellow students which word and picture cards they have. Then, students form themselves into three groups, one for each category of content words. Encourage students to talk about their cards in their groups. Draw a large word web like the example below on chart paper and have students from each group put their word and picture cards in the appropriate place on the web.

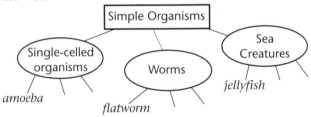

▶ Compound words

> Compound words are two separate words which form one meaning when they are joined together. That meaning may be different than the meaning of either of the individual words (for example: *sand dollar*). Compound words may be written as one word or two words. The following content words are compound words: *flatworm, roundworm, earthworm, jellyfish, sand dollar, sea urchin*.

Point out some of the compound words for students and have them look at Dictionary page 78 to try to find the other compound words. Ask each student to select one compound word and write the two parts of the word on separate index cards. Collect all the cards and redistribute two to each student. Then have students walk around the room asking each other which words they have so that students can trade with each other to get one of the content words. In the process, students may come up with silly or interesting combinations such as *sea jelly, dollar fish*, etc. Encourage students to note this information. Make a separate list of such student creations on the board.

WORKBOOK: Topic 39
See Teacher's Book page 157.

▶ CONTENT

Components: Dictionary pages 78-79, Transparency 39, Wall Chart 39, Content Reading Topic 39, Worksheet Topic 39, Cassette

- Present the content reading. **See pages xvii-xix for general techniques about presenting content readings.**
- Ask the following or similar questions:

  What are two examples of protozoans?
  Name six different sea creatures.
  Can corals and sponges move around?
  Do leeches have segments?
  What are simple organisms?
  What do starfish, sea urchins, and sand dollars eat?

▶ Modal *can*

> We use the modal *can* with other verbs in order to express ability. *Can* is used with all subjects and doesn't change form. The negative *can't* or *cannot* is used for inability to do something. *Cannot* is written as one word.

Point out the use of *can* and *can't* in the content reading and ask students to underline and read aloud all sentences with *can* or *can't*. Ask students to talk about things they can and can't do. They can use some of the phrases from the content reading. Ask students if they can move around, move quickly, or find their own food. Brainstorm with them to come up with a blackboard column of things they *can* do and another column of things they *can't* do. The information can be scientific, such as *I can use my hands to get food* or it can be silly, such as *I can't write with my nose*. When students have filled these two columns with things they can and can't do, have them take turns using the information to ask each other questions with *can*. For example *Can you write with your nose?* Students answer with *Yes, I can* or *No, I can't*.

▶ Adjective clauses with *that*

> We can use an adjective clause to describe a noun. An adjective clause begins with a relative pronoun (*that, who, which, who,* and *whom*) and contains a verb. An adjective clause follows the noun it describes. For example: *Segmented worms have bodies that have many identical sections.*

Point out some of the adjective clauses in the content reading to students, beginning with the first sentence, *Simple organisms are organisms that don't have many parts*. Now ask students to read through the content reading again and define the following simple organisms using adjective clauses with *that*: *corals and sponges, protozoans, segmented worms,* and *jellyfish*.

WORKSHEET: Topic 39
See Teacher's Book page 157.

► CHANTS

Components: Dictionary pages 78-79, Content Chant Topic 39, Cassette

 ## CONTENT CHANT

Flatworms Are Flat

Flatworms are flat.
They're not round.
You won't find one
on the ground.
They like water,
ponds, and streams.
You might see one
in your dreams.

Flatworms are flat,
but that's OK.
I like flatworms anyway.

Roundworms are round,
but they're not fat.
Roundworms are round
and that is that!

- Present the content chant. **See pages xx-xxi for general techniques about presenting chants.**
- Before distributing the chant, have students practice with small chunks of the language from the chant. Divide the class into two groups. Group 1 chants, *Flatworms are flat. Flat, flat, flat *.* Group 2 chants *Roundworms are round. Round, round, round *.* Have students clap where indicated by the asterisk. Groups chant their lines repeatedly, first in turn, and then simultaneously.
- Now, keeping the same groups as the above activity, have each of the groups repeatedly chant one of the following words: *water, ponds,* or *streams.* First groups chant in turn, and then simultaneously.
- Distribute Content Chant 39. Divide the class into three groups and have each group chant one stanza. Encourage students to pantomime as they chant.
- Now select individual students to chant and pantomime each of the three stanzas in the chant.

► EXTENSION

Components: Dictionary pages 78-79, Transparency 39, Wall Chart 39

- Divide students into groups. Ask each group to research one group of sea creatures. The first group researches *jellyfish*, the second group *corals and sponges*, and the third group *starfish, sea urchins and sand dollars*. Then make a chart like the one below. With students, fill in the information about how these creatures move and what they eat. Then have groups research information in the additional categories: the size of the creatures, their physical characteristics, where in the world they live, and any additional interesting information. Encourage students to use science books, encyclopedias and the Internet. Have students add their information to the chart and then share it with the entire class.

Types of Information	Jellyfish	Corals and Sponges	Starfish, Sea Urchins, Sand Dollars
1. movement	They move around	They can't move	They move slowly
2. food	They eat tiny animals	They eat sea plants	They eat animals that live at the bottom of the ocean
3. size			
4. physical characteristics			
5. where they live in the world			
6. additional information			

- Divide the class into groups and have students study the earthworm. Tell students that earthworms can be about 10 inches long and almost 1/2 inch in diameter. Encourage students to find out as many interesting facts as possible about earthworms through the use of science books, encyclopedias, and the Internet. If possible, bring an earthworm to class that students can observe. Have students draw pictures or make clay models showing the segments. Groups write reports about their research on earthworms, make a poster, and present their information to the class.
- If possible, set up a microscope and invite students to view a slide of pond water. Ask students to draw a pictures of the organisms they see on the slide and compare it to those in the Dictionary for this topic. Are they looking at a paramecium or an amoeba? Can they tell the difference? Encourage students to share and discuss their results.
- Ask students if they have ever seen any of the simple organisms in this topic. Ask students to write and illustrate a story about their experience with them. If students haven't seen any of these simple organisms, encourage them to write and illustrate a fantasy about one of these creatures.

►LITERATURE

Suggested Books

Wonderful Worms
written by Linda Glaser; illustrated by Loretta Krupinski.
Millbrook Press, 1992. ISBN 1562940626
This book, written in simple sentences, describes the physical characteristics and behavior of earthworms. The illustrations give a "worm's-eye" view of the earthworm environment, showing how birds, human beings, and dogs might appear to a worm if it had eyes. To extend the topic, students can pretend that they are the worms and act out the illustrations.

Wormology
written by Michael Elsohn Ross;
photographs by Brian Grogan.
Carolrhoda Books, 1996. ISBN 0876149379
There isn't anything common about the common earthworm, as students will learn when they read *Wormology*. Mixing information with activities that include observation, drawing, and mathematics, this book is sure to help students learn more about their backyard neighbors. The language is clever, lively, and simple, usually no more than two lines of text per page, and each line of text can be rephrased to ask a question. Colorful photographs clarify the instructions for the activities, and students can perform the suggested experiments with readily-available household or classroom items. A short glossary and index are included.

Sharing Nature with Children
written by Joseph Cornell.
Dawn Publications, 1979. ISBN 09161242
This classic of outdoor education presents forty-two fun activities that can help students appreciate their natural environment. Children are encouraged to use their senses of sight, smell, hearing, and touch to discover and imagine the world of nature. The activities are ideally-suited to small group work. Many of the activities will enrich students' understanding of simple organisms. This book also complements many of the other topics in Unit 5.

WORKBOOK: Topic 39

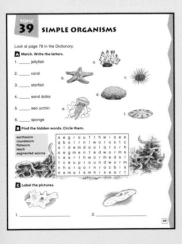

In A, students match the words with the pictures. In B, they find each word in the list in the word search. Words appear horizontally and vertically. In C, they label the two pictures.

WORKSHEET: Topic 39

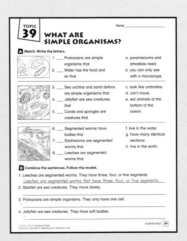

For each picture in A, students choose the correct phrase to complete each sentence. In B, students combine each pair of sentences to make four sentences using *that*.

MOLLUSKS AND CRUSTACEANS

▶ **CONTENT**

Mollusks and crustaceans and their environments

▶ **LANGUAGE**

Verb + noun phrase + infinitive for expressing purpose: *They open their shells to get food.*

Use **+ noun phrase +** *for* **+ gerund for expressing purpose:** *They use their antennae for finding their way.*

Modal *can:* *You can see the shell, but you can't see the mollusk inside.*

CONTENT WORDS

1. octopus
2. squid
3. tentacles
4. sea slug
5. shells
6. scallop
7. clam
8. oyster
9. mussel
10. conch
11. snail
12. lobster
13. shrimp
14. crab
15. claw
16. antennae
17. barnacles
18. crayfish

Mollusks

Crustaceans

 CONTENT READING

Mollusks and Crustaceans

Most mollusks and crustaceans live in the water. Mollusks have soft bodies. Some mollusks, like the scallop, clam, oyster, conch, snail, and mussel, have hard shells on the outside. They open their shells to get food. They also use their shells for hiding from other animals. They close the shell and hide inside it. You can see the shell, but you can't see the mollusk inside. It's safe in the shell.

Other mollusks, like the octopus, squid, and sea slug, have shells on the inside. You can't see their shells. The shells are inside their soft bodies. These mollusks can't hide in their shells, so they defend themselves in other ways. The octopus can change colors to hide from other animals. The squid can squirt ink at other animals. The octopus and the squid also have tentacles. They use the tentacles for catching and holding food.

Crustaceans have pairs of legs. They use their legs for moving around oceans or rivers. They also have two antennae. They use their antennae for finding their way. Some crustaceans, like the lobster, crab, and crayfish, have claws. They use their claws for catching food and for fighting other animals. Lobsters, crabs, shrimp, and barnacles live in salt water, like the ocean. Crayfish live in fresh water, like rivers and lakes.

▶ WORDS

Components: Dictionary pages 80-81, Transparency 40, Wall Chart 40, Workbook page 40, Word and Picture Cards Topic 40, Cassette

- Present the content words. **See pages xiv-xvi for general techniques about presenting content words.**

> **Language Note:** *Antennae* is the irregular plural form of *antenna*. The word *conch* is pronounced with either a final *k* sound as in *clock* or a final *ch* sound as in *watch*. The plural is written as *conchs* (pronounced as *konks*) or *conches* (*kon-chiz*). The plural of *octopus* is either *octopuses* or *octopi*. The prefix *octo* means eight. The plural of *squid* is either *squids* or the noncount form, *squid*. *Shrimp* and *crayfish* are noncount nouns and don't have a plural form.

- If possible, bring in a collection of shells from mussels, oysters, clams, scallops, conches, snails, etc. Ask students to identify these in their native language(s) and draw them. Then invite students to compare these real samples and their drawings with the pictures on Dictionary page 80. Encourage students to discuss the similarities and differences.

- Have students look at the wall chart as you point out the groupings of *Mollusks* and *Crustaceans*. Draw two columns on chart paper. Label one *Mollusks* and the other *Crustaceans*. Put the word cards and the picture cards in two stacks at the front of the room and have students, in turn, select a card from each stack. Students place their cards in the appropriate columns.

- Make a chart like the example below. Ask students to classify the mollusks and crustaceans according to the presence or absence of various characteristics. Students mark ✔ + ✗.

Mollusks and Crustaceans	hard outer shell	tentacles	legs	claws	antennae
1. octopus	✗	✔			
2. squid	✗	✔			
3. lobster	✗	✗	✔	✔	✔

- Help students conduct polls of which mollusks and crustaceans they like to eat, don't like to eat, or have never eaten. Students work in groups using a chart like the one below.

Mollusks and Crustaceans	Like		Don't like		Never tasted	
	Boys	Girls	Boys	Girls	Boys	Girls
1. octopus						
2. squid						

> **WORKBOOK:** Topic 40
> See Teacher's Book page 161.

▶ CONTENT

Components: Dictionary pages 80-81, Transparency 40, Wall Chart 40, Content Reading Topic 40, Worksheet Topic 40, Cassette

- Present the content reading. **See pages xvii-xix for general techniques about presenting content readings.**

- Ask the following or similar questions:

> *Where do most mollusks and crustaceans live?*
> *Do crayfish live in rivers and lakes?*
> *Which mollusks have hard shells on the outside of their bodies?*
> *Which mollusks have tentacles?*
> *What do the octopus and squid use their tentacles for?*
> *Why does the octopus change colors?*

▶ *Use* + noun phrase + *for* + gerund for expressing purpose

> In English, we can express purpose in several ways. In one way, we use the pattern [verb + noun phrase + infinitive]. The infinitive is [*to* + simple form of verb]. The infinitive expresses the purpose. It answers the question *Why?* about the verb. For example: *They open their shells to get food.* (Why do they open their shells? To get food.) Another way to express purpose in certain cases is with the pattern [*use* + noun phrase + *for* + gerund]. For example: *They use their antennae for finding their way.*

Have students underline and read aloud all sentences in the content reading that use the two patterns for expressing purpose explained above. Then divide the class into two groups. Group 1 writes a list of questions on the board about why the mollusks and crustaceans do certain things or use certain parts of their bodies. For example: *Why do mollusks open their shells?* Group 2 writes their answers to Group 1's *Why* questions with sentences expressing purpose. For example: *They open their shells to get food.*

▶ **Expressing purpose with [*use* + noun phrase + *for* + gerund] or [verb + noun phrase + infinitive].** Ask students to think of something they use. It can be a pencil, a basketball, a skateboard, etc. Have students draw a picture of this thing and write a sentence telling about its use. Students can use either pattern for expressing purpose. For example: I *use my basketball to shoot hoops* or *I use my basketball for shooting hoops.*

> **WORKSHEET:** Topic 40
> See Teacher's Book page 161.

MOLLUSKS AND CRUSTACEANS **TOPIC 40** 159

►CHANTS

Components: Dictionary pages 80-81, Content Chant Topic 40, Cassette

 CONTENT CHANT

Do You Like Clams?

Do you like clams?

    Yes, I do.

    I like clams and oysters, too.

Do you eat squid?

    Yes, I do.

    I eat squid and octopus, too.

Do you cook crayfish?

    Yes, I do.

    I cook crayfish and lobster, too.

How about shrimp?

    They're not for me.

    I like shrimp, but they don't like me.

- Present the content chant. **See pages xx-xxi for general techniques about presenting chants.**

- Before distributing the chant, have students practice with small chunks of the language from the chant. Divide the class into four groups. Each group chants in turn, and then simultaneously, one of the following phrases: *clams and oysters*; *squid and octopus*; *crayfish and lobster*; and *shrimp, shrimp, shrimp.*

- Distribute Content Chant 40. Divide the class into two groups. Group 1 chants all the questions in each stanza. Group 2 chants all the answers.

- Note that in the phrase *How about shrimp* the stress is on the word *shrimp*. The initial vowel sound in the word *about* is reduced as it is linked to the word *How*, so that the expression *How about* sounds more like *How 'bout.*

- Select pairs of individual students to practice the chant. One student chants all of the questions and the other student chants all of the answers.

►EXTENSION

Components: Dictionary pages 80-81, Transparency 40, Wall Chart 40

- Have individual students make up as many riddles as they can for the mollusks and crustaceans. Students write each riddle on a separate index card. For example: *I squirt ink at my enemies. Who am I?* Encourage students to make more than one card and to sign their name to each card so they don't get their own cards back. Collect the index cards and redistribute them to the class. Now have individual students read aloud the riddle they received. If the student can't answer the riddle, the other students can help. If no one can answer the riddle, the original riddle writer answers it.

- Refer students back to the poll they conducted in the Words section of this topic. Focus on those items which students say they have never tasted. Ask them if they would like to taste them. Point out that many people do not cook clams and oysters, although others do. Encourage students to express their feelings about trying new foods.

- Have students create a chart similar to the one used in the Words section, substituting *Male* and *Female* for the *Boys* and *Girls* columns. Ask students to conduct this same poll using friends and family members. Each student should ask five people which of these mollusks and crustaceans they like, don't like, or have never tasted. After students report their data to the class, have them work together to combine the data and make bar graphs illustrating the data.

- Have students ask friends and family members for recipes they use for cooking/eating any of the mollusks and crustaceans in this topic. Have students also investigate cookbooks and magazines for recipes. Students can group their recipes by type (all the octopus recipes, all the clam recipes, etc.) and work together to put them on poster board, illustrate them, and present them to the entire class.

- Have students form research groups to find out more information on each of the mollusks and crustaceans listed in this topic. Encourage students to use science books, the books listed in the Literature section of this topic, encyclopedias, and the Internet. Have students investigate the creatures' habitats, life cycles, physical characteristics, enemies, and their methods of giving birth to and caring for their young. Groups write and illustrate their reports and share the information with the entire class. Encourage students to put their information on posters, if appropriate.

►LITERATURE

Suggested Books

Interesting Invertebrates:
A Look At Some Animals without Backbones
written by Elaine Landau.
Franklin Watts, 1991. ISBN 0531200361
This book is a carefully-crafted introduction to the collection of animals in this topic. Each of the seven chapters examines one or two invertebrates and provides information about their physical characteristics, behavior, and environment. Close-up color photographs of each animal clarify and supplement the information. Teachers may wish to match some of the photographs to the word and picture cards. Sections of the text may be shared in small groups.

Octopus
written by Carol Carrick; illustrated by Donald Carrick.
Clarion, 1978. ISBN 0395287774
"Though dangers surrounded her, the female octopus kept careful guard as she searched for a safe place to lay her eggs." So begins *Octopus* by Carol Carrick, a book that combines a good story with accurate scientific facts. Some of the more challenging language can be made familiar to students by reading the book aloud once or twice. Reading the text aloud also will convey the power of the language. The book is an example of how nonfiction can be effectively integrated into literature.

Snailology
written by Michael Ross; photographs by Brian Grogan; illustrations by Darren Erickson.
Carolrhoda books, 1996. ISBN 0876148941
In this easy-to-follow guide, students learn how to locate, collect, and observe snails. Each topic is presented in a one or two-page format and often includes simple activities that ESL students can do after minimal direct instruction. Color photographs often model the activities. Teachers may want to pair second-language and mainstream students for these activities.

WORKBOOK: Topic 40

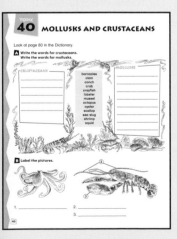

In A, students sort the listed words into two groups by rewriting the words in two new lists, one labeled *Crustaceans* and the other labeled *Mollusks*. In B, they label parts of a squid and a lobster.

WORKSHEET: Topic 40

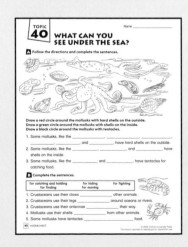

In A, students read the directions and sort the mollusks pictured by drawing different colored circles around those with hard shells, those with shells on the inside, and those that have tentacles. In B, students complete the sentences with choices from the word box.

41 INSECTS AND ARACHNIDS

▶ **CONTENT**
....
Insects and arachnids and the process of metamorphosis

▶ **LANGUAGE**
....
Coordinating conjunctions *and* and *but*: *There are many kinds of insects and arachnids, but people usually just call them bugs. Insects have six legs and arachnids have eight legs.*

Modal *can*: *Arachnids can walk, but they can't fly.*

 CONTENT WORDS

1. caterpillar
2. chrysalis
3. butterfly
4. metamorphosis
5. hive
6. bee
7. ladybug
8. grasshopper
9. cricket
10. fly
11. firefly
12. mosquito
13. ant
14. thorax
15. abdomen
16. cockroach
17. spider
18. web
19. tick
20. scorpion

 CONTENT READING

Insects and Arachnids

There are many kinds of insects and arachnids, but people usually just call them bugs. Insects have six legs and arachnids have eight legs. Insects have three body parts: a head, a thorax, and an abdomen. Arachnids have two body parts. The head and thorax are one part. The abdomen is the other part.

Some insects can walk and other insects can jump or fly. Crickets and grasshoppers can jump. Bees, flies, fireflies, and mosquitoes can fly. Arachnids can walk, but they can't fly.

Insects can bother you, but they can be helpful, too. Ants come to picnics and eat the food. Mosquitoes bite your arms and legs. But, both ants and mosquitoes are good food for birds and bats. Bees sting, but they make honey in their hives, too.

Cockroaches can come into your kitchen and scorpions can sting your feet. Ticks usually bite dogs, but sometimes they bite people.

Ladybugs and butterflies are beautiful. At night, fireflies make light and crickets make music. Spiders make webs and catch flies, mosquitoes, and other bugs for food.

Some insects have a complete metamorphosis. A caterpillar begins its life as an egg. The egg hatches and the caterpillar comes out. It crawls around and it eats leaves. The caterpillar becomes a chrysalis. It grows and changes inside its shell. The chrysalis becomes a butterfly. Caterpillars can walk, but butterflies can fly.

▶ WORDS

Components: Dictionary pages 82-83, Transparency 41, Wall Chart 41, Workbook page 41, Word and Picture Cards Topic 41, Cassette

- Present the content words. **See pages xiv-xvi for general techniques about presenting content words**

  > **Language Note:** The written *ch* in the words *arachnids* and *chrysalis* is pronounced with a *k* sound. The plural of *chrysalis* is *chrysalises*. The plurals of *fly* and *firefly* are *flies* and *fireflies*. A *firefly* is also called a *firebug*, *lightning bug*, or *glowworm*. The plural form of *mosquito* is either *mosquitoes* or *mosquitos*. The word *cockroach* comes from the Spanish word *cucaracha*.

- Have students look at the wall chart as you point to the groupings of *Insects* and *Arachnids*. Draw two columns on chart paper, and label one *Insects* and the other *Arachnids*. Place the word and picture cards in separate stacks. Have students select a card from each stack and place them in the appropriate columns.

- Have students open their Dictionaries to page 82 and look at the pictures and words for Content Word 4, *metamorphosis*. Explain that *metamorphosis* is a process of development with four different stages. In the first stage there is an egg. Ask students to look at the other words on this page and see if they can guess the second, third, and fourth stages of this metamorphosis. If students can't guess, call their attention to Content Words 1, 2, and 3 on this page.

- Enlarge the picture card for *metamorphosis* and make enough copies so that you have one card for every four students. Cut each of these enlarged picture cards into four pieces to separate the four stages. Mix the cards and distribute the pieces randomly, one per student. Students go around the room and ask each other which card they have in order to form groups of four students with the four cards making up a complete metamorphosis. This activity culminates with the students in each of the groups holding their cards and standing in the correct order of the four stages.

- Explain to students that we often associate certain descriptive words with insects and arachnids. For example, we might use the words *beautiful, light, airy, free,* or *happy* to describe a butterfly. By contrast, we might use the words *nasty* or *mean* to describe a mosquito. Divide the class into groups. Distribute a set of picture cards (omitting *chrysalis, metamorphosis, hive, thorax, abdomen,* and *web*) to each group and ask students to write any words that come into their minds about the insect or arachnid on their cards. Encourage students to compare and discuss their words.

WORKBOOK: Topic 41
See Teacher's Book page 165.

▶ CONTENT

Components: Dictionary pages 82-83, Transparency 41, Wall Chart 41, Content Reading Topic 41, Worksheet Topic 41, Cassette

- Present the content reading. **See pages xvii-xix for general techniques about presenting content readings.**

- Ask the following or similar questions:

  How many legs and body parts do insects have?
  Which insects can jump?
  Can arachnids fly?
  What can crickets and grasshoppers do?
  Are any insects helpful?
  What are the four stages of the metamorphosis of a butterfly?

- ▶ **Coordinating conjunctions *and* and *but***

  > We use *and* to connect sentences with similar ideas or to add information. We use *but* to connect two sentences where the second sentence introduces information that is different from the first sentence, but is still related. We use a comma before *but*.

  Point out the use of sentences with *and* and *but* in the content reading. Have students underline and read aloud all sentences connected with *and*. Have students circle and read aloud all sentences connected with *but*.

- ▶ **Coordinating conjunctions *and* and *but*.** Ask students to draw pictures showing an insect and an arachnid. Then have students write sentences under their pictures making comparisons between insects and arachnids using *and* or *but*. For example: *Insects have three body parts, but arachnids have two body parts. Insects can walk and arachnids can walk, too.*

- ▶ **Coordinating conjunctions *and* and *but*, Modal *can*.** Ask students to make up sentences comparing what any two insects or arachnids can or can't do. Ask students to draw a picture of these two insects or arachnids. Students then write two sentences about them, using *can* or *can't*. They combine their sentences with *and* or *but*. For example: *Mosquitoes can bite and ticks can bite, too. Butterflies can fly, but spiders can't.* Have students share their pictures with the class and read their sentences aloud.

- Divide the class into two groups. Ask students to look at the wall chart and make up a story about what is happening in the pictures. Group 1 creates a story about *Insects* using the top part of the chart. Group 2 creates a story about *Arachnids* using the bottom part of the chart.

WORKSHEET: Topic 41
See Teacher's Book page 165.

► CHANTS

Components: Dictionary pages 82-83, Content Chant Topic 41, Cassette

 ## CONTENT CHANT

Ants Walk

Ants walk,
grasshoppers jump,
butterflies fly,
but caterpillars crawl.

Mosquitoes bite,
bees sting,
crickets chirp,
but caterpillars crawl.

Ants walk,
grasshoppers jump,
spiders bite,
but caterpillars crawl.

Spiders bite,
crickets chirp,
butterflies fly,
but caterpillars crawl.

- Present the content chant. **See pages xx-xxi for general techniques about presenting chants.**

- Before distributing the chant, have students practice with small chunks of the language from the chant. Have the whole class chant *caterpillars crawl* as they pantomime caterpillars crawling. Students begin chanting very softly and very, very slowly as they pantomime crawling very, very slowly. Then they speed up gradually and get louder as they repeatedly chant these words while pantomiming crawling.

- Distribute Content Chant 41 and divide the class into seven groups. Each group takes the part of one of the following: *ants, grasshoppers, butterflies, mosquitoes, bees, crickets,* and *spiders*. Each group chants the words that refer to these insects and arachnids in the chant as they pantomime the actions described in the chant. Have each group practice separately first, then have all groups chant in turn. Encourage students to over-emphasize words like *bite* and *sting*. They can chirp the word *chirp*. The entire class chants the line *but caterpillars crawl*.

- Have individual students take turns chanting the parts of each insect and arachnid.

► EXTENSION

Components: Dictionary pages 82-83, Transparency 41, Wall Chart 41

- Have students write an illustrated story about their own experiences with one or more of these insects and/or arachnids. Encourage students to share their work with the class.

- Divide the class into groups and have each group "adopt" an insect or arachnid. The groups do research on their adopted animals. They find out detailed information on size, characteristics, life cycles, and habitats, plus any other interesting information they can find. Have students make diagrams or models of their adopted animals and label all their parts. Have students also make posters describing and illustrating their animals. Groups share their research with the entire class.

- Have students work individually or in groups to make books entitled *A Day in the Life of a* _____. Use Eric Carle's book *The Hungry Caterpillar* as a model.

- Have students make butterflies out of construction paper. Encourage students to make butterflies of various colors, patterns, and sizes. Have each student make a tiny hole in each butterfly and tie a long piece of string or fishing line through the hole. Students can fly their butterflies around the room, or attach several butterflies of different sizes together to make butterfly mobiles.

- If possible, collect butterflies or fireflies in a jar, with a piece of cheesecloth over the top and some holes in the cover of the jar. Put leaves and twigs inside the jar and have students get a close-up view of these insects. If possible, try to find a caterpillar and keep it in a jar with air-holes, cheesecloth, twigs, and leaves. Students observe the process of metamorphosis firsthand and keep a journal of the daily changes. Return the animals to their natural environment after students have finished with their observations.

- If possible, have students build their own ant colonies. They can gently dig up an ant hill with its surrounding dirt and place it in a jar with a wet paper towel to keep the dirt damp. Tape brown or black construction paper around the jar to encourage the ants to dig tunnels in the dirt. Add a few cookie crumbs. Put cheesecloth over the top and then make holes in the top of the jar. Remove the construction paper to observe the ants and especially the tunnels which they made close to edge of the jar.

- Have students sing "The Itsy-Bitsy Spider." Explain to students that *itsy-bitsy* means very, very small.

> The itsy-bitsy spider went up the water spout.
> Down came the rain and washed the spider out.
> Out came the sun and dried up all the rain
> and the itsy-bitsy spider went up the spout again.

► LITERATURE

Suggested Books

The Lady and the Spider
written by Faith McNulty; illustrated by Bob Marstall.
HarperTrophy, 1987. ISBN 0064431525
"Spiders! Ugh!" That's how some students may feel about these unfairly maligned creatures. This Reading Rainbow selection should change their minds. Told from the spider's point of view, this story introduces us to a spider who lives in a head of lettuce. The life of the spider could be cut short if the woman who finds him does not return him to the garden. The book's narrative is gentle and the grammar is easy to manage. The engaging story contains accurate, scientific information, making this book an especially useful classroom tool.

Night Letters
written by Palmyra Lomonaco;
illustrated by Normand Chartier.
Dutton Books, 1996. ISBN 05254537873
Every summer evening, Lily takes a notepad and pencil out to her backyard to record the messages that nature has left her, from the track of a line of ants to the designs on the wings of a moth. The information in this book, conveyed by the story and accompanied by beautiful illustrations, relates directly to the natural world depicted in the Dictionary illustration and highlighted by this topic. A word bank will help students learn unfamiliar words. The story, which includes letter writing and notetaking, provides an instructional model for extending this topic with letter-writing and note-taking activities.

There Was an Old Lady Who Swallowed a Fly
written and illustrated by Simms Taback.
Viking Children's Books, 1997. ISBN 0670869392
This innovative version of the venerable old rhyme catches students' interest with its unique artwork and unusual design. The repetitive rhyming patterns in this well-known poem can be adapted as a classroom chant. The text contains several language patterns that students will have learned, and the illustrations are humorous enough to engage older students. Teachers will find this versatile book useful for reading aloud or for individual practice.

Have You Seen Bugs?
written by Joanne F. Oppenheim; illustrated by Ron Broda.
Scholastic, 1998. ISBN 0590059637
This book celebrates the natural world of insects in rhyme and pictures. The repeated word patterns and the rhymes are especially good for beginners and intermediate students. Teachers can read the book aloud, and then students can read in small groups or in pairs with their mainstream classmates. The illustrations provide a great reference for students who want to create their own bug books.

Butterflies & Moths
written by Bobbie Kalman; illustrated by Tammy Everts.
1994. ISBN 0865057141
Butterflies and moths are depicted in this book in vibrant photographs and drawings. Boldface words in the text signify key terms. These terms are often defined in context, adding vocabulary and content to this topic. The Table of Contents is detailed, which makes it an excellent model for students who are learning how to locate information.

WORKBOOK: Topic 41

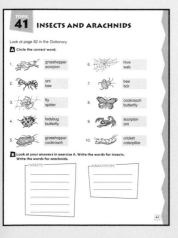

In A, each picture has two words beside it. From each pair, students circle the word that matches the picture. In B, they rewrite the words they circled in A in two lists, one labeled *Insects* and one labeled *Arachnids*. (Only the words for those insects and arachnids pictured in exercise A should be listed in exercise B.)

WORKSHEET: Topic 41

In A, students combine each pair of sentences to write new sentences using *and* or *but*. In B, students number the sentences in the order in which they occur in the life of a butterfly. Then, they label the stages shown in the picture.

CONTENT

Freshwater and saltwater fish

LANGUAGE

Linking verb + *like* for comparisons: *The pipefish looks like a pipe.*

Quantifiers *some, many,* and *all*: *All fish swim very well.*

Compound words: *Bluefish are blue and goldfish are gold.*

CONTENT WORDS

1. bluefish
2. swordfish
3. shark
4. tuna
5. salmon
6. pipefish
7. eel
8. cod
9. sea horse
10. fin
11. gills
12. scales
13. bass
14. minnow
15. trout
16. perch
17. catfish
18. goldfish

Saltwater Fish

Freshwater Fish

CONTENT READING

Fish

All fish live in the water. Saltwater fish live in the ocean. The water in the ocean is very salty. Freshwater fish live in rivers, lakes, and ponds. The water in rivers, lakes, and ponds doesn't have any salt. Some fish can live in fresh water and in salt water.

All fish swim very well. Many fish travel together in groups, or schools. All fish have fins and tails. Many fish also have scales. Fish use their fins and tails to go through the water.

Fish breathe in the water, too. They take water into their mouths. Then, they push the water out through their gills. The gills take oxygen from the water.

There are many different types of fish. Some fish have interesting names. They look like other things. The pipefish looks like a pipe. The sea horse looks

like a horse. The catfish looks like a cat. It has big whiskers. The swordfish looks like a sword. Eels look like snakes, but they are really fish. They have fins and gills.

Bluefish are blue and goldfish are gold. Some people keep goldfish in aquariums because goldfish are very pretty.

▶ WORDS

Components: Dictionary pages 84-85, Transparency 42, Wall Chart 42, Workbook page 42, Word and Picture Cards Topic 42, Cassette

- Present the content words. **See pages xiv-xvi for general techniques about presenting content words.**

  > **Language Note:** The words *bluefish, swordfish, pipefish, sea horse, catfish* and *goldfish* are compound words.

- Have two students at the board and the rest of the students at their seats draw a column of small rebus-like pictures of the following words: *blue, sword, pipe, sea, cat, horse, gold*. Then ask students to draw a small fish next to each of these pictures. Now have students look at Dictionary page 84 and find the actual picture and spelling of their picture puzzle words. Explain that these are compound words. They are real fish which look like a horse, a cat, a pipe, etc.

- Have students look at the wall chart as you point to the groupings of *Saltwater Fish* and *Freshwater Fish*. Now draw two columns on chart paper. Label one *Saltwater Fish* and the other *Freshwater Fish*. Pair students. Place one set of word cards and one set of picture cards in separate stacks. Students, in pairs, take turns selecting a picture card from the picture stack and holding it up as their partners find the matching word card in the word stack. Together the pair decides whether to put their cards on the chart paper in the *Freshwater Fish* or *Saltwater Fish* columns.

- Draw two columns on the board and label one *Freshwater Fish* and the other *Saltwater Fish*. Put one set of picture cards facedown in a large bowl (a fish bowl, if possible). Have student volunteers "go fishing" by putting their hands in the fish bowl and pulling out one picture card. They say the name of the fish and then write it in the appropriate column.

- Divide students into groups and help each group conduct a poll of which fish the students in that group like to eat, don't like to eat, or have never tasted. (Note that all the fish listed in the content words are edible except perhaps for *pipefish, sea horse, minnows,* and *goldfish*.) Students work in their groups and record their data using a chart like the example below. Each group then presents their data to the entire class. Help students combine their data and then make bar graphs to illustrate the combined data. Encourage students to discuss the results.

Fish	Like	Don't like	Never tasted
1. bluefish			
2. swordfish			

▶ CONTENT

Components: Dictionary pages 84-85, Transparency 42, Wall Chart 42, Content Reading Topic 42, Worksheet Topic 42, Cassette

- Present the content reading. **See pages xvii-xix for general techniques about presenting content readings.**

- Ask the following or similar questions:

  Is the water in the ocean salt water or fresh water?
  Do all fish have fins and tails?
  Do all fish have scales?
  What do fish do with their gills?
  Name three freshwater fish and three saltwater fish.
  What does a catfish look like?

▶ **Linking verb + *like* for comparisons**

  > Linking verbs are a type of stative verb. They are intransitive (they don't take direct objects). Linking verbs include *look, appear, seem, feel, sound,* and *taste*. We can use [linking verb + *like*] to make comparisons. For example: *The pipefish looks like a pipe.*

Point out instances of *look + like* in the content reading. For example: *The sea horse looks like a horse.* Have students underline and read aloud all the sentences from the content reading with *look + like*. Now ask students to write ten comparative sentences using *look, feel, seem, sound, appear,* or *taste + like*. For example: *My room looks like a zoo.* Students' sentences can be funny. Encourage students to use their imaginations. Have them read their work to the entire class.

▶ **Quantifiers *some, many,* and *all*.** Use the example diagram below to explain the quantity words *some, many,* and *all*. Explain that they describe different amounts of a whole with *all* representing 100% or the whole.

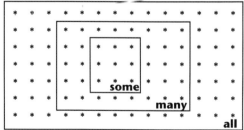

Have students circle all the instances of *some* in the content reading. Have them underline all the examples of *many*, and draw a box around the examples of *all*. Then, students read these sentences aloud. Now divide the class into teams. Have the students on each team look at the wall chart and write ten questions using *some, many,* and *all* for students on the opposite team to answer. For example: *Do all fish live in salt water? (No, they don't.)* Score one point for each correct question and answer.

WORKBOOK: Topic 42
See Teacher's Book page 169.

WORKSHEET: Topic 42
See Teacher's Book page 169.

► CHANTS

Components: Dictionary pages 84-85, Content Chant Topic 42, Cassette

 CONTENT CHANT

Swordfish, Catfish

Swordfish, catfish
tuna fish, shark
Don't go swimming
in the ocean, in the dark.

If you meet a shark
in the middle of the sea,
treat him very
carefully.

Bluefish, goldfish
pipefish, cod
I think catfish
are very odd.

I've never seen one
in the sea,
so I don't know
what they think of me.

- Present the content chant. **See pages xx-xxi for general techniques about presenting chants.**

- Before distributing the chant, have students practice small chunks of the language from the chant. Divide the class into two groups. Group 1 repeatedly chants *swordfish, catfish, tuna fish, shark.* Group 2 repeatedly chants *bluefish, goldfish, pipefish, cod.*

- Distribute Content Chant 42. Before students practice the stanzas, have them practice the longer lines in the chant by chunking them. For example, when teaching the sentence *Don't go swimming in the ocean in the dark,* present the sentence in chunks from the end in order to preserve the rhythm and intonation. Students practice each chunk repeatedly and then add on the preceding chunk. For example, have students repeat *in the dark*, then repeat *in the ocean,* and then combine *in the ocean, in the dark.* Then they practice *Don't go swimming,* and add it to the rest: *Don't go swimming in the ocean in the dark.* Use this same technique with other long sentences in the chant.

- Divide the class into groups and have each group chant one stanza of the chant.

► EXTENSION

Components: Dictionary pages 84-85, Transparency 42, Wall Chart 42

- Ask students if they would like to have goldfish or other tropical fish as pets in an aquarium. Encourage students to talk about their experiences with pet fish, or which fish they would like to have as pets if they haven't had any.

- Divide the class into groups and have each group "adopt" a fish. The groups do research on their adopted fish to find out detailed information on the fish's habitat, size, weight, color, tail shape, life cycle, food and feeding habits, and other interesting characteristics (for example, male sea horses carry the babies). Have students make diagrams or models of their adopted fish and label its parts. Students can also make posters describing and illustrating their fish. Groups share their research with the class.

- Ask students if they have ever gone fishing. If they have not, ask them if they would like to or would not like to. Ask students if they would kill the fish and eat it, or catch it and release it to allow the fish to live. Encourage student discussion and debate.

- Refer students back to the poll they conducted in the Words section of this topic. Encourage students to talk about fish listed in the content words which they have never tasted. Then ask students to talk about fish they eat at home or have eaten in their former countries which are not listed in the content words. Invite those students to describe the fish and if, possible, to bring in a sample for students to taste.

- Have students collect fish recipes from friends, family members, and magazines. Group the recipes according to fish type (if there is more than one recipe per fish) or by fish habitat (fresh water/salt water). If practical, have students experiment with cooking some of the different recipes.

- Ask students to write a process paragraph or an outline of the steps for one of the following: catching a fish, cleaning a fish, or cooking a fish. Encourage students to share and discuss their work.

► LITERATURE

Suggested Books

Fishes

written and illustrated by Brian Wildsmith.
Oxford University Press Children's Books, 1987.
ISBN 0192721518

This book contains brilliant and exuberant paintings of fish, accompanied by traditional and inventive collective nouns such as "a stream of minnows" and "a hover of trout." The text extends students' familiarity with names and features of creatures in the natural world as it entertains them with its wordplay. This book is also useful for teaching Topic 15, The Northwest.

Encyclopedia of Fishes

edited by Dr. John H. Paxton and Dr. William N. Eschmeyer; illustrated by David Kirshner.
Academic Press, 1994. ISBN 0125476604

As the title indicates, this volume offers encyclopedic coverage of fish. The text is divided into two sections: information about the environments of fish and information about the types of fish. Vivid color photographs and illustrations of fish both common and unusual enhance the text. The illustrations are likely to prompt questions that students can answer by reading the accompanying text. Maps, charts, diagrams, and a detailed index make this an excellent teaching tool.

Hungry, Hungry Sharks

written by Joanna Cole; illustrated by Patricia Wynne.
Random House, 1996. ISBN 0394874714

This "Step Into Reading" book is a basic introduction to sharks: their physical characteristics, their behavior, and their many different varieties. The book stays within the reading level of beginners without sacrificing content. Teachers might want to have students take turns examining each two-page spread and reading aloud the words and/or sentences they know. This book also lends itself well to a K-W-L chart reading strategy.

Crinkleroot's 25 Fish Every Child Should Know

written and illustrated by Jim Arnosky.
Simon and Schuster, 1993. ISBN 0027058441

In this book, the jovial woodsman Crinkleroot gives readers a general introduction to fish. The book begins with general information about fish (explaining in very simple terms how they breathe and how they swim), followed by realistic illustrations of twenty-five common fish. This book is recommended for use by beginners in small groups or with partners. Students can match the names of the fish in the book to the pictures in the Dictionary illustration.

WORKBOOK: Topic 42

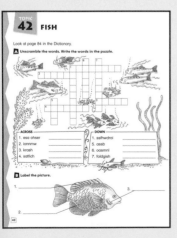

In A, students unscramble the words to complete the crossword puzzle. Writing each word in the puzzle will give them additional clues for unscrambling the other words. In B, students label the parts of the fish.

WORKSHEET: Topic 42

In A, students write *True* or *False* next to each sentence. In B, they complete the sentences with the names of fish, and match the sentences to the pictures of what each fish looks like. In C, they draw four imaginary fish.

43 AMPHIBIANS AND REPTILES

▶ **CONTENT**

Amphibians and reptiles

▶ **LANGUAGE**

Coordinating conjunctions and and but: *Adult frogs and toads don't have gills and tails, but they have webbed feet and their skin feels wet.*

Adverbial clauses of time with as and when: *As they grow, their tails get smaller./ When they are older, they breathe with lungs.*

CONTENT WORDS

1. salamander
2. tail
3. frog
4. webbed foot
5. tadpole
6. toad
7. alligator
8. crocodile
9. garter snake
10. turtle
11. chameleon
12. iguana
13. rattlesnake
14. cobra

Amphibians

Reptiles

 CONTENT READING

Amphibians and Reptiles

Amphibians and reptiles live on land and in the water. Most reptiles live on land. They breathe with lungs. Young amphibians start their lives in the water. They breathe with gills. As amphibians grow, they change. When they are older, they breathe with lungs. They can't breathe under water anymore.

Frogs and toads are amphibians. Young frogs and toads are tadpoles. They live in water and breathe with gills. They use their tails for swimming. As they grow, their tails get smaller. They grow legs. They leave the water and lose their gills. Adult frogs and toads don't have gills and tails, but they have webbed feet and their skin feels wet.

Salamanders are also amphibians. A salamander has legs and a tail. A salamander's skin feels wet, too.

Most reptiles live on land and breathe air. Reptiles have hard scales on their skin. Alligators and crocodiles are reptiles. A crocodile has a wide mouth and an alligator has a narrow mouth.

Turtles, iguanas, and chameleons are reptiles, too. A turtle moves very slowly. Some turtles can hide their heads and legs inside their hard shells. An iguana can run quickly. Iguanas eat plants and insects. A chameleon can change colors. Sometimes it's brown, sometimes it's yellow, and sometimes it's green.

All snakes are reptiles. As snakes grow, they shed their skins. Rattlesnakes and cobras can kill with their poison. Garter snakes don't have any poison. They can't hurt people, but sometimes they scare people.

▶ WORDS

Components: Dictionary pages 86-87, Transparency 43, Wall Chart 43, Workbook page 43, Word and Picture Cards Topic 43, Cassette

- Present the content words. **See pages xiv-xvi for general techniques about presenting content words.**

> **Language Note:** *The a in* toad *is not pronounced. The vowel sound in* toad *is pronounced like* mode. *The* ch *in* chameleon *is pronounced with a* k *sound. The* g *sound in* iguana *sounds like the* g *sound in* good. *The* ua *in* iguana *is pronounced like* wah.

- Have students look at the wall chart as you point to the groupings of *Amphibians* and *Reptiles*. Draw two columns on chart paper, one labeled *Amphibians* and the other labeled *Reptiles*. Put the word cards and the picture cards in two stacks at the front of the room. Have students select a card from each stack and place their word cards and their picture cards in the appropriate columns.

- Have students look at page 86 in their Dictionaries. Explain the concept of syllables and stress. For example, *salamander* has four syllables and is pronounced *SAL-a-man-der*. Tap out the rhythm of the four syllables with a pencil or a ruler on the desk. The word *i-GUA-na* has three syllables. Tap out the rhythm for the students. Be sure to tap loudly on the stressed syllable. Now, model each of the words and have students take turns tapping out the number of syllables and indicating the stress on the correct syllable. When students are comfortable with this, divide the class into two teams. Each team, in turn, identifies a category (*amphibians* or *reptiles*) and then taps out the number of syllables with the correct stress of any word within that category. The other team guesses the word. For example, Team 1 presents *Reptiles: TAP-tap-tap-tap*. Team 2 guesses *alligator*. In some cases, there could be two possible right answers. Score one point for each correct answer.

- Divide the class into groups. Students conduct a poll of which amphibians and reptiles they like, don't like, are interested in, or are afraid of. Students work in their groups using a chart like the example below. Each group then presents their data to the entire class. Help students combine their data and then make bar graphs to illustrate the combined data. Encourage students to discuss the results.

Amphibians and Reptiles	Like	Don't like	Interested in	Afraid of
1. salamander				
2. frog				

> **WORKBOOK:** Topic 43
> See Teacher's Book page 173.

▶ CONTENT

Components: Dictionary pages 86-87, Transparency 43, Wall Chart 43, Content Reading Topic 43, Worksheet Topic 43, Cassette

- Present the content reading. **See pages xvii-xix for general techniques about presenting content readings.**

- Ask the following or similar questions:

  Where do most reptiles live?
  Where do young amphibians live?
  Name four amphibians.
  Do young frogs have tails?
  What is the difference between an adult salamander and an adult frog or toad?
  What happens to frogs and toads as they grow?

▶ **Coordinating conjunctions *and* and *but***

> We use *and* to connect sentences with similar ideas or to add information. We use *but* to connect two sentences when the second sentence introduces information that is different from the first, but is still related. We use a comma before *but*.

Point out sentences with *and* and *but* in the content reading. Have students write at least six sentences describing the pictures in the wall chart using *and* or *but*. These can be general statements or specific descriptions of the picture. For example: *A chameleon is a reptile and a rattlesnake is a reptile* or *The toad is on a rock, but the crocodile is in the water.*

▶ **Adverbial clauses of time with *as* and *when***

> An adverbial clause of time tells when the action of the main clause happens. These clauses with *as* (and sometimes with *when*) show two actions happening during the same time period. For example: *As amphibians grow, they change.* (They change during the time they grow.) These clauses can come before or after the main clause in a sentence (*When they are older, they breathe with lungs* or *They breathe with lungs when they are older*). If the adverbial clause comes first in the sentence, we use a comma after it.

Point out examples of adverbial time clauses in the content reading. Have students underline and read these sentences aloud. Students can then write five sentences about their childhood showing two actions that happened at the same time or during the same time period. Student use *as* or *when* in their time clauses. For example: *As I was growing up, I learned to read in Spanish* or *When I was a baby, I cried all the time.*

> **WORKSHEET:** Topic 43
> See Teacher's Book page 173.

▶ CHANTS

Components: Dictionary pages 86-87, Content Chant Topic 43, Cassette

 CONTENT CHANT

Tadpoles Swim, Rattlesnakes Bite

Tadpoles swim.
Rattlesnakes bite.
Crocodiles crawl around all night.

Garter snakes move very fast.
Turtles usually come in last.

Chameleons love to sit around,
changing color from green to brown.

Salamanders swim.
Iguanas chew.
They have four legs.
You have two.

- Present the content chant. **See pages xx-xxi for general techniques about presenting chants.**

- Before distributing the chant, have students practice with small chunks of the language from the chant. Divide the class into four groups. Each group repeatedly chants two of the following words: *tadpoles, rattlesnakes; crocodiles, garter snakes; turtles, chameleons; salamanders, iguanas.*

- Distribute Content Chant 43. Students practice the longest sentence in the chant (*Chameleons love to sit around, changing color from green to brown*). To preserve the rhythm and intonation, present the sentence in smaller chunks from the end, building up to the whole sentence (see instructions on chunking in Chants section, pages xx-xxi).

- Divide the class into seven groups. Each group takes the part of one of the following: tadpoles, rattlesnakes, crocodiles, garter snakes, turtles, salamanders, and iguanas. Each group chants the words that refer to them as they pantomime the actions described in the chant. Have each group practice separately first, then have all groups chant in turn. The entire class chants the line *Chameleons love to sit around, changing color from green to brown.*

- Have individual students take turns chanting the parts of the seven groups as above.

▶ EXTENSION

Components: Dictionary pages 86-87, Transparency 43, Wall Chart 43

- Have individual students make up as many riddles as they can for the amphibians and reptiles. Students write each riddle on a separate index card. For example: *When I was a baby, I had a tail. What am I?* or *I can change my colors. What am I?* Encourage students to make more than one card and to sign their name to each card so they don't get their own cards back. Collect the index cards and redistribute them to the class. Now have individual students read aloud the riddle they received. If a student can't answer the riddle, other students can help. If no one can answer the riddle, the riddle writer answers it.

- Have students write an illustrated story about their own experiences with one or more of these amphibians and/or reptiles. Encourage students to share their work with the entire class.

- Continue the discussion started in the Words section of this topic about how students feel about these animals. Explain to students that in various parts of the world, some people keep some of these amphibians and reptiles as pets, some people cook them and eat them, and some people buy things (shoes, briefcases, purses, etc.) made from their skins (particularly from the skins of *alligators, crocodiles,* and various types of snakes). Have students conduct a poll in class, and later outside the classroom, to find out what the people they know would do with these animals. Use the example chart below. Have students make bar graphs to show the results. Encourage class discussion.

Amphibians and Reptiles	Questions	Classmates		Other People		Total	
	Would you:	yes	no	yes	no	yes	no
1. frog	a) keep this animal as a pet?						
	b) cook and eat this animal?						
	c) buy something made from its skin?						
2. alligator	a) keep this animal as a pet?						
	b) cook and eat this animal?						
	c) buy something made from its skin?						

- Divide the class into groups and have each group "adopt" an amphibian or a reptile. Each group does research to find out its animal's size, characteristics, life cycle, and habitat, as well as any other interesting information. Have students make diagrams or models of their adopted animals and label all the parts. Have students also make posters describing and illustrating their animals. Groups share their research with the entire class.

► LITERATURE

Suggested Books

Into the Sea
written by Brenda Z. Guiberson; illustrated by Alix Berenzy.
Henry Holt & Co., 1996. ISBN 0805022635
This dramatic and powerful story traces the life cycle of an endangered sea turtle: its birth on a stretch of beach, its adventures in the sea, and its return to the beach as an adult to lay its own eggs. The story is told in the present tense and endeavors to show what the turtle sees, hears, and smells. The straightforward text and exquisite illustrations reinforce the vocabulary of this topic. The text for each picture can be read separately, acted out, or drawn by the students to facilitate the reading and to extend the topic. Teachers may want to refer back to this book when discussing Topic 48, Our Environment.

Amazing Crocodiles & Reptiles
written by Mary Ling; photographs by Jerry Young.
Alfred A. Knopf, 1991. ISBN 06798069X

Amazing Snakes
written by Mary Ling; photographs by Jerry Young.
Alfred A. Knopf, 1990. ISBN 067802258
These two titles from the "Eyewitness Juniors" series give students a close-up look at crocodiles, snakes, and other reptiles. Each volume is full of intriguing facts, as well as colorful photographs and drawings. The text is written in conversational language suited to question and answer practice. The books are good sources of information about the characteristics, habits, and diets of these animals. Each book has an extensive and helpful table of contents.

Reptiles (Predators Discovery Library)
written by Lynn M. Stone.
Rourke, 1993. ISBN 0866254374
This straightforward book describes and illustrates how reptiles such as snakes, lizards, and alligators pursue and capture their prey. Each of the nine topics in the book is accompanied by fascinating, full-color photographs. The short sentences and paragraphs can be read aloud and paraphrased for younger students. Intermediate and advanced students can read the book independently. A short glossary and index aids word-building and research.

WORKBOOK: Topic 43

In A, students match the pictures to the words. In B, they choose words from the word box to write the names of each numbered amphibian or reptile.

WORKSHEET: Topic 43

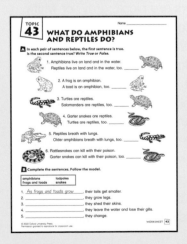

Each number in A has a pair of sentences. The first sentence in each pair is true. Students decide if the second sentence is true or false. In B, students choose words from the word box and follow the model in the first sentence to fill in adverbial time clauses with *as* in the other sentences.

CONTENT

Various kinds of birds and their body parts

LANGUAGE

Possessive nouns: *The goose's neck is long and white.*

Modal *can*: *Penguins can't fly, but they can swim.*

 CONTENT WORDS

1. pigeon
2. sparrow
3. robin
4. cardinal
5. goose
6. duck
7. hummingbird
8. crow
9. chicken
10. turkey
11. seagull
12. eagle
13. nest
14. penguin
15. ostrich
16. peacock
17. parrot
18. beak
19. feather
20. wing

CONTENT READING

Birds

All birds have feathers, beaks, and wings. Feathers cover the bird's body and keep the bird warm. Birds pick up food with their beaks. Most birds use their wings to fly. Some birds build nests. They sit on their eggs in the nests and they sleep there, too.

Birds live in many different places. Pigeons live in cities. A pigeon's feathers are black, gray, or white. Robins, sparrows, and cardinals live in cities, but they also live in the country and the suburbs. A sparrow's feathers are dark brown, and a cardinal's feathers are red. The robin's chest is red, but its back is brown. Hummingbirds live in the country and the suburbs. A hummingbird is very small. The hummingbird's wings can beat 50 to 90 times in one second. Sometimes, its wings move so fast that you can't see them.

The duck, the goose, and the seagull live near water. The duck's neck is short, and brown or green.

The goose's neck is long and white. Ducks, geese, and seagulls can fly, and they can swim, too.

Chickens and turkeys often live on farms. Crows live there, too. But the farmers don't like crows. Crows steal corn.

Some birds live in very cold places. The penguin's fat and thick body keeps it warm in cold water, ice, and snow. Penguins can't fly, but they can swim.

Ostriches live in flat places with tall grass. The ostrich's neck and legs are very long. An adult ostrich can be eight feet tall. Ostriches can't fly and they can't swim, but they can run very fast.

Eagles, peacocks, and parrots are beautiful birds. A bald eagle's head is white. The peacock's feathers are long and blue. The parrot's feathers are red, blue, green, and yellow. Some people keep parrots as pets in cages. Some people teach parrots to talk.

▶ WORDS

Components: Dictionary pages 88-89, Transparency 44, Wall Chart 44, Workbook page 44, Word and Picture Cards Topic 44, Cassette

- Present the content words. **See pages xiv-xvi for general techniques about presenting content words.**

- If possible, bring in bird feathers from different birds to pass around the room. Then have students open their Dictionaries to page 88 and see if they can either match the feathers to the bird, or at least tell whether the feathers belong to a big bird or a small bird. Ask if any of them know the names of these birds in their native languages. If there are students from different language backgrounds, have them place an enlarged picture card on the bulletin board for each bird name they know in their native language(s). Have them write each name in as many different languages as possible.

- Display the transparency. Enlarge one set of picture cards and one set of word cards. Shuffle them together and display them on the chalk tray. Have students, in pairs, take turns finding a picture card and its corresponding word card. Both students pronounce the word together. Then, have one student of the pair circle the picture of their bird on the transparency (use washable markers) while the other student writes the bird's name beside the picture.

- Divide the class into two teams. Distribute one set of picture cards to each team. Students on each team, in turn, hold up a picture card while students from the opposite team describe as many features as possible about that particular bird. For example, if Team 1 holds up *hummingbird*, students from Team 2 might say *a small bird, a green body*, or *a long beak*. Score one point for each correct characteristic.

- **Game: Name That Bird**. Select one student to be "it." That student writes the name of a bird on a paper and places the paper face down. Other students ask *Yes/No* questions to determine which bird the student is thinking of. The student who correctly guesses the name of the bird becomes "it."

- Have each student write one *Yes/No* question about a particular bird on a piece of paper. Then have students fold their papers and put them in a box. Mix the questions. Place one set of mixed picture cards on the chalk tray. Divide the class into teams. Students from each team take turns selecting a question, reading it aloud, pointing to the appropriate card and answering the question. For example, a student who reads aloud the question *Are a seagull's feathers blue and green?* points to the *seagull* picture card and says, *No, a seagull's feathers are white and gray*. Score one point for each correct answer.

WORKBOOK: Topic 44
See Teacher's Book page 177.

▶ CONTENT

Components: Dictionary pages 88-89, Transparency 44, Wall Chart 44, Content Reading Topic 44, Worksheet Topic 44, Cassette

- Present the content reading. **See pages xvii-xix for general techniques about presenting content readings.**

- Ask the following or similar questions:

  Which birds live near water?
  Where do hummingbirds live?
  Name one bird that lives in cities.
  What color is the bald eagle's head?
  Can penguins fly?
  What can ducks, geese, and seagulls do?
  What do birds use their feathers, beaks, and wings for?

▶ **Possessive nouns**

> Possession is shown by adding apostrophe + s ('s) to a noun. If a noun ends in a written s, we just add the apostrophe: *Charles'*.

Play the tape of the content reading. Have students follow along and clap each time they see a word with an apostrophe + s. Play the tape again, but this time have students underline the words with an apostrophe s and circle the owned item (*pigeon's*(*feathers*)). Have each student write an apostrophe + s on one piece of paper and a lowercase s on another. Then have students take turns reading sentences from the content reading that contain either a possessive or regular plural. As the student reads a sentence, the other students hold up the appropriate paper.

▶ **Possessive nouns.** Write the sentence *The feathers of the sparrow are dark brown*. Underline *feathers of the sparrow* and show students that we can replace this with *the sparrow's feathers*. Have students practice with a few other sentences (see also Worksheet Topic 44). Have students write and read aloud five sentences about their classmates using possessives. For example, *Kim's book is red*. Point out to students that when talking about people, it is only correct to say *Kim's book*, and not *the book of Kim*. (Note that in Spanish we do say *el libro de Kim*, so Spanish speakers may need to be reminded that this structure is not correct in English.)

▶ **Modal *can*.** Have students circle and read aloud all the instances of *can* and *can't* in the content reading. Then, divide the class into groups. Have students look at the pictures in the wall chart. Each group writes ten sentences using *can* or *can't* about any of the birds. Encourage students to include information about the various habitats, when possible. For example: *A penguin can live in very cold places.*

WORKSHEET: Topic 44
See Teacher's Book page 177.

►CHANTS

Components: Dictionary pages 88-89, Content Chant Topic 44, Cassette

 CONTENT CHANT

Penguins Can't Fly

Penguins can't fly.
Neither can I.
Eagles do.
Pigeons do, too.

A duck can swim,
but so can you.
Crows are noisy.
Seagulls are, too.

Parrots talk.
Hummingbirds sing.
Peacocks show off
everything.

- Present the content chant. **See page xx-xxi for general techniques about presenting chants.**

- Before distributing the chant, have students practice the names of the birds in the chant. Divide the class into four groups. Group 1 chants *penguins, eagles, and pigeons*. Group 2 chants *a duck*. Group 3 chants *crows and seagulls*. Group 4 chants *parrots, hummingbirds, and peacocks*. Each group chants their words repeatedly, in turn first, and then simultaneously. Have students start chanting their lines slowly and softly and then gradually increase their speed and volume.

- Distribute Content Chant 44. Divide the class into three groups. Each group chants a stanza and pantomimes the action of its lines. They may also make crow and seagull sounds at the appropriate point in the chant.

- Select individual students in groups of three to chant each of the three stanzas and pantomime the actions.

►EXTENSION

Components: Dictionary pages 88-89, Transparency 44, Wall Chart 44

- **Game: Bird Bingo.** Students choose any twelve picture cards and arrange them on a paper in three rows of four squares to make game boards. To play the game, a student caller randomly calls out the names of various birds from another set of cards while the other students try to locate that bird on their game boards. Students place chips, colored paper squares, or other markers on each bird picture as it is called. The first student to cover every square is the winner.

- Divide students into two groups. Have one group research the national bird of the U.S., the bald eagle, and have the other group research the state bird. Have students describe their bird's appearance in detail, and find information about when and why the bird was selected. Include information about where the symbol of the bird appears. For example, the bald eagle is in the logo of the U.S. Post Office, on the Great Seal of the U.S., and on the one-dollar bill. A state bird may appear on the state flag, the state seal, etc. Encourage students to use information from the local library, encyclopedias, and the Internet. Then have each group choose a "class bird" and explain the reasons for their selection. The class votes and makes a poster about the winning "class bird."

- Explain to students that in various parts of the world, some people keep birds as pets, some people cook them and eat them, and some people buy things made from their feathers (earrings, pins, pillows, quilts, etc.). Have students conduct a poll in class, and later in their communities, to find out what the people they know would do with these animals. Use the example chart below. Have students make bar graphs to show the results. Encourage class discussion.

Birds	Questions	Classmates		Other people		Total	
	Would you:	yes	no	yes	no	yes	no
1. duck	a) keep this animal as a pet?						
	b) cook and eat this animal?						
	c) buy something made from its feathers?						
2. peacock	a) keep this animal as a pet?						
	b) cook and eat this animal?						
	c) buy something made from its feathers?						

- Make birdfeeders. Before starting, have students cover the desks with newspaper. To begin, have them attach a piece of wire to a pine cone. Then, they spread peanut butter on the pine cone and roll it in bird seed. Pair students. Each pair selects a safe place outside for their birdfeeder and makes and records observations over several days. Students report their findings to the class.

▶ LITERATURE

Suggested Books

The King of the Birds
written and illustrated by Helen Ward.
Millbrook Press, 1997. ISBN 0761302883
Clear, colorful pictures of birds from all over the world illustrate this retelling of a traditional story about choosing a king. The text includes accessible vocabulary, although there are a few difficult words and sophisticated grammatical structures. In addition to generating discussion about bird identification and characteristics, the story can be used as a starting point for talking about decision-making (who might be king) and expressing opinions.

Bird Egg Feather Nest
written by Maryjo Koch.
Collins Publications, 1994. ISBN 002554569
This lavishly-illustrated book contains fascinating facts about birds of all kinds. The look of the book is extraordinary—handwritten text weaves its way in and around beautiful watercolor art. It is published in cooperation with the National Audobon Society, and so it may be necessary to guide students through the book's authoritative language. However, the text can be paraphrased easily. This book engages students and serves as a springboard for the creation of their own drawings and writings about their favorite birds.

Birds
written and illustrated by Brian Wildsmith.
Oxford University Press, 1980. ISBN 0192721178
Birds contains colorful paintings accompanied by the sometimes unusual collective nouns used to describe groups of different species of birds ("a stare of owls," "a party of jays"). The book's simplicity should appeal to all students who are learning the names of different types of birds, but it will be especially appealing to beginners. It may be effectively compared to and contrasted with *Fishes* (see Topic 42, Literature).

Crinkleroot's 25 Birds Every Child Should Know
written and illustrated by Jim Arnosky.
Simon and Schuster, 1993. ISBN 002705859X
In this book, the jovial woodsman Crinkleroot gives readers a general introduction to birds. The book begins with general information about birds (explaining in very simple terms how they use their feathers for insulation and how they use their wings to fly), followed by realistic illustrations of twenty-five common birds. This book is recommended for use by beginners in small groups or with partners. Students can match the names of the birds in the book to the pictures in the Dictionary illustration.

WORKBOOK: Topic 44

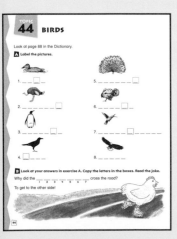

In A, students label the birds. One letter in each word is in a square (except for number 8). Students will use these letters to complete a familiar riddle in exercise B.

WORKSHEET: Topic 44

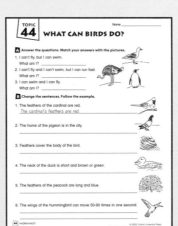

Students answer the riddles in A using the information from the content reading. In B, students change the sentences to use the possessives. The first sentence is done for them as a model.

► **CONTENT**

Domestic mammals and their young

► **LANGUAGE**

Comparative adjective + *than*:
Kids are smaller than goats.

CONTENT WORDS

1. goat
2. kid
3. sheep
4. lamb
5. rabbit
6. bunny
7. dog
8. puppy
9. cow
10. calf
11. cat
12. kitten
13. paw
14. pig
15. piglet
16. horse
17. foal
18. forelegs
19. hind legs
20. hoof

CONTENT READING

Domestic Mammals

Mammals are a type of animal. Domestic mammals live with people on farms or in houses. Other kinds of mammals live in the wild. People are mammals, too.

Some domestic mammals live in the fields. Goats, sheep, and rabbits are domestic mammals. Young goats are kids. Young sheep are lambs. Young rabbits are bunnies. Kids are smaller than goats. Sheep are larger than lambs. Rabbits are bigger than bunnies.

Dogs and cats live in the house. Young dogs are puppies and young cats are kittens. Dogs are older than puppies. Kittens are younger than cats.

Cows, horses, and pigs live in the barn. Young cows are calves. Young horses are foals. Young pigs are piglets. Calves are shorter than cows. Horses are taller than foals. Pigs are fatter than piglets.

Mammals with four legs have forelegs and hind legs. The forelegs are in the front. The hind legs are in the back.

Some mammals have paws. Other mammals have hooves. Cats, dogs, and rabbits have paws. Goats, sheep, cows, pigs, and horses have hooves. Paws are softer than hooves. Hooves are hard.

All young mammals get milk from their mothers. Piglets drink milk from the pig. Kittens drink milk from the cat. Calves drink milk from the cow.

▶ WORDS

Components: Dictionary pages 90-91, Transparency 45, Wall Chart 45, Workbook page 45, Word and Picture Cards Topic 45, Cassette

- Present the content words. **See pages xiv-xvi for general techniques about presenting content words.**

    > **Language Note:** The word *sheep* takes the same form for both singular and plural. In words ending with the written letter *y*, the *y* changes to *i* and we add *-es* to form the plural (*bunny, bunnies; puppy, puppies*). We sometimes use other words such as *doggie, kitty, piggy*, and *horsy* to indicate small, very young, or very cute animals. The word *forelegs* means the legs that are in front. *Fore* means *forward*, not the number *four*.

- Have students look at Dictionary page 90 and ask them the names of the animals in their native languages. Distribute enlarged picture cards to students and have them write the animals' names on the cards. If students are from different language backgrounds, have them write the various names for the same animal on the same picture card.

- Distribute a set of picture cards to students (omit *paw*, *forelegs*, *hind legs*, and *hoof*). Have students walk around the room, asking each other which cards they have. Students try to find the matching adult or baby of an animal pair. For example, the student with the *goat* picture card tries to find the student with the *kid* picture card. Students in their pairs then pronounce the names of their animals.

- Make two columns on the board, one labeled *Adult* and the other labeled *Baby*. Distribute the word cards and have students put them in the appropriate columns.

- Divide the class into two groups. Distribute two sets of picture cards and have students in each group arrange themselves physically according to the size of the animal on their card, in ascending order from the smallest animal to the largest.

- Display picture cards for either the adult or baby versions of each of the animals (excluding *rabbit*). Explain to students that in English we say that certain animals make certain sounds. For example, a dog says *woof*, or *bow-wow*. A cat says *meow*. A cow says *moo*, a sheep says *baa*, a goat says *maa*, and a pig says *oink*. Now point to each animal as students identify them by the sounds they make.

- Ask students if they know words in their native languages for the sounds that animals make. Have students from various language backgrounds pick up an animal card and say the word for the sound the animal makes.

WORKBOOK: Topic 45
See Teacher's Book page 181.

▶ CONTENT

Components: Dictionary pages 90-91, Transparency 45, Wall Chart 45, Content Reading Topic 45, Worksheet Topic 45, Cassette

- Present the content reading. **See pages xvii-xix for general techniques about presenting content readings.**

- Ask the following or similar questions:

    Are people mammals?
    Name eight mammals. Give their adult and baby names.
    What are mammals?
    Where do domestic mammals live?
    Which mammals have paws and which have hooves?
    Where do all young mammals get their milk?

▶ **Comparative adjective + *than***

    > To form a comparative, we generally add *-er* to the base form of an adjective and then add *than*: *smaller than, larger than, younger than*, etc. For certain adjectives, such as *important* or *interesting*, we use *more* + adjective + *than*. For example: *Science is more interesting than math.*

Point out an example of comparative adjectives in the content reading (*Calves are shorter than cows*) and have students underline and read aloud all the other sentences using comparative adjectives + *than*. Divide students into groups. Each group looks at the wall chart and writes as many sentences using comparative adjectives + *than* as they can. For example: *The sheep is larger than the lamb. The rabbit is older than the bunny.* Encourage students to use two different adjectives for the same animals, if they can. Have each group read their sentences aloud while students in the other group check for accuracy. The group with the most correct sentences is the winner.

▶ **Comparative adjective + *than*.** Divide students into groups. Students in Group 1 arrange themselves according to height, make a list of the students in their group in ascending order (from shorter to taller), and put their list on the board. Students in Group 2 arrange themselves according to age, make a list of the students in their group in ascending order (from younger to older), and put their list on the board. Now the whole class looks at the two lists and individual students ask and answer *Yes/No* questions using comparatives. For example: *Is Pedro younger than Aimee? No, he isn't. He's older than Aimee.* (Avoid this activity with students who may be height sensitive.)

- Pair students and have them look at the wall chart. Students take turns role-playing adult and baby pairs of animals. Encourage students to look at the expressions on the faces of these animals and use their imaginations for their role plays.

WORKSHEET: Topic 45
See Teacher's Book page 181.

►CHANTS

Components: Dictionary pages 90-91, Content Chant Topic 45, Cassette

 ## CONTENT CHANT

Dogs Are Bigger Than Puppies

Dogs are bigger than puppies.
Lambs are smaller than sheep.
Horses are not at all like cats.
They stand up when they sleep.

Little pigs are piglets.
A foal is a baby horse.
A little cat is a kitten.
His dad is a cat, of course.

Bunnies hop.
Rabbits run.
Cows stand around
in the sun.

Dogs are bigger than piglets.
Horses are smarter than sheep.
Cats are not at all like cows.
They curl up when they sleep.

- Present the content chant. **See pages xx-xxi for general techniques on presenting chants.**

- Before distributing the chant, have students practice the names of adult and baby animals in the chant. Divide the class into six groups. Each group chants two of the following adult and baby pair words repeatedly, first in turn and then simultaneously: *dogs and puppies; sheep and lambs; horses and a foal; a cat and a kitten; pigs and piglets; rabbits and bunnies.*

- Now distribute Content Chant 45. Divide the class into three groups. The groups chant the first, second, and fourth stanzas, respectively. Instead of chanting all the words as they are written, each group substitutes the sound that the animal makes when they see the name of the animal. For example, in the first stanza, the group would chant (Woof) *are bigger than* (woof). (Baa) *are smaller than* (baa). (Neigh) *are not at all like* (Meow). *They stand up when they sleep.*

- Divide the class into five groups. Groups 1 through 4 chant the four stanzas of the chant and pantomime the actions of the animals mentioned. Group 5 provides all the animal sounds when they occur in each stanza, as the class had previously practiced.

►EXTENSION

Components: Dictionary pages 90-91, Transparency 45, Wall Chart 45

- Explain to students that in various parts of the world, some people keep some domestic animals as pets (*dogs, cats, horses*), some people cook them and eat them (*cows, lamb, horses, dogs*), and some people buy things made from their skin or hair (*wool and angora sweaters, sheepskin rugs, leather belts, coats, jackets*). Have students conduct a poll in class, and later outside the classroom, to find out what the people they know would do with these animals. Use the example chart below. Have students make bar graphs to show the results. Encourage students to be accepting of cultural differences that emerge in class discussions.

Domestic Mammals	Questions	Classmates		Other people		Total	
	Would you:	yes	no	yes	no	yes	no
1. cat	a) keep this animal as a pet?						
	b) cook and eat this animal?						
	c) buy something made from its skin or hair?						
2. sheep	a) keep this animal as a pet?						
	b) cook and eat this animal?						
	c) buy something made from its skin or hair?						

- Have a discussion about the care of pets. Ask students to write and illustrate a story about their pet (or one that they would like to have if they don't have a pet). Have students include the chores they do or would do to take care of their pet and the thing they like best about their pet.

- Review the animal sounds in English and then teach students the song "Old MacDonald Had a Farm." Students form a circle and sing it.

- **Game: Grab Bag Review.** Have students pick a word or picture card from a large paper bag and then tell the class one thing they learned about this animal. Continue playing until students have exhausted their knowledge. Students cannot repeat what someone else has said.

- If possible, have students visit a local farm and upon their return, write and illustrate a report on what some domestic animals are used for. For example: *cows give milk, chickens lay eggs,* etc. If it is not possible for students to visit a local farm, have them do research in encyclopedias and on the Internet for their report.

► LITERATURE

Suggested Books

If You Were Born a Kitten
written by Marion Dane Bauer; illustrated by Joellen McAllister Stammen.
Simon and Schuster, 1997. ISBN 0689801114
This gentle and poetic book describes different kinds of birth, from the birth of a kitten to the birth of a human baby. Each accompanying description uses the language pattern, "If you were..., you would..." The repetitive use of this language structure, along with the large pastel illustrations, makes this book especially useful for read-aloud and read-along activities. This book may also be used with other topics in this unit, as well as with the topics in Unit 4.

The Night I Followed the Dog
written and illustrated by Nina Laden.
Chronicle Books, 1994. ISBN 0811806472
This is a zany story about a curious boy who wants to find out where his dog goes at night. He follows his seemingly ordinary dog to a dog nightclub aptly named "The Doghouse" and is surprised by what he finds there. Key words in the text are highlighted by clever visual imagery. Teachers can encourage students to look closely at the words in the text and use similar techniques to write their own words.

The Day the Sheep Showed Up
written and illustrated by David M. McPhail.
Cartwheel Books, 1998. ISBN 0590849107
The day the sheep shows up is a confusing one for the rest of the barnyard animals. "What is this strange animal?" they ask. Finally, the sheep introduces himself. Although they are unsure at first, the other animals learn to accept the sheep as one of their own. The message of this book is excellent for newcomers. Students will be able to follow the pictures and imitate the sounds of barnyard animals while they act out the story. They can use the story's dialogue as a model when they talk about the story or act it out.

The Cow Buzzed
written by Andrea Zimmerman and David Clemesha; illustrated by Paul Meisel.
HarperTrophy, 1995. ISBN 0064434109
In this chain reaction story similar to the song "Old Macdonald Had a Farm," a bee catches a cold and gives it (and its buzz) to a cow. The cow gives the cold (and its moo) to a pig. Before long, all of the animals on the farm are passing the cold around, adding their own distinctive sounds. Students can have plenty of fun with the simple humor, rhyme, and repetitive refrains of this book. The chain structure of the story also lends itself to acting out.

Nature's Footprints in the Barnyard
written by Q. L. Pearce and W. J. Pearce; illustrated by Delana Bettoli.
Silver Press, 1990. ISBN 0671688286
In this book from the "Nature's Footprints" series, ten animals are presented in sets of two along with their unique footprints. Readers are invited to follow the footprints in the colorful illustrations as they learn about the characteristics of the animals. Many beginner students will be able to read the text individually after hearing it read aloud once or twice. As an extension, students can write short sentences about themselves and illustrate them with their own footprints or handprints.

WORKBOOK: Topic 45

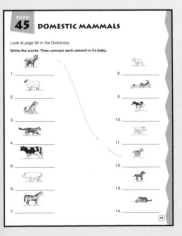

On this page, students write the words for domestic mammals and their babies, and match the picture of each adult to its baby.

WORKSHEET: Topic 45

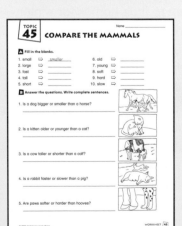

For each adjective in A, students write the comparative form. In B, they answer the questions, using complete sentences with the comparative adjective and *than*.

▶ **CONTENT**
....
Wild mammals and their habitats

▶ **LANGUAGE**
....
Verb + infinitive: *Bears like to eat berries, fish, and honey.*

Modal *have to*: *They live in the water, but they have to breathe air.*

CONTENT WORDS

1. squirrel
2. bat
3. opossum
4. bear
5. deer
6. fur
7. whale
8. dolphin
9. camel
10. kangaroo
11. pouch
12. tiger
13. monkey
14. giraffe
15. lion
16. zebra
17. elephant
18. tusk

CONTENT READING

Wild Mammals

Many mammals live in the wild. Wild mammals need to be near their food supply. They usually don't go near people. You can see them sometimes, but you have to be very quiet.

Squirrels, bears, deer, and opossums live in forests. Squirrels also live in parks. They collect nuts and acorns and bring them to their homes for winter. Bears have to find food in the summer because they sleep all winter. Bears like to eat berries, fish, and honey. Baby opossums ride on their mother's back. They have to hold on tight to her fur.

Bats live in caves and tunnels. They are the only mammals with wings. Bats like to fly at night.

Whales and dolphins look like fish, but they are mammals. They live in the water, but they have to breathe air. Dolphins like to jump and play. Whales like to eat small plants and animals in the sea.

Camels live in the desert. They don't need to drink water very often. They can walk for hours and hours without drinking.

Kangaroos live in Australia. They have long hind legs and strong tails. Kangaroos like to jump. Baby kangaroos live in their mothers' pouches.

Monkeys and tigers live in the hot, wet jungle. Monkeys like to hang from trees in the jungle.

Giraffes, zebras, and lions have to be near grass and water. These mammals live on the plains and grasslands of Africa. Giraffes have very long necks. Zebras have black and white stripes. African elephants have long trunks and long tusks.

▶ WORDS

Components: Dictionary pages 92-93, Transparency 46, Wall Chart 46, Workbook page 46, Word and Picture Cards Topic 46, Cassette

- Present the content words. **See pages xiv-xvi for general techniques about presenting content words.**

  > **Language Note:** The *g* sound in the word *giraffe* sounds like the *g* sound in the word *gentle*. Also, *giraffe* has a silent *e*. The word *tusk* has a final consonant cluster, which is sometimes difficult for some students to pronounce. Be sure that students pronounce both the *s* and *k* sounds.

- To introduce this topic, bring in several stuffed animals of the types featured in this topic. Have students identify the ones they know and then find the matching animals on the Dictionary page.

- While students are looking at the Dictionary page, ask them the names of these animals in their native languages. Distribute enlarged picture cards and have students write the animals' names on them. If students are from different language backgrounds, have them write the various names for the same animal on the same picture card. Display the cards.

- Make a list on chart paper and label it *What We Know About Wild Mammals*. Have students tell any information they already know about any of these animals and record their information on the list.

- Pair students. Place one set of word cards and one set of picture cards in separate stacks. Students take turns selecting a picture card from the picture stack and holding it up as their partners find the matching word card in the word stack. Pairs, in turn, pronounce the name of their animal together.

- Divide the class into two teams. Distribute one set of picture cards to each team. Students on each team, in turn, hold up a picture card while students from the opposite team describe as many features as possible about that particular wild mammal. For example, Team 1 holds up *kangaroo* and students from Team 2 say: *It's a large mammal; It is brown; It holds its baby in its pouch.* Score one point for each correct characteristic. Write any additional characteristics on the *What We Know About Wild Mammals chart.*

- **Game: Name That Wild Mammal.** Select one student to be "it." That student writes the name of a wild mammal on a paper and places the paper face down on the front desk. Other students ask *Yes/No* questions to determine which mammal the student is thinking of. If nobody guesses within twenty questions, the student who is "it" gets another turn. Otherwise, the student who correctly guesses the name of the mammal becomes "it."

WORKBOOK: Topic 46
See Teacher's Book page 185.

▶ CONTENT

Components: Dictionary pages 92-93, Transparency 46, Wall Chart 46, Content Reading Topic 46, Worksheet Topic 46, Cassette

- Present the content reading. **See pages xvii-xix for general techniques about presenting content readings.**

- Ask the following or similar questions:

  Do you have to be quiet to see wild mammals?
  Do whales and dolphins have to breathe air?
  Where do squirrels, bears, deer, and opossums live?
  When do bats like to fly?
  What do bears like to eat?
  What do kangaroos like to do?

▶ **Verb + infinitive**

> Certain verbs in English such as *like, need, try, want, hope, plan,* and *promise* can be followed by an infinitive form of another verb. An infinitive is the word *to* + the simple form of a verb. For example: *Wild mammals need to be near their food supply.*

Point out an example of the verb + infinitive pattern in the content reading (*Bears like to eat berries, fish, and honey*). Have students underline and read aloud all sentences in the content reading that use this pattern. Divide students into groups. Each group looks at the wall chart and writes sentences using verb + infinitive to describe the mammals in the pictures. Suggest to students that they use the verbs *like, need,* and *want* for their descriptive statements. For example: *The dolphin likes to swim in the water.*

▶ **Verb + infinitive.** Students each write five sentences about themselves and the animals in the wall chart using any combination of the above verbs (*like, want, need, try, hope,* etc.) plus an infinitive. For example, *I like to watch squirrels in the park.*

▶ **Modal *have to***

> A modal is an auxiliary verb or helping verb that is followed by the simple form of the main verb. The modal *have to* (*has to* in the third person singular) expresses necessity.

Divide the class into two teams. Team 1 gives orders to students in Team 2 and then teams reverse roles. For example: *Juan has to walk backwards and count backwards from 20 to 1.* The orders must use *have to/has to.* The orders can be funny as long as they are safe and reasonable.

WORKSHEET: Topic 46
See Teacher's Book page 185.

▶ CHANTS

Components: Dictionary pages 92-93, Content Chant Topic 46, Cassette

 CONTENT CHANT

Tiger, Elephant, Kangaroo

Tiger, elephant,
kangaroo.
Wild animals in the zoo.
You like them, but they don't like you.
Tiger, elephant,
kangaroo.

Watch the monkeys.
Look at the lion.
Talk to the zebra in the zoo.

But don't pet the lion.
Don't touch the tiger.
You'll be sorry if you do!

- Present the content chant. **See pages xx-xxi for general techniques for presenting chants.**

- Before distributing the chant, have students practice with the names of the animals in the chant. Divide the class into two groups. Group 1 repeatedly chants *tiger, elephant, kangaroo*. Group 2 repeatedly chants *monkeys, lion, zebra*. Groups chant first in turn and then simultaneously. Students start chanting slowly and softly and then gradually increase their speed and volume.

- Distribute Content Chant 46. Before students practice the stanzas, have them practice the longer lines in the chant by breaking them into smaller chunks from the end in order to preserve the rhythm and intonation. Students practice each section repeatedly and then add on the next one. For example, in the sentence *You like them, but they don't like you*, students chant the following phrases:

  like you/ but they don't/ but they don't like you/ you like them.

  Then they chant the entire sentence: *You like them, but they don't like you*. Have students practice the sentence *You'll be sorry if you do* in the same manner.

- Now divide the class into three groups. Each group chants and pantomimes one of the three stanzas.

▶ EXTENSION

Components: Dictionary pages 92-93, Transparency 46, Wall Chart 46

- Have students pretend to be one of the wild mammals listed in this topic. Students, in turn, pantomime the actions and general behavior of one of the animals and the class guesses which animal it is.

- Have students write about which one of these wild mammals they would like to be if they could, and tell why. Students illustrate their work and share it with the entire class.

- Explain to students that in some parts of the world people hunt wild mammals. Some people hunt these animals to eat them, others hunt them for sport, and still others eat them, but don't hunt them. Have students conduct a poll in class, and later outside the classroom, using the example chart below. Have students make bar graphs to show the results. Encourage class discussion. Include *whale* and *dolphin* in your list of animals.

Wild Mammals	Questions	Classmates		Other people		Total	
	Would you:	yes	no	yes	no	yes	no
1. bear	a) eat the meat of this animal?						
	b) hunt this animal for food?						
	c) hunt this animal for sport?						
2. deer	a) eat the meat of this animal?						
	b) hunt this animal for food?						
	c) hunt this animal for sport?						

- Divide the class into groups and have each group "adopt" a wild mammal. Each group does research to find out detailed information on its animal's habitat, size, weight, color, life cycle, food and feeding habits, and the care of its young. Students can get their information from science books, encyclopedias, and the Internet. Have students make diagrams, drawings or models of their adopted animals and label all their parts. Students also make posters describing and illustrating their animals. Groups share their research. Have students add any generally useful information to the chart done earlier in the Words section of this topic, *What We Know About Wild Mammals*.

► LITERATURE

Suggested Books

Animaze!: A Collection of Amazing Nature Mazes

written by Wendy Madgwick; illustrated by Lorna Hussey.
Alfred A. Knopf, 1992. ISBN 0679826653
In this collection of twelve mazes, children are asked to guide animals through potentially dangerous situations in a variety of natural habitats. As students follow the paths of the mazes, they learn about the habitats and common enemies of a wide variety of animals, many of which are featured in this topic. The mazes, organized by their natural environments, are accompanied by short paragraphs that include information about the animals. The author also poses questions that can generate discussion. For an extension activity, students can create environmental mazes for other creatures that they've studied. This book may also be useful for Topic 53, Climates and Land Biomes.

What the Moon Saw

written and illustrated by Brian Wildsmith.
Oxford University Press Children's Books, 1986.
ISBN 0192721577
The sun brags about everything he can see. While he brags, he introduces readers to many animals from around the world (as well as a useful list of adjectives). The moon responds by pointing out the one thing she can see that the sun never does—the dark. Vibrant collages add color to this tale about everyone's special abilities. The language pattern "There is a.../This is a...," and the simple prose makes the book ideal for beginners. As an extension, students can collect the story's adjectives in a word bank and employ them in other sentences and contexts.

Creatures Small and Furry

written by Donald J. Crump.
National Geographic Society, 1993. ISBN 0870444867
True to its title, this book is a close-up look at a number of small, furry animals such as the dormouse, the opossum, the squirrel, the rabbit, and the shrew. Short paragraphs of lively writing describe the animals pictured in large, full-color photographs. The simple text can be mastered easily in conjunction with the content words for this topic.

The Oxford Book of Animal Poems

compiled by Michael Harrison and Christopher Stuart-Clark.
Oxford University Press Children's Books, 1992.
ISBN 0192761056
This anthology contains poems about the many kinds of wildlife found on Earth. It begins with ocean-dwelling mammals and circles the globe continent by continent. The poems can be used with other topics in Unit 5, as well. Many poems are well suited for read-aloud activities. A useful animal index appears at the back of the book.

WORKBOOK: Topic 46

For each animal pictured in A, students find the word in the word search. Words appear vertically and horizontally. In B, students fill in the sentences by identifying each numbered animal.

WORKSHEET: Topic 46

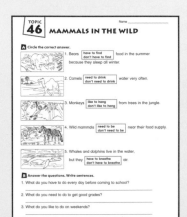

In A, students use the information in the content reading to circle the correct choice from the box in each sentence. In B, they use these verbs with infinitives to answer questions about themselves.

▶ **CONTENT**
....
Prehistoric animals

▶ **LANGUAGE**
....
Simple past: *Smilodons lived less than 2 million years ago./ They ate meat.*

CONTENT WORDS

1. dinosaurs
2. triceratops
3. ankylosaurus
4. apatosaurus
5. anatosaurus
6. diplodocus
7. dryosaurus
8. brachiosaurus
9. stegosaurus
10. spike
11. tyrannosaurus
12. pteranodon
13. allosaurus
14. smilodon
15. saber tooth
16. fossil

Herbivores

Carnivores

CONTENT READING

Prehistoric Animals

Millions of years ago, many different types of animals lived on the Earth. They are called prehistoric animals. Some of these animals were dinosaurs.

Many dinosaurs were herbivores. They only ate plants. The anatosaurus and the dryosaurus were herbivores. The triceratops was an herbivore, too. It had three horns on its head. The ankylosaurus and the stegosaurus were also herbivores. The ankylosaurus had spikes on its back. The stegosaurus had spikes on its tail.

The apatosaurus and the diplodocus were very long dinosaurs. The apatosaurus was 70 feet long and the diplodocus was 90 feet long. The brachiosaurus was one of the tallest dinosaurs. It was 40 feet tall.

Some dinosaurs were carnivores. They ate meat. Sometimes they ate other dinosaurs. The allosaurus was a carnivore. It had very sharp teeth. The tyrannosaurus was a carnivore, too. It had 60 teeth. People call the tyrannosaurus the king of the dinosaurs. The pteranodon was a carnivore, too. Pteranodons could fly.

Dinosaurs lived more than 65 million years ago. Smilodons lived less than two million years ago. The smilodon was a large cat with two large saber teeth. Some people call these cats saber-toothed tigers.

These prehistoric animals are extinct. They are not alive today, but we can see their fossils in museums. Fossils are bones and other parts of prehistoric animals or plants. Fossils can stay in rocks or in the ground for millions of years. Scientists find fossils and study them. We can learn a lot about prehistoric animals from fossils.

▶ WORDS

Components: Dictionary pages 94-95, Transparency 47, Wall Chart 47, Workbook page 47, Word and Picture Cards Topioc 47, Cassette

- Present the content words. **See pages xiv-xvi for general techniques about presenting content words.**

> **Language Note:** The *p* in *pteranodon* is silent. The root word *-saurus*, which occurs in many of the content words in this topic, means *lizard*. *Tyrannosaurus* is often referred to as *Tyranno-saurus Rex*, meaning "King of the Tyrant Lizards."
>
> Dinosaur names with three, four, or five syllables can be difficult for students to pronounce. The chart below illustrates the main or primary stress for each of the names. Many of these have the primary stress on the root word, *saurus*.

Three Syllables	Four Syllables		Five Syllables	
SMIL-o-don	tri-CER-a-tops	steg-o-SAUR-us	an-ky-lo-SAUR-us	brach-i-o-SAUR-us
	Di-PLOD-o-cus	pter-AN-o-don	a-pat-o-SAUR-us	ty-rann-o-SAUR-us
	dry-o-SAUR-us	all-o-SAUR-us	a-na-to-SAUR-us	

- Have students look at page 94 in their Dictionaries. Explain the concept of syllables and stress. For example, *tyrannosaurus* has five syllables and is pronounced *ty-rann-o-SAUR-us*. Tap out the rhythm of the syllables with a pencil (or use a percussion instrument). Be sure to tap louder on the fourth syllable *SAUR*. Model each of the words as you tap out their rhythm and stress. Then have students take turns saying the words as they tap out the number of syllables, tapping louder on the stressed syllable. Distribute a set of picture cards to each of two teams. Students on each team, in turn, pronounce the word for a card and tap out its rhythm and stress in syllables as the other team guesses the word. Score one point for each correct pronunciation and one point for each correct rhythm and stress.

- Point to the groupings of *Herbivores* and *Carnivores* on the wall chart. Draw two columns on chart paper, one labeled *Herbivores* (*Plant Eaters*) and the other labeled *Carnivores* (*Meat Eaters*). Place the word and picture cards in two stacks (omit *dinosaurs*, *spike*, *saber tooth*, and *fossil*). Have students select a card from each stack, pronounce the word, and place their cards in the appropriate columns.

- Many students may be familiar with dinosaurs. Create a *K-W-L* chart (*Know*, *Want to Know*, *Learned*). Ask students what they already know and what they want to know about dinosaurs. Record their answers in the *Know* column and the *Want to Know* column. Add to the chart as you progress through this topic. Any incorrect information can be reviewed for accuracy at the end of this topic.

> **WORKBOOK:** Topic 47
> See Teacher's Book page 189.

▶ CONTENT

Components: Dictionary pages 94-95, Transparency 47, Wall Chart 47, Content Reading Topic 47, Worksheet Topic 47, Cassette

- Present the content reading. **See pages xvii-xix for general techniques about presenting content readings.**

- Ask the following or similar questions:

  Was the triceratops a carnivore?
  Name five dinosaurs that were herbivores.
  What did the allosaurus eat?
  Which dinosaur was the king of the dinosaurs?
  When did dinosaurs live?
  What are fossils?

▶ **Simple past**

> We form the simple past tense by adding *-d* or *-ed* to regular verbs. Irregular verbs have special forms for the simple past. The irregular verbs in the content reading and their simple past forms are: *eat/ate, have/had*. We form *Yes/No* questions in the simple past with [*Did* + subject + simple form of main verb]: *Did he eat? Did they have three horns?* The simple past forms of the verb *BE* are *was* and *were*. *Yes/No* questions with *BE* are formed by inverting subject and verb (*Was he large?*).

Have students underline and read aloud all sentences with the past tense of *BE* that appear in the content reading. Have them circle and read aloud all sentences with regular and irregular past tense forms of other verbs. Now divide students into two groups and ask them to look at the wall chart. Group 1 writes ten sentences using any past tense form to describe the *Herbivores*. Group 2 writes ten sentences using any past tense form to describe the *Carnivores*.

▶ **Simple past.** Have students play *Name that Dino*. Select one student to be "it." That student writes the name of a dinosaur on a piece of paper. Other students ask *Yes/No* questions with *be* and/or other verbs in the past tense to try to guess which dinosaur the student is thinking of.

▶ **Simple past.** Have students each write seven sentences using the past tense to describe what they ate every day last week. Help students compile their data and make bar graphs showing the total numbers of various foods they ate (for example, meats, vegetables, cereal, etc.).

> **WORKSHEET:** Topic 47
> See Teacher's Book page 189.

► CHANTS

Components: Dictionary pages 94-95, Content Chant Topic 47, Cassette

 CONTENT CHANT

Diplodocus Was Very Strong

Diplodocus was very strong.
Diplodocus was ninety feet long.
His teeth were sharp, his neck was strong.
Diplodocus was very long.

Brachiosaurus was very tall.
His tail was long, his head was small.
Brachiosaurus was easy to see.
When he got hungry, he'd eat a tree.

Triceratops was strange to see,
with horns on his head; one, two, three.
He didn't look at all like you or me.
Triceratops was strange to see!

Stegosaurus was a frightening sight.
With spikes on his tail, he was up all night,
munching on plants, munching on trees.
Stegosaurus was easy to please.

Tyrannosaurus Rex was the dinosaur king.
He could do almost anything.
When he got hungry and wanted more,
he'd eat another dinosaur.

- Present the content chant. **See pages xx-xxi for general techniques about presenting chants.**

- Before distributing the chant, have students practice with the rhythm and stress of the dinosaur names in each of the five stanzas. Divide the class into five groups. Each group repeatedly claps out the rhythm and stress of the dinosaur name in its stanza. Group 1 claps out *Di-PLOD-o-cus, (Clap-CLAP-clap-clap)* repeatedly. Group 2 claps out the rhythm and stress for *Brach-i-o-SAUR-us (Clap-clap-clap-CLAP-clap)* and so forth.

- Now distribute Content Chant 47. Keep students in the same groups as in the above activity. Each group chants one stanza respectively, but instead of pronouncing the name of the dinosaur in their stanza, they clap out the rhythm and stress for the name. For example: *Clap-CLAP-clap-clap was very strong. Clap-CLAP-clap-clap was ninety feet long.*

- Now have the students, in their same groups, chant their stanzas including the names of the dinosaurs. Encourage students to pantomime the words in their stanzas as they chant.

► EXTENSION

Components: Dictionary pages 94-95, Transparency 47, Wall Chart 47

- Have individual students make up as many riddles about each dinosaur as they can using the past tense. Students write each riddle on a separate index card. For example: *I had three horns on my head. What am I?* Encourage students to make more than one card and sign their name to each card so they don't get their own card back. Collect the cards, redistribute them to the class, and have individual students read aloud the riddle they received. If a student can't answer the riddle, other students can help. If no one can answer the riddle, the riddle writer answers it.

- Explain to students that the dinosaurs in the Dictionary are just some of the dinosaurs which lived millions of years ago. Have students invent their own dinosaurs and draw pictures of them. Students should create a name for their dinosaurs. Knowing that *saurus* means *lizard*, what interesting and creative combinations can they make up for their imaginary dinosaurs? Have students share their drawings and dinosaur names with the entire class.

- Divide the class into groups. Have each group do further research on a dinosaur from the Dictionary illustration or from other resources on dinosaurs. Students should find out the meaning of the dinosaur's name, its weight, length, and number of limbs, as well as any other identifying characteristics. Students should also find out when their dinosaurs lived and any other interesting facts from dinosaur books, museums, encyclopedias, and the Internet. Each group then writes a report, makes a poster with the important information, and makes a diagram, drawing, or three dimensional clay model of the dinosaur.

- Have students discuss the various facts they have learned about dinosaurs and select the most important information to add to the *K-W-L* chart they began in the Words section of this topic. Have students review the previous information on the chart and check it for accuracy, correcting the information as necessary.

- If possible, take students to a museum to see fossils. Afterwards, have students make their own fossils using leaves, bones, or shells. Students flatten a six-inch square of clay, rub petroleum jelly on the clay, place the object on top of it, and then pour plaster of paris onto the clay and let it set. When it is dry, separate the clay for the plaster and students will have made their own modern-day fossils.

► LITERATURE

Suggested Books

Dinosaur Poems
compiled by John Foster; illustrated by Korky Paul.
Oxford University Press Children's Books, 1997;
ISBN 0192761269
Many of these bouncy, rhythmic, and lively poems can be used for reading in chorus or as springboards for role playing. Some of the language is British English; this may prompt discussion about differences between British and American English. Many of the dinosaurs featured in this topic appear in this humorous collection.

The Magic School Bus In the Time of the Dinosaurs
written by Joanna Cole; illustrated by Bruce Degen.
Scholastic, 1994. ISBN 0590446894
Ms. Frizzle is up to her usual antics as she and the class travel back in time to the days when dinosaurs roamed the earth. This book may be enjoyed first as a read-aloud, just for the adventure and fun. For beginners, the story may be paraphrased as it is read. To help students follow the story, teachers may want to draw a time table on the board. When the story is reread, students may record and illustrate events according to the time table. The reports that the characters in the story write can act as models for students' own reports on the story.

Prehistoric Life
written and illustrated by Dougal Dixon.
Oxford University Press, 1996. ISBN 0195212371
Prehistoric Life divides the prehistoric age into its respective periods and discusses the animal life that developed and thrived in each era. With this book students will learn more about fossils, early animals, and the dinosaurs depicted in the Dictionary illustration. The book is extensively illustrated, and interesting facts accompany almost every picture. Students will need to be guided through the scientific names and terminology, but even beginners will be able to match the word and picture cards to the text.

Gone Forever! An Alphabet Book of Extinct Animals
written by Sandra Markle and William Markle; illustrated by Felipe Davalos.
Athneum, 1998. ISBN 0689319614
The animals in this book did not live during the age of the dinosaurs. However, it is important for students to realize that, like the dinosaurs, animals are becoming extinct even today. In this book, a different extinct animal is featured for every letter of the alphabet. A brief paragraph accompanies each full-page illustration. This collection may prompt students to investigate other endangered species. A short list of addresses of wildlife organizations is included at the end of the book. Teachers may wish to have students work with a mainstream partner to write to one of these organizations.

WORKBOOK: Topic 47

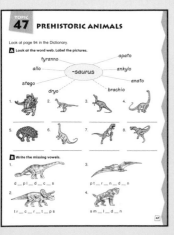

In A, students fill in the names of dinosaurs. To help them, they refer to a web showing the root *-saurus*, and some prefixes that can be added to this root. In B, they fill in the missing vowels in the names of other prehistoric animals.

WORKSHEET: Topic 47

In A, students choose verbs from the word box to fill in the sentences. In B, they answer the questions, based on the information from the content reading.

48 OUR ENVIRONMENT

▶ **CONTENT**
....

The environment

Environmental problems and solutions

▶ **LANGUAGE**
....

Simple past: *Water pollution was one problem./Cans and bottles filled big, ugly landfills.*

Present perfect continuous: *The town has been solving its environmental problems.*

Compound words: *Air pollution was another problem.*

CONTENT WORDS

1. water pollution
2. air pollution
3. soil pollution
4. smog
5. smoke
6. smokestack
7. exhaust
8. oil slick
9. litter
10. garbage
11. can
12. bottle
13. landfill
14. glass
15. plastic
16. metal
17. compost
18. carpool

CONTENT READING

Our Environment

People, plants, and animals all live in the same environment. That environment is the Earth. People and animals need food, water, and air. Plants need food, water, air, and soil.

This town had serious environmental problems several years ago. Water pollution was one problem. There were oil slicks on the lake.

Air pollution was another problem. People drove their cars everywhere and they ignored the exhaust. Hundreds of smokestacks polluted the air with smoke. The smoke mixed with fog and then the town had smog.

Soil pollution was a problem, too. People threw litter and garbage on the sides of the roads. Cans and bottles filled big, ugly landfills.

But things have been changing recently. The town has been solving its environmental problems. People have been reducing their litter. They have been reusing plastic and glass bottles. They have been recycling metal cans and newspapers. Some people have been making compost from their uneaten food, banana peels, and other garbage.

People have been riding together in carpools. Some people have been walking or biking to work. They haven't been polluting the air with their cars.

Now, the sky and the lake are blue, and the trees and grass are green. Plants are growing and people are breathing clean air.

▶ WORDS

Components: Dictionary pages 96-97, Transparency 48, Wall Chart 48, Workbook page 48, Word and Picture Cards Topic 48, Cassette

- Present the content words. **See pages xiv-xvi for general techniques about presenting content words.**

  > **Language Note:** The stress on the word *environment* is on the second syllable (*en-VI-ron-ment*). The *n* sound is heard before the *m* sound in the last syllable. This *n* + *m* cluster is sometimes difficult for students. Have students practice pausing slightly in the syllable break between the *n* and *m* sounds. The *h* is silent in *exhaust*.

- Point out some of the compound words for students and have them look at Dictionary page 96 to find the other compound words. Students each select one compound word and write the two parts of the word on two separate index cards. Collect all the cards and redistribute them, two per student. Have students walk around the room asking each other which words they have so that they can trade with each other to get one of the content words. In the process, students may come up with silly or interesting combinations such as *water pool, land car*, etc. Encourage students to share this information with the class. Make a list of such creations on the board.

- Introduce the word *environment* by asking students to look around the room and tell what they see. Ask them how the room feels. Is it too hot, cold, or noisy? Is it comfortable or uncomfortable? Explain that the classroom is their immediate *environment*, or surroundings. The school and the neighborhood around it is also their environment. Explain, however, that *environment* can also have a more general meaning. When we talk about *protecting the environment*, we use the word *environment* to mean the whole Earth: the sky, the water, and the ground. Ask students which sense of the word is being used in the title of the topic.

- Have students look at the wall chart as you point to the top picture, which shows many environmental problems such as *smog, litter*, etc. Then point to the bottom picture which shows environmental solutions, such as recycling metal, recycling glass, and recycling plastic. Draw two columns on chart paper, label them *Environmental Problems* and *Environmental Solutions*. Place the word cards and the picture cards in two stacks. Have students select a card from each stack, pronounce the word, and place the cards in the appropriate columns.

- Pair students. Have them circle the pictures of each content word on the transparency and write the words next to the item in the picture. (Be sure to have students use washable markers.)

WORKBOOK: Topic 48
See Teacher's Book page 193.

▶ CONTENT

Components: Dictionary pages 96-97, Transparency 48, Wall Chart 48, Content Reading Topic 48, Worksheet Topic 48, Cassette

- Present the content reading. **See pages xvii-xix for general techniques about presenting content readings.**

- Ask the following or similar questions:

  What do people and animals need to survive?
  What do plants need to survive?
  Name three types of pollution which are environmental problems.
  What does the slogan Reduce, Reuse, Recycle *mean?*
  What can people do to reduce air pollution from cars?

▶ **Simple past and present perfect continuous**

  > We use the present perfect continuous for actions that began in the past and continue into the present. We form the present perfect continuous with [*have/has* + *been* + simple form of the main verb + *-ing*]. For example: *We have been recycling for a long time.*

  Point out the difference between the simple past (for actions that began and ended in the past) and the present perfect continuous (for actions that began in the past and continue into the present). Have students underline and read aloud all instances of the simple past in the content reading. Then have them do the same with the present perfect continuous. Form two groups. Group 1 writes ten sentences using the simple past to describe the top picture in the wall chart. For example: *People threw litter everywhere.* Group 2 writes ten sentences using the present perfect continuous to describe the job the people have been doing in the bottom picture. For example: *They have been taking their garbage to the compost pile.*

▶ **Simple past.** Ask students to use a chart to keep track of the number of glass bottles, plastic containers, and metal cans their families recycle in a week. Have students make a bar graph showing the data for the whole class, and discuss the results using the simple past.

Recycled Materials	Mon.	Tues.	Wed.	Thurs.	Fri.	Sat.	Sun.	Week Totals
Glass Bottles								
Plastic Containers								
Metal								

▶ **Present perfect continuous.** Have students each write one sentence about what they and their families have been doing to try to keep our environment clean. For example: *We have been using carpools.* Students write their names next to their sentences. Place their sentences on the bulletin board.

WORKSHEET: Topic 48
See Teacher's Book page 193.

► CHANTS

Components: Dictionary pages 96-97, Content Chant Topic 48, Cassette

 CONTENT CHANT

Pollution Chant

Smog, smoke,
Air pollution.
Smoke, smokestack,
Air pollution.
Cars, trucks,
Air pollution.
    Pollution *
    What's the solution?

Exhaust, *
Air pollution.
Oil slick,
Water pollution.
Landfill,
Soil pollution.
    Pollution *
    What's the solution?

Carpools. *
That's a solution.
Recycling. *
That's a solution.
Don't litter. *
That's a solution.

    Pollution *
    We're the solution!

- Present the content chant. **See pages xx-xxi for general techniques about presenting chants.**

- Before distributing the chants, have the entire class practice the rhythm and stress of the words *pollution* and *solution* by clapping out the syllables. Have students clap their pattern repeatedly (*clap-CLAP-clap*).

- Then divide the class into two groups. Group 1 chants repeatedly, *Pollution* What's the solution?* (Don't forget to have students clap, as indicated by the asterisk.) Group 2 chants repeatedly *Air pollution, water pollution, soil pollution.* Groups start chanting slowly and softly and then increase their speed and volume. Groups chant in turn first and then simultaneously.

- Now distribute Content Chant 48. Divide the class into four groups. Groups 1 through 3 chant the unindented lines in the three stanzas. Group 4 chants the indented lines in each stanza.

► EXTENSION

Components: Dictionary pages 96-97, Transparency 48, Wall Chart 48

- Explain to students the meaning of the word *slogan* as a phrase used in advertising to convince people to do something, or to highlight the meaning of a company or a campaign. *Reduce, Reuse, Recycle* is an important slogan of the conservation movement. These are the "3 R's" of conservation. Have students make posters with this slogan and decorate their posters with drawings or photographs to try to convince people to *Reduce, Reuse, Recycle*. Put the posters on the bulletin board, or if permissible, place them around the school.

- Have students campaign to reduce the amount of waste in their households. Encourage them to reduce the amount of garbage and increase the amount of recyclable materials they discard every week. Ask students to keep a weekly record of the amount of garbage and the amount of recyclable materials discarded by their families every week. At the end of a month, compare the weekly data to see if students' families have reduced the amount of garbage and increased the number of recyclables. Have students tally their data and discuss how their habits at home may or may not have changed.

- Have students find articles about environmental problems in local newspapers. Have them identify ways people can influence others to do something about the problems. Have students select and complete one or more of these actions, such as writing letters, talking to storekeepers in the community, or giving awards to those who care for the environment.

- Have students do research on careers that help to save the Earth, such as forest rangers, park rangers, city planners, geologists, marine biologists, ecologists, etc. Have students find out the training and education required for these careers and what some of the job responsibilities and benefits are.

- Have students bring in recyclable items to create a class sculpture that makes a statement about the environment. Encourage class discussion.

- Take students in small groups on a "Trash Hunt" near or around the school. Give one student in each group a large trash bag. Ask students to pick up trash such as cans, discarded paper, and other items that are safe to handle. See how many of the collected items can be recycled. If possible, visit a recycling center so that students can turn in their collected recyclables.

► LITERATURE

Suggested Books

Earthways, Earthwise
edited by Judith Nicholls.
Oxford University Press Children's Books, 1998.
ISBN 0192722484
This colorfully-illustrated poetry anthology collects poems with an environmental theme. Short rhymes like "The Dodo" and "Hurt No Living Thing" introduce students to serious environmental concerns in a generally lighthearted, easy-to-digest form. Many of the selections work well as chants or read-aloud activities.

Here Comes the Recycling Truck!
written and photographed by Meyer Seltzer.
Whitman, 1992. ISBN 0807532355
This is the story of a real person, Elisa Seltzer, the driver of a recycling truck. The book follows her on a typical day as she picks up items for recycling. Readers see the places she goes and the people she meets. Most importantly, they find out what is done with all the things she collects. The large color photographs show Elisa at work in her town. ESL students will find the simple repetitive text easy to master. The book may also be used to compare and contrast recycling as depicted in the book to recycling in the students' neighborhoods, or recycling in the Dictionary illustration. This book may also be used effectively with Topic 9, People at Work.

Recycling
written by Joan Kalbacken and Emilie U. Lepthien.
Children's Press, 1991. ISBN 0516011189
Recycling is a basic introduction to the actual processes of recycling and the reasons why we do it. Brief yet thorough explanations of the major aspects of recycling are complemented by numerous color photographs. Many of the topic's content words, as well as items in the Dictionary illustration, can be recognized in the pages of this book.

Earth Keepers
written by Joan Anderson; photographs by George Ancona.
Gulliver Books, 1993. ISBN 0152421998
This black-and-white photographic essay tells the stories of three "earth keepers," men and women who have dedicated themselves to revitalizing or preserving a part of the natural world. The book shows students the practical applications and results of conservation and preservation. Each story can be read aloud separately and any difficult passages can be explained. The writing style is similar to the feature-writing style in newspapers and magazines. A word bank will help students learn unfamiliar words. Direct instruction may be necessary for all but the most advanced students.

WORKBOOK: Topic 48

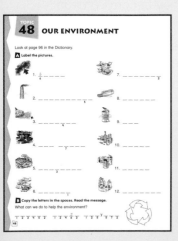

In A, students write the words for each picture. Each word has blanks for each letter. Many of the words have one numbered letter which will be used in the next exercise. In exercise B, students write these numbered letters from exercise A in the appropriate numbered spaces to form a familiar phrase about recycling.

WORKSHEET: Topic 48

In A, students fill in *has been* or *have been* and the correct tense of the verb shown in the circle to form the present perfect continuous in each sentence. In B, they answer the questions about environmental problems and solutions in their own community, using the present perfect continuous.

▶ **CONTENT**

The building blocks of matter

Physical and chemical changes in matter

▶ **LANGUAGE**

Linking verb *become:* *The water freezes and becomes ice.*

Passive voice, simple present: *Together, they are called a compound.*

CONTENT WORDS

1. elements
2. compound
3. atom
4. molecule
5. proton
6. neutron
7. electron
8. solid
9. liquid
10. gas
11. physical change
12. chemical change
13. boil
14. freeze
15. melt
16. evaporate

CONTENT READING

Matter

The Lopez family is making breakfast. Everything in their kitchen is made of matter. Matter is made of different kinds of atoms. Atoms are made of protons, neutrons, and electrons.

Elements are the different types of atoms. Copper (Cu) and silver (Ag) are elements. Elements exist in nature. People can use elements to make things. Mrs. Lopez has pots made of copper and spoons made of silver.

Sometimes two or more atoms combine. Together, they are called a compound. Water is a compound. A water molecule is made of one atom of oxygen and two atoms of hydrogen. The Lopez family uses water every day. They make coffee and tea with water.

Matter can be a solid, a liquid, or a gas. Ice is a solid. Water is a liquid. Steam is a gas. Diego puts water in the ice trays. He puts the ice trays in the freezer. The water freezes and becomes ice. The ice on the counter melts and becomes water again. There is water on the stove. The water boils. Then it evaporates and becomes steam. The molecules stay the same. These are physical changes.

Tina squeezes oranges. They become orange juice. This is another physical change.

Mr. Lopez cooks pancakes. He heats the batter on the grill. The heat from the grill turns the batter into pancakes. The molecules change. This is a chemical change.

▶ WORDS

Components: Dictionary pages 98-99, Transparency 49, Wall Chart 49, Workbook page 49, Word and Picture Cards Topic 49, Cassette

- Present the content words. **See pages xiv-xvi for general techniques about presenting content words.**

  Language Note: The word *molecule* has three syllables with the stress on the first syllable (*MOL-e-cule*). The middle vowel is pronounced like the vowel sound in *sick*. The *eu* in *neutron* is pronounced like the vowel sound in *new*.

- Have students open their Dictionaries to page 98 and look at the words and pictures on the page. Ask students if they know any of these words in their native language(s). For example, point to item 1. The periodic table listings for the elements Copper (Cu) and Silver (Ag) may be familiar to some Spanish-speaking students because they are more closely related to the Spanish words for copper (*cobre*) and silver (*argento*). Ask if students can identify any other familiar words.

- As students are looking at their Dictionary page, explain to them that the first seven items relate to matter and what matter is made of. Items 8 through 10 are the various states that matter can become. Items 11 through 16 are ways in which matter can change. Draw three columns on the board. Label Column 1 *Matter*. Label Column 2 *States of Matter*. Label Column 3, *Actions or Changes in Matter*. Now put the word cards and the picture cards in two stacks at the front of the room. Have students select a card from each stack, pronounce the word, and place the word card and picture card in the appropriate column on the board.

- Make enlarged picture cards of items 8 (*solid*) and 9 (*liquid*). Have students brainstorm various items in the classroom or the school which fall into either of these two categories or states of matter. For example, ink, water, and milk are all liquids. A sandwich, a chocolate bar, and a ruler are all solids. Now divide students into two groups. Group 1 students write the names of as many liquids as they can on the enlarged *liquid* picture card and Group 2 students write the names of as many solids as they can on the enlarged *solid* picture card. Groups read their work aloud to each other and check each other's work for accuracy.

WORKBOOK: Topic 49
See Teacher's Book page 197.

▶ CONTENT

Components: Dictionary pages 98-99, Transparency 49, Wall Chart 49, Content Reading Topic 49, Worksheet Topic 49, Cassette

- Present the content reading. **See pages xvii-xix for general techniques about presenting content readings.**

- Ask the following or similar questions:

  What is matter made of?
  What are elements? Name two elements.
  Is ice a solid or a liquid?
  What happens to the molecules when there is a physical change in matter? What happens when there is a chemical change?
  What happens when Diego puts the ice trays in the freezer?

▶ **Linking verb *become***

  Linking verbs are a type of stative verb. They are intransitive; they don't take direct objects. *Become* is a linking verb.

Explain that we use *become* to show that one thing *has turned into* another thing. For example, *day becomes night. Children become adults.* Sometimes two things combine and *become* a third thing: *Milk and chocolate syrup become chocolate milk.* Ask students to underline and read aloud all sentences using *become* in the content reading. Now divide students into two teams. Each team writes ten questions using *become* that the other team tries to answer. For example, Team 1 asks, *What does water become in the freezer?* and Team 2 answers, *It becomes ice.* Or, Team 2 might ask, *What do water and dirt become together?* and Team 1 answers, *They become mud.* Score one point for every correct question and answer.

▶ **Passive voice, simple present**

  We use the passive voice when we don't know who is performing the action of a sentence or when the doer of the action is not important. We use the simple present tense of *BE* plus the past participle of the main verb [*am/is/are* + past participle] to form these sentences. For example: *Together, they are called a compound.*

Read aloud several examples of the passive voice, simple present in the content reading. Ask students to circle and read aloud all sentences using this pattern. Divide students into two groups. First have all students look at the wall chart and write their own passive voice sentences. For example: *Pancakes are made of batter.* Then, have students go beyond the wall chart and write as many passive voice sentences as they can. The group with the highest number of correct sentences is the winner.

WORKSHEET: Topic 49
See Teacher's Book page 197.

► CHANTS

Components: Dictionary pages 98-99, Content Chant Topic 49, Cassette

 ## CONTENT CHANT

Water Freezes, Ice Melts

Water freezes.
Ice melts.
Water evaporates.
Water boils.

Water freezes.
Water into ice.
Ice melts.
Physical changes.

Water boils.
Water into steam.
Physical changes.
Physical changes.

Flour and water,
pounded into dough,
baked into bread.
Chemical changes.

Flour and sugar,
chocolate chips,
baked into cookies.
Chemical changes.

- Present the content chant. **See pages xx-xxi for general techniques about presenting chants.**

- Before distributing the chant, have students practice small chunks of the language from the chant. Divide into two groups. Group 1 chants *Physical changes*. Group 2 chants *Chemical changes*. Groups chant their words repeatedly, first in turn and then simultaneously. Both groups begin chanting slowly and softly and then increase the speed and volume of their lines as they become more comfortable with the language.

- Distribute Content Chant 49. Divide the class into four groups. Group 1 chants the first three stanzas of the chant. Group 2 chants the last two stanzas. Group 3 chants just the words *Physical changes*. Group 4 chants just the words *Chemical changes*.

- Now have individual students take turns chanting one line of the chant while the entire class chants the lines *Physical changes* and *Chemical changes*.

► EXTENSION

Components: Dictionary pages 98-99, Transparency 49, Wall Chart 49

- Talk to students about temperatures. Explain that water boils at 212° Fahrenheit (100° Celsius) and it freezes at 32°F (0°C). Ask what happens when the temperature outside goes below 32°F. Find out the hottest and coldest temperatures they can remember.

- Ask students why we might boil something. For example, people might boil water to purify it. Or, they might boil it to add it to other foods, such as coffee or soup. People might boil some foods as one method of cooking them. Ask them why somebody might freeze something. For example, people freeze ice cream because otherwise it will melt. They freeze meat to keep it fresh. Have students brainstorm various things we boil or freeze using the graphic organizer below. Then have them write sentences explaining *why* we boil or freeze each of the items. There may be more than one reason for boiling or freezing the same item.

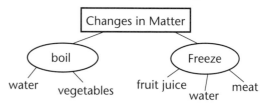

- Have students conduct the following experiment. Each student selects one liquid and one solid to put in a freezer at exactly the same time. They check the freezer to see which of the two items is completely frozen after intervals of 15, 30, 60, 75, and 90 or more minutes. Students enter the data from their observations in a journal and compare their results with the class. Help students make a chart or bar graph showing the various items and the length of time it took to freeze each of them. Ask students to discuss why some items may have frozen faster than others.

- Have students find a copy of the Periodic Table of the Elements in a science book, an almanac, or on the Internet. Explain to students that these elements are arranged according to their atomic numbers (the number of electrons in an element) and chemical properties. For example, the element Magnesium is represented on the chart by its atomic number (12), its symbol (Mg), and its name (magnesium). Tell each student to choose an element and find its name, atomic number, symbol, and melting and boiling points. Have students present their elements to the class and make one combined chart.

- Explain to students that the science of matter is called chemistry. People who work in this field are called chemists. Encourage students to look in the career magazines and on the Internet for various types of chemistry-related jobs and their requirements.

► LITERATURE

Suggested Books

Matter
by Chris Cooper.
DK Publishing, 1992. ISBN 1879431882
Matter is one of the more abstract topics in the Dictionary. This book from the "Eyewitness Science" series is a useful resource for students in need of detailed information about this difficult concept. The text presents concise definitions and illustrates them with photographs, drawings, diagrams, and graphs. An historical overview is also included. While all students will recognize many of the content words in the text, this book is recommended primarily for advanced students.

The Magic School Bus Gets Baked in a Cake
written by Joanna Cole; illustrated by Bruce Degen.
Scholastic, 1988. ISBN 0590403605
In typical fashion, this Magical School Bus story is both lively and informative. While baking a cake for Ms. Frizzle's birthday, the class ends up inside the cake and learns some lessons in basic chemistry. Although second-language students will need help in understanding the idioms and puns, the illustrations provide numerous clues. Teachers can guide students through any difficult patches of text.

A Drop of Water: A Book of Science and Wonder
written and photographed by Walter Wick.
Scholastic Press, 1997. ISBN 0590221973
This Caldecott award-winner explains water-related phenomena such as evaporation, condensation, and the formation of clouds. The book employs simple, readable text and close-up, stop-action photographs to explain these water processes. Its artistic approach to scientific concepts will make a strong impression on students. The spectacular photographs transform the everyday into the amazing. The end of the book includes a list of simple experiments that relate directly to those shown in the photographs.

WORKBOOK: Topic 49

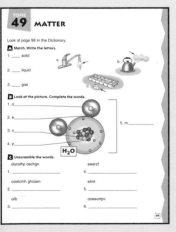

In A, students match the pictures to the words for the three states of matter. In B, they label the parts of a molecule. The first letter of each word is given as a clue. In C, students unscramble six of the content words.

WORKSHEET: Topic 49

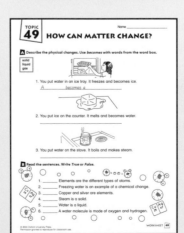

In A, students use the word *becomes* in sentences to describe physical changes. In B, they write *True* or *False* next to each statement, based on the information in the content reading.

50 ENERGY AND MOTION

▶ **CONTENT**

Energy and motion in daily life

Simple machines and how things move

▶ **LANGUAGE**

Verb + noun phrase + infinitive for expressing purpose: *It uses magnetic force to move things.*

Adverbial clauses of time with *when*: *When you put a wedge under a wheel, it doesn't roll.*

CONTENT WORDS

1. simple machines
2. axle
3. pulley
4. wheel
5. wedge
6. inclined plane
7. lever
8. screw
9. magnet
10. gears
11. push
12. pull
13. speed
14. forces
15. friction
16. heat
17. light
18. sound

 CONTENT READING

Energy and Motion

Energy is all around us. Three examples of energy are heat, light, and sound.

When Mr. Fields cooks hamburgers, he uses energy from heat. When Mrs. Fields takes a flash photo, she uses energy from light. When Jenny uses a megaphone, she increases the energy of sound from her voice.

Motion is all around us, too. Simple machines help us to move things or to stop things.

A pulley is a simple machine. A clothesline uses a pulley. When Billy pulls the clothesline, the curtain opens and closes.

Wheels and wedges are simple machines, too. Wheels roll. When you put a wedge under a wheel, it doesn't roll. Nancy's cart won't roll away because the wedges stop the wheels.

Axles are also simple machines. An axle connects two wheels and makes them move together. The red wagon has four wheels and two axles. When Greg and Mary move the dog in the wagon, Greg pulls and Mary pushes. Pulling and pushing are two examples of force.

A lever is another simple machine. It lifts things. A seesaw is an example of a lever. Jimmy lifts his two friends on the seesaw.

An inclined plane is a simple machine, too. A ramp is an inclined plane. Jane uses the ramp to push Andrew up the stairs.

A magnet is another simple machine. It uses magnetic force to move things. Timmy uses a magnet to pick up a screw from the ground.

When Annie and Peter ride their bicycles, they use gears to increase and decrease their speed. Gears are simple machines. When Annie stops her bicycle, the wheels rub against the ground. This friction helps stop the bicycle.

▶ WORDS

Components: Dictionary pages 100-101, Transparency 50, Wall Chart 50, Workbook page 50, Word and Picture Cards Topic 50, Cassette

- Present the content words. **See pages xiv-xvi for general techniques about presenting content words.**

  > **Language Note:** Note the silent *e* at the end of the words *axle*, *inclined plane*, and *force*.

- If possible, bring to class examples of some simple machines, such as a screw, a magnet, or wheels to demonstrate how they work. Toy cars and trucks have several kinds of simple machines which students will recognize.

- Talk about the words *friction, speed,* and *heat.* Explain that *friction* occurs when two objects move across each other. Have students rub their two hands together and feel the friction between their hands. Now have them increase the *speed* until they feel the *heat.* (Suggest that they touch their hands to their faces to feel the heat.) Explain that the friction causes the heat. More speed causes more friction which causes more heat.

- Have students open their Dictionaries to page 100. Ask students if they know any of these words in their native language(s). Explain that items 1 through 10 are simple machines. (They have no moving parts.) Items 11 through 15 relate to motion, and items 16 through 18 are examples of energy. Draw a word web on chart paper like the example below. Then put the word cards and the picture cards in two stacks at the front of the room. Have students select a card from each stack, pronounce the word, and place their word cards and picture cards in the appropriate places on the word web.

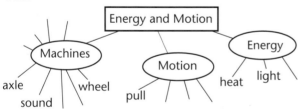

- Divide students into two groups and display the wall chart. Group 1 identifies and counts all the wheels in the picture. Group 2 identifies and counts all the examples of motion and energy in the picture. Groups exchange lists and review the other's list for accuracy.

WORKBOOK: Topic 50
See Teacher's Book page 201.

▶ CONTENT

Components: Dictionary pages 100-101, Transparency 50, Wall Chart 50, Content Reading Topic 50, Worksheet Topic 50, Cassette

- Present the content reading. **See pages xvii-xix for general techniques about presenting content readings.**

- Ask the following or similar questions:

  > *What are three examples of energy?*
  > *What do simple machines help us do?*
  > *Name at least five simple machines.*
  > *What is an example of a lever?*
  > *What happens if you put a wedge under a wheel?*
  > *What are two examples of force?*

▶ **Verb + noun phrase + infinitive for expressing purpose**

> We can use the pattern [verb + noun phrase + infinitive] to express purpose. The infinitive is [to + simple form of a verb]. The infinitive expresses the purpose. It answers the question *Why?* about the verb. For example: *Jane uses the ramp to push Andrew up the stairs.* (Why does Jane use the ramp? To push Andrew up the stairs.) This pattern occurs only with the verb *use* in the content reading, but it can be used with other verbs.

Point out an example of the verb *use* + noun phrase + infinitive in the content reading. (*It uses magnetic force to move things.*) Students underline and read aloud other examples of this pattern with *use.* Divide the class into two groups. Each group writes ten sentences describing why we use various simple machines. For example: *We use a wedge to stop a wheel.* Each group reads its sentences aloud as the other group checks for accuracy.

▶ **Adverbial clauses of time with *when***

> Adverbial clauses of time with *when* are used in complex sentences. They tell when the action of the main clause happens. These clauses can show two actions happening during the same time period. If the adverbial clause comes first in the sentence, we use a comma after it.

Point out an example of this pattern in the content reading (*When Mr. Fields cooks hamburgers, he uses energy from heat*). Students can create their own sentences using this pattern. Be sure students use only simple present verbs. For example: *When I'm in the playground, I'm happy.* Students write their sentences on two index cards, putting time clauses with *when* on one index card and the main clause on another index card. Collect both index cards and put them in two separate piles. Now students randomly choose one card from each pile and read the two parts aloud. This should produce some very funny sentences.

WORKSHEET: Topic 50
See Teacher's Book page 201.

▶ CHANTS

Components: Dictionary pages 100-101, Content Chant Topic 50, Cassette

 CONTENT CHANT

Heat, Light, Sound

Heat, light, sound *
Heat, light, sound *
Feel the heat.
Feel the sun.
See the light.
Look at the sunrise.
Hear the sound.
Listen to the thunder.
Listen to the thunder roll. *

Push it. *
Pull it. *
Put it on wheels.
Put it on wheels.

Push it. *
Pull it. *
Put it on wheels.
Put it on wheels.

Axle *
Pulley *
Put it on wheels.
Put it on wheels.

Push it. Pull it.
Put it on wheels.
Look at it go!
WOW!

- Present the content chant. **See pages xx-xxi for general techniques about presenting chants.**

- Before distributing the chant, have students practice small chunks of the language from the chant. Divide students into three groups. Group 1 chants *Push it (*).* Group 2 chants *Pull it (*).* Group 3 chants *Put it on wheels* twice.

- Now distribute Content Chant 50. Start chanting at a volume that is much too low for students to hear. Ask students why they can't hear you. Direct them to the conclusion that your chanting lacks enough sound. Remind them that sound is a form of energy. Now chant the chant again, but much too slowly. Direct students to the conclusion that your chanting lacks speed. Remind them that speed is also a form of energy.

- Divide the class into two groups. Group 1 chants the first and fourth stanzas. Group 2 chants the second, third, and fifth stanzas. Encourage students to pantomime the words of the chant. Select one or two students to make the sound of thunder when it is mentioned in the first stanza.

▶ EXTENSION

Components: Dictionary pages 100-101, Transparency 50, Wall Chart 50

- Divide the class into three groups. Have students cut pictures from magazines that fit into one of the following three categories: things that produce heat; things that produce sound; things that produce light. Groups make posters displaying their work and present them to the class. Encourage students to discuss their work.

- Have students write an illustrated story about machines they or their family use at home or had used in their home countries (for example, a wheelbarrow, a windmill, a fan, a clothesline, etc.). Have students read their stories aloud and share their drawings. Help the students to identify the simple machines from content words 1-10 that can be found in these objects.

- Practice some *pushes* and *pulls.* Bring in a long piece of rope for a "Tug of War." Divide students into two teams that are approximately equal in total weight. Each team holds one end of the rope. When you say *Pull!*, each team pulls as hard as it can until one team pulls the other team across the room. Then, put a large heavy object such as a desk in the middle of the room. Divide students into two teams approximately equal in size and weight. Each team stands on opposite sides of the desk. When you say *Push!,* each team pushes as hard as it can and tries to move the desk across the room to the other team's side.

- Look around the classroom, school, or playground for examples of simple machines. Have students make lists of the items they find and which simple machines they include. Students might list items such as a wheelchair ramp, a seesaw, or a rolling cart.

- Take the class to the playground. Have one student sit on one end of the seesaw and a smaller, lighter student on the other end. (Avoid choosing students who might be sensitive about their size or weight.) Tell students to hold on with their hands, but not to let their feet touch the ground. Wait for the seesaw to come to a rest. The heavier student will eventually come to rest on the ground, and the lighter student will be in the air on the other end. Help students understand why this happens. Now have the heavier student move closer to the middle of the seesaw. The closer the heavier student moves to the center of the seesaw, the less force he or she will be exerting on his or her end, and the more likely it is that the seesaw will balance. Ask students why they think this happens.

▶ LITERATURE

Suggested Books

Tools

written by Ann Morris; photographs by Ken Heyman.
Lothrop Lee & Shepard, 1992. ISBN 0688101704
Clear, descriptive photographs show people from all around the world using different tools ("simple machines") at their workplaces. The tools are not named on the pages on which they are initially presented so that students can learn to identify them by sight. The picture index in the back of the book names each tool and identifies where it was photographed. Students can refer to it for reinforcement. Many of the objects in the Dictionary illustration are depicted here. This book also works well with Topic 5, The City, and Topic 9, People at Work.

On the Go

written by Ann Morris; photographs by Ken Heyman.
Mulberry Books, 1994. ISBN 0688136370
This simple book describes the ways people from all over the world travel across land, over water, and through the air. A picture index at the back of the book identifies the location of each photograph and a world map places the photos in a geographical context. The book's rhyming structure makes it useful for reading aloud, with independent or paired reading afterwards.

Levers

by Michael S. Dahl.
Children's Press, 1998. ISBN 0516202715

Pulleys

by Michael S. Dahl.
Capstone Press, 1998. ISBN 0516202723

Wheels and Axles

by Michael S. Dahl.
Capstone Press, 1998. ISBN 0516202731

Inclined Planes

by Michael S. Dahl.
Capstone Press, 1998. ISBN 051620274X
All four of these titles are early readers about simple machines. The information is presented in short, simple sentences. Colorful photographs featuring simple machines in close-up amplify the text. Each book concludes with directions for a simple and effective experiment using commonly available materials. Many students will be able to perform the experiments with minimal direct instruction. A simple glossary provides a review of the important terms introduced in each book.

WORKBOOK: Topic 50

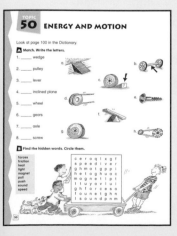

In A, students match the pictures to the words for simple machines. In B, they find and circle the listed words in the word search. The words appear horizontally and vertically.

WORKSHEET: Topic 50

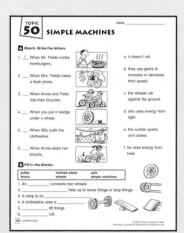

Both activities on this worksheet require information from the content reading. In A, students match to complete the sentences that contain adverbial clauses with *when*. In B, students choose words from the word box to fill in the blanks.

CONTENT

The planets of the solar system

The stars and other astronomical phenomena

LANGUAGE

Simple present: *The Earth is just one planet. All the planets go around the Sun.*

Ordinal numbers: *The Earth is the third planet from the Sun.*

Superlative adjectives: *Pluto is the farthest planet from the Sun.*

CONTENT WORDS

1. solar system
2. planets
3. Sun
4. Moon
5. Mercury
6. Venus
7. Earth
8. Mars
9. Jupiter
10. Saturn
11. Uranus
12. Neptune
13. Pluto
14. star
15. constellation
16. meteor
17. comet
18. galaxy

CONTENT READING

The Universe

Our world is a very small place. The Earth is just one planet. There are nine planets in our solar system. The Sun is the center of our solar system. All the planets go around the Sun. The Earth goes around the Sun once every year.

Mercury is the closest planet to the Sun. Venus is next. The Earth is the third planet from the Sun. Mars is the fourth planet. Jupiter is fifth. It's the largest planet. Saturn is sixth. It has big rings around it. Uranus is seventh. Neptune is eighth. Pluto is ninth. Pluto is the farthest planet from the Sun.

The Moon isn't a planet. It doesn't go around the Sun. It goes around the Earth. The Moon is very close to the Earth. You can see it at night. The Moon is the biggest and brightest light in the night sky.

Comets and meteors are in our solar system, too. Comets are bodies of dust, rock, and gas. Meteors are small rocks in space. Meteors enter the Earth's atmosphere and make bright streaks of light in the sky.

Stars aren't planets. Stars are very large bodies of gas. The Sun is a star. A constellation is a group of stars with a name. Ursa Major is a constellation. It looks like a big spoon, or big dipper. People call it the "Big Dipper." You can see Ursa Major at night.

Galaxies have thousands and thousands of stars. Our solar system is part of a galaxy. Our galaxy is the Milky Way. There are many other galaxies in the universe. They are very far from our solar system.

►WORDS

Components: Dictionary pages 102-103, Transparency 51, Wall Chart 51, Workbook page 51, Word and Picture Cards Topic 51, Cassette

- Present the content words. **See pages xiv-xvi for general techniques about presenting content words.**

   Language Note: The word *meteor* is pronounced as three separate syllables, with the stress on the first syllable. It sounds like *ME-dee-or. Uranus* is pronounced either as UR-a-nus (which sounds like *YOR-a-nus*) or u-RAY-nus (which sounds like *You-RAY-nus*).

- Have students open their Dictionaries to page 102 and look at the words and pictures on the page. Ask students if they recognize any of the items in the picture. Encourage students to share what they know about the universe. Perhaps they know things about the Moon, the planets, the stars, or other galaxies from books, TV, or science fiction movies. Ask students the names of the planets or other content words in their native language(s).

- Enlarge the picture cards and place them along the chalk tray. Invite students to write the content words in their native language(s) on each of the picture cards. Help students create a chart of the different names for the planets, the Moon, and the Sun in the various native languages of the class.

- Display a globe. Show students that Earth is round, just like the other planets. Now show students the wall chart. Point to the third planet on the transparency and show students that Earth is very small compared to some of the other planets. Divide the class into two groups. Group 1 identifies and writes the names of all the planets on the transparency (using a washable marker) next to the appropriate pictures. Group 2 identifies and writes the names of all the other astrological phenomena (*comet, meteor, star*, etc.) next to their pictures.

- Draw a word web on the board like the example below. Distribute a set of word cards and set of picture cards. Have students, in turn, pronounce their words and place their word cards and their picture cards in the appropriate place on the word web.

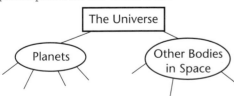

- Divide the class into two teams. Ask each team to make a list of the things that the Sun does. The team with the longest accurate list is the winner.

WORKBOOK: Topic 51
See Teacher's Book page 205.

►CONTENT

Components: Dictionary pages 102-103, Transparency 51, Wall Chart 51, Content Reading Topic 51, Worksheet Topic 51, Cassette

- Present the content reading. **See pages xvii-xix for general techniques about presenting content readings.**

- Ask the following or similar questions:

   How many planets are in the Earth's solar system?
   Name the closest planet to the Sun and farthest planet from the Sun.
   How often does the Earth go around the Sun?
   What does the Moon go around?
   Which planet is the largest?
   What is the name of our galaxy?

- ► **Ordinal numbers**. Write the ordinal numbers *first* through *ninth* in a list on the board. Have students refer to their Dictionaries to locate the *first* planet from the Sun. Ask a volunteer to write the name of this planet next to the word *first* on the board. Continue with the other eight planets until there is a complete list of planets on the board arranged by ordinal numbers.

- ► **Superlative adjectives.** Point out examples of superlative adjectives in the content reading (*the closest, the farthest, the brightest*, etc.). Have students underline and read aloud all sentences with superlative adjectives. Then have students look at the wall chart and create their own sentences with superlative adjectives. You may want to introduce comparative forms (*bigger than, smaller than*) here, too.

- Help students create their own solar system. Assign a content word to each student. Nine students are the planets, one is *the Sun*, and another is the *Moon*. The remaining students are *stars, comets, meteors*, and a *constellation* (the Big Dipper). First, have the nine "planets" line up in order, next to the *Sun*. Ask them each to identify themselves. For example: *I am Mercury. I am the first planet*. Then have the *Moon* walk around the *Earth* and chant repeatedly, *I am the Moon*. Finally, the nine planets each chant their names and ordinal number in terms of closeness to the *Sun* as they slowly walk in concentric circles around the *Sun*. Students who are the furthest away from the *Sun* will take longer to revolve than students who are closer. The students who are *comets, meteors, stars* and the Big Dipper move around the solar system indiscriminately, and chant their names. For example: *I am a comet* or *We are the Big Dipper.*

WORKSHEET: Topic 51
See Teacher's Book page 205.

► CHANTS

Components: Dictionary pages 102-103, Content Chant Topic 51, Cassette

 ## CONTENT CHANT

Look at the Moon

Look at the Moon.
Look at the stars.
Is that Jupiter?
Or is that Mars?

Is that a planet?
Or a very bright star?
You can't see Neptune.
It's too far.

Venus rising
is a glorious sight.
And lots of constellations
will be out tonight.

- Present the content chant. **See pages xx-xxi for general techniques about presenting chants.**

- Before distributing the chant, have students practice small chunks of the language from the chant. Explain to students that the expression "lots of" means *many*. Now, break up the sentence, *And lots of constellations will be out tonight* into smaller chunks from the end of the sentence so students will be able to maintain the rhythm and intonation more easily. Students chant each chunk repeatedly and then add the previous piece. For example: *out tonight / will be / will be out tonight / constellations / constellations will be out tonight / And lots of / And lots of constellations will be out tonight.*

- Distribute Content Chant 51. Select individual students to personify the *Moon,* the *stars, Jupiter, Mars, Neptune, Venus*, and three constellations. Have the rest of the class chant while these students mime or do some action as their words are spoken in the chant.

► EXTENSION

Components: Dictionary pages 102-103, Transparency 51, Wall Chart 51

- Divide the class into nine groups or pairs, one for each planet. Have each group "adopt" a planet and research everything they can about it. Encourage students to find out what the planet is made of, how far it is from the Sun, the temperature on the surface, and the number of days it takes to go around the Sun (the orbital period). Each group can write a report and present it to the class with a poster illustrating key information. When all groups have presented, hang all of the posters on a bulletin board to illustrate the entire solar system.

- Have students research the first landing of a man on the moon and dramatize what happened.

- Have students research the U.S. astronaut program. Students can get extensive information from the Kennedy Space Center in Cape Kennedy, Florida about various launches and astronaut training as well as special programs for students. Encourage discussion about possible career opportunities in space.

- Introduce the zodiac. Explain that each sign of the zodiac refers to a constellation. For example, people born between January 10 and February 18 are the zodiac sign Aquarius. (A full copy of the zodiac can be found in an almanac or encyclopedia, or on the Internet.) Astrologists predict people's behavior and events by their zodiac sign. Ask students if they have seen horoscopes in their native language(s) or in American newspapers and magazines. Bring in magazine or newspaper horoscopes. Ask students to form groups according to their zodiac signs and distribute the horoscopes for each sign. Help students with any difficult language. Then ask students whether they believe what their horoscopes say, and why or why not.

- On a day when the forecast is clear, tell students to look at the stars when they go home at night. Show them the Big Dipper in the picture. Tell them to look for the Big Dipper when they look at the stars. The next day have students tell what they saw.

- Explain to students that in some cultures, people look at the stars or the Moon and make a wish. Teach students this poem, often said when wishing upon the stars:

  Starlight, star bright,
  First star I see tonight,
  I wish I may, I wish I might,
  Have this wish I make tonight

Ask students to share songs or poems in their language which talk about the stars or the Moon.

- Ask students to write and illustrate science fiction stories about extraterrestrial creatures coming to Earth. Have students read their stories aloud to their classmates and show their pictures.

► LITERATURE

Suggested Books

The Young Oxford Book of Astronomy
by Simon Mitton and Jacqueline Mitton.
Oxford University Press Children's Books, 1998.
ISBN 0195214455
The Young Oxford Book of Astronomy is a well-organized, scientifically up-to-date introduction to the study of the planets and stars. The authors, who are both professional astronomers, have a clear, direct writing style that is complemented by the remarkable photographs and diagrams of space. This book is a useful reference for this topic and others in the unit.

My Place in Space
written by Robin and Sally Hirst;
illustrated by Roland Harvey with Joe Levine.
Orchard Books, 1992. ISBN 0152006133
A bus driver doesn't know what he is in for when he asks two very well-informed children where they live. In great detail, the children stake out their place in the universe, from their street address in a small Australian town to their galaxy and beyond. The text, although constructed as a narrative, is very informative, and the illustrations blend a raw, cartoony style full of amusing details with expansive paintings of space. Teachers can have students write and draw about their own place in space using this book as a model.

New Moon
written by Pegi Deitz Shea; illustrated by Cathryn Falwell.
Boyds Mills Press, 1996. ISBN 15397410X
Vincena's big brother shows her the full moon one night and teaches her the word "moon." This gentle book about the moon and its phases features beautiful cut-paper illustrations that capture the joy of learning and sharing. The simple text combines dialogues and descriptive adjectives that can be used to enhance language learning. The book provides good material for question-and-answer exchanges with students about what happens in the story and why.

Our Solar System
by Seymour Simon.
William Morrow & Co., 1992. ISBN 0688099920
Stunning photographs accompany the text of this well-designed book. The language is clear, concise, and easy-to-read. Interesting diagrams show the relative size of the planets and offer information about each one. The book also covers other aspects of the solar system such as asteroids and meteors.

WORKBOOK: Topic 51

On this page, students write the words on the blank lines for the planets and objects numbered in the picture.

WORKSHEET: Topic 51

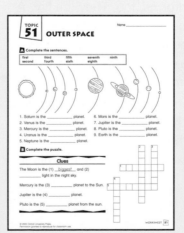

In A, students choose ordinal numbers from the word box to complete the sentences about the order of the planets. Activity B is a crossword puzzle. Students fill in the blanks in the clues and in the puzzle, based on their knowledge of the content reading.

52 THE EARTH AND ITS LANDFORMS

► **CONTENT**
....
Geographic features of the Earth

► **LANGUAGE**
....
Have as a main verb: *The Earth has many different landforms.*

Prepositional phrases: *An ocean is a very large body of salt water.*

CONTENT WORDS

1. mountain	10. wetland
2. volcano	11. peninsula
3. lava	12. isthmus
4. plateau	13. island
5. glacier	14. layers
6. valley	15. crust
7. river	16. mantle
8. gulf	17. outer core
9. ocean	18. inner core

 ## CONTENT READING

The Earth and Its Landforms

The Earth has many different landforms. The highest landforms are mountains. Many mountains have ice and snow on them. Some mountains are volcanoes. They have hot, fiery lava inside. Sometimes, a volcano erupts and lava comes out of the top.

Plateaus are high landforms, too. They are flat. A glacier is a landform of ice and snow. A glacier moves slowly down a mountain into a valley. Valleys are low landforms between mountains or hills. Some valleys have rivers in them.

A river often flows from the land to the ocean. An ocean is a very large body of salt water. Oceans cover three-quarters of the Earth's surface. Sometimes, the ocean extends into the land. This is a gulf.

A wetland is a landform with both land and water. Sometimes, the wetland is dry. Then you can walk on it. Sometimes, the wetland is wet. Then it is under water.

A peninsula is a landform with water on three sides. An isthmus is a thin piece of land with water on two sides. An isthmus connects two larger landforms. An island is a landform with water on all sides.

All these landforms are on the Earth's surface, or crust. The Earth has other layers below its crust. The first layer below the crust is the mantle. The next layer is the outer core. The inner core is deep within the Earth.

▶ WORDS

Components: Dictionary pages 104-105, Transparency 52, Wall Chart 52, Workbook page 52, Word and Picture Cards Topic 52, Cassette

- Present the content words. **See pages xiv-xvi for general techniques about presenting content words.**

  > **Language Note:** The *cier* in *glacier* is pronounced like *sher*. The *cean* in *ocean* is pronounced like *shun*. The *teau* in *plateau* is pronounced like the word *toe*. Its plural is *plateaus* or *plateaux*. The *th* in *isthmus* is silent. It is pronounced like *ISS-muss*. The *s* in *island* is silent. *Island* is pronounced like *EYE-land*.

- Have students open their Dictionaries to page 104. Ask if they recognize any of the landforms on the page. Encourage students to share what they know, especially if they live or have lived on a *mountain*, on a *plateau*, on an *island*, in a *valley*, or near a *river*. Ask students the names of any of these landforms in their native language(s).

- Enlarge the picture cards and place them along the chalk tray. Invite students to write the words in their native languages(s) on each picture card. Compare the similarity of many of the words (cognates or near cognates) in different languages, especially those for *mountain, volcano, plateau, glacier, valley, river, gulf, ocean, peninsula,* and *island*.

- To demonstrate the concept of the earth's layers, bring an onion to class. Explain that the earth has many layers, like an onion. Peel off the shiny outer skin of the onion and tell students this is like the Earth's *crust*. Now peel off another layer and explain that this is like the *mantle*. Peel off more layers and explain that these are like the Earth's *outer core*. Finally, peel down the onion until you can't peel off any more layers. Explain that this remaining portion is like the Earth's *inner core*.

- Divide the class into three groups and have students look at the wall chart. Display the transparency. Group 1 identifies and write the names on the transparency (using a washable marker) of all landforms that have water in, on, or around them. Group 2 writes the names of all the landforms that don't have water in, or, or around them. Group 3 writes the names for the various layers of the Earth.

- Distribute one set of word cards and one set of picture cards. Students walk around the room and ask each other questions until they find matching pairs of word and picture cards. Draw three columns on chart paper, one labeled *Landforms with Water*, another labeled *Landforms without Water*, and the third labeled *Layers of the Earth*. Have students place their matching word and picture cards in the appropriate column.

WORKBOOK: Topic 52
See Teacher's Book page 209.

▶ CONTENT

Components: Dictionary pages 104-105, Transparency 52, Wall Chart 52, Content Reading Topic 52, Worksheet Topic 52, Cassette

- Present the content chant. **See pages xvii-xix for general techniques about presenting content readings.**

- Ask the following or similar questions:

  What are the highest landforms on the Earth?
  Which landform has water on three sides?
  What is a glacier?
  Where is the Earth's mantle?
  What does an isthmus do?
  Where do some rivers flow?

- ***Have* as a main verb.** Have students underline and read aloud all instances of *have/has* in the content reading. Divide the class into two groups. Have students look at the wall chart. Each group makes up as many sentences as possible describing the landforms in the wall chart using *have/has* or *don't have/doesn't have*. For example: *The island has water on all of its sides. The plateau doesn't have water.* Each group reads their sentences aloud as the other groups checks for accuracy.

- Have students write riddles using *have* on index cards for each of the landforms. For example: *I have both water and land. What am I?* (a wetland) Students exchange index cards and take turns reading a riddle aloud and trying to answer it.

▶ **Prepositional phrases**

  > A prepositional phrase consists of a preposition followed by its object. Prepositional phrases can show location (*between mountains or hills, on them*) direction (*from the land to the ocean*), a fraction or part of a whole (*of the Earth's surface, of land*) or what something is made of (*of ice and snow, of salt water*).

Point out some of the prepositional phrases in the content reading. For example: *Many mountains have ice and snow on them*. Students circle all the prepositional phrases and then read them aloud.

- **Game: It's in This Room.** Select one student to be "it." That person leaves the room. Another student hides something *inside, near, on, under, over,* or *between* something. The student who is "it" re-enters the room and asks *Yes/No* questions about the location of the hidden object using prepositional phrases. For example: *Is it in the desk? Is it under the chair?* The student can ask 20 questions to guess where the object is. Then another student gets a chance to be "it" and the class hides another object.

WORKSHEET: Topic 52
See Teacher's Book page 209.

▶ CHANTS

Components: Dictionary pages 104-105, Content Chant Topic 52, Cassette

 CONTENT CHANT

Island, Ocean, River, Valley

Island, ocean, river, valley
Mountain, * volcano *

Island, ocean, river, valley
Mountain, * volcano *

Sail to the island.
Dive in the ocean.
Fish in the river.
Walk in the valley.

Sail to the island.
Climb the mountain.
See the volcano.
Walk on the lava bed.

Sail to the island.
Dive in the ocean.
Fish in the river.
Walk in the valley.

Climb the mountain.
See the volcano.
Walk on the lava bed.
WOW!

- Present the content chant. **See pages xx-xxi for general techniques about presenting chants.**

- Before distributing the chant, have students practice small chunks of the language from the chant. Divide the class into two groups. Group 1 chants *Island, ocean, river, valley.* Group 2 chants *Mountain,* * *volcano** with the appropriate claps.

- Now distribute Content Chant 51. Ask students if they know the meanings of the verbs *sail, dive, fish, walk, climb,* and *see.* If not, pantomime these actions or select individual students to pantomime these actions. Then have the entire class pantomime these actions as you call out the word.

- Explain that a lava bed is an area where hot lava once came down from the mountain but is now settled and cool. You can walk on a lava bed and you won't get burned. Bring in pictures from magazines showing cooled lava beds. The lava is usually dark red or black in a lava bed.

- Divide the class into four groups. The entire class chants the first two stanzas and the last word of the chant, *WOW!* Groups 1-4 each chant one stanza and pantomime their actions as they chant.

▶ EXTENSION

Components: Dictionary pages 104-105, Transparency 52, Wall Chart 52

- Ask students to name a mountain or island in your area. If you have a map of the area, ask them to locate the island or mountain on the map.

- Bring in a fairly detailed map of some local area. It may be a map of your state, a map of your city, a map of the region, or something similar. Make three or four copies, or bring in three or four different maps. Divide students into as many groups as you have maps or copies of maps. Each group studies its map and make lists of all the *mountains, volcanoes, plateaus, rivers, gulfs, oceans, wetlands, peninsulas, isthmuses,* and *islands* found on the map. Students make separate lists for each geographical feature, and show where the feature can be found on the map by listing the map coordinates (for example, *Catalina Island,* Section A-3, etc.). After each group has compiled its list, they exchange maps and lists of features. The new group looks at the lists of geographical features and attempts to find them by using the map coordinates.

- Divide students into groups of two or three. Assign a famous river to each group, or a local river in your area. Have the group research interesting facts about the river. Encourage students to use almanacs, encyclopedias, textbooks, atlases, or the Internet. Students write reports about the information they have found. They can also make a poster showing a photograph or drawing and facts about their river, such as its location, where it begins, where it ends, its length, what people use the river for, etc. Groups present their work to the other students, who then ask questions about each presentation.

- Divide students into small groups. Display a world map. Assign a different continent or section of the map to each group. Each group makes a list of all the islands it can find in that section of the map. Then groups exchange their lists and check each other's work. Each group tries to find all the islands listed by the first group, and then see if they can add more islands to the list.

- Bring in several different colors of play dough. Have students build a model of the different kinds of landforms and make a legend to explain what the colors mean.

► LITERATURE

Suggested Books

Let's Go Rock Collecting

written by Roma Gans; illustrated by Holly Keller.
HarperCollins Juvenile Books, 1997. ISBN 0064451704
English-language learners are sure to feel confident
reading this very basic introduction to geology. The text
presents rock collecting as an interesting exploration of
rocks of different colors, structures, and origins. The
diagrams and photographs show what kinds of rocks
children may find on vacation, at home, or in their own
schoolyard. This book is an excellent activity-driven
extension for this topic. It is also useful for teaching Topic
14, The West.

What Makes Day and Night

written by Franklyn M. Branley;
illustrated by Arthur Dorros.
HarperCollins Publishers, 1986. ISBN 0064450503
Clear diagrams and pictures illustrate a simple text that
explains how Earth's rotation in relation to the sun
changes day to night. The text also contains a visit to the
moon and a brief explanation of its phases. As with other
books in the "Let's Read and Find Out" science series,
this book includes an activity that students can replicate
using everyday classroom items. This book can also be
used effectively with Topic 50, Energy and Motion, and
Topic 51, The Universe.

Blast Off to Earth!: A Look at Geography

written and illustrated by Loreen Leedy.
Holiday House, 1998. ISBN 0823414094
In a cute and clever approach to geography, readers travel
along with a group of robotic aliens on a visit to Earth.
First, the aliens see the blue planet floating in space, then
they drop down to visit the oceans and continents. The
illustrations are charming and full of details which are
sure to generate discussion. The language is
conversational, with short, declarative, and interrogative
sentences set in speech bubbles. The book can be used to
prompt students to invent their own dialogues about
visiting a new place.

The Water's Journey

written and illustrated by Eleanore Schmid.
North-South Books, 1990. ISBN 1558580131
This illustrated account of the water cycle explains
water's journey from mountain snow all the way to the
ocean. Each full-page illustration can be a point of entry to
discuss this topic and Topic 53, Climates and Land
Biomes. The illustrations can be used to generate
questions such as "What is happening in the picture?"
and "Where is this happening?"

WORKBOOK: Topic 52

In A, students write the
words from the word box
to identify the numbered
portions of the picture. In
B, they label the layers of
the Earth.

WORKSHEET: Topic 52

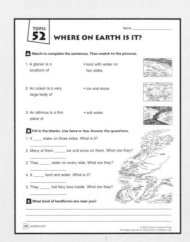

Activities A and B are
based on the content
reading. In A, students
match parts of sentences
using prepositional
phrases. Then they match
these sentences to the
appropriate pictures. In B,
students fill in *have* or *has*
in each question and then
answer the questions. In
C, students write about
the landforms where they
live.

► **CONTENT**

Climates and environments

► **LANGUAGE**

Adverbs of frequency
(***always, usually, never***): *The weather is always hot and dry. It never snows.*

CONTENT WORDS

1. temperate forest
2. deciduous tree
3. taiga
4. evergreen tree
5. tundra
6. moss
7. lichen
8. tropical rain forest
9. vines
10. grassland
11. grass
12. desert
13. sand
14. polar zones
15. temperate zones
16. tropical zone

Temperate forest	Tundra	Grassland
Taiga	Tropical rain forest	Desert

CONTENT READING

Climates and Land Biomes

The Earth has different types of land biomes. Each land biome has a different climate and different kinds of plants and animals. The climate is the kind of weather an area has over a long time.

The temperate forest is one type of land biome. Winters are usually cold and summers are usually warm there. The green leaves of deciduous trees turn orange, yellow, and red in the fall. Then they fall off the trees. Most of the eastern United States and Europe is temperate forest.

The taiga is another biome. Winters are very cold and summers are warm. There are many evergreen trees. Evergreen trees are always green. Many areas in northern and western Canada are taiga.

The tundra is another biome. The weather is always very cold and very dry. There are no trees on the tundra. The ground is covered with ice and snow in the winter. Moss and lichen grow in the summer. Most of the Canadian Arctic is tundra.

The tropical rain forest is another biome. The weather is always warm and it rains almost every day. The trees are always green. There are many plants and vines in the rain forest. Many parts of Brazil are tropical rain forest.

Another type of biome is grassland. There are many kinds of grass, but very few trees. The weather is usually dry and windy. Many parts of Africa are grassland.

The desert is another type of biome. The weather is always hot and dry. It never snows. There is a lot of sand in the desert. There are large areas of desert in Africa, the Middle East, and Australia.

The climates of the Earth are divided into zones. The polar zones are at the top and bottom of the globe. The tropical zone is near the Equator. The temperate zones are between the polar zones and the tropical zone.

► WORDS

Components: Dictionary pages 106-107, Transparency 53, Wall Chart 53, Workbook page 53, Word and Picture Cards Topic 53, Cassette

- Present the content words. **See pages xiv-xvi for general techniques about presenting content words.**

  Language Note: *Lichens* is pronounced like the word *likens*. *Taiga* has two syllables, TAI-ga. The *ai* is pronounced like *eye*. The final *e* is silent in the words *temperate*, *vines*, and *zones*. Note the difference between the biome *desert* (DES-ert) and *dessert* (des-SERT), the sweet dish at the end of a meal. Give students this helpful mnemonic device to help them distinguish between the two words: *Desert* only has one *s* because you only want to go through the desert once, but *dessert* has two *s's* because everybody wants two desserts.

  Content Note: The word *evergreen* refers to trees whose leaves don't change color. They are forever green. The word *deciduous* refers to trees that lose their leaves when the season changes.

- Have students open their Dictionaries to page 106. Ask if they recognize any of the words or pictures. Perhaps they have firsthand experience with tropical rain forests, deserts, or evergreen trees. Ask students to name as many of the content words in their native language(s) as they can. Encourage them to share any firsthand experiences.

- Display the wall chart. Explain that the color codes in the legend at the bottom of the page match the colored borders of each of the biomes on the page. For example, the color in the legend for *temperate forest* is pink. The top left picture, *temperate forest*, has a pink border. The same color coding system is used to show the biomes on the world map on the transparency. Now divide the class into six groups, one for each biome. Students in each group look at their biome and, in turn, describe what they see. Students try to identify all the content words in their picture. They write the name of their biome on the colored borders on the transparency (using a washable marker) as well as the names of each of the content words which occur within their biomes. For example, students in Group 1 write *temperate forest* and *deciduous tree* in the top left picture.

- Select six students to draw a picture of one of the biomes on the board. The class names the biome shown in each picture. Then have these students label their drawings. Now distribute the word and picture cards to the rest of the class. Students, in turn, pronounce the word on each of their cards and place them under the appropriate picture on the board.

WORKBOOK: Topic 53
See Teacher's Book page 213.

► CONTENT

Components: Dictionary pages 106-107, Transparency 53, Wall Chart 53, Content Reading Topic 53, Worksheet Topic 53, Cassette

- Present the content reading. **See pages xvii-xix for general techniques about presenting content readings.**

- Ask the following or similar questions:

  Name the six land biomes.
  Are summers cool in a temperate forest?
  Does it usually snow in the desert?
  Where does it rain almost every day?
  What is the weather like in a grassland?
  What kind of climate zone is near the Equator?

- ► **Adverbs of frequency (*always, usually, never*)**

  Adverbs of frequency tell how often something happens. An adverb of frequency follows the verb *BE* (*The weather is* always *hot and dry*), but it comes before other simple present verbs (*It* never *snows*).

- Point out examples of adverbs of frequency in the content reading. Have students underline and read aloud all sentences with these adverbs. Call students' attention to the difference in position of the adverb depending on whether it is used with the verb *be* or other simple present tense verbs. Now divide the class into two groups and have them look at the wall chart. Each groups makes up as many sentences as possible describing the conditions in the various biomes using *always, usually*, and *never*. Each group reads their sentences aloud as the other groups check for accuracy.

- Divide the class into two teams and have each team write as many sentences as they possibly can with *always, usually,* or *never*. Suggest that students write about the weather in their area, as well as about other topics such as what happens at school or at home. For example: *It always rains in November. We never study English in the afternoon. The mailman usually comes to my house at 2 o'clock.* Students on each team take turns reading their sentences aloud. The team with the most correct sentences is the winner.

- Have students look at the map on the transparency and find the area where they live. Have them identify the biomes in this area. Then have them identify the biomes in their native countries. Ask students about the types of plants and animals that are found in these areas. Ask them their feelings about living in such places. Encourage class discussion.

WORKSHEET: Topic 53
See Teacher's Book page 213.

▶CHANTS

Components: Dictionary pages 106-107, Content Chant Topic 53, Cassette

 ## CONTENT CHANT

It's Great to Live in the Polar Zones

It's great to live in the polar zones,
if you're a penguin or a polar bear.
It's great to live in the polar zones,
though I wouldn't want to live there.

It's tough to live in the tundra.
I don't know what I'd do
if I had a house in the tundra
with all those caribou.

It's fun to live in the tropical zone
with monkeys in the trees.
You won't need a sweater, scarf, or gloves.
Your hands will never freeze.

The grassland's great, if you like grass.
The desert's fine, if you love sand.
The taiga's OK if you're a bear.
If not, it might not be so grand.

But it's great to live in the polar zones,
if you're a penguin or a polar bear.
It's great to live in the polar zones,
though I wouldn't want to live there.

- Present the content chant. **See pages xx-xxi for general techniques about presenting chants.**

- This chant has some complex sentences. There is also additional vocabulary which you may want to pre-teach, such as *caribou, penguin, polar bear, scarf, gloves.* Decide which sentences and vocabulary your students need help with. There are some examples of how to chunk sentences below.

- Before distributing the chant, have students practice, in three groups, the following chunks of its language. The groups, in turn, chant one of the following lines: *in the polar zones, in the tundra,* or *in the tropical zone.* Then they chant the first half of their lines: *It's great to live…, It's tough to live…,* and *It's fun to live….* Now each group puts both parts together (*It's great to live in the polar zones,* etc.).

- Now distribute Content Chant 53. Continue to break up sentences into chunks first, if your students are having trouble with sentence length. Then divide the class into four groups and have each group chant one of the stanzas. Encourage students to pantomime as many words in their stanzas as possible.

▶EXTENSION

Components: Dictionary pages 106-107, Transparency 53, Wall Chart 53

- Have students form six groups, one to study each biome. Each group looks at the climate map on the wall chart to find the areas that are examples of their biomes. Then they look at a detailed political map of the world to find the countries, states, or regions which are part of their biome. For example, the *Taiga* group looks for all the purple areas on the climate map. Then, looking at the political map, they make a list of as many places as they can find which correspond to the purple areas on the climate map. Each group makes a poster showing the places in the world where its biome exists and presents the information to the entire class.

- Have students work in their same biome groups as in the above activity to find out as much information as possible about the types of plants, animals, and weather in the areas of their assigned biome, as well as the lifestyles of people in those areas. Encourage students to explore textbooks, nature magazines, ecological groups, and the Internet. Students write descriptive illustrated reports of their biomes and present their information to the class. Some students may wish to draw a picture of their biome or to make a collage with pictures and words from magazines and newspapers. Encourage variety.

- Divide the class into two teams. Teams, in turn, name a country, state, or region and give its climate zone. For example: *Argentina, in the temperate zone.* The opposing team names the biome for that country, state, or region. If there is more than one biome in that area, students get extra points for naming each one. For example, the biomes for Argentina are *temperate forest* plus some *grassland* and some *desert.* Score one point for each correct climate zone and one for each correct biome.

- Take a class field trip to a nearby park or area where there are a lot of trees. Ask students to look at different trees and say whether they are deciduous (the leaves fall off every year) or evergreen (always green). Students can count the number of trees of both kinds and make a class mural of the trees they saw.

► LITERATURE

Suggested Books

Desert Voices
written by Byrd Baylor; illustrated by Peter Parnall.
Macmillan, 1981. ISBN 068971691
The "voices" of ten different desert animals are heard describing their lives and homes in this exceptional book. The illustrations convey a vivid sense of the desert biome. Each vignette, usually on a two-page spread, can be presented separately to introduce relevant vocabulary and language points. The text is in the present tense and the description lends itself to acting out the desert scenes.

Sunshine Makes the Seasons
written by Franklyn M. Branley;
illustrated by Giulio Maestro.
HarperTrophy, 1985. ISBN 0064450198
In simple language, astronomer Dr. Branley explains how the tilt of the Earth in relation to the sun causes the seasons to change. The text hinges on an easy experiment that students can do, individually or with the whole class. The illustrations mix drawings of everyday situations with informative diagrams.

The Reasons for Seasons
written and illustrated by Gail Gibbons.
Holiday House, 1996. ISBN 0823412385
This book explains the science of the seasons by showing the effects of the Earth's tilt and orbit on the activities of people and animals. The text is simple and straightforward, and the pictures and words can be used as a starting point for talking about change and climate.

WORKBOOK: Topic 53

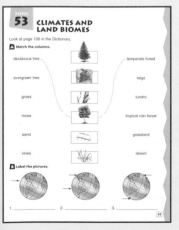

Students match the words in A with the corresponding pictures. Then they match these pictures to the names of the biomes. In B, they write words to label the different zones of the Earth.

WORKSHEET: Topic 53

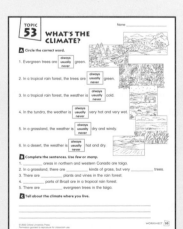

Activities A and B are based on the content reading. In each sentence in A, students circle *always*, *usually*, or *never*. In B, they fill in the sentences with *few* or *many*. In activity C, students tell about the climate where they live.

▶ **CONTENT**

Weather descriptions and forecast

A weather map

▶ **LANGUAGE**

Future with *going to*: *The snow is going to stop this evening.*

Expressions: *How's the weather?*

CONTENT WORDS

1. forecaster
2. sunshine
3. snow
4. wind
5. cloud
6. lightning
7. rain
8. rainbow
9. temperature
10. storms
11. blizzard
12. hurricane
13. fog
14. tornado
15. sleet
16. atmosphere

CONTENT READING

Weather

The Weather Forecast

Bob: I'm your weather forecaster, Bob Storm. Our team is going to tell you about today's weather. First, we're going to see the weather in the Northwest with Eve Chen. Can you hear me, Eve?

Eve: Yes, I can, Bob. There's a blizzard in the northwest mountains today. There is snow everywhere. The snow is going to stop this evening.

Bob: Thank you, Eve. Sam Powers is in Florida. How's the weather there, Sam?

Sam: Well, Bob, we're in the middle of a hurricane. There's going to be wind and rain with some lightning until tomorrow morning. Tomorrow, we're going to see clouds and some sunshine. After the storm, I think we're going to see a rainbow.

Bob: Thanks, Sam. Nona Murphy is in Boston. How's the weather there, Nona?

Nona: Well, we aren't going to see much through all this fog today. We don't know when it's going to clear up.

Bob: Thanks, Nona. Jim Kirby is in Oklahoma. There's a tornado outside Tulsa. What's happening there, Jim?

Jim: Well, Bob, you can see the tornado. I'm going to stay right here in this basement.

Bob: Be safe, Jim. Tyrone Preston is outside Cleveland. Tyrone, how's the weather?

Tyrone: We have sleet, Bob. It's freezing. The ice is very slippery! When the temperature rises this afternoon, the sleet is going to turn to rain.

Bob: Finally, Melanie Garber reports from high above the atmosphere in the space shuttle.

Melanie: Hello from outer space, Bob. What a day! I can see different weather all over the Earth.

▶ WORDS

Components: Dictionary pages 108-109, Transparency 54, Wall Chart 54, Workbook page 54, Word and Picture Cards Topic 54, Cassette

- Present the content words. **See pages xiv-xvi for general techniques about presenting content words.**

  > **Language Note:** The letters *ture* in the word *temperature* sound like *chur*. *Temperature* can be pronounced as a four syllable word which sounds like *TEM-per-a-chur*, or more often, in conversation, as a three syllable word which sounds like *TEM-pra-chur*. The word *lightning* is a two-syllable word with the stress on the first syllable: LIGHT-ning. Note the silent *e* in *forecaster*, *hurricane*, and *atmosphere*. The *ph* in *atmosphere* is pronounced like an *f* sound.

- Have students open their Dictionaries to page 108 and look at the words and pictures on the page. Ask if they recognize any of the words or pictures. Ask students to name as many of the content words in their native language(s) as they can.

- Distribute one set of word cards and one set of picture cards to the class. Have students ask each other questions and trade cards to make word and picture matches. Each student should end up with a matching picture card and word card.

- Divide the class into groups. Students conduct a poll about how they feel about different types of weather. Students work in their groups using a chart similar to the example below. Have all students agree on the types of weather and the types of feelings to put in their charts. Each group then presents their data to the entire class. Help students combine their data and then make bar graphs to illustrate the combined data. Encourage students to discuss the results.

Types of Weather	Like		Don't like		Don't care		Makes me happy		Makes me sad	
	Boys	Girls	Boys	Girls	Boys	Girls	Boys	Girls	Boys	Girls
sunshine										
rain										
snow										

WORKBOOK: Topic 54
See Teacher's Book page 217.

▶ CONTENT

Components: Dictionary pages 108-109, Transparency 54, Wall Chart 54, Content Reading Topic 54, Worksheet Topic 54, Cassette

- Present the content reading. **See pages xvii-xix for general techniques about presenting content readings.**

- Ask the following or similar questions:

  Where is the blizzard?
  When will we see the rainbow?
  Is there sleet in Florida?
  How's the weather in Boston?
  What happens to sleet when the temperature rises?
  What can you see from high above the Earth's atmosphere?

▶ **Future with *going to***

  > We use the future with *going to* to express future time. We use [*am*, *is*, or *are* + *going to* + the simple form of the main verb]. The word *gonna* is a reduction of *going to* and is used in conversation, but not in writing. The future with *going to* structure is often interchangeable with the future with *will*.

  Point out examples of the future with *going to* in the content reading. Have students underline and read aloud all sentences with this pattern. Now ask students to look at the wall chart and dramatize the weather report. Challenge students to make as many sentences using future with *going to* as they possibly can. Provide these three models for the content words: *It's going to snow*; *We're going to have a blizzard*; *We're going to see clouds*.

▶ **Future with *going to*.** Distribute the picture cards. Students, in turn, give a mini-weather report about tomorrow's weather using the information on their cards and sentences with the future with *going to*. For example, the student who gets the card *tornado* might say *We're going to have a tornado tomorrow*.

- Have students make a large calendar on chart paper for the current month. Divide students into groups. Each group copies the calendar on a piece of paper and puts their group's name on it. Students in each group predict the weather for each week by putting copies of the appropriate picture card (*sunshine, snow, wind, rain, fog,* etc.) on each day. Make as many copies of the picture cards as students need for their predictions. Each day, the whole class checks the actual weather and puts the appropriate picture card on that day on the large calendar. Check at the end of the week to see which group(s) had the most accurate predictions.

WORKSHEET: Topic 54
See Teacher's Book page 217.

► CHANTS

Components: Dictionary pages 108-109, Content Chant Topic 54, Cassette

 CONTENT CHANT

> ### Will It Rain Today?
>
> Will it rain today?
> Or will it snow?
> Don't listen to the forecaster.
> He doesn't know.
> When he says
> "We won't have wind or rain,"
> we'll probably get a hurricane.
>
> He promised us sunshine,
> and what did we get?
> We got very, very wet!

- Present the content chant. **See pages xx-xxi for general techniques about presenting chants.**

- This chant has some complex sentences. There are some examples below of sentences you may want to break up into smaller chunks, depending on your students' needs. Also, this chant can be read as a poem, if you prefer.

- Break up the following lines into smaller chunks from the ends of the sentences so students will be able to maintain the rhythm and intonation more easily.

  Don't listen to the forecaster. He doesn't know.

  He promised us sunshine, and what did we get?

- Distribute Content Chant 54. Select one student to be the forecaster and stand at the front of the room with a big smile on his or her face. (If the forecaster is female, change the pronouns for the forecaster to *she*.) The forecaster says only one line, *We won't have wind or rain*, with great certainty. The entire class or other individual students, in turn, say the rest of the chant.

► EXTENSION

Components: Dictionary pages 108-109, Transparency 54, Wall Chart 54

- Explain that every country in the world uses the Celsius scale to measure temperature except the United States which uses the Fahrenheit scale. Draw this chart:

Celsius		Fahrenheit
30 - 40	hot - very hot	90 - 105
18 - 29	warm - very warm	65 - 89
8 - 17	cool - very cool	45 - 65
0 - 7	cold - very cold	32 - 44
-18 - -1	freezing	0 - 31

Divide the class into two teams. Students from each team, in turn, say a number either from the Celsius scale or the Fahrenheit scale. The student from the other team then says one of the describing words in the middle of the chart. For example, if a student from Team 1 says *It's 7 degrees Celsius*, a student from Team 2 says, *It's cold* or *It's very cold*. Then teams reverse roles. Score one point for accuracy.

> **Content Note:** There is a mathematical formula for converting between the two scales, but you can get an approximate equivalent much more easily. To convert from Fahrenheit to Celsius, subtract 30 and divide by two. For example, 70 degrees Fahrenheit (°F) minus 30 equals 40. Forty divided by two is 20 degrees Celsius (°C). So, 70°F is approximately 20°C. To convert from Celsius to Fahrenheit, multiply by two and add 30. For example, 7 degrees Celsius (°C) times two is 14, plus 30 is 44 degrees Fahrenheit (°F). So, 7°C is approximately 44 °F.

- Introduce the names of the seasons: *winter, spring, summer, fall.* In the United States, winter is from December to March, spring is March to June, summer is June to September, and fall is September to December. Encourage discussion about the typical conditions where you live for each season, and the differences in the seasons in students' native countries.

- Teach students weather adjectives (*sunny, windy, clear, cloudy, stormy, rainy, foggy, icy*) using the model sentence *It's <u>cloudy</u> today.* Teach the verbs *rain* and *snow* using the model sentences *It's <u>raining</u> today* or *It's going to <u>snow</u> tomorrow.* For homework, students find an actual weather forecast in a newspaper, on the radio, or on television and write down what the forecaster predicts. Encourage them to listen for words such as *sunny* or *cloudy,* the high and/or low *temperature* of the day, and whether it's going to *rain* or *snow,* etc. The next day, students report the forecast to the class. Record the various forecasts. Now, with students, measure the temperature outside, and check the sky. Is it sunny? Is it cloudy? Is it raining or snowing? When you go back inside, check to see which forecaster was correct.

► LITERATURE

Suggested Books

Storms
by Seymour Simon.
William Morrow and Co., 1989. ISBN 0688074138
This Reading Rainbow title explains how hurricanes, tornadoes, and thunderstorms develop in the atmosphere and how they impact people and places. The text may be too difficult for beginners and some intermediate students to read, but the spectacular photographs can be used to prompt discussion. Students should be able to locate many of the content words in the text. Information in the text can be paraphrased and shared to prompt discussion about students' experiences in stormy weather.

Weather Words and What They Mean
written and illustrated by Gail Gibbons.
Holiday House, 1992. ISBN 082340952X
Like many of Gail Gibbons' books, this one is a treasure for English-language learners. Bright cartoons illustrate simple sentences about weather conditions and the science that explains them. Speech balloons throughout show identifying words and examples of how people talk about the weather. The last page features a chart of interesting weather facts.

Cloudy with a Chance of Meatballs
written by Judi Barrett; illustrated by Ron Barrett.
Aladdin Paperbacks, 1982. ISBN 0689707495
Imagine a country where food falls from the sky. That's the subject of this modern classic, the silly, delightful story of Chewandswallow, where the people eat whatever the weather provides. Children will find familiar words for foods, and cooking and eating implements. The unfamiliar setting will amuse them and inspire them to invent their own weather menus and tall tales.

A Year Full of Poems
selected by Michael Harrison and Christopher Stuart-Clark.
Oxford University Press Children's Books, 1996.
ISBN 0192761498
This collection of funny and famous poetry has selections for all seasons. The illustrations that accompany each poem are diverse and show many examples of the content words. The poems span many reading levels and provide a variety of language patterns and grammar.

WORKBOOK: Topic 54

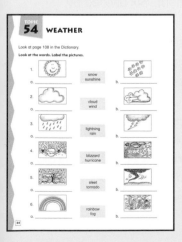

On this page, there are six pairs of pictures and words. Students write the appropriate word from each word pair underneath each picture.

WORKSHEET: Topic 54

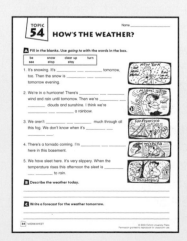

For each sentence in A, students write *going to* plus a verb from the word box. They base their choices on the information in the pictures. In B, they describe the weather for that day where they live, and in C, they write a weather forecast for the following day.

CONTENT

Whole numbers, fractions, and simple mathematical functions

 LANGUAGE

Modal *can*: *You can add numbers.*

Direct and indirect objects: *You give each friend 2 sweet rolls.*

Math expressions: *Seven minus three equals four.*

CONTENT WORDS

1. number line
2. digits
3. even numbers
4. odd numbers
5. add
6. sum
7. subtract
8. difference
9. multiply
10. product
11. divide
12. quotient
13. comparisons
14. whole number
15. fraction
16. mixed number

CONTENT READING

Exploring Math

Math is about numbers. We can show numbers on a number line. Numbers greater than 0 are positive numbers. The number 2 is a positive number. Numbers less than 0 are negative numbers. The number −2 is a negative number.

All numbers are made of digits. Digits are 0 through 9. The number 4 has one digit. The number 12 has two digits. The number 110 has 3 digits.

Some numbers are even and some numbers are odd. Even numbers end in 0, 2, 4, 6, or 8. Odd numbers end in 1, 3, 5, 7, or 9.

You can add numbers. You have 4 cookies. Then, your friend gives you 1 more cookie. Now, you have 5 cookies. Five is the total, or the sum. Four plus one equals five. You can subtract numbers, too. You have 7 brownies. Then, you give your friend 3 brownies. Now, you have 4 brownies. Four is the difference. Seven minus three equals four.

You can multiply numbers. You have 4 friends. Each friend wants 3 cupcakes. So you multiply 4 by 3. You need 12 cupcakes. Twelve is the product. Four times three equals twelve. You can divide numbers, too. You have 6 sweet rolls, and you have 3 friends. So you divide 6 by 3. You give each friend 2 sweet rolls. Two is the quotient. Six divided by three equals two.

In math, you can compare numbers. You can make comparisons with special symbols. Five is greater than four. Two is less than five. One plus one is equal to two.

Numbers can be whole numbers, mixed numbers, or fractions. One (1) is a whole number. One-half ($1/2$) is a fraction. One and one-half ($1\,1/2$) is a mixed number. A mixed number is a whole number and a fraction.

► WORDS

Components: Dictionary pages 110-111, Transparency 55, Wall Chart 55, Workbook page 55, Word and Picture Cards Topic 55, Cassette

- Present the content words. **See pages xiv-xvi for general techniques about presenting content words.**

    Language Note: The letters *ti* in the words *quotient* and *fraction* are pronounced with a *sh* sound like the *ti* in *motion*.

- Have students open their Dictionaries to page 110 and ask if they recognize any of the words or symbols on the page. Ask students to name as many of the content words in their native language(s) as they can. Say the words in English for each of the pictures or symbols on the page. Point out the different ways we refer verbally to some of the same symbols. Make one or more charts to help students learn the various words associated with the symbols (see the chart below).

    Language Note: The content words *add, subtract, multiply,* and *divide* are represented by the mathematical symbols +, -, ×, and ÷. However, when we read these symbols in a mathematical equation, we say *plus, minus, times,* and *divided by.*

    The comparison symbol > means *is greater than* and < means *is less than.*

    The symbol = is said as *equals,* or *is equal to.*

    The chart below summarizes the various terms associated with each mathematical symbol.

Symbol	Action (verb)	Operation (noun)	Result (noun)
+ plus	add	addition	sum
− minus	subtract	subtraction	difference
× times	multiply	multiplication	product
÷ divided by	divide	division	quotient

- Divide the class into four groups. Each group makes up ten equations with a mathematical operation. Group 1 makes equations with the operation *add*. Groups 2, 3, and 4 use the operations *subtract, multiply,* and *divide*. Each group puts their equations on index cards. Collect the cards and redistribute them. Students read the equations aloud and correct any mathematical errors. For example, a student would read 5 - 2 = 3 as *five minus two equals three*, or *five minus two is three*.

- Divide the class into two teams. A student from one team says a whole number and a student from the opposite team tells whether the number is odd or even. Teams take turns and then reverse roles. Continue until all students have participated in the game. Score one point for each correct answer.

WORKBOOK: Topic 55
See Teacher's Book page 221.

► CONTENT

Components: Dictionary pages 110-111, Transparency 55, Wall Chart 55, Content Reading Topic 55, Worksheet Topic 55, Cassette

- Present the content reading. **See pages xvii-xix for general techniques about presenting content readings.**

- Ask the following or similar questions:

    Is -2 a positive or negative number?
    Give one example of an even number and one example of an odd number.
    How many digits are in the number 2,345?
    What is 4 plus 5?
    What is the product of 9 and 2?
    Is 7 > 5?

► **Modal *can*.** Point out examples of *can* in the content reading. Ask students to underline and read aloud all sentences using *can*. Divide the class into two teams. Students on each team ask each other if they can do certain mathematical equations. If students on the opposing team can do the problem, they say *Yes, we can!* and one student gives the answer. For example, a student from Team 1 says *Can you add 4 plus 9?* Students on Team 2 say *Yes, we can!* Then a student from Team 2 answers *Four plus nine equals 13.* If students on the opposing team can't do the problem, they say *No, we can't*, forfeit the point, and try to do the next problem. Teams take turns and reverse roles. Score one point for each correct answer.

► **Direct and indirect objects**

    A direct object answers the question *what* about the verb. In the sentence *I ate two rolls, rolls* is the direct object. An indirect object answers the question *who* about the verb. In the sentence *I gave Alex one roll, Alex* is the indirect object. We can also say *I gave one roll to Alex.*

    Point out all the examples of direct and indirect objects in the content reading. Divide the class into groups. Students in each group refer to the wall chart and write five mathematical problems on index cards using items in the picture (as direct objects) and the names of their classmates (as indirect objects). For example: *I had one and one-half cakes. I gave one to Paul. How many do I have left?* Groups exchange index cards. Students in each group read a problem aloud and solve it.

WORKSHEET: Topic 55
See Teacher's Book page 221.

►CHANTS

Components: Dictionary pages 110-111, Content Chant Topic 55, Cassette

CONTENT CHANT

Even Numbers, Odd Numbers

Even numbers
    2, 4
Odd numbers
    1, 3
Even numbers
    2, 4, 6, 8, 10 *
Even numbers
    2, 4
Odd numbers
    1, 3
Odd numbers
    1, 3, 5, 7, 9 *

Add, subtract, and multiply.
Add, subtract, and multiply.
Add *
    2 plus 2.
    2 plus 2 is 4. *
Subtract *
    4 minus 2.
    4 minus 2 is 2.
Multiply *
    4 times 2.
    4 times 2 is 8.
Add, subtract, and multiply.
Add, subtract, and multiply.

- Present the content chant. **See pages xx-xxi for general techniques about presenting chants.**

- Before distributing the chant, have students practice with small chunks of the language from the chant. Divide the class into two groups. Group 1 chants *Add, subtract, and multiply* repeatedly. Group two repeatedly chants *Subtract*, Multiply** with the appropriate claps. Groups chant in turn and then simultaneously. Groups start slowly and softly and then increase their speed and volume.

- Now distribute Content Chant 55. Divide the class into two groups. Group 1 chants all the unindented lines. Group 2 chants all the indented lines. Once students are familiar with their roles, have them reverse roles. Group 2 now chants the first voice (unindented lines) and Group 1 chants the response (indented lines). Have groups hold up number cards or their fingers as they say the numbers.

- Select pairs of students to do the chant in the same manner as the groups did above.

►EXTENSION

Components: Dictionary pages 110-111, Transparency 55, Wall Chart 55

- Divide students into two teams. Make a pile of the word and picture cards that express arithmetic functions (*add, subtract, multiply, divide*) and *comparisons*. A student from Team 1 names any two numbers. A student from Team 2 picks a card from the pile, and performs the arithmetic function indicated on that card with the two numbers. For example, if the two numbers are 10 and 7, and the card says *multiply,* the student multiplies 10 by 7 and gives the product (70). If the card is *comparisons,* the student from Team 2 says *10 is greater than 7*. If your class is already doing long division, encourage students to divide numbers to get exact quotients. Otherwise, have them use calculators or use simple division with remainders. Score one point for each correct answer.

- Introduce Roman numerals (I, II, III, IV, V, VI, VII, VIII, IX, X, etc.). Explain that I stands for 1, V stands for 5, X stands for 10, L stands for 50, C stands for 100, D stands for 500, and M stands for 1,000. Every number is expressed as some combination of these numerals. If a smaller numeral appears after a bigger numeral, it means add the two numbers. If the smaller numeral appears in front of the larger numeral, it means subtract the smaller numeral from the larger. For example, XI is 10 + 1. IX is 1 subtracted from 10. Have students come to the board in turn and write the numbers from 1 to 100 in Roman numerals.

- Talk to students about Roman and Arabic numerals. Which do they like better? Which are easier to remember? Ask students to name some places where they have seen Roman numerals (the Super Bowl, watches or clocks, chapters of books, etc.). Ask students to name some places where they have seen Arabic numbers (phone numbers, addresses, birthdates, etc.). Ask students to imagine what would happen if they could not use any numbers for a whole day. Create a group story or divide the class into groups and have them write and illustrate their ideas. Encourage class discussion.

- Create a class arithmetic problem. Have each student write a plus or a minus sign followed by a number on a piece of paper. Collect all the pieces of paper. Write the number 50 on the board, then after it, write each of the students' additions or subtractions, and finish it with an = sign. Your equation might look something like this:

50 - 32 + 19 - 18 + 44 + 701 - 90 - 104 + 1 - 32 + 3 - 46 = ____

Have students do all the addition and subtraction in the long equation and provide the correct answer. Check the answer with a calculator.

►LITERATURE

Suggested Books

Mathematics Dictionary and Handbook
written by Eugene D. Nichols and Sharon L. Selwartz.
Nichols Schwartz Publishing, 1997. ISBN 1882269071
This excellent resource comprehensively covers math terms from basic through advanced math in an easy-reference format that is both teacher and student friendly. Most definitions are accompanied by pictures. Teachers may find it helpful to match the word and picture cards for Topics 55-60 to the definitions in this book. It is also useful for presenting and reviewing dictionary skills.

Pigs Will Be Pigs: Fun with Math and Money
written by Amy Axelrod;
illustrated by Sharon Mcginley-Nally.
Simon & Schuster, 1994. ISBN 002765415
With nothing at home to eat, the pig family decides to go to a restaurant. Unfortunately, a quick survey reveals that they have no money. So begins a hunt through the homestead for misplaced and forgotten funds. Students will enjoy seeing how the pigs gradually accumulate their money, and once they get to their favorite restaurant, how they order to suit their budget (the menu is reproduced in full). In comic prose and lively Southwestern-flavored art, this imaginative book teaches students how to count money and perform simple math problems.

Eating Fractions
written by Bruce McMillan.
Scholastic Trade, 1991. ISBN 0590437704
In this photo-based book, fractions are taught by showing whole foods that are then cut into halves, thirds, and fourths. Recipes are included at the end of the book, some of which are wonderfully silly. This is a very basic concept book, best for beginners. Like the Dictionary illustration, it conveys how math is used in everyday life.

If You Made a Million
written and illustrated by David M. Schwartz.
Mulberry Books, 1994. ISBN 0688136346
Marvelossimo the Mathematical Magician leads a group of children on further investigations into the nature of money and its proper use (see Topic 59, Number Patterns, Functions, and Relations). This book can be applied to the more advanced mathematical terms used in this topic. It is a good book for practicing with the functions shown in the Dictionary illustration as they apply to money and the use of money. The language patterns presented also help students to learn *if* clauses and conjunctions.

Fraction Action
written and illustrated by Loreen Leedy.
Holiday House, 1996. ISBN 082341244X
This cute and accessible book is about a classroom of animals who learn about fractions with the help of their teacher, Miss Prime. Students can locate the content words in the colorful, detailed illustrations. The text presents language for problem-solving that students can apply to their own classroom situations. Students will find this book about one of the most difficult concepts of basic math amusing and enlightening.

WORKBOOK: Topic 55

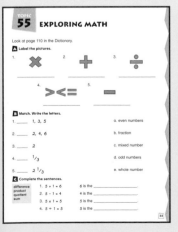

In A, students write the content words represented by the mathematical symbols. In B, they match the numbers or sets of numbers to the words that describe them. In C, they choose words from the word box to describe the answers to the four mathematical equations.

WORKSHEET: Topic 55

On this page, there are five number problems. Students match the problems with the sentences describing operations you can do with numbers. Then, they solve the problems. Following the model in number one, they give each answer in numbers and symbols, and then write it out in words.

▶ CONTENT
·······································
Plane figures, solid figures,
lines, and dimensions

▶ LANGUAGE
·······································
Have as a main verb: *Plane
figures have two dimensions.*

CONTENT WORDS

1. plane figures
2. square
3. rectangle
4. triangle
5. circle
6. pentagon
7. octagon
8. solid figures
9. cube
10. sphere
11. cylinder
12. cone
13. rectangular prism
14. lines
15. line segment
16. parallel
17. perpendicular
18. ray

CONTENT READING

Geometry I

Geometry is about plane figures, solid figures, and lines. We see examples of lines and figures around us every day.

Plane figures have two dimensions. You can measure plane figures up and down, and side to side. Squares, rectangles, triangles, circles, pentagons, and octagons are plane figures, or flat shapes. A triangle has three sides. A rectangle has four sides. A square is a special rectangle. Every side is the same size. A pentagon has five sides. An octagon has eight sides. A stop sign is an octagon. A circle doesn't have sides. It's round. A wheel is a circle.

Solid figures have three dimensions. You can measure solid figures up and down, side to side, and front to back. Cubes, spheres, cylinders, cones, and rectangular prisms are solid figures. A cube has six equal sides. Every side is the same size. A ball is a sphere. A can is a cylinder. A step is a rectangular prism.

Lines have only one dimension. You can measure lines up and down or side to side. Lines go forever in two directions. Parallel lines are next to each other and never cross, or intersect. Perpendicular lines intersect like a cross or a plus sign. A ray starts at one point and continues forever in one direction. A line segment has a beginning and an end.

▶ WORDS

Components: Dictionary pages 112-113, Transparency 56, Wall Chart 56, Workbook page 56, Word and Picture Cards Topic 56, Cassette

- Present the content words. **See pages xiv-xvi for general techniques about presenting content words.**

  > **Language Note:** *Pentagons* and *octagons* are types of *polygons*, closed plane figures bounded by three or more line segments. The prefixes in the word *pentagon* and *octagon* mean *five* and *eight*, respectively.

- Have students open their Dictionaries to page 112 and ask if they recognize any of the words or shapes on the page. Ask students to name as many of the content words in their native language(s) as they can.

- Introduce the concept of dimensions. Draw a line (see Figure A below). Explain that a line has only one dimension. A line has size in only one direction, up and down or side to side. Now use the line as one side of a square and add the other three sides (see Figure B). Show students that the square has size in two directions, or dimensions: up and down *and* side to side. Now use the square as the front face of a cube and draw in the other three visible faces in perspective (see Figure C). Show that the cube has size in three dimensions: up and down, side to side, and front to back.

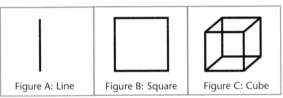

| Figure A: Line | Figure B: Square | Figure C: Cube |

- Make a table like the example below. Distribute one set of picture cards and one set of word cards. Have students, in turn, pronounce the words as they place each of their cards in the appropriate columns.

PLANE FIGURES Two Dimensions	SOLID FIGURES Three Dimensions	LINES One Dimensions
square	cube	line

- Have students look at the wall chart to find additional examples of *plane figures, solid figures*, and *lines*. For example, the *diamond* on the *triangle* flag is actually a *square* tilted on its side. The ball on top of the flagpole is a *sphere*. The white crossing marks on the street are *rectangles*. There are *lines* on the concrete pavement. The manhole cover is a *circle*. Divide the class into teams. Each team makes a list of as many of these shapes, solids, and lines as they can find in the picture. Each team reads their list aloud and points to the appropriate picture on the wall chart as they read the list. Score one point for each correct response.

WORKBOOK: Topic 56
See Teacher's Book page 225.

▶ CONTENT

Components: Dictionary pages 112-113, Transparency 56, Wall Chart 56, Content Reading Topic 56, Worksheet Topic 56, Cassette

- Present the content reading. **See pages xvii-xix for general techniques about presenting content readings.**

- Ask the following or similar questions:

  > *How many dimensions do plane figures have?*
  > *How many sides does a rectangle have?*
  > *Does a circle have sides?*
  > *Which figure has five sides?*
  > *Do parallel lines intersect?*
  > *Is a stop sign a square or an octagon?*

▶ ***Have* as a main verb**

  > *Have/has* can be used as a main verb. Sometimes *have/has* functions as an action verb. For example: *They're having a party. Have some coffee.* Sometimes *have/has* functions as a stative verb. It is stative when it means *possess* or *own*. For example: *Plane figures have two dimensions. Have/has* functions as a stative verb in the content reading.

Point out the occurrences of *have/has* in the content reading. Ask students to underline all examples of the word *have* and circle all examples of the word *has*. Then ask students to read aloud the sentences with these words. Divide the class into two teams. Each team writes 20 True/False statements using *have/has* in the following format.

Statement	True	False
An octagon has five sides.		
Plane figures have two dimensions.		
A pentagon has five sides.		

The teams exchange their statements and each team write their answers to the other team's True/False statements. Score one point for each correct answer.

- Place a set of picture cards in a paper bag. Have individual students, in turn, draw a card from the bag and describe the figure using *have/has* without showing the card or naming the figure. For example: *It has six equal sides.* The other students identify the figure, again using *have has*. For example: *You have a sphere.*

- Divide the class into groups. Ask each group to make up a story about what is happening in the wall chart picture. Have groups dramatize their story. Encourage students to use their imaginations.

WORKSHEET: Topic 56
See Teacher's Book page 225.

► CHANTS

Components: Dictionary pages 112-113, Content Chant Topic 56, Cassette

CONTENT CHANT

Geometry Chant

Plane figure
octagon
Plane figure
square *

How many sides in an octagon?
How many sides in an square? *

Plane figure
octagon
Plane figure
square *

Eight sides in an octagon
Four sides in a square *

How many sides in an octagon?
Eight sides
Stop sign

How many sides in a pentagon?
Five sides
Cross-walk sign

Solid figure, cylinder
Plane figure, square

Cylinder, garbage can
Plane figure, square *

- Present the content chant. **See pages xx-xxi for general techniques about presenting chants.**

- Before distributing the chant, have students practice small chunks of the language from the chant. Divide the class into two groups. Group 1 chants the questions: *How many sides in an octagon? How many sides in a square? How many sides in a pentagon*? Group 2 responds to each question in turn, chanting the responses: *Eight sides in an octagon, Four sides in a square*, *five sides in a pentagon*.

- Now distribute Content Chant 56. Divide the class into two groups. Students in Group 1 chant the questions as they did in the above activity. Group 2 chants everything else in the chant.

- Have individual students volunteer to "be" the figures referred to in the chant. First they draw either the shapes (an octagon, a square, a pentagon, a cylinder) or the objects (stop sign, cross-walk sign, garbage can) in the chant. Then, as the class chants, these students hold up their pictures and say their words as they occur in the chant. When students are familiar with the chant, they can substitute the words for other plane and solid figures in the appropriate places in the chant.

► EXTENSION

Components. Dictionary pages 112-113, Transparency 56, Wall Chart 56

- Give students the following directions. They should draw exactly what you say without looking at their classmates' pictures.
  1. *Draw a large circle in the center of your paper.*
  2. *Draw a cylinder to the left of the circle. One side of the cylinder should touch the circle.*
  3. *Draw another cylinder to the right of the circle. One side of the cylinder should touch the circle.*
  4. *Draw one small circle in the middle of the larger circle.*
  5. *Draw two triangles next to each other above the small circle.*
  6. *Draw one small square below the circle.*

The drawings should look something like this:

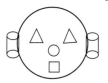

- Divide the class into two teams. Students walk around the classroom looking for everyday examples of planes or solid figures. For example, the blackboard is a *rectangle*. A desk is a *rectangular prism*. A trash can is a *cylinder*. A ball is a *sphere*. Each team makes a list of all the figures they can find. Score one point for each correct example on the list.

- Introduce the three special kinds of triangles. An *isosceles* (eye-SOS-o-leez) triangle has two sides that are the same length. The triangle in the picture is an isosceles triangle. An *equilateral* triangle has three sides of the same length. A yield sign is an equilateral triangle. A *right* triangle has one angle that is a right angle, or 90°. Draw a diagonal line between the corners of a rectangle to form two right triangles. Have pairs of students practice making the three kinds of triangles. Students can check each others' work by measuring the sides.

- Write the prefixes *hexa-*, *septa-*, and *nona-* and the numbers 6, 7, and 9 next to them. Explain that the prefixes mean the numbers 6, 7, and 9. Ask students what you might call a plane figure with six sides (a *hexagon*), a plane figure with seven sides (a *septagon*), or a plane figure with nine sides (a *nonagon*). Explain that the pentagon and the octagon in the picture are both regular, or equilateral, figures. All of their sides are the same length. But all plane figures do not have to be regular. Each side of a pentagon, hexagon, septagon, octagon, or nonagon can be any length at all. (Note that a rectangle is a special kind of plane figure, with four right angles. In a rectangle, each pair of opposite sides must be the same length; in a square, all four sides must be the same length.) Ask students to draw irregular pentagons, hexagons, septagons, octagons, and nonagons.

► LITERATURE

Suggested Books

I Read Symbols
written and photographed by Tana Hoban.
William Morrow & Co., 1988. ISBN 0688023320
This is a wordless picture book of common road signs and the symbols on them. Twenty-seven different signs with symbols appear on a page each; the last two pages show each of the signs with its appropriate English-language label. Some of the signs seen in the Dictionary illustration are presented in the photographs. This book is recommended for generating language about traffic signs and geometric shapes. As a follow-up activity, teachers can take students on a walk outside the school to identify other everyday signs and shapes. This book also works well with Topic 6, The Suburbs.

When a Line Bends...a Shape Begins
written by Rhonda Gowler Greene;
illustrated by James Kaczman.
Houghton Mifflin, 1997. ISBN 0359786061
In lively, rhyming text and simple drawings, the author shows how all shapes can be made from a bent line. The illustrations for this book will appeal to students of all ages. The simple rhyme scheme will help put the content words into practice. The objects named in the rhyme can be recognized in many illustrations throughout the Dictionary.

The Straight Line Wonder
written by Mem Fox; illustrated by Marc Rosenthal.
Mondo Publishing, 1997. ISBN 1572552050
"Once upon a time, there were three straight lines who were the best of friends," begins *The Straight Line Wonder*. When one line decides that he no longer wants to be straight, however, their friendship is challenged. The expressiveness of the prose and pictures makes this an ideal book for students to act out while learning the words and language. Frequent use of verbs, especially in participle forms, gives students the opportunity for extensive verb practice.

WORKBOOK: Topic 56

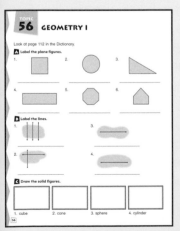

In A, students label the plane figures. In B, they label the lines. In C, they draw the solid figures.

WORKSHEET: Topic 56

In A, students unscramble the words and write them in sentences describing the number of sides for each plane figure. In B, they identify solid figures in the picture. They fill in the blanks to describe which solid figure each object is. Then, they write how many of each solid figure are found in the picture, and match the sentences.

▶ **CONTENT**

Angles, areas, and other advanced geometric functions

▶ **LANGUAGE**

Simple present: *The circumference is the distance around the outside of the circle./The diameter passes through the exact center of the circle.*

Modal *must*: *She must multiply the width by the length.*

 ## CONTENT WORDS

1. compass
2. circumference
3. diameter
4. angles
5. right angle
6. acute angle
7. obtuse angle
8. straight angle
9. intersecting lines
10. perimeter
11. area
12. height
13. length
14. width
15. base
16. edge
17. symmetrical
18. congruent figures

CONTENT READING

Geometry II

Mrs. Ling is an architect. She's designing a playhouse for her daughter.

She uses geometry to draw her plans. She must use a ruler to draw lines and a compass to draw circles. She must measure the height, length, and width of the playhouse.

Mrs. Ling's plan has many angles. The corners of the house are right angles. The roof of the house is an obtuse angle. An obtuse angle is larger than a right angle. The bottom of the roof is an acute angle. An acute angle is smaller than a right angle. The bottom of the house is a straight angle. A straight angle looks like a straight line.

Mrs. Ling wants a round window on the side of the house. She must measure the circumference and the diameter of the window. The circumference is the distance around the outside of the circle. The diameter is the longest distance across the inside of a circle. The diameter passes through the exact center of a circle.

Mrs. Ling also wants to know the size of the playhouse floor. She must find the area. The area is the total floor space inside the playhouse. She must multiply the width by the length.

Mrs. Ling wants to know the perimeter of the playhouse. The perimeter is the distance around the outside of the playhouse. Mrs. Ling must add the lengths of the four sides at the base of the playhouse. The sides of the playhouse meet at edges.

Mrs. Ling wants two windows on the front side of the playhouse. She wants the playhouse to be symmetrical, so it will look the same on the left and the right. The windows must be congruent figures. They must have the same size and shape. Mrs. Ling draws intersecting lines on each window. These lines divide each window into eight panes.

► WORDS

Components: Dictionary pages 114-115, Transparency 57, Wall Chart 57, Workbook page 57, Word and Picture Cards Topic 57, Cassette

- Present the content words. **See pages xiv-xvi for general techniques about presenting content words.**

  > **Language Note:** The word *angle* has a silent *e* and its second syllable is pronounced like *gull*. The vowel, *a*, is pronounced like the vowel in *sang*. The *gh* is silent in the words *right*, *straight*, and *height*. *Length* is pronounced in various ways. The vowel can sound like the vowel sound in *end* or *ate*. Some people say the word either with a *k* sound before the final *th* as in *lenkth* or without the *k* sound as in *lenth*. The word *width* is pronounced with the *d* sound as *width* or without it as *with*. There is no *d* sound in the word *edge*. The *g* sounds like the *g* in *gentle*.

- Have students open their Dictionaries to page 114. Ask students if they recognize any of the words or shapes on the page. Ask them to name as many of the content words in their native language(s) as they can.

- Have students look at the wall chart. Divide the class into two groups. Group 1 looks at the blueprint hanging on the wall in the picture. Group 2 looks at Mrs. Ling, the drafting board, and the model playhouse in the foreground. Each group makes a list of as many content words as they can find contained in that portion of the picture. There are multiple examples of some of the content words (*intersecting lines, height, length, acute angle*, etc.) in both sections of the wall chart. Groups, in turn, read their lists aloud and point to the example of each word in their lists. Encourage students from both groups to find as many additional examples as they can in either section.

- Divide the class into two teams. Distribute a set of picture cards to each team. Students from each team walk around the classroom looking for actual objects representing the content words. For example, the blackboard has *right angles* and the windows have *intersecting lines* on the panes. *Height, length,* and *width* dimensions exist on tables, desks, etc. Students then put the picture card with their team name on the object. Score one point for every correct picture card.

- Put a set of word cards in a pile on the front desk. Have each student select a card from the pile, read the word aloud, and draw an example of it on the board. Have the entire class review the pictures and say the words to label each picture.

WORKBOOK: Topic 57
See Teacher's Book page 229.

► CONTENT

Components: Dictionary pages 114-115, Transparency 57, Wall Chart 57, Content Reading Topic 57, Worksheet Topic 57, Cassette

- Present the content reading. **See pages xvii-xix for general techniques about presenting content readings.**

- Ask the following or similar questions:

  What is the circumference of a circle?
  What is the diameter of a circle?
  What kind of angle is the bottom of the house?
  Are the door and the window of the playhouse congruent figures?
  Is an obtuse angle smaller than or larger than a right angle?
  How does Mrs. Ling find the area of the playhouse?

► **Modal *must***

  > We use the modal *must* plus a main verb to express necessity. We use the one form *must* for both singular and plural subjects.

Point out examples of *must* in the content reading. Have students underline and read aloud all sentences with *must*. Now have each student write two true or false statements using *must* on two separate index cards. For example: *Mrs. Ling must use a compass to draw a circle. She must measure the length to find the circumference.*

Collect all the index cards. Have the students form a circle. Redistribute the index cards, making sure that no student receives his or her own two index cards. Each student, in turn, reads a sentence and other students volunteer answering them as *true* or *false*. When a student gives a correct answer, that student takes one step toward the center of the circle. The first student to reach the center of the circle is the winner.

► **Simple present.** Divide the class into two groups. Each group makes a list of ten classroom objects for the opposite group to measure and states which dimension is to be measured (height, length, or width). For example: *Measure the length of the table. Measure the width of the bookshelf. Measure the height of a chair.* The groups finish their measurements and then ask and answer questions using the simple present of *BE* or any other verbs. For example, a student from Group 1 might ask, *What is the height of the table?* A student from Group 2 could answer *It is 32 inches.* If either group thinks a measurement is not accurate, they can challenge the other group to prove it. You may want to take this opportunity to introduce the words *high, long,* and *wide.*

WORKSHEET: Topic 57
See Teacher's Book page 229.

► CHANTS

Components: Dictionary pages 114-115, Content Chant Topic 57, Cassette

 CONTENT CHANT

Right Angle, Straight Angle

Right angle
Straight angle
Intersecting lines

Compass
Diameter
Intersecting lines

Circumference
Symmetrical
Intersecting lines

Compass
Diameter
Intersecting lines

Height, width, length *
Intersecting lines

Height, width, length *
Intersecting lines

How high is it?
    It's very high.
How long is it?
    It's very long.
How wide is it?
    It's very wide.

Intersecting lines *

- Present the content chant. **See pages xx-xxi for general techniques about presenting chants.**

- Before distributing the chant, have students practice with small chunks of language from the chant. Have all students practice the words *intersecting lines* until they are comfortable with them. Then divide the class into three groups. Each group chants one of the following words: *diameter, circumference*, or *symmetrical*. Then the entire class chants *intersecting lines*.

- Now distribute Content Chant 57. Select individual students to chant and draw the content words in this chant, except for *intersecting lines*. Have the individual students hold up their drawings as they chant their words. The entire class chants the words *intersecting lines* whenever they occur. Select two students to chant the three question and response lines beginning with *How high is it?* Everyone chants the last *Intersecting lines* with a rousing shout and clap.

- Encourage other students to substitute additional content words (and hold up their drawings) in the first six stanzas, while the entire class repeats the refrain *intersecting lines*. For example: *Obtuse angle. Edge. Intersecting lines.*

► EXTENSION

Components: Dictionary pages 114-115, Transparency 57, Wall Chart 57

- Prepare a variety of pairs of figures, congruent and non-congruent, out of construction paper. Among your figures should be two congruent triangles, two congruent circles, two congruent squares or rectangles, several noncongruent triangles, rectangles, and circles, and some other irregular polygons. Display the figures randomly. Point to any two figures and ask students whether the figures are congruent. Continue pointing to figures until students recognize the congruent figures. Make sure the congruent figures aren't so close to each other that the point of the activity becomes obvious.

- Have students use only a compass and a ruler to draw a picture with geometric shapes. Encourage students to use the geometric shapes and figures they learned in this topic and in Topic 56. Students' drawings can be concrete or abstract. Encourage students to use their imaginations. Have students share their drawings and discuss.

- Set up a movie screen and overhead projector. Show students how to make shadow figures. Pair students. Have them use their fingers and hands to create as many different shadow angles as they can. Ask the class to identify the angles each pair makes.

- Have students practice measuring the areas and perimeters of various rectangular objects in your classroom such as desks or tables. Have them also measure the area and perimeter of the entire room and make a scale drawing of the room on graph paper, using one square on the graph paper to equal one foot. Have students cut out scale model desks and other objects and place them on the scale drawing. Encourage class discussion of the process.

- Take a large coffee can or other round object and trace the perimeter on the board or a piece of paper. Tell students you want to know the circumference of this circle. Demonstrate how to measure the circumference using a piece of string. Take a piece of string and arrange it around the same circle. Hold your fingers where the two ends meet. Then unwind the string and hold it against a ruler to measure the circumference. Then discuss another way. The formula for measuring the circumference of a circle is equal to the diameter times a constant called *pi* (π). Pi (pronounced PIE) is equal to approximately 3.14. The diameter is the longest distance across a circle. Have students measure from one end of the circle to the other until they find the longest distance. They now multiply that distance by 3.14. The answer should be similar to the one you found by unwrapping the string. Have students practice measuring the circumference of other circles found in your classroom (such as the bottoms of cups, soda cans, bottle caps, etc.) using both methods and compare the results.

► LITERATURE

Suggested Books

Not Enough Room
written by Joanne Rocklin and Marilyn Burns; illustrated by Cristina Ong.
Cartwheel Books, 1998. ISBN 0590399624
Two sisters are faced with the problem of equally dividing the room they are forced to share. How do they do it? Mathematically, of course! The two sisters divide their room into triangles, squares, and rectangles in an effort to partition the space fairly. Like Topics 56 and 57 in the Dictionary, this book shows geometry applied to a practical situation. The end of the book contains a section of math activities and riddles about geometry words. Young intermediate students will be challenged. For beginners, guided reading will help reinforce the words and concepts.

How a House Is Built
written and illustrated by Gail Gibbons.
Holiday House, 1996. ISBN 0823412326
What happens after the blueprint for a house (like the one seen in the Dictionary illustration) is completed? Gail Gibbons' book finishes the story by showing exactly how a house is built, from plan to finished home. This practical information is conveyed in the simple present tense and passive voice. Numerous, detailed illustrations help explain the text. The content words can be demonstrated in this book as it is read aloud. This book can also be used effectively with Topic 3, The House, and Topic 9, People at Work.

The Greedy Triangle
written by Marilyn Burns; illustrated by Gordon Silveria.
Scholastic Inc., 1994. ISBN 0590489917
This fun book recounts the adventures of a triangle who gets bored with being a triangle and decides to have an angle added to his frame. This doesn't satisfy the triangle, however, and he wants to add more and more angles. In the end, his desire to be something other than what he is has unforseen consequences. This book's eye-catching illustrations and easy-to-follow story make it perfect for reading aloud. As it is read aloud, teachers can pause to let the students identify the content words that they see in the illustrations. Students can also point to or trace the shapes as they pronounce the words. At the end of the book is a teacher's section with additional math-related activities. This book can also be used with Topic 55, Exploring Math.

WORKBOOK: Topic 57

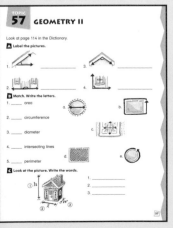

In A, students label the types of angles in parts of the house. In B, they match the words with the pictures. In C, they write the words for the dimensions represented in the picture.

WORKSHEET: Topic 57

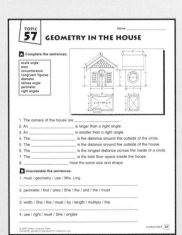

In A, students choose words from the word box to fill in the blanks, based on information from the content reading. In B, they unscramble the sentences using *must*.

▶ **CONTENT**
....
U.S. customary system and the
metric system

▶ **LANGUAGE**
....
***There + BE (there is/there's/
there are):*** *There are 100
centimeters in a meter.*

Simple present: *A thick
pencil is about a centimeter
wide./The metric system
measures length in meters.*

CONTENT WORDS

1. centimeter
2. meter
3. inch
4. foot
5. weight
6. gram
7. kilogram
8. ounce
9. pound
10. ton
11. mile
12. teaspoon
13. tablespoon
14. cup
15. liter
16. pint
17. quart
18. gallon

CONTENT READING

Measurement

Almost every country in the world uses the metric system of measurement. But the United States uses the metric system and the U.S. customary system.

The metric system measures length in meters. A meter is about the length of a baseball bat. There are 100 centimeters in a meter. A thick pencil is about a centimeter wide. There are 1,000 meters in a kilometer. A kilometer is about 10 football fields.

The U.S. customary system measures length in inches, feet, yards, and miles. There are 12 inches in a foot and there are three feet in a yard. An inch is about two and a half centimeters. A football is about a foot long. There are 5,280 feet (or 1,760 yards) in a mile. A mile is about 17 football fields. A yard is a little smaller than a meter.

The metric system measures weight in grams. A kilogram is 1,000 grams. The U.S. customary

system measures weight in ounces and pounds. A pound is 16 ounces. A kilogram is about two pounds. A ton is 2,000 pounds. Most small cars weigh about a ton.

The metric system measures volume in liters. The U.S. customary system uses cups, pints, quarts, and gallons. There are two cups in a pint and there are two pints in a quart. There are four quarts in a gallon. A quart and a liter are about the same.

The metric system uses milliliters for small volumes. There are 1,000 milliliters in a liter. The U.S. customary system uses teaspoons and tablespoons for small volumes. There are three teaspoons in a tablespoon and there are 16 tablespoons in one cup. A teaspoon is about five milliliters.

▶ WORDS

Components: Dictionary pages 116-117, Transparency 58, Wall Chart 58, Workbook page 58, Word and Picture Cards Topic 58, Cassette

- Present the content words. **See pages xiv-xvi for general techniques about presenting content words.**

  Language Note: The chart below illustrates the abbreviations used for all the content words. They are identical for singular and plural. We use periods with abbreviations in the U.S. customary system, but not in the metric system.

centimeter	c	foot	ft.	ounce	oz.	mile	mi.
kilogram	kg	quart	qt.	meter	m	pound	lb.
teaspoon	tsp.	liter	l	gallon	gal.	inch	in.
tablespoon	tbsp.	ton	tn.	cup	c.	gram	g
pint	pt.						

- Have students open their Dictionaries to page 116. Ask them if they know any of the words in their native language(s). Explain that items 1-4 and 11 describe *length or distance*. Items 6-10 describe *weight* (how heavy something is). Items 12-18 describe *volume* (the amount of liquid that can be put in a container).

- Draw three columns labeled *Length or Distance*, *Weight*, and *Volume*. Put the word and picture cards in two stacks. Students select a card from each stack, pronounce the word, and place their cards in the appropriate columns on the chart. Keep this chart for the activities below.

- Divide the class into two teams. Each team writes a list of items and classifies them as to whether we measure them by *length or distance*, *weight*, or *volume*. For example, a street is measured by *length or distance*. Meat is measured by *weight*. Juice is measured by *volume*. Groups write their words in the appropriate column on the chart.

- Explain to students that in the United States we use two systems of measurement: the U.S. customary system and the metric system. (The rest of the world uses only the metric system.) Show students a ruler with both centimeters and inches. Point out that the metric system uses centimeters and the U.S. customary system uses inches. Have students look at the chart from the above activity. Now draw an additional column as in the example chart below and ask students to guess which word and picture cards belong in each system. Students rearrange the cards in each column so that they are in the appropriate rows.

Systems of Measurement	Length or Distance	Weight	Volume
U.S. Customary	inch foot	ounce pound	pint quart
Metric	centimeter meter	gram kilogram	liter

WORKBOOK: Topic 58
See Teacher's Book page 233.

▶ CONTENT

Components: Dictionary pages 116-117, Transparency 58, Wall Chart 58, Content Reading Topic 58, Worksheet Topic 58, Cassette

- Present the content reading. **See pages xvii-xix for general techniques about presenting content readings.**

- Ask the following or similar questions:

  How does the metric system measure length? weight? volume?
  How does the U.S. customary system measure length? weight? volume?
  How many centimeters are there in a meter?
  How much do most cars weigh?
  Is a yard bigger than or smaller than a meter?

▶ ***There + BE (there is/there's/there are).*** Point out examples of *there are* in the content reading. (There are no instances of *there is* in this content reading, and there are no examples of the contracted form *there's*, which is used more in conversation than in formal writing.) Have students underline all instances of *there are* and read aloud the sentences in which they appear. Divide the class into two teams. Each team writes 10 questions about the content using *are there*. For example: *How many inches are there in a foot? How many cups are there in a pint*? The teams exchange their questions and each team writes their answers to the other team's questions using *there are*. For example: *There are twelve inches in a foot. There are two cups in a pint.* Have each team read aloud the questions and their answers. Score one point for each correct answer.

▶ **Simple present.** Distribute rulers that can measure both inches and centimeters. Have students brainstorm a list of twenty objects in the classroom that can be measured by length. Divide the class into two groups. One group measures each of the items in *inches*. The other group measures each of the items in *centimeters*. Then, students from each group, in turn, give the results of their measurements using the simple present of the verb *BE* or of other verbs. For example: *The book is 8 inches long* or *The book measures 20 centimeters*. If either group thinks a measurement is not accurate, they can challenge the other group to prove it.

- Have students look at the wall chart. Divide the class into two groups. Each group writes a story describing everything that is happening in the picture using as many references to the units of measurement as they can. Encourage students to use their imaginations and expand on what they see. Each group then does a dramatic reading of their stories.

WORKSHEET: Topic 58
See Teacher's Book page 233.

► CHANTS

Components: Dictionary pages 116-117, Content Chant Topic 58, Cassette

 ## CONTENT CHANT

Sixteen Ounces, One Pound

Sixteen ounces
    One pound
Two thousand pounds
    One ton

How many pounds?
    Two thousand pounds.

Hey! *
That's heavy! *

Two pints of milk
    One quart
Four quarts of milk
    One gallon

How much milk?
    One gallon.

My, my! *
That's a lot of milk!

- Present the content chant. **See pages xx-xxi for general techniques about presenting chants.**

- Before distributing the chant, have students practice with small chunks of the language from the chant. Divide the class into four groups. Group 1 chants *Sixteen ounces, one pound.* Group 2 chants *two thousand pounds, one ton.* Group 3 chants *two pints of milk, one quart.* Group 4 chants *four quarts of milk, one gallon.* Groups chant repeatedly, first in turn, and then simultaneously. Have the groups start slowly and softly and then increase their speed and volume.

- Now distribute Content Chant 58. Divide the class into two groups. Group 1 chants all of the unindented lines. Group 2 chants the indented lines. Have students say the lines, *Hey!* * *That's heavy!* and *My, my!* * *That's a lot of milk!* with exaggerated expression.

- Have individual students take turns doing the chant in pairs in the same style as the groups. Encourage students to rewrite the chant using other units of measurement.

► EXTENSION

Components: Dictionary pages 116-117, Transparency 58, Wall Chart 58

- Talk to students about distances. To give students an idea of what a mile is, talk about some places that are about a mile away from the school. Ask students if they can walk a mile or ride their bikes one mile. Ask students how far they live from the school and how they get to school in the morning. Encourage class discussion.

- Explain to students how to convert inches and centimeters. One inch is equal to approximately 2.54 centimeters. To convert *inches* to *centimeters*, multiply by 2.54. To convert *centimeters* to *inches,* divide by 2.54 (or multiply by 0.39). Now divide the class into two teams. Students from each team, in turn, give a number (between 1 and 100) of either inches or centimeters. For example: *13 inches.* Students from the opposite team give the corresponding number of centimeters equal to 13 inches. In this case, they would multiply 13 by 2.54 and say *33.02 centimeters.* (Students can use calculators if desired.) Teams reverse roles. Continue the game until all students have had a chance to participate.

- Measure students' height. On a very large piece of chart paper, mark off half-inch increments, starting with 30 inches and ending with 72 inches. Write the whole numbers next to each inch mark (*30, 31, 32, 33,* etc.). Tape the bottom of the chart paper to a spot exactly 30 inches off the ground on an accessible wall. Measure each student's height and make a mark on the piece of chart paper and write the student's name next to each mark. When all students have been measured, have students check their marks against the numbered increments on the chart paper to find their height in inches. Then have students convert their height in inches to their height in centimeters.

- Have students plan to make a five-foot long hero sandwich and calculate the various amounts of ingredients (cheese, meat, onions, etc.) as well as the length of the bread necessary for such an enormous sandwich. If possible, suggest that students actually make such a sandwich and sell it to raise money for a local charity or school project.

- Have a class debate on the use of the metric system versus the U.S. customary system for all units of measurement. Ask students to form three groups: two debating teams (one for each system) and one group to judge the effectiveness of each debating team. Both teams list five reasons why their measurement system is easier, better, or more efficient. Encourage students to ask questions and interact. The judges decide which team has given more persuasive arguments. After the debate, encourage all students to express their feelings about which system they prefer.

▶ LITERATURE

Suggested Books

The Story of Weights and Measures
by Anita Ganeri.
Oxford University Press, 1997. ISBN 019513289
The Story of Weights and Measures presents an overview of systems of measurement from early times to the present day. The book's unit on "Measurement in Action" is particularly useful for applying the abstract concepts in this topic to everyday situations. The many illustrations are helpful in extending the topic's vocabulary and activities.

Over in the Meadow
illustrated by Ezra Jack Keats.
Scholastic Trade, 1991. ISBN 059044848X
This modern classic by Ezra Jack Keats illustrates a traditional Appalachian counting rhyme about animals in the meadow. The rhyme helps students learn grammatical patterns using prepositional phrases as they practice counting from one to ten. The colorful cut-paper collages make this book as attractive as it is useful. Its rhyming text makes this book especially good for reading aloud. This book also works well with Topic 55, Exploring Math.

Measuring Penny
written and illustrated by Loreen Leedy.
Henry Holt and Company, 1997. ISBN 0805053601
At some point, all ESL students need to learn the basic system of measurement used in American classrooms. *Measuring Penny* is a likeable introduction to this basic information. In the story, a girl named Lisa uses her dog Penny as the subject of her class project on measurement. As Penny gets measured, concepts of height, length, weight, and temperature are all addressed. Students should have little difficulty isolating the content words in the clearly-captioned illustrations. As a follow-up, teachers can assign an activity similar to Lisa's in which students use their own pets.

WORKBOOK: Topic 58

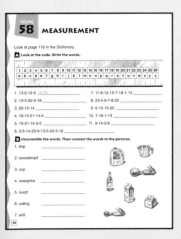

Activity A has a code. Each letter of the alphabet is represented by a number. Eleven content words are given in code. Students look up the letter for each number to write the words. In activity B, students unscramble more content words.

WORKSHEET: Topic 58

In A, students sort words for length, weight, and volume in the two systems of measurement by circling them in three different colors. In B, they fill in the blanks with these words. (For each blank, there are several possible answers.) In C, they use *there are* to describe various measurements, based on the content reading.

59 NUMBER PATTERNS, FUNCTIONS, AND RELATIONS

▶ **CONTENT**

....

Number patterns, tables, and graphs

▶ **LANGUAGE**

....

Adjective clauses with *that*:
Graphs are pictures that compare numbers.

CONTENT WORDS

1. graphs
2. x-axis
3. y-axis
4. coordinates
5. coordinate plane
6. ascending order
7. descending order
8. random order
9. Venn diagram
10. table
11. chart
12. sequence
13. finite set
14. infinite set

CONTENT READING

Number Patterns, Functions, and Relations

Coach Watson's class uses graphs, diagrams, and tables to show information. Graphs are pictures that compare numbers. Graphs have coordinates. Coordinates are points on a coordinate plane. The x-axis is the line that goes from left to right. The y-axis is the line that goes from bottom to top. Every point on the graph has an x-coordinate and a y-coordinate. The bottom left corner of a graph has an x-coordinate of 0 and a y-coordinate of 0.

There are two graphs on the wall above the chalkboard. The first graph shows the favorite sports of the students in the classroom. The second graph shows the weights of four people in descending order. The heaviest person is first and the lightest person is last. The paper that is on the chalkboard shows the heights of those four people in ascending order. The shortest person is first and the tallest person is last.

Diagrams are pictures that show groups of numbers or other information. In the Venn diagram on the board, boys are in one group and girls are in another group. A third group has both boys and girls. The third group is the area that is between the two circles.

Some groups of numbers are infinite. "All even numbers" is an infinite set. It continues forever. Some groups of numbers are finite. "Whole numbers between 10 and 20" is a finite set. There are only nine whole numbers between 10 and 20.

Tables show lists of numbers. People use tables to compare many different kinds of numbers. Ken charts the heights and weights of four people in a table. The table is in random order. The information is not in any special order or sequence.

▶ WORDS

Components: Dictionary pages 118-119, Transparency 59, Wall Chart 59, Workbook page 59, Word and Picture Cards Topic 59, Cassette

- Present the content words. **See pages xiv-xvi for general techniques about presenting content words**

  Content Note: It is customary to express the location of a point on a graph in terms of where its x- and y-coordinates meet. The coordinates are expressed in parentheses with a comma between the values: (value of x axis, value of y axis). For example: *(8, 28)*. In the Dictionary illustration, the line graph illustrates a point of (2,89), showing that the x-axis is 2 and the y-axis is 89.

  Language Note: The word *chart* (item 11) illustrates the verb. The noun *chart* (not listed) could refer to a *table* or a *graph*. We use the word *table* to refer to illustrated data in rows and columns. The letters preceding the hyphen in *x-axis* and *y-axis* are pronounced like the names of the letters *x* and *y*, not like their sounds. *Finite* has the stress on the first syllable (FI-nite) and the letter *i* in both syllables is pronounced like the vowel sound in *my*. *Infinite* has the stress on its first syllable (IN-fi-nite) and the sound of the first and last *i* is pronounced like the vowel sound in *it*. *Coordinates* has the stress on the second syllable (co-OR-di-nates). The first written *o* is pronounced like the vowel sound in *coat*. The second written *o* sounds like the vowel in *or*.

- Divide the class into two groups. Distribute a set of word cards and picture cards to each group and place a large piece of chart paper on the board. Groups, in turn, read a word card aloud and the opposite group produces the matching picture card for that word card. The students put the matched set on the chart paper.

- Pair students. Give each pair a set of word and picture cards. The first student arranges the cards in *ascending order*, from Card 1 to Card 14, and then returns the cards to *random order*. The second student arranges the cards in *descending order*, from Card 14 to Card 1, and then rearranges the cards in *random order* again. After students have done this a few times, have a contest to see which pair of students can do this the fastest.

- Divide the class into two teams. Each team makes a set of number cards from 1-30. Each team in turn, asks the other team to arrange their numbers in a particular order (*ascending, descending, random*) or *sequence* (by 2's, 3's or 5's). Score one point for each correct response.

WORKBOOK: Topic 59
See Teacher's Book page 237.

▶ CONTENT

Components: Dictionary pages 118-119, Transparency 59, Wall Chart 59, Content Reading Topic 59, Worksheet Topic 59, Cassette

- Present the content reading. **See pages xvii-xix for general techniques about presenting content readings.**

- Ask the following or similar questions:

  Which axis goes from bottom to top?
  Which graph shows weight in descending order?
  Do people use tables to compare numbers?
  What are graphs?
  What are coordinates?
  Is "3, 4, and 5" a finite or infinite set?

- ▶ **Adjective clauses with *that***

  We use adjective clauses to describe nouns. An adjective clause can begin with a relative pronoun (*that*). An adjective clause contains a verb and follows the noun it describes. For example: *Graphs are pictures that compare numbers.*

  Point out examples of sentences with adjective clauses in the content reading. Have students underline the adjective clauses and circle the nouns they describe. For example: *Graphs are (pictures) that compare numbers.* Ask students to read these sentences aloud. Select five students to copy one sentence each from the content reading onto cardboard cards. Cut these cards into sentence strips after the noun, separating the main clause (*Graphs are pictures*) from the adjective clause (*that compare numbers*). Have students mix up all of the strips. Then invite individual students to put these sentences back together.

- ▶ **Adjective clauses with *that*.** Have students write sentences with *that* clauses. Divide the class into two groups. Each group writes five main clauses ending with a noun. For example, Group 1 might write *A Venn diagram has three circles* or *Baseball is a game*. The groups exchange their five main clauses and add on the adjective clauses to the other group's sentences. For example, Group 2 might write *A Venn diagram has three circles that intersect* or *Baseball is a game that everyone loves*. Groups reverse roles and read their final sentences aloud.

- Note that Anna's weight is not shown on the weight graph. Her weight is greater than 60, but less than 71. Encourage the class to look at the weight chart and approximate Anna's weight.

- Divide the class into two groups. Groups either role play or tell a story about what is happening in the wall chart. Encourage students to use their imaginations.

WORKSHEET: Topic 59
See Teacher's Book page 237.

►CHANTS

Components: Dictionary pages 118-119, Content Chant Topic 59, Cassette

 CONTENT CHANT

Ascending Order, Going Up

Ascending order
Going up
Gaining weight
Getting taller

Descending order
Coming down
Losing weight
Getting smaller

Look at the chart.
Study the chart.
Ken's getting taller every day.

Look at the table.
Study the table.
Anna's getting thinner every day.

- Present the content chant. **See pages xx-xxi for general techniques about presenting chants.**

- Before distributing the chant, have students practice with small chunks of the language from the chant. Divide the class into two groups. Group 1 chants *ascending order* and Group 2 chants *descending order.* When the groups are comfortable with these lines, add the next chunk. Group 1 chants *Ken's getting taller every day.* Group 2 chants *Anna's getting thinner every day.* Then have each group combine their two lines.

- Now distribute Content Chant 59. Divide the class into two groups. Group 1 chants the first and third stanzas. As they chant, they pantomime "going up," or getting taller (they can start off in a crouched or bent position and slowly unfold to full height). Group 2 chants the second and fourth stanzas as they pantomime descending order.

- Encourage students to substitute fellow students' names and other comparatives in the line *Ken's getting taller every day.* For example: *Abdulla's getting happier every day. Keiko's getting smarter every day.*

►EXTENSION

Components: Dictionary pages 118-119, Transparency 59, Wall Chart 59

- Talk to students about ascending and descending order. Give them some examples of ordered numbers, such as the pages in a book, the floors in a building, or a top ten list. Ask students if the numbers in these examples are in ascending or descending order. Discuss. Then, ask students to talk about some other kinds of orders, such as alphabetical order, chronological order, order of importance, and random order. Ask students how they order their music collections, their clothes, or their toys. Encourage class discussion.

- Divide the class into groups. Each group discusses their favorite sports, days of the week, months of the year, colors, or some other topic that has a limited number of answers. Each group creates a bar graph to reflect their data and presents it to the class. Encourage class discussion.

- Bring in a yardstick and a bathroom scale. Have students measure their heights and weights and construct various graphs and charts to display their data. Have them compare their charts and their data with those on the wall chart. Note: Adjust this activity if you have height or weight sensitive students.

- Although the heights shown in the wall chart are given in inches, we generally express height in feet and inches. For example, if a person is 70 inches tall, we say that the person is *five feet ten inches,* or *five feet ten.* Generally, in conversation, we say *five-ten* and we write it as *5'10".* To convert a height in inches to feet, we count the number of full feet (12 inches) and then add the remaining number of inches. For example, in 70 inches, there are 5 full feet (60 inches) + 10 more inches, so the person is 5'10". Somebody 75 inches tall is 6 full feet (72 inches) + three inches, or 6'3". Have students convert the heights of the students on the wall chart to feet and inches, and then make a diagram showing these heights, expressed in ['] and ["] in ascending order. Now have students make a diagram of their own heights in ascending order.

- Have students bring to class various examples of tables, bar graphs, line graphs, Venn diagrams, or pie charts from magazines, newspapers, or the Internet. Students present their graphics to the class and try to explain what the graphic is illustrating. Encourage students to ask and answer questions about the different data displays. Encourage discussion about students' preferences for certain types of graphics.

► LITERATURE

Suggested Books

How Much Is a Million?
written by David Schwartz; illustrated by Steven Kellogg.
William Morrow & Co., 1985. ISBN 0688040497
The concept of large numbers is presented in a fresh way in this popular book. Detailed, exaggerated illustrations visually impress upon students just how large numbers can get. The simple text corresponds to each picture so that students can relate the numbers to the associated vocabulary. Interrogatives, comparatives, and *if* clauses are the chief grammar points highlighted by the text. This book can be used in conjunction with its sequel, *If You Made a Million* (see Topic 55, Exploring Math), for extended practice with numbers.

Math Curse
written by Jon Scieszka; illustrated by Lane Smith.
Viking Children's Books, 1997. ISBN 0670861944
What is a math curse? For the girl in this story, it's the realization that anything and everything can be made into a math problem. As her day progresses, the math problems she encounters and creates become more and more complex, and more and more absurd. Students will love this wacky story about math anxiety pushed to the limit. The design may make the book challenging reading for beginners, but with teacher guidance, students should become accustomed to the unusual text placement. The text itself will give students practice in recognizing word problem structure and decoding colloquial language. *Math Curse* is an excellent combination of narrative and mathematical concepts.

A Remainder of One
written by Elinor J. Pinczen;
illustrated by Bonnie MacKain.
Houghton Mifflin, 1995. ISBN 0395694558
Joe the soldier bug has a problem: no matter how he tries, he can't seem to avoid being the "odd bug out" when his squadron is on the march. Joe struggles to figure out the correct way to divide the ranks so that he fits in evenly. This struggle is the basis of *A Remainder of One*, an entertaining story about the rewards of problem-solving. Colorful, woodcut-like illustrations show students the problems visually while the rhyming text tells the story. For an extension activity, students can reconstruct the book's number problems with pennies, or teachers can have students play the army bugs and act out the problems.

The Story of Numbers and Counting
written by Anita Ganeri.
Oxford University Press, 1996. ISBN 0195212584
Many ESL students may already be on grade level in math. They may only need to acquire English proficiency in order to solve word problems. This book takes students beyond mathematical symbols and gives them math vocabulary. *The Story of Numbers and Counting* presents an overview of counting systems, mathematics, and counting machines. Small sections of the collage-like layout can be isolated and discussed with students in relation to the Dictionary illustration.

WORKBOOK: Topic 59

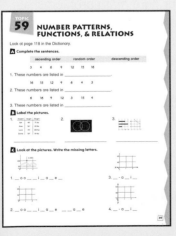

In A, students determine whether the sets of numbers are in ascending, descending, or random order. In B, they label the pictures of graphs, diagrams, and charts. In C, they write the missing letters in each of the content words.

WORKSHEET: Topic 59

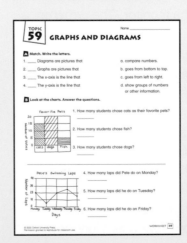

In A, students match to complete the sentences that contain *that*. In B, they answer questions based on each of the charts.

CONTENT WORDS

▶ **CONTENT**
....
Components of computers and calculators

▶ **LANGUAGE**
....
Imperatives: *Sit in front of the computer./Let's try it.*

Modal *can*: *You can also use the arrow keys on the keyboard.*

Expressions: *upside down*

1. personal computer (PC)
2. monitor
3. cursor
4. keyboard
5. mouse
6. disk drive
7. diskette
8. compact disc (CD)
9. switch
10. cable
11. power supply
12. display
13. operations keys
14. equals key
15. unit key
16. fraction bar
17. percent key
18. clear key
19. decimal point key
20. memory recall

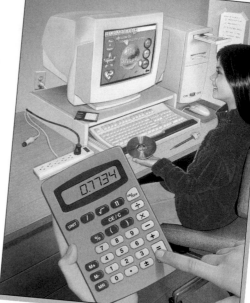

CONTENT READING

Computers and Calculators

Personal computers (or PCs) and calculators are machines. They make life easier for people. You can write a book, play games, or find information on a computer. Let's try it.

Sit in front of the computer. Turn on the power supply. A cable connects the power supply to the computer. Then, turn the on-off switch to "ON." You should see an arrow on the monitor. The arrow on the monitor is the cursor.

Move the cursor with the mouse. You can also use the arrow keys on the keyboard. The mouse and the arrow keys control the cursor. Type some words using the keyboard.

Compact discs (or CDs) and diskettes store information. Look at the disk drive. Is there a diskette in the drive? Push the button under the CD drive. Is there a CD in the drive? Is it a game? Play the game.

You can add, subtract, multiply, and divide on a calculator. Calculators have four operations keys.

They also have an equals key, a fraction bar key, a decimal point key, a percent key, and a clear key. Some calculators have a unit key. It displays the whole number portion of a mixed number. Some calculators also have memory. It is used to store a number. The memory recall key displays the number stored in the memory.

You can use a calculator for hard math problems. Enter the numbers. Then, use the operations keys. Press the equals key and look at the display. The answer will be there. Try it. Let's divide 15.468 by 20. First, press the clear key. You should see a 0 in the display. Now, enter the number 15.468. Don't forget the decimal point key. Now, hit the division key (÷). It's one of the operations keys. Now, enter the number 20 and press the equals key. The answer is in the display. It's 0.7734.

Now, turn the calculator upside down and read the display. What does it say?

►WORDS

Components: Dictionary pages 120-121, Transparency 60, Wall Chart 60, Workbook page 60, Word and Picture Cards Topic 60, Cassette

- Present the content words. **See pages xiv-xvi for general techniques about presenting content words.**

  > **Language Note:** A computer *diskette* is often called a *disk*. The word *disk* can be spelled as *disk* or *disc*. Some people also call it a *floppy disk* or a *floppy* (originally, the diskette was actually floppy).

  > **Content Note:** You may want to point out to students that a computer CD is similar to a music CD. Computer CDs contain information that a computer reads and turns into text and/or pictures. Music CDs contain information that a CD player reads and turns into music.

- If you have a computer and/or a calculator in your classroom, have students sit around them. Distribute one word and picture card to each student. Have each student read his or her card aloud and then point to the corresponding place on the actual computer or calculator in your classroom.

- Display all the picture cards and all but one word card for content words referring to the computer. Have students refer to Dictionary page 120 to find the missing word. Repeat this procedure with the calculator, but omit two word cards. Continue the procedure, omitting more and more word cards each time. Each time, challenge students to find the missing words.

- Divide the class into two teams. Make two rows on the board. Write the abbreviations or symbols listed below in the first row. Ask students to copy the abbreviations or symbols in the first row and write the words which they stand for in the second row. (They are the words in callouts 1, 8, and 13-20.) The team which has the most accurate responses in five minutes is the winner.

PC	CD	−/+/×/÷/	=	UNIT	/	%	CE/C	.	MR

- Mix a set of picture cards and word cards and place them face down on a table. Have students stand around the table and take turns selecting two cards each, turning them over, and pronouncing them. Have the student explain how the two cards are related. For example: *A mouse and a keyboard are both used with a computer.* If the student's answer is correct, that student keeps the cards. The student with the most cards at the end of the game is the winner.

WORKBOOK: Topic 60
See Teacher's Book page 241.

►CONTENT

Components: Dictionary pages 120-121, Transparency 60, Wall Chart 60, Content Reading Topic 60, Worksheet Topic 60, Cassette

- Present the content reading. **See pages xvii-xix for general techniques about presenting content readings.**

- Ask the following or similar questions:

  What connects the computer and the monitor?
  Name two things that move the cursor.
  Where do you put the diskette?
  What does the memory recall key do?
  What is this key? $\boxed{=}$
  What are the four operations keys?

► **Imperatives**

  > We use imperative sentences to give directions, orders, and advice. Imperative sentences use the simple form of the verb. There is no expressed subject. (The subject *you* is understood.) For example: *Open the door.* We can use imperative sentences for polite requests by adding *please*: *Please open the door.* We can also use imperative sentences with *Let's* to make suggestions which include the speaker: *Let's go to the movies.*

  Point out examples of imperatives in the content reading. Ask students to underline all the imperative sentences and circle the verbs in those sentences. For example: *Let's (try) it* and *(Sit) in front of your computer.* Divide the class into two teams. Each team makes index cards for each of the verbs they just circled in the content reading. (There should be a total of 14 different verbs, including the two-word verbs *turn on* and *look at*). Students on each team draw a card and make up a new imperative sentence using the verb on their card. For example, if a student draws the card *sit,* he or she gives a command to a student on the opposing team using *sit* (*Sit on the table*). Students on each team follow the commands of the opposite team. Score one point each for the correct imperative sentence and one point for each correct execution of the command.

► **Modal *can.*** Explain to students that the modal *can* is used to suggest ability or possibility. It is used for *possibility* in the content reading. Have students underline and read aloud all examples of *can* in the content reading. Divide the class into two groups. Each group writes ten sentences using *can* about computers or calculators. For example: *You can use a computer for research. You can use a calculator to figure out percentages.* Groups exchange lists and check each other's work for accuracy.

WORKSHEET: Topic 60
See Teacher's Book page 241.

►CHANTS

Components: Dictionary pages 120-121, Content Chant Topic 60, Cassette

 ## CONTENT CHANT

PC Chant

Cursor, keyboard
monitor, mouse
There's a personal computer
in my house.

Diskette, disk drive
Where's the CD?
My personal computer
is looking for me.

Cursor, keyboard
monitor, mouse
I like that PC
in my house.

It's user-friendly
if you try,
but don't forget to switch on
the power supply.

- Present the content chant. **See pages xx-xxi for general techniques about presenting chants.**

- This chant can be said as a poem. There are some unusually long sentences which can be broken up into smaller chunks from the ends of the sentences so students can maintain the rhythm and intonation more easily. Divide the class into groups. Groups practice with each of the following separate lines:

  There's a personal computer in my house.
  My personal computer is looking for me.
  It's user-friendly if you try,
  but don't forget to switch on the power supply.

  Groups switch lines when they are comfortable with those they have practiced. Any of the four lines above can be broken up into smaller chunks, as in the example below. Students practice with each chunk separately and then hook it on to the previous chunk. For example:

  the power supply / to switch on / to switch on the power supply / but don't forget / but don't forget to switch on the power supply.

- Now distribute Content Chant 60. Explain that *user-friendly* means something is easy to use. Divide class into two groups. Group 1 chants the first two lines of each stanza. Group 2 chants the last two lines of each stanza.

►EXTENSION

Components: Dictionary pages 120-121, Transparency 60, Wall Chart 60

- Discuss with students how technology influences our daily lives. Record their ideas on the board. Have students take a class survey. Ask them what each of them thinks is the most important product of technology (examples: the computer, the electric light, the telephone, television, etc.). Have students chart the data. Then, ask students to write stories about what our daily lives would be like without these inventions.

- Divide the class into groups. Students research how computers have changed in the past 25 years. They write illustrated reports and present their information to the class. Ask each group to predict what they think computers will be like in the year 2050.

- Pair students. Give both students the same five addition, subtraction, multiplication, or division problems to solve. Give one student a calculator. Tell the other student to solve the problems on paper. The student with the calculator should also write his or her answers on a piece of paper. The student with the calculator will, of course, finish much more quickly. Students should compare their answers to make sure they got the correct answers. If their answers disagree, they should both do the calculations again on the calculator to find the correct answer. Then have students reverse roles and do five more math problems. Ask them to discuss their feelings about using a calculator or doing the math themselves.

- Have students practice the expression *upside down*. Hold a pencil with the point down and the eraser up. Now turn it *upside down*. Explain that the "up" side (the eraser) is now down. Turn the pencil again so that the point is facing down again. Explain that it is now *right side up*, because the right (or correct) side is up. Divide students into two teams. Students from one team hold up objects, and students from the other team say whether the object is *upside down* or *right side up*.

- If students haven't already done the simple math problem in the content reading, ask them to do it now on a calculator. When they turn the calculator upside down, they should see the computer representation of the word *hello*. Have them turn page 121 in the Dictionaries upside down and see *hello* again. Now have students do the math problems below which make other words on a calculator when it is turned upside down. Then challenge students to make their own math problems like this.

A.	B.	C.
4763 - 1256 = 3507 (lose)	2276 2 = 1138 (bell)	415 + 222 = 637 (leg)

▶ LITERATURE

Suggested Books

Cybermama: An Extraordinary Voyage to the Center of Cyberspace
written and directed by Alexandre Jardin.
DK Publishing, 1997. ISBN 0789418061
Set in the 21st Century, this futuristic tale about a group of children who enter a computer's memory through a virtual transporter is an unusual way to introduce students to the technical world of computers. The stunning graphics and progressive design may be challenging for some ESL students, but this adventurous book is worth the effort. The fantastic photographs and illustrations will encourage students to talk about technology and how it has impacted on their lives. (Recent immigrants to America may have interesting stories to share about the technological differences between their former country and America.) The graphics can be used for story starters, predicting, and generating *Wh-* questions.

Science and Technology
edited by Jill Bailey and Catherine Thompson
Oxford University Press, 1993. ISBN 0199101434
This book is the ideal starting point for clear information on computers and calculators. Designed and written in a friendly and accessible way, it will reinforce the content words that students see in the Dictionary illustration. Short selections may be chosen to isolate other content words introduced in this unit.

WORKBOOK: Topic 60

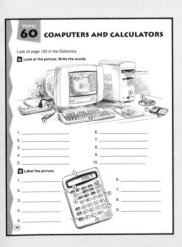

In A, students write the words for parts of the computer, as numbered in the picture. In B, they write the words to label the parts of the calculator.

WORKSHEET: Topic 60

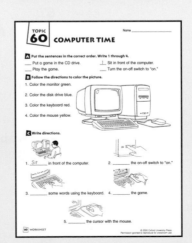

In A, students write numbers to give the order in which the directions should occur. In B, students read and follow directions for coloring parts of the computer in the picture. In C, they fill in verbs to create imperative sentences.

WORD LIST

The numbers to the right of the entries indicate the topic in which the word is introduced. Words in italics appear in a topic's title or can be found as labels or text within a topic's main illustration.

A

abdomen **41**
across **27**
actor **17**
actress **17**
acute angle **57**
Adams, John **24**
add **55**
adobe **21**
advertisement **11**
Africa **Appendix**
afternoon **Appendix**
agriculture **13**
air pollution **48**
airplane **7**
Alabama **10**
Alaska **10**
Alaska Pipeline **15**
alligator **43**
allosaurus **47**
ambulance **8**
American Samoa **10**
ammunition **27**
amoeba **39**
amphibians **43**
anatosaurus **47**
angles **57**
angry **33**
animals **35**
ankle **30**
ankylosaurus **47**
ant **41**
Antarctica **Appendix**
antennae **40**
Anthony, Susan B. **29**
apartment building **5**
apatosaurus **47**
apple **38**
Appomattox **27**
apprentice **22**
April **Appendix**
arachnids **41**
arch **21**
Arctic Ocean **Appendix**
area **57**
Arizona **10**

Arkansas **10**
arm **30**
around **26**
arrow **19**
artery **31**
ascending order **59**
Asia **Appendix**
asparagus **Appendix**
assembly line **12**
Atlantic Ocean **Appendix**
atmosphere **54**
atom **49**
attic **3**
auditorium **2**
August **62**
aunt **4**
Australia **Appendix**
avocado **38**
axle **50**

B

baby **4**
bacon **Appendix**
ballot **28**
banana **38**
bandage **8**
bank **5**
bark **36**
barn **7**
barnacles **40**
barrel **25**
Barton, Clara **29**
base **57**
baseball cap **Appendix**
basement **3**
basket **19**
basketball **6**
bass **42**
bat **46**
bathrobe **Appendix**
bathroom **3**
bathtub **3**
battle **23**
bay **22**
bayonet **23**
beak **44**

bear **46**
beautiful **16**
bed **8**
bedroom **3**
bee **41**
bell **21**
Bell, Alexander Graham **29**
belt **Appendix**
bicycle **6**
Bill of Rights **28**
bills **Appendix**
birds **44**
black **Appendix**
blacksmith **22**
blanket **8**
blizzard **54**
block **6**
blood vessels **31**
blouse **Appendix**
blue **Appendix**
bluefish **42**
boat **15**
body **30**
boil **49**
bone **31**
book **1**
boots **Appendix**
born **24**
both **59**
bottle **48**
bow **19**
boys room **2**
bracelet **Appendix**
brachiosaurus **47**
brain **31**
branch **36**
bread **Appendix**
breakfast **Appendix**
bridge **7**
bright **32**
broccoli **37**
brother **4**
brown **Appendix**
bud **36**
buffalo **14**
bulb **36**
Bull Run **27**

WORKBOOK ANSWER KEY

TOPIC 1
Exercise A
chalkboard	bulletin board
pencil sharpener	wastebasket
computer	table
desk	chair
map	overhead projector

Exercise B
cassette player	book
pencil	pen
crayon	paper
notebook	ruler

TOPIC 2
Exercise A
1. office	2. secretary
3. principal	4. library
5. librarian	6. media center
7. hall	8. boys room
9. girls room	10. custodian
11. cafeteria	12. auditorium
13. gym	14. coach
15. playground	

Exercise B
Places (circled): office, library, media center, hall, boys room, girls room, cafeteria, auditorium, gym, playground
People (underlined): secretary, principal, librarian, custodian, coach

TOPIC 3
Exercise A
1. roof	2. attic
3. bedroom	4. bathroom
5. living room	6. kitchen
7. porch	8. basement
9. window	

Exercise B
1. sink	2. toilet
3. bathtub	4. shower
5. door	

TOPIC 4
1. grandmother	2. aunt
3. sister	4. mother
5. brother	6. father
7. uncle	8. grandfather
9. grandparents	10. parents
11. cousins	12. baby

TOPIC 5
Exercise A
1. movie theater	2. traffic light
3. police station	4. post office
5. department store	6. garbage truck
7. parking garage	8. apartment building

Exercise B
1. bus	2. bank
3. restaurant	4. hotel
5. taxi	6. newsstand

TOPIC 6
1. garage	2. bicycle
3. corner	4. street
5. mailbox	6. stop sign
7. gas station	8. park
9. swimming pool	

TOPIC 7
1. barn	2. silo
3. road	4. truck
5. chicken coop	6. fence
7. pond	8. wagon
9. tractor	10. hills
11. stream	12. bridge
13. airplane	14. orchard

TOPIC 8
Exercise A
1. patient	2. paramedic
3. nurse	4. doctor

Exercise B
1. blanket	2. cast
3. crutches	4. bed
5. medicine	6. pillow
7. wheelchair	8. bandage
9. stethoscope	10. thermometer

TOPIC 9
Exercise A
1. police officer	2. computer operator
3. dental assistant	4. mail carrier
5. construction worker	

Exercise B
1. electrician	2. firefighter
3. mechanic	4. messenger
5. writer	6. plumber
7. pharmacist	8. salesperson

TOPIC 10
Exercise A
1. New Mexico	2. New Hampshire
3. New York	4. New Jersey
5. North Carolina	6. North Dakota
7. South Carolina	8. South Dakota
9. West Virginia	10. Rhode Island

Exercise B
1. Arizona	2. California
3. Georgia	4. Hawaii
5. Massachussetts	6. Nebraska
7. Pennsylvania	8. Texas
9. Utah	10. Washington

TOPIC 11
Exercise A
1. studio	2. newscaster
3. television	4. satellite
5. telephone	6. radio
7. magazine	8. advertisement
9. newspaper	10. headline

Exercise B
1. Liberty Bell	2. The White House
3. Statue of Liberty	

TOPIC 12
Exercise A
1. cotton	2. rice
3. sugarcane	4. port
5. factory	6. plantation
7. furniture	8. sugar

Exercise B
1. worker	2. thread
3. cloth	4. assembly line
5. lumber	

TOPIC 13
Exercise A

```
w r t v (d a i r y b a r n) b h k g z p c
m (f a r m h o u s e) o r e b x (c a z a x
(h) g a r a h o u a i n (s) x (h) a o b v r n
a m (p) g w q s a t h j o (t) a y m a k m p
r o l r c s d u t o m y q (y) w b t l w k
v (p l a n t) a l p t g b h o p i s x o j
e d f i j l a s v b n e k l o n a y u n
s y u n o i w q x f (c a t t l e) d d s (c)
t (n (w h e a t) r t y b (n) v z s a e p e o
r d r e s w g y h z a s b n h y s d r (r)
a (p l o w) x (g r a i n e l e v a t o r) n
```

Exercise B
1. Mount Rushmore	2. Great Plains
3. Great Lakes	

TOPIC 14
Exercise A
1. corral	2. cowgirl
3. graze	4. herd
5. cowboy	6. peak
7. buffalo	

Exercise B
1. Rocky Mountains
2. Continental Divide
3. Old Faithful
4. Yellowstone National Park

TOPIC 15
Exercise A
1. redwood	2. logging
3. sawmill	4. wood
5. cannery	6. rainfall

Exercise B
1. e	2. a
3. c	4. b
5. f	6. d

Exercise C
1. Puget Sound	2. Space Needle
3. Alaska Pipeline	

TOPIC 16
Across:
1. hydroelectric plant	2. drill
3. irrigation canal	4. electricity

Down:
5. pipeline	6. dam
7. oil	8. well
9. refinery	10. cactus
11. gasoline	12. tank

TOPIC 17
Exercise A
1. filmmaking
3. actor
5. script
7. set
2. director
4. camera
6. actress

Exercise B
1. c
3. b
5. d
2. e
4. a

TOPIC 18
1. a. longitude, b. latitude
2. a. pyramid, b. totem pole
3. a. compass rose, b. legend
4. a. money, b. silver
5. a. state, b. province
6. a. national border, b. capital

TOPIC 19
Exercise A
1. pictograph
3. tepee
5. cliff dwelling
2. wampum
4. hide
6. longhouse

Exercise B
1. d
3. a
2. b
4. c

TOPIC 20
Exercise A
1. mast
3. crew
5. oar
7. sailor
9. wave
2. cargo
4. rope
6. knot
8. prow

Exercise B
1. Ponce de León
2. Christopher Columbus
3. Leif Eriksson

TOPIC 21
Exercise A
1. g
3. h
5. b
7. f
2. c
4. a
6. d
8. e

Exercise B
1. gate
3. trading post
5. fort
7. ride
2. patio
4. pueblo
6. teach
8. adobe

TOPIC 22
Exercise A
1. blacksmith
3. meetinghouse
5. common
7. mill
2. inn
4. stockade
6. courthouse
8. harbor

TOPIC 23
Exercise A
People: redcoat, Continental soldier, Paul Revere, minutemen
Things: tomahawk, steeple, lantern, tea

Exercise B
1. cannon
3. cannonball
5. musket
2. powder horn
4. bayonet
6. rifle

TOPIC 24
Exercise A
founding fathers
Thomas Jefferson
King George III
John Adams
Benjamin Franklin
John Hancock
printing press
Independence Hall

Exercise B
Across:
1. draw 2. cartoon 3. quill
Down:
4. pamphlet 5. write 6. signature

TOPIC 25
Exercise B
1. trapper
3. journal
5. cabin
2. barrel
4. oxen
6. campsite

TOPIC 26
Exercise A
1. hammer
3. nail
5. pick
2. pan
4. shovel

Exercise B
1. prospector
3. across
5. tent
2. mule
4. around

Exercise C
1. Levi Strauss
2. Sutter's Mill

TOPIC 27
Exercise A
1. Confederacy
3. slave
5. knapsack
7. uniform
9. Yankee
2. Rebel
4. canteen
6. flag
8. Union
10. ammunition

Exercise B
1. Robert E. Lee
3. Abraham Lincoln
2. Ulysses S. Grant

TOPIC 28
Exercise A

Exercise B
1. President
2. Congress
3. Senate
4. House of Representatives
5. Supreme Court

TOPIC 29
Exercise A
Women:
Clara Barton
Eleanor Roosevelt
Harriet Tubman
Margaret Mead
Sacajawea
Helen Keller
Pocahontas
Susan B. Anthony
Men:
Alexander Graham Bell
Cesar Chavez
Frederick Douglass
George Washington
Henry Ford
Martin Luther King, Jr.
Sequoya
Thomas Edison

TOPIC 30
1. head
3. elbow
5. hand
7. toe
9. mouth
11. knee
2. nose
4. arm
6. leg
8. eye
10. neck
12. foot

TOPIC 31
1. skull
3. jaw
5. muscle
7. brain
9. stomach
11. intestine
2. bone
4. spine
6. skeleton
8. lungs
10. heart

TOPIC 32
1. a. bright, b. dark
2. a. soft, b. loud
3. a. rough, b. smooth
4. a. foul, b. fragrant
5. a. sour, b. sweet

TOPIC 33
1. hungry
3. thirsty
5. hot
7. sick
2. tired
4. sad
6. cold
8. happy

TOPIC 34
Exercise A
1. fire extinguisher
3. safety glasses
2. first aid kit

Exercise B
1. e
3. f
5. d
7. a
2. c
4. g
6. b

Exercise C
1. model
3. collection
5. data
2. diagram
4. exhibit
6. chart

TOPIC 35
Exercise A
1. cell wall
3. cytoplasm
5. chromosome
7. nucleus
9. chromosome
2. cell membrane
4. nucleus
6. cell membrane
8. cytoplasm

Exercise B
1. monerans
3. fungi
5. animals
2. protists
4. plants

TOPIC 36

Exercise A
1. flower   2. pistil
3. stamen   4. stalk
5. bud   6. bulb
7. leaf   8. root
9. petal

Exercise B
1. limb   2. branch
3. trunk   4. tree
5. needle   6. pinecone

TOPIC 37

Exercise A
1. celery   2. broccoli
3. cabbage   4. peas
5. carrot   6. peppers
7. onion   8. yam

Exercise B
1. radish   2. potato
3. cauliflower   4. string bean
5. lima beans   6. cucumber

TOPIC 38

Exercise A
1. orange   2. lemon
3. lime   4. cherry
5. apple   6. peach
7. pineapple   8. strawberry
9. pear

Exercise B
1. watermelon   2. grapefruit
3. cantaloupe

TOPIC 39

Exercise A
1. e   2. a
3. b   4. f
5. c   6. d

Exercise B

```
s e g r o u f t h w i a e e
q b o l r n l w o r o s t c
a l d e m d a o l a t o r h
s e g m e n t e d w o r m s
t e a r t h w o r m e d s l
l c e u p r o u n d w o r m
v h a r q o r n r a c b i s
n e m a t s m h i x e a r t
```

Exercise C
1. amoeba   2. paramecium

TOPIC 40

Exercise A
Crustaceans:
barnacles   crab
crayfish   lobster
shrimp
Mollusks:
clam   conch
mussel   octopus
oyster   scallop
sea slug   squid

Exercise B
1. tentacles   2. antennae
3. claw

TOPIC 41

Exercise A
1. grasshopper   2. ant
3. spider   4. ladybug
5. cockroach   6. web
7. tick   8. butterfly
9. scorpion   10. caterpillar

Exercise B
Insects:
grasshopper   ant
ladybug   cockroach
butterfly   caterpillar
Arachnids:
spider   tick
scorpion

TOPIC 42

Exercise A
Across:
1. sea horse   2. minnow
3. shark   4. catfish
Down:
1. swordfish   5. bass
6. salmon   7. goldfish

Exercise B
1. fin   2. scales
3. gills

TOPIC 43

Exercise A
1. c   2. d
3. b   4. a

Exercise B
1. cobra   2. rattlesnake
3. chameleon   4. alligator
5. garter snake   6. turtle
7. crocodile   8. iguana

TOPIC 44

Exercise A
1. duck   2. ostrich
3. penguin   4. crow
5. peacock   6. turkey
7. hummingbird   8. eagle

Exercise B
Why did the *chicken* cross the road?

TOPIC 45
1. goat   2. sheep
3. dog   4. cat
5. cow   6. pig
7. horse   8. lamb
9. puppy   10. calf
11. piglet   12. kid
13. foal   14. kitten

TOPIC 46

Exercise A

```
k a n g a r o o
d l t d r v x e
j u i o f w m j
o c g l s h o h
e l e p h a n t
y a r h v l k c
f z g i b e e a
l i o n p w y m
k g i r a f f e
z e b r a n s l
```

TOPIC 46

Exercise B
1. bear   2. squirrel
3. opossum   4. deer
5. bat

TOPIC 47

Exercise A
1. stegosaurus   2. dryosaurus
3. anatosaurus   4. brachiosaurus
5. ankylosaurus   6. apatosaurus
7. tyrannosaurus   8. allosaurus

Exercise B
1. diplodocus   2. triceratops
3. pteranodon   4. smilodon

TOPIC 48

Exercise A
1. smoke   2. smokestack
3. exhaust   4. oil slick
5. landfill   6. litter
7. garbage   8. bottle
9. can   10. glass
11. metal   12. plastic

Exercise B
reduce reuse recycle

TOPIC 49

Exercise A
1. c   2. b
3. a

Exercise B
1. atom   2. electron
3. neutron   4. proton
5. molecule

Exercise C
1. physical change   2. chemical change
3. boil   4. freeze
5. melt   6. evaporate

TOPIC 50

Exercise A
1. c   2. d
3. f   4. a
5. g   6. h
7. b   8. e

Exercise B

```
c e r o q l x g f
s p e e d i v e r
g h m a t g p p i
h e t o g h u a c
m a g n e t t l t
t t u y a v l u i
g h f o r c e s o
f o u n e t g h n
l s o u n d p n m
```

TOPIC 51
1. Sun   2. Mercury
3. Venus   4. Earth
5. Moon   6. Mars
7. Jupiter   8. Saturn
9. Uranus   10. Neptune
11. Pluto   12. comet
13. star   14. meteor
15. constellation

TOPIC 52
Exercise A
1. mountain
2. plateau
3. glacier
4. valley
5. river
6. wetland
7. isthmus
8. peninsula
9. gulf
10. ocean
11. island
12. volcano
Exercise B
1. outer core
2. inner core
3. mantle
4. crust

TOPIC 53
Exercise A
deciduous tree, temperate forest
evergreen tree, taiga
grass, grassland
moss, tundra
sand, desert
vines, tropical rain forest
Exercise B
1. tropical zone
2. temperate zones
3. polar zones

TOPIC 54
1. a. sunshine, b. snow
2. a. cloud, b. wind
3. a. rain, b. lightning
4. a. blizzard, b. hurricane
5. a. sleet, b. tornado
6. a. rainbow, b. fog

TOPIC 55
Exercise A
1. multiply
2. add
3. divide
4. comparisons
5. subtract
Exercise B
1. d
2. a
3. e
4. b
5. c
Exercise C
1. sum
2. difference
3. product
4. quotient

TOPIC 56
Exercise A
1. square
2. circle
3. triangle
4. rectangle
5. octagon
6. pentagon
Exercise B
1. parallel
2. perpendicular
3. ray
4. line segment

TOPIC 57
Exercise A
1. acute angle
2. straight angle
3. obtuse angle
4. right angle
Exercise B
1. d
2. e
3. a
4. c
5. b
Exercise C
1. height
2. length
3. width

TOPIC 58
Exercise A
1. mile
2. meter
3. ton
4. pound
5. ounce
6. centimeter
7. kilogram
8. weight
9. foot
10. gram
11. inch
Exercise B
1. pint
2. tablespoon
3. cup
4. teaspoon
5. quart
6. gallon
7. liter

TOPIC 59
Exercise A
1. ascending order
2. descending order
3. random order
Exercise B
1. table
2. Venn diagram
3. graphs
Exercise C
1. coordinates
2. coordinate plane
3. x-axis
4. y-axis

TOPIC 60
Exercise A
1. cursor
2. monitor
3. power supply
4. disk drive
5. compact disc
6. switch
7. diskette
8. mouse
9. cable
10. keyboard
Exercise B
1. display
2. fraction bar
3. unit key
4. clear key
5. operations keys
6. percent key
7. equals key
8. memory recall
9. decimal point key

WORKSHEET ANSWER KEY

TOPIC 1
Exercise A
1. There is/There's
2. There are
3. There is/There's
4. There are
5. There is/There's

Exercise B
1. There is/There's a book on the desk.
2. There are crayons on the table.
3. There is/There's a piece of paper in the wastebasket.
4. There are two pencils on the notebook.

TOPIC 2
Exercise A
1. third
2. second
3. first
4. second
5. first
6. third

Exercise B
1. on
2. in
3. in front of
4. in
5. in
6. near

TOPIC 3
Exercise A
1. U, on
2. A, over/above
3. P, between
4. R, on
5. B, below
6. O, next to
7. D, over/above
8. C, over/above

Exercise B
The cheese is <u>in</u> the <u>cupboard</u>.

TOPIC 4
Exercise A
1. older
2. younger
3. oldest
4. youngest

Exercise B
1. Their
2. mother's
3. Our
4. His

TOPIC 5
Exercise A
1. There is a building across the street from the bank.
2. There's a helicopter over the movie theater.
3. There's a hotel near the parking garage.
4. There is a taxi between the bus and the traffic light.

Exercise B
in front of, across, between, behind

TOPIC 6
Exercise A
1. He is washing the car.
2. They are playing basketball in the driveway.
3. She is riding her bicycle in the park.
4. They are swimming in the swimming pool.

Exercise B
1. There are many beautiful blocks.
2. There are clean streets and friendly people.
3. This is a quiet neighborhood.
4. Some gardens have pretty flowers.
5. There are big houses.

TOPIC 7
Exercise A
1. d
2. a
3. b
4. f
5. c
6. e

Exercise B
inside, outside, next to, from, into, across, over

TOPIC 8
Exercise A
1. True
2. True
3. False
4. True
5. False

TOPIC 9
Exercise A
1. c, paint
2. h, writes
3. d, cuts
4. b, play
5. g, fight
6. e, sells
7. a, fixes
8. f, delivers

TOPIC 10
Exercise A
1. larger
2. smallest
3. smaller
4. largest
5. smaller
6. larger
7. large
8. small

TOPIC 11
Exercise A
1. a
2. c
3. b

Exercise B
1. The Statue of Liberty is in New York City.
2. The Liberty Bell is in Philadelphia.
3. The White House is in Washington, D.C.

TOPIC 12
Exercise A
1. furniture, lumber
2. sugar, sugarcane
3. cloth, cotton

Exercise B
1. furniture, clothing, sugar
2. cotton, lumber, sugarcane, rice
3. restaurants, supermarkets
4. Kennedy Space Center, historic plantations

TOPIC 13
Exercise A
1. a
2. b

Exercise B
1. will go
2. will keep
3. will make
4. will become
5. will take

TOPIC 14
Exercise A
1. have lived
2. have raised
3. has erupted
4. have built
5. have used
6. have grazed

TOPIC 15
Exercise A
Top to bottom:
4, People use wood to build furniture and houses.
1, Lumberjacks cut the trees down with chain saws.
3, Workers at the sawmills cut the timber into boards.
2, Lumberjacks drive logging trucks into the forests and take the timber to sawmills.

Exercise B
1. The Alaska Pipeline is 800 miles long.
2. The three states of the Northwest are Alaska, Washington, and Oregon.
3. The Space Needle is in Seattle.

TOPIC 16
Exercise A
1. Natural resources are so valuable that people spend a lot of money looking for them.
2. In some parts of the Southwest there is so little water that people have to build reservoirs, dams, and irrigation canals for water storage.
3. Sometimes oil wells pump so much oil that people have to put it in tanks.
4. The Grand Canyon is so beautiful that millions of people visit it every year.

TOPIC 17
Exercise A
1. True
2. False
3. False
4. True
5. False
6. False

Exercise B
1. California, Hawaii
2. filmmaking, technology
3. fiber optics, lasers
4. surfing, swimming
5. northern, southern

TOPIC 18
Exercise A
1. capital
2. states
3. national border
4. north
5. east
6. south
7. west

Exercise B
1. Ottawa
2. Mexico City
3. Canada
4. Mexico

TOPIC 19
Students' answers may vary.
Pacific Northwest:
They lived along the Pacific Ocean.
They made boats, houses, and masks from wood.
They danced at ceremonies on special days.
They wore animal masks.
Great Plains:
They lived in tepees.
They hunted for animals.
They dried animal hides in sun.
They made clothes from the hides.
Southwest:
They lived in cliff dwellings.
They drew pictures about their lives.
They made pottery and baskets.
They used looms to weave beautiful baskets.
East:
They lived in wooden longhouses.
They hunted for animals.
They gathered fruit and nuts.
They made belts from wampum.

TOPIC 20
1. Ponce de León, was
2. Vikings, were
3. Columbus, was
4. were, cargo
5. explorers, were
6. Natives, were
7. Leif Eriksson, was
8. prow, was
9. was, jewelry
You will make an important <u>discovery</u>.

TOPIC 21
Exercise A
1. surround, surrounded
2. build, built
3. ring, rung
4. make, made
5. buy, bought
6. arm, armed
7. sell, sold
Exercise B
1. were armed
2. was rung
3. were bought and sold
4. were built
5. was surrounded
6. were made

TOPIC 22
Exercise A
1. c<u>ame</u>
2. b<u>uilt</u>
3. m<u>ade</u>
4. w<u>as</u>
5. g<u>rew</u>
6. g<u>round</u>
7. h<u>ad</u>
Exercise B
1. came, England
2. had, common
3. made, pans
4. grew, tobacco
5. built, Atlantic
6. ground, mill
7. was, services

TOPIC 23
1. When
2. before
3. After
4. when
5. When
6. before
7. When
8. Before
9. After

TOPIC 24
Exercise A
1. a
2. b
3. a
4. b
Exercise B
1. wrote
2. signed
3. met
4. declared
5. printed

TOPIC 25
(Order may vary.)
1. Wagons travelled together in wagon trains because it was safer that way.
2. Hunters and trappers trapped animals because they could sell the pelts to make fur coats.
3. The pioneers were proud of their homesteads because they had worked so hard and traveled so far.
4. Many Americans wanted to go west because the West had a lot of land and very few people.

TOPIC 26
Exercise B
1. More prospectors kept coming.
2. Prospectors began panning in the streams for gold.
3. Levi Strauss started selling clothes to gold diggers.

TOPIC 27
Exercise A
1. True
2. False
3. False
4. True
Exercise B
2, 5, 1, 6, 4, 3

Exercise C
1. The Union soldiers wore blue uniforms.
2. Abraham Lincoln wrote the Emancipation Proclamation.
3. The Yankees won the Battle of Gettysburg in 1863.
4. Yes, people in the Confederacy had slaves.

TOPIC 28
Exercise A
1. President
2. citizens
3. Congress
4. citizens
5. President
Exercise B
1. The judges of the Supreme Court are appointed by the President.
2. The Supreme Court is governed by nine judges.
3. The members of Congress are elected by the citizens of the U.S.
4. The judges are approved by Congress.
Exercise C
1. are called, Rights
2. are listed, ballot
3. is divided, two

TOPIC 29
1. d
2. a
3. b
4. c
5. f
6. e
7. h
8. g

TOPIC 30
Exercise A
1. b
2. e
3. a
4. d
5. c
Exercise B
1. watches, listens
2. stands
3. puts
4. bends
5. falls

TOPIC 31
Exercise A
1. What does the heart do?
2. What does the brain do?
3. What do the muscles and tendons do?
4. What do the veins do?
5. What do the lungs do?
6. What does the esophagus do?
Exercise B
(Answers may vary.)
1. The joints connect your bones.
2. The skull protects your brain.
3. The spine supports your skull.
4. The bones protect and support your body.

TOPIC 32
Exercise A
1. Look
2. Listen
3. Taste
4. Smell
5. Touch
Exercise B
1. They look
2. They sound
3. It tastes
4. It smells
5. It feels

TOPIC 33
Exercise A
1. He is excited. He is happy. He is sad.
2. She is surprised. She is scared. She is angry.
Exercise B
1. Jim is very tired.
2. They are really hungry.
3. My brother is very thirsty.

TOPIC 34
Exercise A
1. b
2. c
3. e
4. a
5. f
6. d
Exercise B
1. Planning
2. Observation
3. Classification
4. measurement
5. Experimentation
6. Reporting

TOPIC 35
1. have, have, have
2. has, don't have, have, have
3. has, doesn't have
4. have

TOPIC 36
Exercise A
1. A
2. A and B
3. A
4. A and B
5. B
6. B

Exercise B
1. make
2. spread
3. start
4. are
5. fall
6. have
7. hold
8. open, becomes
9. carries

TOPIC 37
Exercise A
1. a head of
2. a pound of
3. two heads of
4. three heads of
5. three
6. six
7. two
8. four
9. one

TOPIC 38
Exercise A
1. b, like
2. a, doesn't like
3. d, likes
4. c, don't like
Exercise B
1. She is looking at the apples.
2. He is thinking about the apples.
3. She is putting the tomatoes on the table.

TOPIC 39
Exercise A
1. b
2. a
3. e
4. c
5. d
6. g
7. h
8. f
Exercise B
1. Leeches are segmented worms that have three, four, or five segments.
2. Starfish are sea creatures that move slowly.
3. Protozoans are simple organisms that only have one cell.
4. Jellyfish are sea creatures that have soft bodies.

TOPIC 40
Exercise A
(Word order may vary.)
1. scallop, clam, oyster, conch, snail, mussel
2. octopus, squid, sea slug
3. octopus, squid
Exercise B
1. for fighting
2. for moving
3. for finding
4. for hiding
5. for catching and holding

TOPIC 41
Exercise A
1. Arachnids have eight legs and insects have six legs.
2. Fireflies make light and crickets make music.
3. Insects have three body parts and arachnids have two body parts.
4. Some insects can only walk and other insects can also jump or fly.
5. Arachnids can walk, but they can't fly.
6. Ticks usually bite dogs, but sometimes they bite people.

Exercise B
1. The caterpillar begins its life as an egg.
2. The egg hatches and the caterpillar comes out.
3. The caterpillar crawls around.
4. The caterpillar becomes a chrysalis.
5. The chrysalis becomes a butterfly.
6. The butterfly flies around.

egg, caterpillar, chrysalis, butterfly

TOPIC 42
Exercise A
1. True
2. False
3. False
4. False
5. False
6. True
Exercise B
1. b, horse
2. a, cat
3. d, sword
4. c, pipe

TOPIC 43
Exercise A
1. True
2. True
3. False
4. True
5. True
6. False
Exercise B
1. As frogs and toads grow
2. As tadpoles/amphibians grow
3. As snakes grow
4. As amphibians/tadpoles grow
5. As amphibians/tadpoles grow

TOPIC 44
Exercise A
1. a penguin
2. an ostrich
3. a seagull
Exercise B
1. The cardinal's feathers are red.
2. The pigeon's home is in the city.
3. Feathers cover the bird's body.
4. The duck's neck is short and brown or green.
5. The peacock's feathers are long and blue.
6. The hummingbird's wings can move 50–90 times in one second.

TOPIC 45
Exercise A
1. smaller
2. larger
3. faster
4. taller
5. shorter
6. older
7. younger
8. softer
9. harder
10. slower
Exercise B
1. A dog is smaller than a horse.
2. A kitten is younger than a cat.
3. A cow is taller than a calf.
4. A rabbit is faster than a pig.
5. Paws are softer than hooves.

TOPIC 46
Exercise A
1. have to find
2. don't need to drink
3. like to hang
4. need to be
5. have to breathe

TOPIC 47
Exercise A
1. lived
2. were
3. ate
4. was
5. was
6. were
7. could
8. had
Exercise B
1. The tyrannosaurus ate meat.
2. The triceratops had three horns on its head.
3. The diplodocus was 90 feet long.

TOPIC 48
Exercise A
1. has been reusing
2. have been recycling
3. have been making
4. has been riding
5. have been biking

TOPIC 49
Exercise A
1. A liquid becomes a solid.
2. A solid becomes a liquid.
3. A liquid becomes a gas.
Exercise B
1. True
2. False
3. True
4. False
5. True
6. True

TOPIC 50
Exercise A
1. f
2. d
3. b
4. a
5. e
6. c
Exercise B
1. axle
2. Simple machines
3. inclined plane
4. pulley
5. Levers
6. Wheels

TOPIC 51
Exercise A
1. sixth
2. second
3. first
4. seventh
5. eighth
6. fourth
7. fifth
8. ninth
9. third
Exercise B
1. biggest
2. brightest
3. closest
4. largest
5. farthest

TOPIC 52
Exercise A
1. A glacier is a landform of ice and snow.
2. An ocean is a very large body of salt water.
3. An isthmus is a thin piece of land with water on two sides.
Exercise B
1. has, a peninsula
2. have, mountains/volcanos/glaciers
3. have, islands
4. has, a wetland
5. have, a volcano

TOPIC 53

Exercise A

1. always
2. always
3. never
4. never
5. usually
6. always

Exercise B

1. Many
2. many, few
3. many
4. many
5. many

TOPIC 54

Exercise A

1. going to snow, going to stop
2. going to be, going to see, going to see
3. going to see, going to clear up
4. going to stay
5. going to turn

TOPIC 55

Exercise A

1. d, 3+1=4, Three plus one equals four.
2. a, 3x3=9, Three times three equals nine.
3. e, 5-2=3, Five minus two equals three.
4. c, 4÷2=2, Four divided by two equals two.
5. b, 5>4, 3<5

TOPIC 56

Exercise A

1. rectangle
2. triangle
3. pentagon
4. octagon
5. square
6. circle

Exercise B

1. cube, 2
2. sphere, 2
3. cylinder, 3
4. cone, 3
5. rectangular prism, 5

TOPIC 57

Exercise A

1. right angles
2. obtuse angle
3. acute angle
4. circumference
5. perimeter
6. diameter
7. area
8. Congruent figures

Exercise B

1. Mrs. Ling must use geometry.
2. She must find the area and the perimeter.
3. She must multiply the width by the length.
4. She must use right angles.

TOPIC 58

Exercise A

Circled in red: inches, feet, yards, miles, meter, centimeter, kilometer
Circled in yellow: ounces, pounds, ton, grams, kilograms
Circled in black: cups, pints, quarts, gallons, teaspoons, tablespoons, liters, milliliters

Exercise B

Possible answers:
1. inches/feet/yards/miles
2. ounces/pounds/tons
3. cups/pints/quarts/gallons/
   teaspoons/tablespoons
4. centimeters/meters/kilometers
5. grams/kilograms
6. liters/milliliters

Exercise C

1. There are 12
2. There are 3
3. There are 16
4. There are 2
5. There are 2
6. There are 4
7. There are 3
8. There are 100
9. There are 1000
10. There are 1000
11. There are 1000

TOPIC 59

Exercise A

1. d
2. a
3. c
4. b

Exercise B

1. 15
2. 5
3. 20
4. 20
5. 5
6. 16

TOPIC 60

Exercise A

1. Sit in front of the computer.
2. Turn the on-off switch to "on."
3. Put a game in the CD drive.
4. Play the game.

Exercise C

1. Sit
2. Turn
3. Type
4. Play
5. Move

INDEX OF
FEATURED GRAMMATICAL STRUCTURES

Numbers following these featured grammatical structures refer to the Dictionary topics.